W9-CNR-588

History of Modern Chinese Literature

Edited by **Tang Tao**

FOREIGN LANGUAGES PRESS BEIJING

First Edition 1993
Second Printing 1998

ISBN 7-119-01459-5

Published by Foreign Languages Press
24 Baiwanzhuang Road, Beijing 100037, China

Printed by Beijing Foreign Languages Printing House
19 Chegongzhuang Xilu, Beijing 100044, China

Distributed by China International Book Trading Corporation
35 Chegongzhuang Xilu, Beijing 100044, China
P. O. Box 399, Beijing, China

Printed in the People's Republic of China

Contents

Publisher's Note

The *History of Modern Chinese Literature* is a survey of the major writers of the first half of the twentieth century and their works in the context of the events which transformed Chinese society in that period.

In 1911 the Qing Dynasty came to an end and the Republic of China was founded. However, Chinese politics and society had still not shaken off the vestiges of feudalism and the suffering caused by feudal thinking is well-illustrated in modern Chinese literature. As well as the suffering caused by feudalism and imperialism, there were many political events and upheavals in China reflected in the literature as the Chinese writers strove to depict their society with all of its complexities and contradictions.

The themes of modern Chinese literature were quite different from those of the classics. The new literature explored such themes as peasants, women and intellectuals, as well as the urban problems of alienation and isolation, replacing the intrigues of the emperors, generals and scholars of classical literature. The new literature was more reflective of the whole society and not just the aristocracy and the Confucian scholar-officials which had dominated traditional literature. As feudalism approached its demise there was more emphasis on the liberation of the individual reflected in such themes as free marriage and the yearning for a new social order.

The *History of Modern Chinese Literature* outlines the major events which provide the backdrop for modern Chinese literature: the collapse of the Qing Dynasty and feudalism, the Russian Revolution, the May Fourth Movement, the May 30th Movement, the anti-Japanese war, the oppression of the Kuomintang (KMT) government, the civil wars and finally the Liberation in 1949. Against the background of these events Chinese authors describe the lives of their characters. By providing a socio-political context for the reader the *History of Modern Chinese Literature* aids the reader in understanding the literature in its own cultural framework.

The book tells about major modern Chinese writers such as Lu Xun, Guo Moruo, Mao Dun, Lao She, Ba Jin, Ai Qing, Ding Ling and Cao Yu. It also introduces lesser-known writers, so the reader has a guide to China's modern authors and their works.

The book describes the Chinese literary scene and its development, starting at the turn of the century with intellectuals like Liang Qichao who advocated refining classical style to later reformers like Chen Duxiu and Hu Shi who were in favour of using the vernacular in writing. Eventually the transition to the vernacular was made, ending the 2,000-year dominance of writings of classical style. The effect was to bring literature closer to the people which accordingly began to reflect their interests.

The book also looks at the influence of Western literature on Chinese literature. Chinese writers, literary magazines and societies introduced Western literature in translation and soon the techniques of romanticism, realism and naturalism began to appear in Chinese literature. This cultural melange revitalized Chinese literature which had developed primarily in isolation up to that point.

The *History of Modern Chinese Literature* gives an overview of the thirty-year period from the May Fourth Movement in 1919 to the Liberation in 1949, showing the events and ideologies that shaped modern Chinese literature. This historical and cultural framework helps the reader understand the themes and trends of contemporary Chinese literature.

INTRODUCTION

An Outline of the Development of Modern Chinese Literature

I. The Literary Revolution and Its Development

Modern Chinese literature came into being during the May Fourth Movement of 1919. Essentially political in nature, the Movement intensified the literary revolution begun earlier, giving it character and direction. Thenceforth, Chinese literature changed its course. It linked up with the literature of the advanced nations and made great strides in coming closer to the ordinary people of the country. Significantly, the May Fourth literary revolution opened a new chapter in the history of Chinese literature.

The literature of feudal China has a long history and it is adorned with numerous works of excellence. But as the feudal system was collapsing at the turn of the century and as China by then had been reduced, both politically and economically, to a semi-colonial state, the end of feudal literature became more and more apparent even though it refused to die a natural death. For their part, many reformists, while seeking to bring about social changes, had also tried to revitalize the old literature by introducing what they considered literary innovations. However, all their attempts failed to produce the anticipated results because social and historical conditions at that time were not conducive to the revival of feudal literature.

After the outbreak of the First World War, the European imperial powers were fully engaged in fighting among themselves. For a while, they loosened their grip on China. Consequently, Chinese national industries developed on a relatively large scale and this led to a marked expansion of capitalist power. At the same time, however, the proletariat also grew in strength, and the balance of class forces definitely made conditions favourable for revolution. It was in these historical circumstances that the progressive intellectuals, chief among whom was Chen Duxiu, editor of the *New Youth* magazine, devoted themselves wholeheartedly to the propagation of new ideas. These intellectuals were influenced by the new trends of thought prevailing in the West, and the literary revolution they launched soon played a significant part in the New Culture Movement. Led by the spirit of democracy and science, the literary revolution came as a proper response to the demand for fundamental change in thinking and outlook. It was also seen as an appropriate answer to the need, generally felt, that Chinese literature should be taken into a new stage of development.

The formal proposal for a literary revolution was made by Chen Duxiu in the February number of the *New Youth* magazine for 1917, although the desire for change had been expressed before in other progressive periodicals. In its early numbers, the *New Youth*, which first appeared in September 1915 under the name of *Youth Magazine*, published articles such as "On the History of Modern European Literature and Art." Specifically aimed at the contemporary literary circles, these articles sought to introduce to the reader the development of Western trends of thought in literature and art from classicism to romanticism, realism and naturalism. In December 1915, Chen Duxiu pointed out clearly the need for literary reform. He wrote in his "Reply Letter to Zhang Yongyan":

> Our literature and art are still in the ages of classicism and romanticism. From now on the trend should be towards realism. In literature, we should emphasize the truthful recording of facts and events; in painting, the drawing of scenes from real life. Only thus can we get rid of the evils of ornateness and decadence.*

Li Dazhao, too, wrote in the first number of the *Morning Chimes*, August 1916:

* *Youth Magazine*, Vol. I, No. 4, December 1915.

> The birth of a new culture is always heralded by the arrival of a new literature and art, whose growth depends especially on the efforts of a few who dare defy general opinion in promoting their beliefs. They spread their ideals, solidify their self-assumed authority, and made their desperate self-awakening call, thereby arousing the masses from their deep sleep.*

As the enlightened thinking spread and gained support, the eagerly-awaited birth of the literary reform movement was only a matter of time.

In January 1917, came the first systematic proposals for literary reform. They were put forward by Hu Shi in his article "Modest Proposals for the Reform of Literature," published in the *New Youth* magazine for that month. He suggested eight specific ways of treating the ills of the old literature, such as its formalism, and the writers' addiction to archaism in their literary creations. In Hu Shi's views, the writer must (1) make sure his writing has substance, (2) try not to imitate the old writers, (3) pay full attention to the precision of grammar and style, (4) stop complaining without any legitimate cause, (5) never use cliches and outworn diction, (6) avoid using classical allusions, (7) avoid using parallelism,** and (8) feel free to use colloquial expressions, if necessary. He maintained that genuine literature should "depict present-day social state of affairs" and "contain lofty thoughts and sincere feelings." In addition, he suggested, positively, that the written language should be brought close to ordinary daily speech and argued that *bai hua* (the vernacular) should replace *wen yan* (classical Chinese) as the language for literature.

Compared with Liang Qichao and other reformists at the end of the Qing Dynasty, Hu Shi had gone far ahead in advocating a new literary style. To Liang Qichao, it should be noted, the new style meant improvement upon *wen yan* (classical Chinese), that is to say, further refinement of the antiquated literary language and style. Also, Hu Shi's ideas had much greater influence because they

---

* Li Dazhao, "The Mission of the *Morning Chimes*", *Morning Chimes*, Inaugural Number, August 15, 1916.

** The literary device of matching both sound and sense in two lines or sentences — [tr.]

came at the right time, following the trend of history. However, the fact still remains that his proposals were concerned more with the "reform" of the *means* of literary expression than with the *content* of the literature itself. Even in his article "On the Constructive Literary Revolution," published in the *New Youth* for April 1918, all he could say, and it was said very clearly, was: "The only aim of my theory on the construction of a new literature can be summed up in a few words: 'a vernacular literature and a literary vernacular.' We advocate the literary revolution only because we want to create a vernacular literature for China." Precisely because there was no emphasis on new content, Hu Shi can be seen as moving further back into the stronghold of conservatism, well protected by the walls of stylistic innovations. Indeed, Lu Xun most appropriately pointed out: "Decadent thinking can be expressed in the classical language as well as in the vernacular."* In other words, if Hu Shi's suggestions had been followed, there would have been only changes in the means of literary expression, that is in the adoption of *bai hua* (the vernacular). There could never have occurred the fundamental change in content and outlook. In short, modern Chinese literature would never have come into being.

The true holder of "the banner of the literary revolution," borne out by later developments, was Chen Duxiu, prime representative of the radical democratic intellectuals. In his article "On the Literary Revolution," published in the *New Youth* for February 1917, he proposed three major principles in his clarion call for action against feudal literature. They were:

(1) Get rid of the ornate, adulatory aristocratic literature; create a simple, honest and expressive national literature.

(2) Get rid of the stale, ostentatious literature in the style of classics; create a fresh, sincere and realistic literature.

(3) Get rid of the obscure and difficult literature of hermit style; create a lucid and popular literature.

Chen Duxiu's criticism was aimed at feudalism. Not only did he speak out against the ills of formalism and ornateness of the old literature; he strongly opposed the feudal thinking behind literary

* Lu Xun, "China Without a Voice," *Three Leisures.*

works, vilifying it as "impenetrable darkness" and "long-accumulated filth." To him, the literary revolution would most effectively usher in a new culture and bring about change in national outlook. In turn, he believed, this would lead to political reform. With the nineteenth-century bourgeois European literature as model, he demanded that the new literature in China should truthfully express emotion and realistically depict life. He also wrote in his reply letter to Hu Shi: "It is indisputable that the vernacular should be the language for literature in the reform of Chinese literature. We must not give our opponents even the privilege of discussion."* Chen Duxiu's stand was a lot firmer than that of Hu Shi, who had written to express his doubts that "our proposals may not provide the right answers." It can also be said that Chen Duxiu, more than anybody else, had unflinchingly carried on the work of the bourgeois literary reformists of the late Qing Dynasty, taking their movement to its height.

Favourable response to the *New Youth*'s call for a literary revolution came from Qian Xuantong and Liu Bannong, among many other writers and scholars. In a series of open letters to the editors of the *New Youth* magazine, Qian Xuantong fiercely attacked the old literature and condemned the blind imitations of *pian wen*** and other antiquated prose styles. He strongly advocated the theory that the spoken and the written languages should be the same. The development of the Chinese language, he stressed, had made the adoption of *bai hua* (the vernacular) a foregone conclusion. Liu Bannong published articles including "My Views on the Reform of Literature" and suggested that writers should free themselves from their superstitious belief in the antiquated literary forms and styles. Some of his specific suggestions included the adoption of a new prosody and the use of a new system of punctuation.

Unquestionably, the literary revolution launched by the *New Youth* magazine in early 1917 accomplished a great deal in its attack of feudalism and the old literature. Its achievement, in this respect, will always be acknowledged in literary history. However,

* Chen Duxiu, "Reply Letter to Hu Shi," *New Youth*, Vol. III, No. 3, May 1917.

** Rythmic prose characterized by parallelism and ornateness. — [Tr.]

its proposals for the creation of a new literature were not clear or specific enough. What was meant by "a simple, honest and expressive national literature," "a fresh, sincere and realistic literature," or "a lucid and popular literature"? The leaders of the literary revolution often belittled classical literature. Indeed, at times they negated its excellence altogether as they tried to turn the reader's attention totally to the West. But what kind of Western bourgeois literature would best serve as a blue-print for the new literature in China? On this, they were not all that clear. Of course, they wanted to introduce particularly the works of Western writers who followed realism, hoping that its literary principles would provide a proper direction for Chinese literature. However, at the same time they highly praised aesthetic writers such as Oscar Wilde and others who advocated the doctrine of "art for art's sake." They did not sufficiently understand the subsequent European movement of naturalism and promoted it as the newest direction to be followed by the Chinese writers. Even the ideas of Chen Duxiu, derived from Western bourgeois literary concepts, were not without contradictions which revealed his confusion of thought. He suggested, for example, that literature should play a significant role in intellectual enlightenment as well as in political reform. At the same time, however, he could also ask: "If literature has extraneous functions to perform, apart from its own expression, there will be pre-existing conditions for literary creation. How then can literature preserve its own independent worth without drastically destroying its intrinsic value?"* Not surprisingly, for well over a year the literary revolution, from its first signs to its public proclamation, still remained in the stage of exploration of theories. No truly epoch-making masterpieces had appeared so far; neither was it a widespread movement.**

In essence, the literary revolution launched by the *New Youth* magazine was guided by Western social and literary thinking. But

* Chen Duxiu, "An Answer to Zeng Yi's Letter," *New Youth*, Vol. III, No. 2, April 1917.

** The works which received acclaim in the *New Youth* were the novels of Su Manshu and the vernacular poems of Hu Shi written in lines of five or seven words each.

before it developed further and revealed more weaknesses, a new historical age had been ushered in by the October Revolution of 1917 in Russia. Consequently, with the spread of Marxism, many new factors appeared in the course of revolution in China. Li Dazhao, Lu Xun, Qian Xuantong, Shen Yinmo, Gao Yihan and Hu Shi joined the editorial board of the *New Youth* magazine, which had become, in effect, the centre of the cultural united front, drawing strength from three different groups: intellectuals who had leanings towards communist ideology, revolutionary petty-bourgeois intellectuals and bourgeois intellectuals. Then came the May Fourth Movement of 1919, which brought the proletariat on the historical stage and marked the beginning of the new democratic revolution period in China. It was inevitable that the literary revolution soon underwent changes which eventually gave it a completely new character.

The very first sign of change, clear enough, came in May 1918 when Lu Xun's story *The Diary of a Madman* appeared in the *New Youth.* Inspired by the spirit of the times, the work was a declaration of total war on feudalism. It immediately started a conflagration, as it were, which was going to burn down the cannibalistic feudal system of the past several thousand years. The literary revolution had finally gone beyond its early stage in which it was preoccupied with theoretical work. Now the revolution in the content of literature had begun. A thorough revolutionary, Lu Xun remained utterly firm in his opposition to literary formalism, which he described as the phenomenon of "changing the label, not the goods." He believed that "in the inculcation of a healthy scholarship, literature and art, the first task has to do with the reformation of thought."* In his works that followed, through his incisive style, he poignantly exposed the root causes of the ills of the old society. Pervading all his works are revolutionary ideas and fervent hopes that the oppressed people will eventually be liberated. He highlighted many serious problems such as the future of the peasants, women and the intellectuals, as he treated hitherto unexplored themes in Chinese literature.

* Lu Xun, "Crossing Rivers and Leading the Way," *New Youth*, Vol. V, No. 5, November 1918.

Other new works of this period also drew their material from real life, such as Liu Bannong's poem "Separated by a Sheet of Paper" and Ye Shaojun's novel *Is That a Human Being, Too?* (also entitled *Life*). In these works, the writers, imbued with the new thinking of the age, exposed class oppression and class antagonism. They deeply sympathized with the people from the lower social strata. Significantly, after the outbreak of the May Fourth Movement of 1919, the new literature sought to especially embrace the prevailing ideas which supported social reform, women's liberation and the belief in the sanctity of labour. For example, the poems of Guo Moruo published in the *Lantern of Learning*, such as "The Nirvana of the Phoenixes" and "Ode to Bandits," have a very strong rebellious tone and express a deep yearning for the new social system. His poems fired the imagination of numerous young people and aroused their intense passion. Similarly, many of the works by other writers are characterized by the authors' thoroughly democratic thinking and their as yet unclear socialist aspirations. Truly reflecting the mood of the times, they are the outstanding achievements of the literary revolution in a new historical age.

The drastic change in literary content of necessity called for and indeed brought about the emancipation of form and style from the tyranny of the classical tradition. Increasingly, the vernacular was being used. In the May issue of 1918, for example, the *New Youth* switched completely to the vernacular in all its pages. Following the call for "the liberation of poetry," many advocates of the new literature movement cast aside the fetters of traditional prosody and used the vernacular for the new poetry. The periodicals founded after the *New Youth* such as the *Weekly Review* and the *New Tides* also published literary works written in the vernacular as well as translations. In particular, the second half of the year 1919 saw a surge of vernacular periodicals. Consequently, in the following year, out of business necessity even well-established periodicals such as the *Short Story Monthly* and the *Eastern Magazine*, hitherto controlled by disciples of the old school, had to make the linguistic change gradually. In 1920, faced with the *fait accompli* that the vernacular had replaced the outmoded classical language, the Ministry of Education of the Beiyang (Northern Warlord) government conceded that the vernacular had become the *guo yu* (national language), and that it should be adopted in all the schools. Thus, in a remarkably short time after the May Fourth Movement of 1919, the reign of the classical literary language, which had a long history of over two thousand years, came to an end.

The achievements of the literary reformers indicated that feudalism had fallen into decay. They also clearly demonstrated the irresistible force of the new democratic cultural revolution. It should be specially noted that conceptually these pioneers had gone far beyond the stage in which they were concerned only with the evolution of a new language. Indeed, they had acquired a completely new starting point. For example, when Lin Shu and the other disciples of the old literary school dismissed the vernacular as "vulgar and shallow" and that it was not even "worth a sneer" because, as they pointed out, it was "the language of hawkers and peddlers,"* Lu Xun retorted: "What a pity! The words that came out of four hundred million Chinese mouths are not even 'worth a sneer'!"** In his rebuttal, Lu Xun considered the problem of literary tools from the point of view of the masses. Hence the reference to the "four hundred million Chinese mouths." The May Fourth literary revolution and the vernacular movement had marked the beginning of the popularization of literature and art, thus paving the way for later movements which sought to bring literature and art closer to the masses.

After 1918, there were changes in the concept of literature and its function. Realism prevailed as more and more people accepted the idea that "literature should serve life" and that it should "reflect life." Based on this principle, periodicals such as the *New Youth*, the *Weekly Review* and the *New Tides* began their fierce attack on the novels of "the dark curtain school." Attention was also drawn to the reform of the old opera, which some extremists dismissed altogether as "the dance of a hundred beasts." Meanwhile, some of the intellectuals who had been initiated into communism began to observe and analyse all spiritual phenomena including literature

* Lin Shu, "Letter to Cai Heqing," *Public Voice*, Beijing, March 18, 1919.
** Lu Xun, "Murderers Today," *New Youth*, Vol. VI, No. 5, May 1919.

from the standpoint of historical materialism. Their conclusion was that "changes in the economic structure would automatically affect any spiritual structure, thus giving rise to corresponding political and legal changes as well as changes in morals and philosophy."* They firmly believed that the new literature had a bright future. At the same time, they made new demands on the role it was going to play and explained what they thought its nature and function should be. For example, in the article "What Is New Literature?" Li Dazhao offered views which were different from those held by Hu Shi and others who actively preached the belief that "the aim of the literary revolution is only to create a national vernacular literature"** or that "the new literature simply means vernacular literature."*** "As I see it," Li Dazhao wrote, "the new literature is not merely something written in the vernacular. Neither is its creation a matter of introducing a few new ideas and new facts, depicting new people or acquiring new terms."† He also sharply criticized some writers of the new literary works for their "fame-seeking" mentality. "The new literature we would like to see," he went on to say, "is that which realistically depicts life and society, not that which is designed to bring fame to the individual writers." His advice was that writers should "get rid of the old poison of feudalism and the new poison of capitalism." For the new literature to flourish, there had to be rich soil and deep roots: that is, "profound thoughts and theories, firmly held ideology, artistic excellence and the spirit of fraternity." The article was written in December 1919, shortly after "the battle of ideologies." It can be assumed that the "firmly held ideology" he mentioned was communism, which Hu Shi vehemently opposed and which he himself strongly defended. In spite of Li Dazhao's somewhat hazy understanding of communism at times, the article was a significant piece of work by an intellectual who had acquired a preliminary knowledge of the ideology. It made a positive contribution to the study

* Li Dazhao, "My Views on Marxism" (I), *New Youth*, Vol. VI, No. 5, May 1919.

** Hu Shi, "On the Constructive Literary Revolution," *New Youth*, Vol. IV, No. 4, April 1918.

*** Fu Sinian, "How to Use the Vernacular," *New Tides*, Vol. I, No. 2, February 1919.

† *Sunday*, January 4, 1920. (Special number on social problems)

of the major problems facing the literary revolution, particularly in the choice between revolution and reform, between proletarian collectivism and bourgeois individualism.

Another major activity of the May Fourth literary revolution was the extensive introduction of foreign literature. In its special Ibsen number of 1918, the *New Youth* published translations of his works including *A Doll's House.* Thus a new era began in the introduction of foreign works, unprecedented both in scope and influence. Among the leading translators were Lu Xun, Liu Bannong, Shen Yanbing, Zheng Zhenduo, Qu Qiubai, Geng Jizhi, Zhou Zuoren and Tian Han. Almost all the progressive periodicals and newspapers published translations of foreign works, and the Chinese reader was given a systematic introduction to the famous works of Russian, European, Japanese and Indian writers. Through the influence of these translations, the Chinese writers were further encouraged to free themselves from the fetters of the old literature. The new literature developed rapidly a character of its own as it acquired a certain "common language," so to speak, with the progressive literatures of other nations.

However, as yet many people at the time had not thoroughly grasped the theories of historical materialism. As a result, in the introduction of foreign literary works through translation, they sometimes failed to distinguish between works of excellence and those of little worth, the positive and the negative. Thus, one finds among the works translated not only first-rate pieces but also quite a few which are mediocre or even reactionary. Furthermore, the influence of foreign literature was not always healthy. For example, some of the supporters of the new literature, especially those connected with the *New Tides* magazine, even went as far as blindly suggesting "total Westernization," advocating what they called "a Europeanized vernacular" and "a Europeanized Chinese national literature."* Understandably, their well-intentioned efforts had a negative effect on the development of the new literature. On balance, however, the introduction of foreign literary works during the May Fourth period did make a valuable contribution to the

* Fu Sinian, "How to Use the Vernacular," *New Tides*, Vol. I, No. 2, February 1919.

overall progress of the new literature in China. Many of the works of Lu Xun, Guo Moruo and others show that indeed these writers had been influenced, positively, by foreign writers.

In their study and introduction of foreign literature, the literary pioneers gave top priority to the works of progressive Russian writers. They found new hope for national liberation in the October Revolution of 1917. Furthermore, in Russian literature they could see "the good souls of the oppressed, their miseries and their struggles." They fully understood that the world was made up of two kinds of people: "The oppressor and the oppressed."* Thus, Qu Qiubai observed in his essay written in March 1920:

> The study of Russian literature seems to have become most popular in China. Why? The main reason is that the Russian Bolshevik Red revolution has brought about gigantic political, economic and social changes which have influenced people's thinking all over the world. Everybody wants to trace the distant causes of the revolution and examine its culture. The result is that inevitably world attention has been focussed on Russia and Russian literature. In the dark and miserable Chinese society, everybody is trying to find a new way out of his plight. The sound of the crumbling old Russian society is most welcome, like the sound of footsteps in a deserted valley promising life. It arouses great interest in people. That is why they want to study and discuss Russia. Consequently, Russian literature has become the target of the Chinese scholars.**

Russian literature had become the "target" of the Chinese scholars because its progressive tradition appealed to the Chinese reader. In the literary domain, the Chinese progressives were determined to follow the direction pointed out by the October Revolution. And this was a special historical phenomenon of the May Fourth Movement which could not have occurred before. In the progressive Chinese literary circles, the attention hitherto paid to the West had now been switched to Russia. It was clear that the literary revolution had begun undergoing fundamental changes.

In a few years, then, the May Fourth literary revolution had

* Lu Xun, "A Tribute to Sino-Russian Linguistic Friendship," *Mixed Dialects.*

** Qu Qiubai, Preface to *Famous Russian Short Stories*, New Chinese Magazine Press, Beijing, July 1920.

achieved extraordinary results. It came as demanded by the times and it was in complete accord with the spirit of the age. Its success was due mainly to the spread of Marxism, as the Chinese revolution entered a new phase and the proletariat claimed the historical stage. The literary revolution started earlier by the *New Youth* had now been intensified and taken to greater heights. Of course, the May Fourth literary revolution had its weaknesses, too. At times, its judgment on some specific matters showed an absence of historical criticism. It did not manage, neither could it have been possible, to take the new literature even closer to the masses. All in all, however, it was truly a monumental and thorough revolution without any parallel in the history of Chinese literature.

Of course, the theme of anti-feudalism can be found in the progressive literature produced immediately before the May Fourth literary revolution; indeed, it can also be found in classical Chinese literature. But there had never been, neither could there have been, a new literature such as that created by the May Fourth Movement which fundamentally and completely negated the whole feudal system as well as the feudal mentality. The new literature, imbued with the modern democratic spirit, portrayed new themes. New characters appeared, drawn from the peasants, workers and the new intellectuals, replacing the usual heroes and heroines in the old literature: that is, emperors and generals, scholars and beauties. Even the theme of striving for freedom of choice in marriage, frequently found in literary works of the past, was now treated in a different way. It sought to express the new thinking which prompted the combined desires for the liberation of the individual, itself inseparable from national liberation, and the successful adoption of socialism in the country. In the content of thought, the May Fourth new literature made a complete break with feudal literature. It had gone far beyond the achievement of the old masterpieces with democratic inclinations. It has also moved ahead of the average contemporary bourgeois literary works. Consequent upon national awakening, the new literature faithfully followed the call of socialism in its total commitment of the cause of anti-feudalism and anti-imperialism.

The May Fourth literary revolution rejected the antiquated

literary language. It advocated the adoption of the vernacular as the language for literature, the creation of a new poetry and the reform of the old drama. All this produced unprecedented results. For ages Chinese literature had remained far too removed from the masses and such a phenomenon can be explained, of course, in socio-political terms. However, it had also to do with the long-sanctified, difficult, orthodox and outmoded classical literary language. The adoption of the vernacular alone enabled the new literature to come closer to the masses than ever before. From theory to creative writing, from content to artistic expression, the May Fourth literary revolution brought in new approaches. Indeed, just as it reflected the achievement of the Chinese people in their struggles against feudalism and imperialism, it also, appropriately, opened a new chapter in the history of Chinese literature.

II. The Literary Societies and the Initiation of Revolutionary Literature

After 1921, the new literature movement entered a new stage of development. One after another, literary societies were founded and literary and art magazines began to appear in different parts of the country. Gradually, the movement gained independence, separating itself from the other reform movements. Different schools came into being. There was a rapid increase in the number of works published and their quality, in general, also improved. The literary revolution, which flourished in the enlightened period of the May Fourth Movement of 1919, was now bearing more and better fruits.

At the beginning of the literary revolution in 1917, and even during the early days of the May Fourth Movement of 1919, there were no literary societies. The holders of "the literary revolutionary" banner, that is, the *New Youth* and later the *New Tides* and *Young China* as well, were magazines with contents designed to appeal to the diverse interests of the readers. It was not until 1921 that literary societies and exclusively literary magazines appeared. In January of that year, the Literary Research Society was founded in Beijing. Among the twelve founders were Zheng Zhenduo, Shen Yanbing, Zhou Zuoren, Ye Shaojun, Wang Tongzhao, Xu Dishan, Guo Shaoyu and Geng Jizhi. The magazine published by their society was the *Short Story Monthly*, which had already been taken over and improved upon by Shen Yanbing, the new editor. Later, the society also published, separately in Shanghai and Beijing, the *Literary Xunkan* (*Literary Ten Days*)—the one which came out in Shanghai later changed its named to the *Literary Weekly*. Other publications of the society included *Poetry*, a monthly, and a series of almost a hundred literary works. As membership of the society grew, branch societies were formed outside Beijing and Shanghai, in cities such as Guangzhou, Ningbo and Zhengzhou. These branch societies all had their own local publications.

In July 1921, the Creation Society was formed by Guo Moruo, Yu Dafu, Tian Han, Cheng Fangwu, Zheng Boqi, Zhang Ziping and others, who were then all studying in Japan. They began publishing a series of books in Shanghai. The following year saw more of their publication such as *Creation*, a quarterly, *Creation Weekly*, *Creation Daily*, *Flood* and *Creation Monthly*. Its membership reached as many as several dozens of people. More and more literary societies were soon founded and they put out their own magazines promoting the new literature. According to the statistics collected by Mao Dun, by the end of 1925 well over one hundred literary magazines were published in different parts of the country. Among the more active societies were the following:

(A) In Shanghai: 1. The Popular Drama Society, founded by Ouyang Yuqian, Shen Yanbing and Zheng Zhenduo. It published *Drama*, a monthly.

2. The Mi Sa Society with its monthly publication *Mi Sa* and other collections of works, founded by Hu Shanyuan and others.

3. The Southern China Society and the fortnightly *The Southern China*, run by Tian Han.

4. The Hurricane Society, directed by Gao Changhong and others first in Beijing and then in Shanghai. It twice published the weekly *Hurricane*.

(B) In Hangzhou: The Lakeside Poetry Society formed by Feng Xuefeng, Pan Mohua, Ying Xiuren and Wang Jingzhi. It published collections of poetry such as *Lakeside* and the magazine *China February*.

(C) In Changsha: The Hu Guang Literary Society (Shimmering Lake Waters), organized by Li Qingya and others, with its half-monthly *Hu Guang*.

(D) In Wuhan: The Yi Lin Society (Artistic Circles), set up by Liu Dajie and others. It published the magazine *Yi Lin* every ten days.

(E) In Tianjin: The Green Waves Society, formed by Zhao Jingshen, Jiao Juyin and others. It published *The World of Poetry* and *Green Waves* every ten days and the magazine *Short Stories*.

(F) In Beijing: 1. The Tattler Society, formed by Lu Xun, Sun Fuyuan, Qian Xuantong, Chuan Dao and Zhou Zuoren. Its publication was the weekly *The Tattler*.

2. The Sunken Bell Society, organized by Feng Zhi, Yang Hui, Chen Weimo and Chen Xianghe. It published *The Sunken Bell* as a weekly and a half-monthly, and also distributed a book series.

3. The Unnamed Society, organized by Wei Suyuan, Li Jiye and Tai Jingnong under the supervision of Lu Xun. It published jointly with the Hurricane Society the weekly and half-monthly *The Wilderness* and later, independently, the half-monthly *The Unnamed* as well as three series of books.

4. The New Moon Society, formed by Xu Zhimo, Wen Yiduo, Liang Shiqiu, Hu Shi and Chen Yuan. They published poetry and drama in special sections of the paper *The Morning Daily*. Later, they had their own monthly the *New Moon*.

As they multiplied, these literary societies and their publications nurtured a large number of writers who gradually came to the fore in the literary movement. It was certainly a very productive period. Of the short stories published, Lu Xun's *Call to Arms* and *Wandering* distinguished themselves in content, thought and style. Other fine works came from accomplished writers such as Ye Shaojun, Yu Dafu, Wang Tongzhao, Lu Yan and Tai Jingnong. Medium-length and full-length novels, too, began to appear. In poetry, the major event was the publication of Guo Moruo's *The Goddesses*, which made free verse extremely popular although poets such as Wen Yiduo and Xu Zhimo soon advocated a new kind of prosody, distinctly different from that of classical poetic composition. Lyrical prose, in particular, reached a very high level of achievement. The works of Lu Xun, Zhou Zuoren, Bing Xin, Zhu Ziqing and Yu Dafu received extensive praise and were seen as a proper challenge to the old literature. In drama, the trend changed from the translation of foreign works to creative writing, and the one-act comedies of Ding Xilin were particularly noteworthy. It should be noted that the first generation of writers of the new literature movement were all active members of these literary societies.

Different literary schools gradually came into being. The basic assumption of the Literary Research Society was "literature for life's sake." In their works the members emphasized detailed and exact depiction of life as well as depth of analysis, thus gradually showing they were following the principles of realism. Writers of the Creation Society, on the other hand, inclined towards self-expression, paying relatively little attention to objective description. The strong emotions in their works clearly indicated that from the very beginning they were moving in the direction of romanticism. Both these two groups of writers were influenced by the works of different European and American literary schools. The other groups, in literary thinking, were close to either of the two societies. The Tattler Society and Unnamed Society, for example, leaned towards the Literary Research society, while others such as the Mi Sa, the Southern China and the Sunken Bell societies were more in tune with the Creation Society. In other words, realism and romanticism were the main trends in the early period of the new literature in China although symbolism and aestheticism also had a certain influence in the literary circles, thus resulting in the formation of other relatively more complex schools.

In any event, the flourishing of these societies and the increase in the number of publications proved to be beneficial to the literary front in the struggle against the feudal revivalist schools. From 1922 to 1925, the magazine *Criterion*, published in Nanjing and the *Jia Yin Weekly* in Beijing, launched their attack on the new literature. They vilified the vernacular as an improper language for literature and were opposed to the new thinking. Simultaneously and spontaneously, members of the new literature movement made their counterattack, whether they belonged to the Literary Research Society, the Creation Society, the Tattler or any other group. In this anti-feudalism battle, they each made their valuable contribution on the ideological front. In particular, through his incisive prose, Lu Xun, who was connected with the Literary Research Society, the Tattler Society and the Unnamed Society, fully exposed the absurd arguments of the two revivalist schools in Nanjing and Beijing.

However, unhealthy tendencies were also noticeable during this productive period of literary creation. As yet young writers of bourgeois or petty-bourgeois background had not acquired a proper understanding of society and practical life. In the face of difficulties which made the future look gloomy enough, they felt it was impossible to find a way out of their predicament. Consequently, they easily gave vent to their feelings of loneliness and despair. They could not objectively view the desertion of the new cultural united front by people like Hu Shi. Also, their uncritical acceptance of Western bourgeois ideas and Western literature inevitably had a negative influence on their outlook and their works. As Gorky pointed out, "the basic and central theme of nineteenth-century European literature is that of pessimism, caused by the individual's feeling of his own helpless state in society."* Indeed, pessimistic thinking and feelings pervaded the works of quite a number of young writers. Their themes are narrow—one finds the phenomenon of "thou" and "love" invading every piece and indeed almost every line. These works were often merely an outlet for their morbid sentiments and self-pity. Some of them show that their authors were seriously affected by escapism, decadence, and the feeling of doom. As Mao Dun observed, "the whole literary world before the eve of the May 30th Incident**

* Gorky, "A Talk with Young Writers," *Essays on Literature*, People's Literature Press, November 1958, p. 299.

** On May 15, 1925, a Chinese worker was killed by the Japanese capitalists in Shanghai. On May 30, over 10,000 students and workers in the city demonstrated and protested in the city's concessions. British police opened fire, killing 11 demonstrators and wounding dozens more. This was also known as the "May 30th Massacre."

of 1925 was shrouded in an atmosphere of frustration and anxiety."*

The early Communists recognized these unhealthy tendencies in the works of the new literature and they promptly offered criticism and guidance. At the conference of the Young Chinese Association held in Hangzhou in July 1922, Li Dazhao and Deng Zhongxia put forward written proposals for the "creation of an effective literature that can awaken the masses." They urged young Chinese writers to "participate in revolutionary, democratic movement." The Socialist Youth League at its first national congress also called for "the 'proletarianization' of learning, literature and art." In June 1923, the quarterly *New Youth*, the periodical of the Chinese Communist Party under the chief editor Qu Qiubai, published "The New Manifesto" pointing out that "the current Chinese literary thinking is influenced by bourgeois poetics, and it often inclines towards decadence." The manifesto stated clearly that the Chinese revolutionary and literary movements "cannot achieve anything unless they are under the leadership of the working class." Through the quarterly *New Youth*, the weekly *Chinese Youth*, the supplement "Awakening" of the Shanghai *Republic Daily* and other progressive periodicals, the Communists published many articles, propagating their revolutionary literary ideas and proposals. For example, essays such as Deng Zhongxia's "For the New Poets" and Yun Daiying's "On the Eight-Legged Style" criticized in earnest the young writers' tendency to follow "individualism without any social consideration." They urged the writers to "produce more works which reflect the noble national spirit" so that the new literature "can inspire people with the desire to participate in the movement of national independence and democratic revolution." In his essay "The New Mission of the Writers," Shen Yanbing also pointed out that "their mission at present is to capture the spirit of the revolutionary movement of the oppressed people and the class. They should let this spirit pervade their masterpieces so that it can spread far and wide." This would "lead to even greater and more vigorous revolutionary movements."

* Mao Dun, "Preface to *The Short Stories*," Vol. I, *Major Branches of New Chinese Literature*.

These above-mentioned writers also clearly explained how revolutionary literature could be created. The writer must be concerned about social reality; he must identify himself with the labouring masses and participate in revolutionary activities. "If you want to be a revolutionary writer, the first thing you should do is to get yourself involved in revolutionary work and let your revolutionary feelings grow." "First, there must be revolutionary feelings. Only then will there be revolutionary literature."* In his essay "Literature and Revolutionary Literature," Shen Zemin also explained that writers should not lack revolutionary thinking or life experience.

Under the influence and guidance of the early Communists, some literary societies began to appear in 1924, formed specially to promote revolutionary literature and related literary activities. In Shanghai, for example, the Spring Thunder Society was founded by Jiang Guangchi, Shen Zemin and other young writers. Every week they published articles about revolutionary literature in the special literary section, "Awakening," of the *Republic Daily*. Poems, too, appeared, the best known being Jiang Guangchi's "Lament for China." In Hangzhou, the students of Zhijiang University founded the Awakened Society and published the periodical *Awakened*. Their aim was to "promote revolutionary literature and revolutionary zeal." In Beijing, besides the *Raging Fire*, a publication of the Communist Youth League, there was also *Fireball*, published by the Society for the Study of Literature and Art of the Labouring Class. The aim of the society was to "study the realities of life and to save romantic literature and art from degeneration." The appearance of all these societies indicated that the influence of revolutionary thinking had been growing among young people who were devoted to literature and art.

The literary views of the early Communists, however, were not entirely without errors of judgment. In some of the essays, the writers could not see clearly the boundary of thought between Marxism and bourgeois democracy. Other essays leaned too much to the "Left," typified by Jiang Guangchi's "Modern Chinese Society

* Yun Daiying, "On Literature and Revolution," "The Writers China Needs," *Chinese Youth*, Nos. 31 and 80.

and Revolutionary Literature." In general, the early Communists tended to over-negate the works of the petty-bourgeois writers who, in fact, constituted the main force in the Chinese literary circles then. Some also overlooked, in various degrees, the special characteristics of literature and art. Consequently, many of them did not fully appreciate the significant contribution of Lu Xun to the cultural front and the immense value of his works.

After the May 30th Incident of 1925, when the revolutionary war in the country reached another climax, even greater response to the call for a revolutionary literature came from numerous petty-bourgeois writers and young people who were devoted to literature and art. The literary movement gained momentum, now that a new political situation had emerged consequent upon the alliance of the Nationalist and the Communist parties. Since, by nature, it was impossible for the petty-bourgeoisie to follow an independent political line, many of the progressive writers stood by the proletariat and the labouring masses during the struggles in the wake of the February 7th* (1923), May 30th (1925) and March 18th (1926)** incidents. As a result, they were influenced by revolutionary thinking. In particular, the nationwide, stupendous May 30th Movement of 1925 left its indelible mark, and literary works continued to appear, portraying anti-imperialist themes. Other works also grew in number which depicted, directly or indirectly, the revolutionary struggles of the masses, such as Jiang Guangchi's volumes of poetry "The New Dream" and "Lament for China" and his novels *The Young Vagabond* and *On the Yalu River*.

Among writers who took part in the national revolutionary struggle were Shen Yanbing, Guo Moruo, Cheng Fangwu, Ying Xiuren and Pan Mohua. In 1926 Guo Moruo published his essays

---

* In February 1923, the Beijing-Hankou Railway workers established their trade union. Warlord Wu Peifu used armed force to prevent the workers from holding meetings. When the workers went on a protest strike, Wu Peifu ordered his troops to open fire, killing many workers. This large-scale massacre came to be known as the "February 7th Incident."

** On March 18, 1926 several thousand students and people of all walks of life in Beijing held an anti-imperialist demonstration at Tian'anmen Square. Warlord Duan Qirui ordered his troops to open fire on the demonstrators, killing about fifty people and over two hundred more were seriously wounded. This was referred to in history as "March 18th Incident."

"Revolution and Literature" and "The Awakening of Writers and Artists," urging young writers and artists to "go to the factories, live among the soldiers and the people, and throw themselves into the whirlpool of revolution." He pointed out that the literature and art in urgent demand was that which "speaks for the oppressed classes," "sympathizes with proletarian socialism" and "speaks from the standpoint of the fourth class." After the March 18th Incident of 1926, Lu Xun went south and published some of his famous talks, including "Literature of the Revolutionary Age." Other writers such as Ye Shaojun, Zheng Zhenduo, Ouyang Yuqian, Tian Han, Yu Dafu and Wen Yiduo were also moved by the spirit of the great revolution. They either publicly supported the revolutionary struggle led by the Communist Party or went to cities like Guangzhou and Wuhan, where they helped to spread the revolution through their work in literature and art. In his writings, for example, Zhu Ziqing lauded the Communist heroes who were determined "to build a Red Paradise on earth." There was also a steady increase in the number of works by young writers who depicted the lives of the poor. During the period of the Northern Expedition against the warlords, many writers promptly responded to the call that "literature should speak for the fourth class." Some of their works may not be literary masterpieces, but they are nevertheless full of the spirit of revolutionary struggle. Thanks to the revolutionized thinking of the writers and the unfailing effort of the literary groups and societies, the revolutionary literature advocated by the early Communists had finally established itself in the Chinese literary world. All their activities had created favourable conditions for further development of the proletarian literary movement and for the creation of a truly revolutionary literature.

III. The Proletarian Literature Movement and the League of Left-Wing Writers

A major literary event after 1927 was the proletarian revolutionary literature movement, also known as the Left-wing literature movement, initiated by the Creation Society and the Sun Society in early 1928. Then came the controversies which members of these two societies had with Lu Xun, Mao Dun and others. In March 1930, the Chinese League of Left-Wing Writers was founded (also known as the Left League) and the "Left-wing literature" subsequently became a powerful force. The Left League was dissolved in 1936, of its own accord, so that a united front against the Japanese aggression could be formed during the war. By then, in a matter of eight or nine years, the proletarian revolutionary literature movement had produced an army of writers whose influence was keenly felt in China.

What gave rise to the proletarian revolutionary literature movement? Why did it develop to such an extent when circumstances surely would have crippled it from the start? After all, the Great Revolution of 1927 had failed and the persecution of cultural workers by the Kuomintang government had already claimed several hundred thousand lives.

First of all, the proletarian revolutionary literature suitably answered the needs of the times. After the April 12th Incident* of 1927, the class relationships in the country underwent great changes. The original united front broke up; the upper bourgeoisie had betrayed the revolution and for a while the majority of the national bourgeoisie followed the moves of the reactionary forces. As a result, the Chinese revolution was led solely by the proletariat. Both the bitter class struggle which ensued and the new revolutionary conditions required that the proletariat should make its stand clear on matters related to literature and art. In the words of Li Chuli, one of the literary revolutionaries, the task was to take the "mixed revolutionary literature" of the first decade into a new stage, that of "proletarian literature."**

Secondly, in literary terms, the rise of the Chinese proletarian literature at the time was not an isolated phenomenon. About 1928, the international proletarian literature movement had gained momentum in Russia, Western Europe, Japan and Korea. These international developments further inspired the Chinese revolutionary

* On April 12, 1927, Chiang Kai-shek staged a counterrevolutionary coup in Shanghai and ordered a mass slaughter of workers and Communists.

** See his article "An Answer to Lu Xun's 'Obscurity in the Drunken Eyes'."

writers. In 1928 and 1930, two conferences of international revolutionary writers were held in Moscow and Kharkov respectively. The "League of International Revolutionary Writers" formed at the second conference, in particular, had a great influence on literary circles in China.

Thirdly, the proletarian literature movement began in early 1928 also because many revolutionary intellectuals had flocked to Shanghai after the failure of the Great Revolution in 1927. The foreign "concessions" provided sanctuary for these revolutionaries whose lives would have been endangered elsewhere. Guo Moruo and Shen Yanbing, for instance, were on the arrest list of the Kuomintang because they had participated in revolutionary activities during the period of the Northern Expedition against the warlords. In Shanghai, they could hide themselves and appear incognito. Others like Yang Hansheng, Li Yimang, Cheng Fangwu, Qian Xingcun and Hong Lingfei came after the abortive Nanchang Uprising of 1927 or after their local Party organizations had been destroyed by the Kuomintang. Still others like Shen Duanxian and young writers of the Creation Society such as Feng Naichao, Li Chuli, Peng Kang and Zhu Jingwo returned from Japan because of the persecution of Left-wing intellectuals in that country. All these writers, one after another, found shelter in Shanghai. They were indignant at the Kuomintang's counterrevolutionary massacres and dissatisfied with the literary united front which had failed to live up to their expectations in the revolutionary struggle. Consequently, some of the original members of the Creation Society and those who had been closely associated with it, reorganized the society and resumed publication of the *Creation Monthly*. They also put out new magazines such as *Cultural Criticism* and *Quicksand*. Jiang Guangchi, Qian Xingcun and Meng Chao formed the Sun Society and published the *Sun Monthly*. Later, Hong Lingfei and Du Guoyang founded Our Society with its monthly publication *Ourselves*. These groups were all working for the promotion of proletarian literature or revolutionary literature and they each made a valuable contribution to the Left-wing literature movement.

Some of the earliest articles advocating proletarian revolutionary literature were: Mai Ke'ang's (Guo Moruo's) "The Heroic Tree,"

Cheng Fangwu's "From Literary Revolution to Revolutionary Literature," Jiang Guangci's (Jiang Guangchi's) "On Revolutionary Literature" and Li Chuli's "How to Construct a Revolutionary Literature?" In these articles, the writers discussed the class nature of literature, emphasizing literature as a useful weapon in class struggle. They also clearly explained the social origin of proletarian literature and indeed its historical mission. They believed that before proletarian literature could be created, writers "must strive to acquire proletarian consciousness" and "get rid of their petty-bourgeois nature." In addition, they pointed out that proletarian literature "should be for the peasants, workers and the masses" and that it should use "a language close to that of the common people."* Their ideas came at the right time, for after the failure of the Great Revolution of 1927 many intellectuals had lost faith in revolution. The appearance of proletarian revolutionary literature inspired people with hope, revitalized the writers and pointed out a clear direction for them. Yin Fu, Ye Zi and Sha Ting, for example, who later became major Left-wing writers, owed much to the enlightenment and nurture of this proletarian literature movement.

It must be said in retrospect, however, that many advocates of proletarian literature were themselves going through the process of change, from petty-bourgeois to proletarian thinking. As yet they had not fully grasped the theories of Marxism. Not surprisingly, therefore, they were not immune from the faults of one-sidedness or absolutism in their views. So they displayed the conviction that only they were the embodiment of revolution—"I, myself, am revolution."* Their analyses of the revolutionary situation were not all that accurate and their literary judgment was affected by their irresponsible assumptions. For instance, in some of their articles they exaggerated the function of literature and art, propagating the idealist-inclined belief that literature could "organize life," "create life" and that writers could "go beyond the age."

* Cheng Fangwu, "From Literary Revolution to Revolutionary Literature," *Creation Monthly*, Vol. I, No. 9, February 1928.

* Jiang Guangchi, "Modern Chinese Literature and Social Life," *Sun Monthly*, January 1928.

In emphasizing that "literature is communication," they overlooked the special characteristics of literature and art, and the important role played by life experience in literary and artistic creation. They argued that literature was merely "a reflection of the desire to fulfil class-oriented aspirations" and even publicly declared that they would leave literary techniques to "the writers of yesterday."* To them, the change in a person's world view could be done through the acceptance of dialectical materialism as propounded in books and that, indeed, the change could be easily completed overnight.

Because they did not sufficiently understand the nature of the Chinese society then and the tasks of the revolution, the Creation Society and the Sun Society first of all focussed their criticism on Lu Xun when they started the proletarian literature movement. They failed to clearly see the dividing line between the bourgeois democratic and the socialist revolutions. To them, the bourgeoisie and even the petty-bourgeoisie were, in general, the targets of the revolution. They argued that "most of the writers belong to the counterrevolutionary camp" and called for an end to "the literature of the petty-bourgeois scholars and masters." They negated the achievements of the May Fourth new literature, which they saw as the literature of the bourgeoisie. It was imperative, they felt, that writers like Lu Xun, Ye Shengtao and Yu Dafu should be criticized. Thus, Lu Xun was vilified not only as "the drop-out of the times" and "the best spokesman" for the bourgeoisie, but also among "the dregs of feudalism" and "a double counterrevolutionary vis-à-vis socialism."** In making these unjustifiable accusations, members of the two societies showed that they did not sufficiently understand the reality of Chinese society and the revolutionary situation. Indeed, they were merely applying Marxist terminology dogmatically. It should be noted, too, that they were very much under the influence of the predominating political thinking of Qu Qiubai

* The quotations are from Li Chuli's "How to Construct a Revolutionary Literature," "Book Review of *The Life of Ying Lan*," and "Epilogue to *Walking on the Same Dark Path*."

** The quotations are from the following articles: "Dance of the Tables," "Foreword to the First Number of *Quicksand*," "A Reply to Lu Xun's 'Obscuriy in Drunken Eyes' " and "Dregs of Feudalism Found on the Front of Literature and Art."

within the Communist Party and of the Japanese Leftist Communist Chiburi Fukumoto. As Lu Xun put it later, "they had not done a meticulous analysis of Chinese society and they mechanically applied the methods which could work only under Soviet Russian rule."*

The criticism of Lu Xun and others by the Creation Society and the Sun Society led to well over a year's debates and arguments within the camp of the advocates of the new literature. Throughout this period Lu Xun was resolute and completely positive in his support for the revolutionary literature and the proletarian literature. In his article "Literature, Art and Revolution" he stated clearly: "All literature and art are means of communication.... If so, it stands to reason that they can be used to promote the cause of revolution. It is a kind of tool, as it were." He went on: "Revolution often breaks out in the world. Naturally, there will be revolutionary literature. Some of the people in the world have woken up.... Naturally, there will be literature of the people. To put it plainly, it is the literature of another class, the fourth class."** In his criticism of the Creation Society and the Sun Society, Lu Xun pointed out that apart from their hazy understanding of the revolutionary situation and the targets of revolution their efforts to create a proletarian revolutionary literature were led by their own opinion, not by the true spirit of Marxism.*** In his judgment, the Creation Society had exaggerated the power of literature and art, believing that "they can change heaven and earth."† As Lu Xun saw it, many of those who advocated the view that "literature is communication" were in fact trying to "climb the literary ladder to get into the castle of idealism." †† They underestimated the contribution of life experience and the significance of technique in literary creation. In Lu Xun's words, they were "more interested in upholding the signboards than in improving the quality of the goods they sell." He sincerely urged them to pay primary attention to "the substantia-

---

* Lu Xun, "A Glympse of Literature and Art in Shanghai," *Two Hearts.*

** Lu Xun, "Literature, Art and Revolution," *Three Leisures.*

*** Lu Xun, "Flat and Thin," *Ibid.*

† Lu Xun, "Literature, Art and Revolution," *Ibid.*

†† Lu Xun, Foreword to *Translations Under the Wall.*

tion of content and improvement of literary techniques" in their revolutionary writings.* The special character of literature and art, he emphasized, should not be overlooked. Thus he wrote: "Of course, I believe that all literature and art are means of communication. But not all means of communication are literature or art. It is the same as saying that all flowers have colour (white is also a colour), but not everything which has colour is a flower. Revolution needs slogans, posters, reports, telegrams and textbooks, but it also needs literature and art — precisely because of their literary and artistic nature."** In his articles such as "Obscurity in Drunken Eyes" and "Current Concepts of the New Literature," Lu Xun analysed, from the class point of view, the causes of "obscurity and confusion" which still plagued the Creation Society in spite of "its change of direction." He especially emphasized that petty-bourgeois writers should adopt a realistic attitude while they were going through the ideological remolding process. In his words, "they should not be afraid of self-criticism, they should be brave enough to speak the truth." He further advised: "Don't keep the remnants of old ideas in your mind, deliberately hiding them, and point your finger at your own nose much like an actor on the stage, saying 'Only I represent the proletariat.' " Lu Xun's sharp comments were most valuable to the advocates of proletarian literature.

In Autumn 1929, after the debates had come to an end and the real opponents of proletarian literature had been exposed and denounced by both sides, the Communist Party suggested the amalgamation of all the societies and groups. The idea was to form a united organization of revolutionary writers and its core was to be made up of the founders of the Creation Society, the Sun Society, Lu Xun and his followers. The writers welcomed the idea with great enthusiasm and preparatory work was soon undertaken by Feng Naichao of the Creation Society, Shen Duanxian (Xia Yan), who had good relations with the Sun Society; and Feng Xuefeng, who knew Lu Xun before most others and had co-edited books with him introducing Marxist theories on literature and art. On

* Lu Xun, "Literature, Art and Revolution," *Three Leisures.*

** *Ibid.*

March 2, 1930, the Chinese League of Left-Wing Writers came into being in Shanghai. The founding members, besides Lu Xun, included Shen Duanxian, Yang Hansheng, Yu Dafu, Feng Naichao, Feng Xuefeng and Zheng Boqi. Guo Moruo and Mao Dun were not in the country at the time but they had agreed to be listed as founders. The founding of the League was a major event in the history of modern Chinese literature. It marked the beginning of a new era in the development of revolutionary literature. Also, it indicated that the forces of the Chinese proletariat had grown and its vanguards, the Chinese Communist Party, had strengthened its leadership in matters concerning revolutionary literature and art.

The inaugural meeting of the Left League was attended by over forty members. Guidelines for theory and practice were adopted and the League made its stand clear as it declared:

> Our art is necessarily devoted to the "victory-or-death," bloody struggle.
>
> If the content of art is that of the joys and sorrows of mankind, then our art of necessity expresses the feelings of the proletariat in this dark, "medieval," class-ridden society.
>
> Therefore, our art is against the feudal and the capitalist classes. We are also against the inclinations of the petty-bourgeois class, which has lost its social status. We must not only help but also participate in the production of proletarian art.*

At the meeting, Lu Xun gave an important talk.** He emphasized that if the Left-wing writers were merely pursuing romantic fantasies and did not get involved in the actual struggle, "they can easily create whatever 'Leftist' image for themselves. But the moment they encounter reality, they will fail to pass test." These Left-wing writers, he warned, would "just as easily become Right-wing writers." Many revolutionary writers at the time truly believed that they had already been "proletarianized." In truth, however, they had not yet acquired a deep understanding of what would be involved in the long and arduous process of ideological remoulding; perhaps they had not paid enough attention to that process itself. Lu Xun's forthright admonition was therefore most

---

* Printed in *Germination Monthly*, Vol. I, No. 4, April 1930.

** Lu Xun, "Suggestions for the League of Left-Wing Writers," *Ibid.*

appropriate. Particularly perceptive was his theory that the revolutionary world view could be formed only in practical revolutionary struggle, during which that world view would be severely tested. He also explained that writers should never feel that they were above other people or that they should be given privileges after the success of the revolution. In his words, "the intellectuals have their own work to do, and its importance should not be underestimated. But working class is not obligated to give poets and writers preferential treatment." He analysed the relation between literary work and the working people, and the analysis was beneficial particularly to those who had joined the revolutionary literature movement mainly because, perhaps unknown to themselves, they were lured by their own illusions. Above all, he elaborated on what should be done in order to complete the four main tasks facing the League. As he put it, "in the protracted struggle against the old society and the old forces, one should be resolute, constantly mindful of one's strength"; "the battleline should be extended"; "a large number of new fighters should be created"; and "there should be a common goal because that is the essential condition for the existence of the united front." For a long time, Lu Xun had been watching the changes in the Chinese literary circles and the trends of thought followed by the Russian writers after the October Revolution. In his talk at the inaugural meeting, he systematically summed up his observations, dwelling especially on the lessons learned from the experience of the proletarian revolutionary literature movement in its initiation stage. He put forward most valuable suggestions on how to deal with the "Left" tendency and solve the key problems related to the creation of a revolutionary literature. In short, he explained clearly how Marxist theories could be applied effectively in the fields of literature and art.

After it was founded, the Left League began publishing periodicals such as *The Pioneers*, *Germination Monthly*, *Partisan*, *World Culture*, *Crossroads*, *The Dipper* and *Literary Monthly*. At the same time, it put out magazines for underground circulation such as *Literary Guide*,—the first number appeared under the name *Outpost*—and *Literature*, a half-monthly. It also reorganized or took over other publications including *Popular Literature and Art*, *Modern*

Short Stories and *News on Literature and Art*. By comparison, there were even more periodicals edited or published by the founding members of the League. In Beijing and Tokyo, branches of the League were set up and smaller organizations in Guangzhou, Tianjin, Wuhan and Nanjing were also created. The branches and some of these small organizations had their own publications. More and more Left-wing young writers and artists joined the League, and it soon had over 270 members. As Feng Naichao pointed out in one of his articles, "Any one will be regarded as a comrade of the League if he understands the necessity of revolution and social reform, works for the cause of revolution and carries on the struggle led by the League and its principles."* Under the leadership of the Communist Party, the League united the various factions, and accelerated the proletarian revolutionary literature movement. Its significance in the development of modern Chinese revolutionary literature cannot be overstated.

The formation of the League of Left-Wing Writers and its activities brought about a close relation between literature and art and revolution. It openly showed itself as a unit of the revolutionary forces under the leadership of the proletariat. Dedicated to the struggle against imperialism and the reactionary groups, it further developed the May Fourth new literature tradition. It regularly sent representatives to take part in the activities of other revolutionary organizations. Consequently, it established close links with these organizations, thus fulfilling one of the objectives of the League adopted at its inaugural meeting. In addition, it joined the League of International Revolutionary Writers as its branch in China.

Since the formation of the League, "almost all its members are determined to get involved in the actual social struggle."** Some of them joined the progressive political organizations such as the League for Freedom in China and the China League for the Defence of Civil Rights. A great number of them took part in workers' movements and threw themselves into the anti-Chiang Kai-shek

* "The Chinese Proletarian Literature Movement and the Historical Significance of the Founding of the *Left League*," *Germination Monthly* (renamed *New Land Monthly*), Vol. I, No. 6, June 1930.

** "From the Editor," *Germination Monthly*, Vol. I, No. 4, April 1930.

and anti-imperialist revolutionary struggles. After the September 18th Incident* of 1931 and the January 28th Incident** of 1932, the Left-wing writers published *A Declaration to the World from the Shanghai Cultural Circles* and formed the Association of Anti-Japanese Chinese Writers. In their anti-Japanese and anti-Chiang Kai-shek activities, they widely spread the revolutionary cause, awakening people to the urgency of the struggle for national survival. The League encouraged writers to produce works which made practical contribution to the revolution. Some of the publications carried information about land reform in the Chinese Soviet areas and news of the latest successful battles against the Kuomintang's "encirclement campaigns." In order that literature and art could still better serve the revolution, the Left-wing writers began exploring ways of bridging the gap between their works and the masses. Hence the subsequent discussions on the popularization of literature and art and on the creation of works which could reach a wider audience.

During this period, the revolutionary writers and artists were particularly active and their works had a great popular appeal. Consequently, the Kuomintang intensified its suppressive measures and severely persecuted those who associated with the proletarian revolutionary literature movement. In the autumn of 1930, the year when the League was found, the Left-wing actor Zong Hui was assassinated in Nanjing. The following year, on February 7, Li Weisen (Li Qiushi),*** a Left-wing cultural worker, and four members of the League were murdered in the Kuomintang Police

---

* When the Japanese troops stationed in Northeast China attacked Shenyang on September 18, 1931, the Chinese army in the city and the Northeastern Army, upon Chiang Kai-shek's order of nonresistance, retreated to the south of Shanhaiguan Pass. So Japanese troops quickly occupied Liaoning, Jilin and Heilongjiang provinces. This is commonly known to the Chinese people as the "September 18th Incident."

** Japanese marines launched an attack at Shanghai on January 28, 1932. Disregarding the nonresistance policy of the Kuomintang government the Nineteenth Army of the Kuomintang and the people of Shanghai resisted. But their resistance was betrayed by Chiang Kai-shek and Wang Jingwei and ended in failure.

*** Li Weisen was not a member of the Left League. However, because of his close relation with the League, he was included in the memorial service for the four members assassinated by the Kuomintang. He is remembered as one of the five martyrs.

Headquarters in Longhua, Shanghai. The four members were Rou Shi, Hu Yepin, Yin Fu and Feng Keng. In May 1933, without any search warrant, the Kuomintang agents arrested Ding Ling, Pan Zinian and others, killing the poet Ying Xiuren on the spot. The same year saw the murder of writer Hong Lingfei in Beijing and the imprisonment of Pan Mohua in Tianjin. The latter died in jail the following year. For a long time, Lu Xun was under arrest and was on the assassination list of the Kuomintang agents. Even today it is still difficult to give an accurate number of young writers and artists who were imprisoned and murdered in different parts of the country.

Furthermore, the Kuomintang government banned revolutionary literary and art works and broke up progressive literary and art organizations. In February 1934 alone, about 150 kinds of books were banned not counting the numerous works held back, edited and rewritten by the Kuomintang. After the Creation Society was forced to disband in February 1929 and the Shanghai Art Drama Society in April 1930, more and more progressive literary and art organizations met with the same fate. The methods of suppression, too, became more despicable and vicious. In 1933, the Kuomintang agents wrecked the Shanghai Yihua Film Company and then intimidated all the cinemas in the city that they should not show films directed by Tian Han and Shen Duanxian. Bookshops, too, such as the Hufeng, Beixing and Liangyou were forced to close down. Throughout the period of the Second Revolutionary Civil War (1927-37), as Lu Xun pointed out, "proletarian revolutionary literature and the revolutionary labouring masses suffered the same suppression and faced the same imminent destruction. They were involved in the same struggle, sharing the same fate."* That common experience, however, led to the cementing of the most valuable tradition of the Left League and the proletarian revolutionary literature.

It was in these difficult and dangerous circumstances that the League fought bravely for the cause of proletarian revolutionary literature and achieved good results. Through common struggle, it

* Lu Xun, "Chinese Proletarian Revolutionary Literature and the Blood of the Vanguards," *Outpost*, Vol. I, April 25, 1931.

gained solidarity with those who worked for newspapers and bookshops and with members of other cultural organizations. Its influence continued to grow. Under the surveillance of the Kuomintang government, many periodicals published by the League had to change their names frequently. Lu Xun invented the famous "art of slipping through the net," a product of his remarkable tactical thinking. He also suggested that the League should seek unity with as many writers as possible. "Some people," he said, "may not be able to give us much help. But they do not have any ill-will towards us, either. Therefore, they are not our enemies, certainly not at the moment. It will be our loss indeed, if through our harsh words and stern looks we turn them away."* During his convalescence period from the late spring and early summer of 1931 to early 1934, Qu Qiubai, in close co-operation with Lu Xun, also did "a lot of useful cultural work."**

In response to new situations created by the rising anti-Japanese and anti-Chiang Kai-shek feeling after the September 18th Incident of 1931, the Left League with Lu Xun as leader was engaged in forming links and establishing solidarity with the progressive writers. It showed tenacity and flexibility in all such work. Consequently, the proletarian literature movement spread wide. At the same time, it managed to avoid, partially, the influence of the "Leftist" line when it made its appearance for the third time. Originally, the League was formed so that preliminary work could be done in order to get rid of the factionalism which had emerged in the initiation period of proletarian literature. It did not manage to eradicate the old "Leftist" sentiments; hence the resurgence of closed-doorism and factionalism after the Wang Ming political line had assumed supremacy. However, the League did gradually forge closer links with most of the progressive writers. In some areas of literature and art, the united front was extended, and the achievements in theatre and film, for example, were particularly outstand-

* Lu Xun, "Letter to Wang Zhizhi," *Letters*, People's Literature Press, Vol. II, 1976, p. 1060.

** See *Resolutions on Some Historical Problems*, prepared by the Central Committee of the Communist Party. The resolutions were passed at the Seventh Plenary Session of the Sixth Central Committee of the Communist Party of China on April 20, 1945.

ing. All in all, the work done by the League had created favourable conditions for the formation later of the national united front of writers and artists against the Japanese aggression.

The League also paid a good deal of attention to the study of theory and criticism. It made great efforts in the propagation of Marxist theories on literature and art and was engaged in fierce battles on the front of literature and art. At the inaugural meeting of the League in 1930, the resolution was passed that "Marxist theories of literature and art, and Marxist principles of criticism should be firmly established." Consequently, the League set up a society for the study of these theories. Some of the members of the League risked their lives in translating the works of Marx, including his writings on literature and art. Lu Xun's translation of Plekhanov's *On Art* and his other works had much influence in the literary circles. Qu Qiubai translated the works related to the theories of literature and art by Engels, Lenin, Plekhanov and Lafargue. These works were introduced to the Chinese reader. Throughout the Second Revolutionary War, the Left-wing writers and theorists, in their concerted effort, translated and published three series of works related to Marxism: *A Small Collection of Theories on Literature and Art*, edited by Chen Wangdao; *Scientific Theories on Art*, edited by Feng Xuefeng; and *A Collection of Theories on Literature and Art*, edited by the Tokyo branch of the League. During this period, revolutionary writers effectively used Marxist theories in their literary battles with the opposing groups such as the "New Moon School" and the fascist "Movement of National Literature and Art." They also exposed the misleading ideas of those who promoted themselves as the so-called "democratic people" and "third kind of people" in the world of literature and art. While engaged in all these literary battles, they further spread Marxist theories.

There were also outstanding achievements in literary creation. Writers who began their career during the May Fourth Movement or slightly later had been given the baptism of the new revolutionary fire. As their world view changed, their works changed accordingly. Lu Xun's essays and his novel *Old Tales Retold* are ample evidence of his new exploration and development in thinking and artistic expression. In the intense political struggles of the time, his essays with their razor-sharp critical analyses were particularly effective and powerful. Mao Dun's *Midnight* and his short stories were the other major achievements of this period. Jiang Guangchi also turned out distinguished works, including *The Roaring Land*. Nurtured by the League, new writers continued to emerge. Most of them had been inspired by the May Fourth new thinking and they were steeped in the tradition of the new literature. As the proletarian revolutionary movement spread, they began their writing careers and many of their works brought new life and spirit to the literary circles. Among these writers were Ding Ling, Zhang Tianyi, Yin Fu, Ye Zi, Sha Ting, Ai Wu and others who became major writers during or after this period.

The most striking feature found in the literary works of this period was the treatment of new topics and themes which had great social significance. For subject matter, many writers turned to the brave struggles, under white terrorism, of the revolutionaries and the labouring masses. As the revolution took deeper roots among the peasants, the life and struggles in the villages gradually appeared in the writers' creative vision. Indeed, quite a few writers themselves were originally from the villages; some of them had also taken part in these struggles and therefore they were writing from their solid, first-hand experience. Through their artistic portrayal, they vividly and realistically depicted the collapse of the villages, the plight of the peasants as well as their awakening and struggles. The unstable, turbulent city life of the 1930s was also truthfully and intensely described in other literary works. After the September 18th Incident of 1931 and the January 28th Incident of 1932, there was a gradual increase in works which echoed the voice of the people in their call for national salvation against Japanese aggression. Most of these reveal the powerful fighting spirit, intense emotion and abundant optimism of the period.

Some serious faults and shortcomings, however, were noticeable in the League's activities during the proletarian revolutionary literature movement. In politics, sometimes it followed the views held by the Leftist leaders of dogmatism within the Communist Party. So it emphasized the "anti-Rightist" and "anti-capitalist class" lines, which were quite inappropriate at times. Instead of making effective use of the legal means of struggle, it wanted to organize "flying rallies," "festival parades" and "general alliance strikes" in cities where the enemy was in great strength. It even advocated "armed riots." The result was that it easily laid itself open to attack and consequently suffered many setbacks. After the September 18th Incident of 1931, it adopted slogans such as "Only Russia is our mother country" and "Protect Russia through military means." These were empty slogans which did not reflect the feeling of the masses. Indeed, the League's theoretical work was not built on sufficient understanding of the Chinese society then and the realities of the literary movement. At times, in solving problems, it mechanically applied the methods used in foreign countries, without realizing it was merely following dogmatism. In organizational matters, the League was treated as if it were a political party with its own strict regulations. It had not done enough to unite more progressive writers in carrying out the common struggle. All these showed, in different degrees, the faults of being too closed and factionalized. Quite a number of the literary works were still marked by strong petty-bourgeois consciousness, lacking in Chinese colour and spirit. Some of the works, too, were obviously written by following certain formulas and theories. Lu Xun, for his part, offered many suggestions which were perceptive, fair and practical. However, sometimes they were not properly understood, let alone accepted by members of the League. These problems brought things to a head in 1936, when the revolutionary situation reached a new and critical point. Controversies once again arose in the inner circles of the Left-wing writers and artists over the choice between the two emphases: "literature of national defence" and "popular literature of national revolutionary war." There were dangerous signs that the League was going to be torn apart.

All these facts indicated that although most of the Left-wing writers were determined to devote themselves to the work of proletarian revolution, they still retained strong petty-bourgeois thoughts and sentiments. As Lenin put it, "Proletarian movement anywhere in the world does not and cannot come about 'on the instant,' with its class nature untainted.... Only through the arduous undertaking and long struggles of the most progressive workers, indeed all the awakened workers, can the proletarian class movement rid itself of the various petty-bourgeois impurities, limitations, narrow-mindedness and other defects. Only then can it gain strength."* In a word, the shortcomings of the proletarian revolutionary literature movement had much to do with the "petty-bourgeois impurities, limitations, narrow-mindedness and other defects" found in the thoughts and sentiments of the revolutionary writers. However, the truth of this apart, accounts of the contribution of the League of Left-Wing Writers can easily fill the pages of a chapter in the history of modern Chinese literature.

During the period of the Second Revolutionary Civil War, there were other literary activities pursued by writers who were not associated with the proletarian revolutionary movement. These writers did not have a well-organized body like the League of Left-Wing Writers. Neither did they form literary societies such as those which were in existence before the League. Very often they worked together, publishing periodicals, editing books and sharing their activities because they held much the same literary views. In general, these writers can be divided into two different categories.

The first group was represented by progressive and democratic writers such as Zheng Zhenduo, Wang Tongzhao, Ba Jin and Jin Yi. The best-known periodicals they published included *Literature*, edited by Zheng Zhenduo and Wang Tongzhao; *Literary Quarterly*, by Zheng Zhenduo; *Literary Monthly*, by Ba Jin and Jin Yi; and *Literary Miscellany*, by Jin Yi. Of these periodicals, *Literature* enjoyed the longest period of publication and it also had the greatest influence. Other publications such as *Good Companion Literary Series*, *New Magazine of Enlightened Literature*, Life Books shop's *Literary Treasure House*, and *Literary Collections* edited by Ba Jin, also contained many distinguished works. In their activities, many of the writers of this group experienced political and economic suppression by the reactionary forces. At the same time, however, they received unfailing co-operation and valuable help from the League of Left-Wing Writers and its members. During this period,

* Lenin, "History of the Russian Workers' Newspapers and Periodicals," *Complete Works* (Chinese translation), Vol. XX, p. 248.

they produced many works, some of which were notably sombre in tone and gloomy in outlook. In general, these writers tried to expose the evils of the old society. They condemned the corruption and decadence found in the upper class, as they described in depth the misfortunes and sufferings of the down-trodden. Some of these works also expressed the yearning for a bright future which could be created through human effort. Among the outstanding works published were Ba Jin's *The Family*, Cao Yu's *Thunderstorm* and *Sunrise* and Lao She's *Camel Xiangzi*. Together with the distinguished works of the Left-wing writers, these masterpieces took the modern Chinese novel and drama to a high level of achievement.

Writers of the other groups, as represented by Zhou Zuoren, Lin Yutang and Shen Congwen, had leanings towards liberalism. The periodicals they published included *Camel Grass*, edited by Zhou Zouren in Beijing and *Analects*, *Human World* and *Wind of the Universe*, all edited by Lin Yutang at different periods. In their works writers of this group tried to steer clear of social realities as they promoted humour and followed "divine inspiration." Their poetry and prose are rather light in content and simple in approach. A common and distinct feature of the novels such as those by Shen Congwen is the depiction of the natural charm of village life. Most of these writers were in northern China and accordingly they were known collectively as the "Beijing School." Unlike the first group of writers aforementioned, writers of this school kept a certain distance from the League of Left-Wing Writers. At times on certain issues, they even adopted an opposing stand. However, some of the young writers nurtured by the "Beijing School" such as He Qifang, Bian Zhilin and Xiao Qian underwent marked changes after the outbreak of the War of Resistance Against Japan.

IV. The Literary Movement after the Outbreak of the War of Resistance Against Japan

The anti-Japanese war brought about changes in all aspects of life in the country, including, as can be expected, the conditions under which the writers worked. After the fall of Shanghai in November 1937, hitherto the cultural centre, and other cities along the coast, literary and publishing activities were severely hampered. Some of the major periodicals which had a relatively longer history and greater influence such as *Literature, Literary Miscellany, Light* and *Midstream*, ceased publication and consequently, many writers were denied the opportunity of seeing their works in print. As large territories fell one after another into enemy hands, the tide of anti-Japanese feeling also rose throughout the country. It was the chaotic and turbulent life of wartime, and the writers had to cope with an entirely new experience. Many of them were forced by circumstances to leave their "garrets" and moved out of their small world. They went to the interior areas, the countryside or the front. Instead of pursuing their previous literary plans, they devoted their time and energy to a different kind of work which was directly and immediately related to the War of Resistance Against Japan. The primary concern, naturally, was how to ensure the survival of the country.

For a while during the early period of the anti-Japanese war, therefore, literary creativity was at a fairly low point. There was a rapid decrease in the publication of works of any considerable length. In their place, were the numerous shorter works which could immediately bring home to the people the reality of war and the urgency of national salvation, such as correspondence from the front, reportage, street drama, poetry written for declamation in streets and elsewhere and popular literature. These works had a great appeal for the people and were very effective in moving them into action. The circumstances of war made new demands on literature, which, accordingly, changed its character as it responded to the call of necessity.

As the writers were exposed to the harsh realities of life during wartime, they underwent changes in their hearts and minds. Close contact with the common people and, consequently, a better understanding of their lot gave them a wider vision of life. Their works became richer in content. In their efforts to make sense of life and literary creation under war conditions, they gradually realized "how distant the new literature and art have been from the soldiers and the masses for the past twenty years." They fully understood that "literature and art should reach out to the people"* and felt that "because their works have not met the needs of the people they now want to search for something new."** As a result, a fault commonly found in the May Fourth new literature movement began to be remedied, that is, the remoteness of literature and art, in various degrees, from the common people. (It was against this background that the debate on forms of national literature and style took place from 1939 to 1940.) Although, as it turned out, the paths ahead were far from smooth, these changes in the writers' approach to life and literary creation greatly influenced the movement of revolutionary literature and art. Significantly, they marked the beginning of a new period which was characterized by the writers' deep involvement in practical life as they moved freely in the midst of workers, peasants and soldiers.

Of the extensive anti-Japanese cultural activities after the outbreak of the war, particularly striking were those related to drama. Societies were founded such as the Association of Chinese Dramatists and the Shanghai Drama Society for National Salvation. Of the drama performances, most noteworthy were those of *The Defence of Lugou Bridge*, which was written collectively. Other major events were the formation of the Shanghai Drama Troupe for National Salvation and its departure ceremony conducted before it went to other parts of the country to give performances. All these activities revealed the new spirit of the anti-Japanese cultural movement.

After the fall of Shanghai in November 1937, the centre of cultural activities shifted to Wuhan, now the home of a large number of writers who had come from Shanghai, Beijing, Tianjin and Northeast China. At first, these writers did not have any well-run organization, although they were all "pursuing the same goal of extending cultural feelers as far as they could to reach the

* Lao She, "Defence of Wuhan and the Role of Literature and Art," *Wartime Literature and Art*, Vol. I, No. 12, July 9, 1938.

** Mao Dun, "The Development of Revolutionary Literature and Art in the Struggle Against the Oppressive Reactionary Forces," *Essays in Celebration of the National Congress of Literature and Art Workers.*

masses."* Particularly lacking was leadership ideology, and their anti-Japanese fervour often failed to produce the anticipated results. There was, in fact, very little co-ordination of the activities related to literary creation, publishing, and the propaganda work done through literature and art. Their activities also betrayed, in various degrees, their misguidedness and confusion in ideological matters.

In December 1937, Zhou Enlai came to Wuhan as chief representative of the Communist Party on the anti-Japanese national united front and as vice-director of the Political Department of the Military Council. He was very concerned about the development of the anti-Japanese cultural movement and duly worked out guidelines for the activities to be pursued in the Kuomintang-ruled areas with Wuhan as the centre. Through the Office of the Eighth Route Army in the city, the Communist Party newspaper *Xinhua Daily* circulating in the Kuomintang-ruled areas, and through his participation in various important anti-Japanese cultural activities, Zhou Enlai did a good deal of co-ordinating work. A large number of literary and art workers in Wuhan were subsequently organized. Some went to Yan'an or other anti-Japanese democratic bases. Most of them, however, joined the anti-Japanese national united front, through the arrangements of the National Federation of Anti-Japanese Writers and Artists and the Third Office, under the charge of Guo Moruo, of the Military Council's Political Department. Thus, a powerful anti-Japanese cultural army was formed, and their activities were numerous. Almost instantly the streets of Wuhan were echoing their anti-Japanese songs. Everywhere theatrical performances were given and public poetry readings held. Publications multiplied and the morale of the writers was high. This new development in literature and art was characterized by extraordinary vitality as it responded to the new political situation which promised better days to come.

The National Federation of Anti-Japanese Writers and Artists, founded in Wuhan on March 27, 1938, was the first nationwide organization of its kind to appear after the formation of the Society

* Guo Moruo, *Mighty Waves*, 1959 edition, p. 91.

of Anti-Japanese Dramatists. The founders of the Federation comprised ninety-seven representatives from the literary circles. At its inaugural meeting Zhou Enlai gave a significant talk.* Among the forty-five executive members elected were Guo Moruo, Mao Dun, Feng Naichao, Xia Yan, Hu Feng, Tian Han, Ding Ling, Wu Zuxiang, Xu Dishan, Lao She, Ba Jin, Zheng Zhenduo, Zhu Ziqing, Yu Dafu, Zhu Guangqian, Zhang Daofan, Yao Pengzi, Chen Xiying and Wang Pinling. Zhou Enlai, Sun Ke and Chen Lifu were elected honorary executive members, while Lao She was put in charge of the daily work of the Federation. Soon after it came into being, the Federation set up several dozen branches and correspondence offices in different parts of the country. Through the work of the Party members of the Federation and the progressive writers, the Communist Party effectively provided leadership in organizing anti-Japanese cultural activities. Similar nationwide associations were also formed by those who were working in music, film and painting.

The founding of the National Federation of Anti-Japanese Writers and Artists well indicated that for the cause of national liberation, the most extensive united front had been formed. The slogan adopted at its inaugural meeting was: "Take literature to the countryside; take literature to the army." Guided by this principle, the Federation organized visits to the front. These and other activities made a great impact on the writers as more and more of them felt the urge to "go to the countryside, go to the army." The Federation's periodical *Wartime Literature and Art* was the only all-comprehensive publication during the War of Resistance Against Japan. In all, seventy-one issues were published from May 4, 1938 to May 1946 and the periodical played a significant role in the cultural activities of that period.

About the same time the Federation was founded, the Third Office of the Military Council's Political Department was established in Wuhan in April 1938, under the charge of Guo Moruo. Led directly by Zhou Enlai, the Department's vice-director, and by a special branch of the Communist Party in the office, the Third

---

* Quoted in the Wuhan edition of *Xinhua Daily*, March 28, 1938.

Office organized the literary and art workers who had come to Wuhan and the cultural societies in the city in a united attempt to extend the anti-Japanese cultural activities, including various kinds of performances and street propaganda work. Troupes were sent to the front, cultural supply centres for the front were formed and rallies and public addresses were organized. The cultural activities in the early period of war soon reached their climax. Of all these activities, the most influential were the dramatic performances. In August 1938, the Third Office organized the drama troupes and cultural workers who had come to Wuhan, including the all-important Shanghai Drama Troupe for National Salvation. This resulted in the creation of nine anti-Japanese drama teams, four anti-Japanese propaganda teams, a children's drama group and a film-showing team. After the reorganization of the Third Office, the thirteen drama and propaganda teams merged and were re-structured to form ten groups instead, all being given the same name of Anti-Japanese Drama Propaganda Team. These and the other groups went to different parts of the country to do anti-Japanese cultural propaganda work. For eleven years the drama teams were active, against all odds. Some of them were banned by the Kuomintang government for a long period. Some of the members including the well-known dramatist Liu Baoluo, former secretary of the Federation of Left-Wing Dramatists, lost their lives. But most of these teams survived the severe disruptive measures taken by the Kuomintang designed to bring about their reorganization, disintegration or dissolution. However, in spite of the adverse political conditions, material and other restraints, they remained firm in their struggles and continued their cultural activities, which contributed greatly to the War of Resistance Against Japan and to the democratic movement in the country.

After the fall of Wuhan in October 1938, the Japanese gradually stopped their strategic attack on the Kuomintang-ruled areas. Their main military forces were shifted to the battlefields of the Communist-led anti-Japanese democratic bases. At the same time, they intensified their efforts to lure the Kuomintang into political surrender. As Chairman Mao observed: "The Kuomintang government then began to change its policy, gradually shifting the emphasis from resistance to Japan to opposition to the Communist Party and the people."* In the areas under its rule, the Kuomintang began to restrict and even ban various kinds of anti-Japanese activities. It brutally persecuted, first and foremost, the Communists although others who maintained an anti-Japanese stand also met with the same fate. The large-scale anti-Communist campaigns it launched soon reached one climax after another. Particularly shocking was the Southern Anhui Incident** of January 1941. As the Kuomintang continued its persecution, it adopted more and more severe measures in an effort to stamp out anti-Japanese cultural activities. To strengthen its control over what was considered anti-Japanese literature, it established the Central Censorship Board with branch committees in different parts of the country. A number of the anti-Japanese cultural groups were forced to reorganize themselves, some were disbanded, and quite a few cultural workers were sent to concentration camps (for example, Feng Xuefeng) or even murdered.

In these circumstances of persecution, the Party's Central Committee decided to preserve talent and strength. Also because of Zhou Enlai's personal concern about their safety, a number of the cultural workers and a few drama teams moved to Yan'an and other anti-Japanese democratic bases. In spring 1941, some of them went to Hong Kong and other places. As the persecution escalated, many of the progressive writers in the Kuomintang-ruled areas had to leave for other cities such as Chongqing, Guilin and Kunming, where their activities were also severely restricted. Consequently, during the period from the fall of Wuhan in October 1938 to the Southern Anhui Incident in January 1941, the cultural movement in the Kuomintang-ruled areas suffered a setback. There was a marked decrease in the

* Mao Zedong, "On Coalition Government," *Selected Works*, Foreign Languages Press, Beijing, 1965, Vol. III, p. 217.

** The Southern Anhui Incident occurred on January 7, 1941, when the Communist New Fourth Army and the Kuomintang Army agreed to join forces to repel the Japanese invaders. On the way north, in southern Anhui Province, the nine thousand troops of the New Fourth Army fell into an ambush by eighty thousand Kuomintang troops and—but for a thousand or so who managed to break through—were wiped out. The commander of the army Ye Ting was seriously wounded and taken prisoner, and the deputy commander of the army Xiang Ying got killed.

once-abundant production of anti-Japanese works; in particular, theatrical performances were heavily reduced. The feeling of anxiety and frustration pervaded some of the full-length novels and plays, in sharp contrast with the generally optimistic tone found in the works of the early period of the war.

Though out of necessity many of the writers had to retreat to the interior, quite a few stayed behind and continued the bitter struggle, under the leadership of the Communist Party. The play *Foggy Chongqing* by Song Zhidi, published in 1940, further developed the trend set by Zhang Tianyi earlier with his short story *Mr Hua Wei*, which sought to expose the corruption in the Kuomintang-ruled areas. *Panning Out Gold*, a full-length novel, also received much acclaim in the literary circles for its perceptive delineation of the lives of the peasants. Later, appeared works such as *Corrosion* and *Qu Yuan*, in which the writers made use of contemporary and historical material respectively in their attack on the fascist rule of the Kuomintang. These works highlighted the sharp struggles of the writers, whose only weapon was the pen, against the stubborn reactionaries. Their achievements were remarkable. In the literary battles, too, they successfully refuted the theory held by Liang Shiqiu and others that "literature and art have nothing to do with the War of Resistance Against Japan" and the proposal by Zhang Daofan that "writers should not write only about the dark side of society." Above all, they exposed the strategy of the "Gang of the Warring States" who openly advocated the political views of the fascist agents.

In September 1940, after the Political Department of the Military Council had been reorganized, Guo Moruo with the support of Zhou Enlai left the Third Office in protest against the government's order that all staff members of the Third Office should join the Kuomintang. Two months later, in November, he founded the Cultural Work Committee in Chongqing with himself serving as chairman and Yang Hansheng as vice-chairman. Prominent members of the Committee included Shen Junru, Mao Dun, Lao She, Jian Bozan, Du Guoyang, Tian Han and Hong Shen. The Committee's work was divided into three areas: international studies, analysis of the information about the enemy, and cultural studies which included drama, poetry, music and the other fine arts. Until it was disbanded by the Kuomintang government on March 30, 1945, the Committee was the centre of the progressive cultural circle in the Kuomintang-ruled areas during the later period of the War of Resistance Against Japan.

In the early period of the war, the cultural movement was gaining momentum in East China, with its centre in the "lone island" of Shanghai. Although after the fall of Shanghai in November 1937, a large number of writers and artists fled to the interior or went to the front and the anti-Japanese democratic bases, the anti-Japanese cultural activities in Shanghai did not stop. For over four years up to the Japanese attack on Pearl Harbour on December 8, 1941, the progressive writers and patriotic cultural workers rallied round the Communist underground organizations. They took advantage of the peculiar environment of the British, French and other foreign "concessions," where they carried out anti-Japanese cultural activities openly or secretly and started what was known as the Shanghai "lone island" literary movement. Through the stage and the newspapers, they continued their unwavering patriotic struggle and anti-Japanese propaganda work, even though they were operating under difficult conditions created by the political forces of the Japanese, the traitors and their supporters. They published a number of patriotic and progressive works such as *The Complete Works of Lu Xun*, *Literary Works of the Great Age* and *A Collection of Drama* in four volumes each containing ten plays. The works, including translations, of Fang Zhimin and Qu Qiubai were also published, as was the Chinese translation of Edgar Snow's *Red Star Over China*. They attacked the so-called "Great Far Eastern literature" and "the literature of peace" advocated by the traitorous writers who fawned on Japanese imperialism. The works of these writers, they pointed out, were hallmarks of a slave mentality. They also attacked the pornographic nature of these works and published "The Declaration Against Pornographic Culture." In addition, they did everything they could to extend the work of the national united front in the literary and art circles. They united and organized the patriotic writers, artists and other cultural workers including folklore artists in their common struggle against the forces of the Japanese, the traitors and the reactionaries.

Before the Southern Anhui Incident of January 1941, the cultural movement in the "lone island" of Shanghai was full of vigour. Drama, in particular, flourished. The most active group was the Shanghai Drama Society, but the newly-formed troupes also made their contribution. In producing modern, historical and progressive foreign plays as well as adapting classical and folk operas, all the drama groups took full advantage of the stage to heighten the people's national consciousness and arouse their patriotic feelings. For example, they dramatized the lives of the national heroes who had fought against foreign invasion and the performances achieved great success in inspiring the spectators to follow in their footsteps. Among the plays which drew a large audience and had a wide political influence at the time were Yu Ling's *Shanghai at Night*, *Weeping Flowers* and the historical play *Heroes of the Ming Dynasty*, Ah Ying's (Qian Xingcun's) historical play *The Legacy of Hate from the Ming Dynasty* (later renamed *Flowers of Blood*) and Romain Rolland's *Le Jue de L'amour et de la Mort*, translated by Li Jianwu.

The essay was also popular for quite sometime in the "lone island" of Shanghai. Writers found it most effective in exposing and satirizing the vices of the day. Their essays appeared mainly in the periodicals such as *Essays Series*, *Lu Xun Feng* (*Lu Xun Wind*) and in the supplements of newspapers. Particularly influential was *The Border Drum*, a collection of essays by six writers, published by the newspaper *Wen Hui Bao*. As the number of essays increased and their influence grew, these publications drew the attention of the enemy and the traitors. In these harsh circumstances, the progressive writers found themselves divided in their views on the role expected to be played by the essay. Controversy arose between Ba Ren (Wang Renshu) and Ah Ying over the essays published in *Lu Xun Feng*. Shortly after this, however, the progressive writers and artists sorted out their differences and expressed their collective thinking in a joint publication, "Our Views on the *Lu Xun Feng* Essays," which confirmed the belief that the essay was a powerful weapon in the struggle against the enemy. They also forcefully answered the attacks of the traitorous writers and successfully refuted their arguments.

After the outbreak of the Pacific War at the end of 1941, however, the political situation in the "lone island" rapidly deteriorated and many writers and artists were forced to move out of Shanghai or to go underground. As a result, cultural activities gradually came to standstill. It was not until July 1943 that the writers who were still in Shanghai resumed writing, upon the instigation of Ke Ling when he became editor of the commercial magazine *Phenomena*. The contributors included Wang Tongzhao, Shi Tuo, Xu Tiaofu, Lou Shiyi, Fu Lei and other young writers who later became accomplished essayists and novelists.

Compared with what was going on in the Kuomintang-ruled areas and in the "lone island" of Shanghai, the cultural scene in the Communist-led anti-Japanese bases was very different. In a free and democratic political atmosphere, the writers and artists had close contact with the workers, peasants and soldiers. They enjoyed freedom of movement and could go even as far as the front. Furthermore, their work was fully supported by the Communist Party and the various administrative organizations. After the Red Army arrived in northern Shaanxi Province, the Federation of Chinese Writers and Artists was formed first in Bao'an and then in Yan'an. (It was later renamed the National Federation of Anti-Japanese Writers and Artists, the Shaanxi-Gansu-Ningxia Border Region Branch). Cultural activities for the masses were further increased. After the Lugouqiao Incident* of July 7, 1937, many writers and artists came to Yan'an and other anti-Japanese democratic bases from different parts of the country including, of course, Shanghai. They joined the local writers and artists, sharing their work and participating in their activities. Consequently, the literature and art movement was given an even greater impetus. More

* On the night of July 7, 1937, Japanese troops bombarded Wanping Town and Lugouqiao (known to the Westerners as Marco Polo Bridge) southwest of Beijing. The Chinese troops stationed there fought back. This has been known as the Lugouqiao Incident, also July 7th Incident, which marked the beginning of China's War of Resistance Against Japan.

literary periodicals appeared such as *The Literature and Art Front*,* *Battle Song*, *Poetry Construction*, *Blades of Grass* and *Spring Rain*. Many literary and art societies also came into existence. In Yan'an and some other bases, anti-Japanese songs, declamatory poetry, street poetry and leaflet poetry were extremely popular. A number of writers went to the front or behind enemy lines and what they wrote from their observations was both realistic and moving. Indeed, they fully deserved Mao Zedong's praise of the creative works of literature at the time.

Shortly before and after 1939, drama and other cultural activities began to flourish in the vast countryside of the anti-Japanese bases. These activities were heavily supported by professional organizations such as the Northwest Battlefield Service Group, Yan'an Lu Xun Academy of Arts, Taihang Mountain Drama Group, Anti-Japanese Drama Society and the Central Hebei Front Line Drama Society. In the North China base area alone, there were over a hundred relatively well-established village drama groups in 1940. By the time the Japanese started the May 1st mopping-up campaign of 1942, the number of drama groups and propaganda teams had gone well beyond one thousand in the central Hebei and Beiyue regions.** Their activities enriched the cultural life in the countryside.

January 1940, Mao Zedong published his essay "On New Democracy" in which he gave a clear, perceptive analysis of the cultural activities since the May Fourth Movement and of the revolutionary culture prevailing at the time. The essay was extremely influential in providing guidance for the progressive writers and artists throughout the country. It also made great impact on the literary and art movement in the border regions and democratic base areas. At its first congress, for example, the Shaanxi-Gansu-Ningxia Border Region Branch of the National Federation of Anti-Japanese Writers and Artists issued a declaration

---

* *The Literature and Art Front* was edited in Yan'an and published in the Kuomintang-ruled areas.

** These figures are taken from Sha Kefu's address, "The Drama Movement in the Villages of North China and the Reform of the People's Art," given at the first National Congress of Literary and Art Workers. The address was published in *Essays in Celebration of the National Congress of Literary and Art Workers.*

urging all the cultural workers to participate in the creation of national, democratic and scientific new culture. Under the guidance of the professional writers and artists, and through the cultural activities of the masses, many people's poets began to make their presence felt, such as Li Jisheng in Shanxi Province and Sun Wanfu in northern Shaanxi Province. In their works, which were well loved by the readers, they used a new style to depict the new life of the people who were engaged in the anti-Japanese struggle led by Communist Party. And that was definitely a new feature of the literature and art which came out of the democratic base areas in the early period of the War of Resistance Against Japan.

However, there were problems, too. Of these, the most serious was that writers and artists with a petty-bourgeois background could not integrate with the workers, peasants and soldiers, who were now the leaders. As Mao Zedong pointed out, "it does not necessarily follow that, having come to the base areas, they have already integrated themselves completely with the masses of the people [there]."* He went on: "Intellectuals who want to integrate themselves with the masses, who want to serve the masses, must go through a process in which they and the masses come to know each other well. This process may, and certainly will, involve much pain and friction."** To remove the pain and the friction, one had to undergo severe tests over a long period. Similarly, He Qifang explained in his article "Remould Oneself, Remould Literature and Art": "During the war, many writers and artists followed the dictates of circumstances and went to the front. They were of course also led by their fervour. One can say that has been the general trend. But it has to be said that most of them had only a vague idea of what they could offer in the war against the enemy. They did not have sufficient understanding of how they could best serve the workers, peasants and soldiers. Besides, many of them went to

---

* Mao Zedong, "Talks at the Yan'an Forum on Literature and Art," *Selected Works*, Foreign Languages Press, Beijing, 1965, Vol. III, p. 70.

** *Ibid.*, p. 96.

the front only to collect material for their writing later."* Indeed, even though they had chosen to come to Yan'an, some of the cultural workers never mixed with the workers, peasants and soldiers.

The many weaknesses of these petty-bourgeois intellectuals became all too clear when the anti-Japanese war was at a stalemate. Their true selves were revealed particularly in 1941 and 1942, when the democratic bases faced the joint attacks from the Japanese and traitorous troops and Chiang Kai-shek's armies. Severe damage was done to production and the economy, and that made living conditions extremely harsh. In these circumstances, many of the writers looked for friends only in the intellectual circles. The focus of their writing, too, was shifted to the lives of these intellectuals. They did not know the workers, peasants or soldiers well and they often felt like "a hero with no place to display his prowess." To them, writing was a means of portraying their own petty-bourgeois selves, and this approach accounted for the morbid tone and prejudiced outlook in their works. In observing life in the revolutionary bases, some of them were influenced by the petty-bourgeois concepts of individualism, ultra-democracy and egalitarianism. They could not submit themselves to the strict organizational discipline and frequently complained about the conditions under which they lived and worked. They were discontented with both the material and the spiritual life in Yan'an. Indeed, they had forgotten that the conditions and the duties of the cultural workers in the revolutionary bases were entirely different from those in the Kuomintang-controlled areas. So they said: "Chongqing is not the only place shrouded in fog. The fog is here, too." They proposed to expose the "wrongs" found in Yan'an. The situation was further affected by factionalism as the writers published satirical essays in the periodicals put out by their own clique. In these circumstances, it is understandable that Wang Shiwei, in order to attract as much attention as possible, published essays such as "Wild Lilies," "Politicians and Artists" and many other articles, which gave distorted accounts of the revolutionary base areas.

---

* Published in *The Liberation Daily*, April 3, 1943.

All in all, however, the emergence of the aforementioned problems did not mean that the cultural workers in Yan'an were retreating from their original progressive stand. Quite the contrary, these problems indicated that revolutionary literature and art had in fact entered another stage of development in the base areas. Only when the problems were made known could proper solutions be found. The time had finally come to tackle some of the fundamental problems deeply rooted in the Chinese revolutionary literary and art movement.

V. The Yan'an Forum on Literature and Art and Literature in the Liberated Areas

In May 1942, Mao Zedong delivered his "'Talks at the Yan'an Forum on Literature and Art," which eventually solved the long-existing and basic problems that had been plaguing the movement of revolutionary literature and art. He summed up the historical experience gathered from the trends and developments since the May Fourth Movement of 1919. In addition, he correlated the state of cultural activities in Yan'an with that in various other anti-Japanese democratic base areas and offered solutions to many problems concerning theory and policy. The "Talks" took Marxist theories on literature and art one stage further and it has since proved to be a significant piece of work in the history of Chinese literature and art as well as in the history of ideology.

In the "Talks," the first topic of discussion, to which the greatest attention is subsequently given, is the fundamental principle that literature should "serve the masses" and its related question of "how it serves the masses." That he tackled the key issues and provided solutions to the problems which troubled the literary world then, showed his acute power of perception as a Marxist thinker. True, in the late 1920s and the early 1930s the theories of Engels and Lenin on the relation between literature and the labouring masses had been introduced into China. But in practice the question of what kind of people literature and art should serve had not been properly dealt with. In the early years of the May Fourth Movement, some writers did advocate the idea of "literature of the common people" and "literature of the masses." Later, they even suggested specifically that literature and art should belong to the workers and the peasants. Indeed, their many discussions on these topics revealed signs that they were making some headway. However, as it turned out, what they meant by "common people" and "the masses" were in fact the urban petty bourgeoisie and its intellectuals. To many of them, "the popularization of literature and art" was only a matter of using popular means of expression in their choice of form and style. Of course, the revolutionary writers had produced some good works which depicted the struggles of the workers and peasants. But because of the conditions at the time, historically determined, and because of the as yet unclear thinking of the writers, the integration of literature and art with the workers and peasants had not been given serious attention. Quite a few Left-wing writers, in fact, "betrayed their petty-bourgeois feelings and thoughts, which they mistakenly regarded as those of the proletariat."*

The many problems in the literary and art circles in Yan'an clearly revealed the weakness of the May Fourth Movement. It had become even more obvious around 1941 because of the new historical conditions. Mao Zedong emphatically stated: "The question of 'for whom?' is fundamental; it is a question of principle.... [We must] achieve a complete and thorough solution."** Based on his understanding of the conditions existing in China then, he pointed out specifically: "Our literature and art are first for the workers.... Secondly, they are for the peasants.... Thirdly, they are for the armed workers and peasants, namely the Eighth Route and the New Fourth Armies and the other armed units of the people.... Fourthly, they are for the labouring masses of the urban petty bourgeoisie and for the petty-bourgeois intellectuals." He called on the literary and art workers "to take the class stand of the proletariat." Repeatedly, he stressed that literature and art should be, first

* Zhou Yang, Preface to *Marxism and Literature and Art*.

** Mao Zedong, "Talks at the Yan'an Forum on Literature and Art," *Selected Works*, Foreign Languages Press, Beijing, 1965, Vol. III, pp. 78, 79. Unless otherwise stated, the quotations in this section are taken from the "Talks," *Ibid.*, pp. 69-97.

and foremost, "for the workers, peasants and soldiers"; in other words, the masses. And that had always been his starting-point in considering the various problems related to culture. As early as 1938, he had already stated in the article "The Role of the Chinese Communist Party in the National War" that the new culture should be characterized by a "fresh, lively Chinese style and spirit which the common people of China love."* In 1940, he also emphasized in another article, "On New Democracy," that the culture of the new democracy was to be "a national, scientific and mass culture" and that "it should serve the toiling masses of workers and peasants who make up more than 90 percent of the nation's population and should gradually become their very own."** This line of thinking links together all his ideas in the "Talks." In his view, "a thing is good only when it brings real benefit to the masses of the people."

In dealing with the relation between raising standards and popularizing literature and art, Mao Zedong, as always, had the masses uppermost in his mind. He explained: "Only by starting from the workers, peasants and soldiers can we have a correct understanding of popularization and of the raising of standards and find the proper relationship between the two." The broad masses of workers, peasants and soldiers—particularly the peasants—had long been under the yoke of the exploiting classes, bound by feudal superstition, ignorance and the shackles of the force of habit of various petty producers. They desperately yearned for cultural emancipation and the liberation of thinking. They wanted to see a widespread movement of enlightenment, eagerly waiting for works of literature and art and welcomed cultural knowledge which could meet their urgent needs and which they found easy to absorb. In short, they wanted a culture which could add fuel to their revolutionary flames, a culture which could strengthen their belief that they would win in the common struggle against the enemy. For them, the prime need was not "more flowers on the brocade" but "fuel in snowy weather." Naturally, "popularization is

---

* Mao Zedong, "The Role of the Communist Party in the National War," *Selected Works*, Foreign Languages Press, Beijing, 1965, Vol. II, p. 210.

** Mao Zedong, "On New Democracy," *Ibid.*, pp. 380, 381.

the more pressing task." However, popularization needed guidance because once that goal had been achieved, people would demand higher standards, including the kind needed by the cadres. Therefore, while emphasizing the popularization of literature and art, one should not neglect raising standards at the same time. Mao Zedong put forward his well-known formula: "The raising of standards is based on popularization, while popularization is guided by the raising of standards." Consequently, much of the hitherto confused thinking about the relation between the two was cleared away. He also pointed out that "since our literature and art are basically for the workers, peasants and soldiers, 'popularization' means to popularize among the workers, peasants and soldiers and 'raising standards' means to advance from their present level." Raising standards, he continued, did not mean "raising the workers, peasants and soldiers to the 'heights' of the feudal classes, the bourgeoisie or the petty-bourgeois intellectuals; it means raising the level of literature and art in the direction in which the workers, peasants and soldiers are themselves advancing." Mao Zedong's expositions on the relation between popularization and the raising of standards proved to be of great value as guiding principles not only for literary and art workers but also for those who were working in other areas.

The significant historical contribution of the "Talks" is that it linked the laws of literature and art closely together with their special characteristics. Then it proceeded to solve scientifically the key problems encountered in the development of proletarian literature. Mao Zedong tackled these problems from two starting-points: the feelings and thoughts of the writers and the source of social life. Works of literature and art, he explained, "are products of the reflection in the human brain of the life of a given society. Revolutionary literature and art are the products of the reflection of the life of the people in the brains of revolutionary writers and artists." The establishment and development of proletarian literature and art, therefore, depended not only on "the brains of revolutionary writers and artists," the subjective conditions, but also on "the life of the people" as source of material, the objective conditions. Only after the writers had solved these two key problems—that is, the change in thinking and feelings and the acquisition of social life as source of creative material—"can we have a literature and art that are truly for the workers, peasants and soldiers, a truly proletarian literature and art." That was why Mao Zedong suggested that while studying Marxism the writers should go into the "very midst and into the thick of practical struggles of the workers, peasants and soldiers."

In tackling the first key problem, Mao Zedong attached great importance to the internal changes undergone by writers with a petty-bourgeois background. He gave a new definition of the popularization of literature and art: "Many comrades like to talk about 'a mass style.' But what does it really mean? It means that the thoughts and feelings of our writers and artists should be fused with those of the masses of workers, peasants and soldiers." Using his own experience as an example, he earnestly and specifically explained that it was necessary and possible to undergo the change in thinking and feelings in the process of integration with the workers, peasants and soldiers. Lenin, too, had suggested, in his letter to Gorky shortly after the October Revolution in 1917, that writers and artists should go and live among the workers, peasants and soldiers. He maintained that even a great writer like Gorky, who had been a factory worker and who had a wide spectrum of life experience, should try to observe more how the workers, peasants and soldiers lived, observe more what was new, in order to feel deeply the pulse of the revolution and of the age. This would eventually enable a writer to control his unhealthy sentiments. In the 1940s, the Chinese proletariat together with the other revolutionary classes had established their government in certain regions of the country. The writers and artists were living in the midst of the workers, peasants and soldiers who were now in power. A large number of petty-bourgeois intellectuals through long and practical struggle had also acquired the experience of remoulding themselves into proletarian revolutionaries. Under these new historical conditions in China, Mao Zedong developed Lenin's ideas into a complete theory which became a useful and practical guide for writers in the process of "proletarianization."

The other key problem in developing proletarian literature and art was whether the writers and artists could draw enough from life experience as their source of material. This, in effect, was the same question as how well they understood the masses of workers and peasants. On this issue, some of the early promoters of proletarian literature were rather muddled in their thinking. They thought it was a fallacy that "literary creation hinges entirely upon the writer's experience." Observation and imagination, they maintained, would make it unnecessary for them to get involved in actual life experience. Thus Jiang Guangci could argue: "To describe the lives of the bandits, you have to become a bandit yourself. To describe the life of a prostitute, you have to be a prostitute. Isn't that rather ridiculous?"* This view, plausible indeed, was refuted by Lu Xun in his article "A Glimpse of the Literature and Art in Shanghai." He pointed out: "A writer living in the old society is familiar with what goes on there and he has got used to people in that society. That is why he can 'observe.' He cannot write about people and what goes on in the proletarian class if he has never had anything to do with them before. His accounts, if indeed he tries to write about them, will be inaccurate. That is why a revolutionary writer must at least live with the revolution, or deeply feel the revolutionary pulse." Lu Xun's analysis was perceptive and incisive. However, it did not attract enough attention because the Kuomintang government "prevented the workers, peasants and soldiers from having access to revolutionary literature and art." That segregation hampered the development of proletarian literature and art. Thus some of the writers who arrived at Yan'an and other anti-Japanese democratic bases were out of tune with the workers, peasants and soldiers. They felt that their mission was in sharp contradiction with the existing conditions. As the Chinese saying goes, "even the most capable housewife cannot make a meal out of nothing." In other words, writers could not write about the workers, peasants and soldiers without showing a lack of proper understanding of them. "When they do depict them," Mao Zedong noted, "the clothes are the clothes of working people but the faces are those of petty-bourgeois intellectuals."

* Hua Xili (Jiang Guangci), "On the Old and New Writers and Revolutionary Literature," *The Sun Monthly*, April number, 1928.

There were even worse distortions of truth in the writers' delineations. To solve the problem, Mao Zedong urged: "China's revolutionary writers and artists, writers and artists of promise, must go among the masses; they must for a long period of time unreservedly and wholeheartedly go among the masses of workers, peasants and soldiers, go into the heat of the struggle, go to the only source, the broadest and richest source, in order to observe, experience, study and analyse all the different kinds of people, all the classes, all the masses, all the vivid patterns of life and struggle, all the raw materials of literature and art. Only then can they proceed to creative work."

Through the process of going into the very midst of the masses and into the thick of practical struggles, then, cultural workers could remould their thinking and acquire the source of their creative works. That, Mao Zedong pointed out, was the essential condition for the development of Chinese proletarian literature and art. His propositions are of great value because they are in complete accord with the characteristics of literature and art. Of course, literature and art should reflect, and therefore be faithful to, objective life. But such depictions are done through the thinking and artistry of the creator, and without this refraction, so to speak, there will be no works of literature and art. Herein lies the relevance of a writer's subjective feelings and thoughts and, indeed, his understanding of life. For a piece of work to move the reader, these feelings should have been deeply felt by the writer himself first. In that sense, the work is a product of his heart and soul. However, because these feelings and thoughts have found their home in the writer's works, they should be in harmony with the realities of life; otherwise, they will be mere outbursts of shallow emotions and empty talk, which do not have the moving power of literature and art. On the other hand, if a writer depicts life without any feeling, any concern at all, he will likewise find it hard to produce works which can move the reader. The laws of literature and art require the integration of the creator's subjectivity, that is to say his thinking and feelings, with the objective observations of life in his works. In the creation of proletarian literature, therefore, these laws lend special significance to the writer's remoulding of his thinking and feelings. They also demand that the writer should follow a special route to the source of artistic creation, a journey through which he can achieve the fusion of the internal with the external, the subjective with the objective elements. Upon this very concept of fusion, Mao Zedong developed his ideas on literature and art in the "Talks." As he saw it, in proletarian literary works the writer's feelings and thoughts were never out of touch with the realities of life, and the works in turn would be enriched by what had come out of the writer's heart and mind.

In the "Talks," Mao Zedong analysed the relation between literature and art and politics. He also discussed the relation between the work done by the Party in literature and art and the Party's work as a whole. While clearing up the muddled thinking found in the cultural circles, he confirmed the glorious and militant tradition of revolutionary literature and art which had its origin in the May Fourth Movement. More than twenty years before the Yan'an Forum, Chinese revolutionary literature and art had already played a significant political role in the New Democratic Revolution. As Mao Zedong put it, "literature and art have been an important and successful part of the cultural front since the May Fourth Movement" and they had made "a great contribution" to the revolution. Two erroneous tendencies had emerged in the past, however, with regard to the relation between literature and art and politics. The first originated in the view advocated by Trotsky in the 1920s that literary and artistic creation "is a subconscious process," that "art and political theories cannot be unified,"* and that proletarian literature and art "will never come into existence."** According to this view, literature and art could only go in the opposite direction of proletarian politics. This belief had a negative influence on a number of people in the Chinese progressive literary and art circles. The other erroneous tendency was to

* The quotations are taken from Trotsky's address delivered at the conference on the Party's policies on literature and art, convened by the Central Committee of the Soviet Communist Party on May 9, 1924.

** See Trotsky's Foreword to *Literature and Revolution*. The Chinese translation was published in the *Unnamed Series*, No. 13, February 1928.

see literature and art only as tools serving political purposes such as justifying and publicizing certain policies.

Mao Zedong criticized the dualism of Trotsky's view with regard to the relation between literature and art and politics. He also pointed out the undesirable tendency, at the other extreme, of oversimplification and vulgarization. He explained: "In the world today, all culture, all literature and art belong to definite classes and are geared to definite political lines. There is in fact no such thing as art for art's sake, art that stands above classes or art that is detached from or independent of politics. Proletarian literature and art are part of the whole proletarian revolutionary cause; they are, as Lenin said, cogs and wheels in the whole revolutionary machine." He emphasized the objective law that literature and art must not be separated from politics. Literature and art are a kind of social ideology which is built upon a certain economic base, serving the needs of that base itself. But because it is "an ideology much higher, that is, much farther away from its economic base,"* it often needs politics as a link in rendering its service. Politics is "the concentrated expression of economics"** and, as Mao Zedong observed, "only through politics can the needs of the class and the masses find expression in concentrated form." Therefore, revolutionary literary and art workers must pay attention to the relationship between literature and art and politics. At the same time, to avoid the debasement of the relation between literature and art and politics, he stressed in the "Talks": "When we say that literature and art are subordinate to politics, we mean class politics, the politics of the masses, not the politics of a few so-called statesmen." True proletarian politics, he reminded the cultural workers, would always stand for the basic interests of the people in accordance with the objective realities of life; that which went against the interests of the people and the objective realities of life could never even pretend to be proletarian politics. Of course, proletarian politicians sometimes made mistakes, too. That was why the ques-

* Engels, "Ludwig Fuerbach and the End of Classical German Philosophy," *Selected Works of Marx and Engels*, Vol. IV.

** Mao Zedong, "On New Democracy," *Selected Works*, Foreign Languages Press, Beijing, 1965, Vol. II, p. 340.

tion of literature and art serving proletarian politics should not be separated from the other question of their function which was to depict life truthfully. In an honest approach to life, however, the political nature of literature and art and their truthfulness to life could become one. This union was emphasized by Mao Zedong when he distinguished between the proletarian and the bourgeois politicians. He wrote:

> Revolutionary statesmen, the political specialists who know the science or art of revolutionary politics, are simply the leaders of millions upon millions of statesmen—the masses. The task is to collect the opinions of these mass statesmen, sift and refine them, and return them to the masses, who then take them and put them into practice. They are therefore not the kind of aristocratic 'statesmen' who work behind closed doors and fancy they have a monopoly of wisdom. Herein lies the difference in principle between proletarian statesmen and decadent bourgeois statesmen. This is precisely why there can be complete unity between the political character of our literary and artistic works and their truthfulness. It would be wrong to fail to realize this and to debase the politics and the statesmen of the proletariat.

To avoid oversimplifying the relation between literature and art and politics and to avoid a too narrow and mechanical understanding of politics, Mao Zedong specifically explained in the "Talks" that literature and art should serve "the revolutionary tasks set by the Party in a given revolutionary period." This could turn out to be quite a long period. Also, these "revolutionary tasks" were undertaken in the interest of the proletariat and the masses of other labouring people as an answer to the practical needs during their struggle in that particular period. To complete these tasks was the goal not only of the Party but also the whole nation, and the guidelines for their completion would be welcomed by all. Revolutionary literature and art, as a component of the proletarian revolutionary machine, would function effectively only when they were serving the cause of revolution.

For literature and art to be properly integrated with politics, the integrity of their special character should be maintained and respected. In the process of creation, literature and art follow their own inherent laws. Violate these laws, and the perfect fusion of literature and art with politics can never be achieved. That was why Mao Zedong showed his utmost respect for these laws in his explanations of the relation between literature and art and politics. He emphasized: "Politics cannot be equated with art, nor can a general world outlook be equated with a method of artistic creation and criticism." To him, "Marxism embraces but cannot replace realism in literary and artistic creation." It would be extremely naive and harmful to believe that correct political thinking can warrant the violation of the internal laws of art. The characteristics of art can be seen not only in the finished product. They manifest themselves throughout the process of creation, in the emergence of form and content which together give art its distinctive being. According to the theory of dialectical materialism, everything in nature and in the human society is a dialectic unity of its own substance and form. The uniting of politics with art, therefore, does not simply mean finding suitable artistic forms of expression for the political content. It demands that artists should, out of the furnace of life experience, smelt their own metal which bears the hallmark of their own political inclinations and artistic excellence. In artistic creation, then, the main question is how to explore life experience under the guidance of the laws of art, how to evolve naturally an integrated political-artistic content. Many great works of art have a pungent and deep political content which is conveyed in accordance with the special laws and demands of art. This is done not by mechanically giving politics an attractive appearance, reducing abstract phenomena to concrete shapes, or by lending easily recognizable cloaks to profound concepts. Precisely because he objected to the mindless following of formulas and concepts, Mao Zedong believed that "politics cannot be equated with art" and that "to study Marxism means to apply the dialectical materialist and historical materialist viewpoint in our observation of the world, of society and of literature and art; it does not mean writing philosophical lectures into our works of literature and art."

The significance Mao Zedong attached to the special characteristics of literature and art can be seen throughout his "Talks." He suggested, for example, that the "primary task" of revolutionary writers "is to understand people and know them well," and that "they should conscientiously learn the language of the masses." He believed that "we must take over all the fine things in our literary and artistic heritage." Literature and art, he also maintained, have their own special "questions of methods and style." He suggested: "Our criticism ought to permit the free competition of all varieties of works of art." As he saw it, "works of art which lack artistic quality have no force, however progressive they are politically. Therefore we oppose both the tendency to produce works of art with a wrong political viewpoint and the tendency towards the 'poster and slogan' style which is correct in political viewpoint but lacking in artistic power. On questions of literature and art we must carry on a struggle on two fronts." All this shows Mao Zedong's thorough thinking on the relation between literature and art and politics.

Many other issues were also discussed in the "Talks." For example, he explained that "man's social life is the only source of literature and art" and that "life as reflected in works of literature and art can and ought to be on a higher plane, more intense, more concentrated, more typical, nearer the ideal, and therefore more universal than actual everyday life." He gave many precise and penetrating comments on the proper use of cultural legacy, the ways of improving the heritage, the united front in the literary and art circles and so on. These enlightening comments have greatly enriched Marxist theories on literature and art.

The publication of the "Talks" brought about another literary revolution since the May Fourth Movement of 1919. After Yan'an forum on literature and art, the literary movement in the liberated areas made rapid progress, producing many works of high quality. Compared with those published before, these works are marked by their distinctly new characteristics. First of all they definitely show that the writers had undergone changes as a result of their integration with the workers, peasants and soldiers. Gone in their works were the empty feelings, the groans and moans of the intellectuals of yesterday. Replacing the self-pity expressed in their works was the portrayal of the struggles of the masses. Underlying the descriptions of the lives of the common people were the revolutionary sentiments which had brought the writers and the masses close together. According to Zhou Yang's statistics, for example, of the 177 pieces of work collected in the *People's Literature Series*, "101 are about the anti-Japanese war, the people's liberation war, the people's army and its relationship with the people. Forty-one are about problems in the countryside and other anti-feudal struggles, including the people's fight for rent reduction, their efforts to get even with the landlords, their determination to bring about land reform and the work they did in tackling feudal superstition, illiteracy, unhygienic practices and forced marriage. Sixteen pieces are about industrial and agricultural production; seven are about historical events, mainly stories about the agrarian revolution in northern Shaanxi Province. The remaining twelve have other themes such as the work-styles of cadres."* Through their descriptions of national and class struggles and problems of production, many of these works truthfully depict the changes which had taken place and the new life of the people in the liberated areas. Among the outstanding full-length novels of this period are Ouyang Shan's *Uncle Gao*, Ding Ling's *The Sun Shines over the Sanggan River* and Zhou Libo's *The Hurricane*. The works of Zhao Shuli and other writers are full of the freshness of the countryside, enlivened by the simplicity, sincerity, humour and cheerfulness of the peasants. Other novels, particularly those of Sun Li and Kang Zhuo, are marked by the writers' poetic sentiments and the beauty they had found in the lives and struggles of the masses. These features of the literature of the liberated areas were definitely something new.

Secondly, in literature and art as in real life, the workers, peasants, and soldiers had now come to the fore. Mao Zedong pointed out in his "Letter to the Yan'an *Pingju* (Beijing) Opera Theater, after Watching *Driven to Joint Liangshan Mountain Rebels*": History is made by the people, yet the old opera (and all the old literature and art, which are divorced from the people) presents the people as though they were dirt, and the stage is dominated by lords and ladies and their pampered sons and daughters." He

---

* See "New Literature and Art of the People" in *Essays in Celebration of the National Congress of Literary and Art Workers*, pp. 70-71.

thought this was "historical reversal" and the revolutionary writers and artists should therefore "reverse this reversal" in order to restore the truth of history. Many of the distinguished literary works which came out after Mao Zedong's "Talks" made their contribution precisely in this respect. The heroes and heroines in the prominent literary works such as Xiao Erhei, Li Youcai, Xi'er, Liu Hulan, Wang Gui and Li Xiangxiang all had the same background of the labouring class. They were presented with utter honesty and accuracy, a far cry from past practice when the characters were given "the clothes of working people but the faces are those of petty-bourgeois intellectuals." In their different ways, these characters indicated a new generation of peasants had arrived, peasants who were no longer the stereotyped objects of humiliation and oppression as described by the writers before. Even the white-haired girl, for example, who had had enough of her share of the landlord's brutal treatment, showed the indomitable spirit of the labouring masses in their struggle against oppression. Her will to live never deserted her, and her determination to get even with the oppressor was equally unwavering. In the new literary works, the labouring people were presented as the real driving force for the social development. These works effectively told the truth the once emancipated, the oppressed people in the old society could give full rein to the expression of their wisdom, ability and personality. Of course, they were not portrayed as super-heroes who could do no wrong, but as real people from real life who had grown up in the revolution and passed its many tests. In short, they were from the masses, representing the masses and that fact alone made them special. Even though at times some writers tended to romanticize or idealize what they saw, in general they succeeded in creating characters who were both credible and likeable. Most of these writers closely followed the principles of realism in their delineation of the common people.

Thirdly, the literary works in the liberated areas amply showed that the writers had achieved distinction in using the language of the masses and the artistic forms which appealed to them. In their works they maintained a close relation with the traditions of national and, in particular, local folk literature and art. To increase the sources of inspiration, they turned to various artistic forms of expression which were popular among the Han people such as the *yangge* dance, folk operas, folk songs, ballads and *kuaiban* storytelling which are told to the rhythm of bamboo sticks. Thus a new style of *yangge* dance was developed from the songs and dance in the border and other areas. *The White-Haired Girl*, with its features of the new national opera, in fact, had its origin in the *yangge* dance. Its story came from the legends circulating in the Shaanxi-Chahar-Hebei Border Region and the language used in the opera is that of the peasants in northern China, simple and colourful. Likewise, the lyrics and tunes retained their local flavour, though they had been suitably adapted in the creation of an opera distinctly characterized by its national spirit and style. In his long poem *Wang Gui and Li Xiangxiang*, Li Ji followed closely the structure of the popular folk song *xintianyou* from northern Shaanxi Province. Every two lines in the poem form a unit, and the language is simple and fresh. The rhythm throughout is natural and smooth, and its verbal music is keenly felt particularly when the poem is read aloud, adding to the richness of its figurative descriptions of events. Many of the novelists adopted the manner of narration which was familiar to the common people. Although Zhao Shuli did not follow this popular practice, he also used the simple language of the masses in his novels and his achievement in this respect was particularly outstanding. He was steeped in the tradition of the classical novel and that of the folk art of storytelling. Zhou Yang's evaluation of his works is well worth quoting:

> In his works Zhao Shuli has most skillfully used the language of the masses. His mastery of the vernacular is beyond dispute whether it is used for dialogue or general narration. We can see that his works are deeply rooted in the tradition of the Chinese novel. He has indeed absorbed much that has lent strength to the old novel, especially in the use of language. What he has created is not a replica of the old form and style; rather, it is a genuinely new and national model. His language is the lively language of the masses. In literary creation, he

is not bound by convention. Indeed, he is an innovator and a creator.*

However, some misjudgments were apparent in the evolution of a literature which served the workers, peasants and soldiers in the liberated areas. In emphasizing that literature and art should serve politics, some people tended to be too narrow-minded or mechanical in approach. Their understanding of the nature of literature and art was also questionable. Thus, they made simplistic demands that literature and art should be used to suit all major tasks including propaganda work. Some writers, too, had been inappropriately given assignments according to the needs of the moment, without any consideration of their specific qualifications and interests. While the literary and art workers were strongly urged to learn from the labouring masses, not enough attention was paid to the adverse influence of the thinking of the small producers. The result was that such thinking pervaded some of the literary works. Also, more writers could have received benefit from studying the techniques of foreign writers.

Still, in spite of all these faults and shortcomings, literary creation had undergone great changes in a few years. These changes indicated that the new literature was definitely moving in a new direction. In the development of a new literature in China, they were indeed of epoch-making significance because of their deep and far-reaching influences.

VI. New Literary Developments in the Kuomintang-Controlled Areas

While the literature in the liberated areas flourished, the progressive literature and art movement in the Kuomintang-controlled regions also made headway after 1942 in spite of the government's severe measures of suppression. Following the Southern Anhui Incident of 1941, the die-hard reactionaries tightened their control over the progressive cultural workers. In July

* Zhou Yang, "The Creative Writings of Zhao Shuli," *Liberation Daily*, August 26, 1946.

1941, the Kuomintang's Central Committee on the Examination of Books and Periodicals in one sweep banned as many as 961 titles. The following year, articles by Zhang Daofan and Liang Shiqiu appeared in the September and October numbers of the *Vanguards of Culture*, the official publication of the Kuomintang's Central Committee on Cultural Movement. In these articles, entitled "The Literary and Art Policies We Need" and "On Literary and Art Policies" respectively, they promoted themselves as upholders of the Three People's Principles and preached the theory that "literature and art should be aimed at all the people." According to them, literature and art should stress the "national consciousness of loyalty, filial piety, benevolence, love, faithfulness, righteousness and peacefulness." At the eleventh plenary session of the Kuomintang's fifth national congress, held in September 1942, the reactionary "Programme for the Cultural Movement" was passed. Two months later came the "National Cultural Construction Movement Week" in Chongqing.

As things stood, there was nothing wrong originally in using terms such as "national culture" and "national literature," especially in the circumstances of acute national contradictions. But, first, the Kuomintang set national contradictions against class contradictions. It urged progressive writers not to "adopt the standpoint of the workers and peasants" and turn out works which carried "hate" against the exploiting classes.* Secondly,he Kuomintang did not make any distinction between "national consciousness" and feudal thinking. In promoting what it called "national culture," it was in fact propagating the ideas of feudalism. Their slogans were: "The country must come first, the nation must come first," and "One party, one ideology and one leader." Adopted in the name of culture, these slogans were meant to serve, in essence, the political interests of the Kuomintang. By "national" in whatever context it was used, they meant in fact the extremely small number of big landlords and big capitalists in the vast nation.

The measures of suppression and persecution adopted by the Kuomintang government created most serious problems for the

* Liang Shiqiu, "On Literature and Art Policies," *Vanguards of Culture*, Vol. I, No. 8, October 20, 1942.

progressive literature and art movement. Politically, the writers had no protection; in literary creation they were denied freedom of expression. Their works were censored or banned. Economic factors also adversely affected their cultural activities. The rapid rise in the cost of paper and printing and the heavy taxes imposed by the government—the tax on drama performances in Chongqing, for example, was as high as 55 percent of the price of the ticket—inevitably made it difficult for the publication or performance of excellent works. Understandably, the development of the cultural movement was seriously hampered. In these harsh circumstances, however, the progressive writers and artists, led by the Communist Party continued to maintain and strengthen the extensive cultural united front. They never wavered in the struggle against the reactionary forces. In the words of Mao Dun, "these progressive revolutionary writers and artists never stopped adapting themselves to the unfavourable conditions. They made all the necessary manoeuvres in the battles, they never gave up, but took full advantage of any available opportunity and they fully supported one another. Eventually, they broke through the forces of the reactionaries, whose suppressive measures proved to be of little avail. In short, they won."* The National Federation of anti-Japanese Writers and Artists and its branches in various Kuomintang-controlled areas remained active. They united anti-Japanese cultural workers from various sections of society and got them involved in many activities.

After the Southern Anhui Incident of January 1941, the Communist Party, through its Cultural Work Committee, a united front organization which had legal status in the Kuomintang-controlled areas, rallied many progressive cultural workers as well as a large number of those who had hitherto remained in the middle politically. Subsequently, they made a valuable contribution by their activities, which were all related to the following aims: for the resistance against Japan, against defeatism; for unity, against divisionism; for progress, against regression. For instance, in the midst

* Mao Dun, "The Development of Revolutionary Literature and Art in the Struggle Against the Oppressive Reactionary Forces," *Essays in Celebration of the National Congress of Literature and Art Workers.*

of the Kuomintang's clamorous National Cultural Construction Movement Week, *Xinhua Daily* published the editorial entitled "The Prerequisites for Cultural Construction," clearly pointing out that the culture to be constructed must serve the masses, which made up over 90 percent of the country's population. Its aim should be "fighting for the liberation and freedom of the Chinese people." With the support of Zhou Enlai, the progressive literary and art circles accelerated the revolutionary literature and art movement through various special means. Thus, they made full use of occasions such as the commemoration of Lu Xun and the celebrations of the birthdays of other writers. The periodicals *Cultural Life*, *Wartime Literature and Art*, and *Literature Sentry*, for example, published special issues in honour of the fiftieth birthday of Guo Moruo and Mao Dun in 1941 and 1945 respectively (also to mark the twenty-fifth year of their career as writer), and the twentieth year of Lao She's writing career in 1944. These special issues extolled their outstanding contribution to the cultural revolution, summed up the experience of the literature movement and outlined work to be done. Activities such as these strengthened unity and raised the fighting spirit of the literary and art workers.

In July 1944, the National Federation of Anti-Japanese Writers and Artists started a campaign to raise funds for the foundation in aid of poor and sick writers. The campaign was undertaken in view of the sad fact that "quite a few of them cannot afford medical fees and many who died were not given burial." Another objective was to "strengthen the link between the public and the cultural workers." The campaign was enthusiastically supported by the general public and it brought the democratic movement to a climax in the following year. In January and February 1945, the Democratic League and the various social groups from the industrial, commercial, women's, youth and cultural circles, issued their declarations for the cause of democracy. Among these, *The Suggestions of the Cultural Circles on the Current Situation*, drafted by Guo Moruo, made the greatest impact. It called for an emergency conference to discuss the wartime political guiding principles, the formation of a wartime united government, the removal of various government measures which had made a mockery of democracy. Specifically, it proposed "the abolition of the Kuomintang's partisan indoctrination in education so that there will be no interference with the freedom of academic research or with the cultural movement." It demanded "an end to all the activities of the Kuomintang agents, genuine guarantee of personal freedom, and the immediate release of political prisoners including the patriotic youths in jail." The *Suggestions*, signed by over 370 people, spoke for all the cultural workers. It was published in the *Xinhua Daily* on January 22, 1945 and received great response from the public.

As the democratic movement gathered momentum, it strengthened the literature and art movement and the two became one united force. Many meetings for the cause of democracy were held in the format of seminars and talks on literature and art. A large number of writers joined the democratic movement and their works were most influential. In his play *Before and After the Qingming Festival*, Mao Dun exposed the harm done to national industry by the bureaucratic capitalists. He made it very clear indeed that only when the national capitalist class joined forces with the people in the common struggle for democracy could "the shackles be broken which have been destroying the life of the country's industry." Satirical poems, comedies and essays by other writers, also deeply hurt the Kuomintang authorities because of the bitter criticism conveyed through literary means. Even Zhang Henshui, in his novel *The Eighty-First Dream*, satirized the dark realities of the Kuomintang-controlled areas. The poet Wen Yiduo, inspired by the spirit of revolution and the Communist Party, came to the forefront of the democratic movement. He was passionately involved in revolutionary public activities, giving speeches and reciting poems. The path he took indicated the change of direction made by quite a number of bourgeois and petty-bourgeois writers and artists who had remained for some time at the ideological crossroads during this period of revolution.

The progressive writers and artists in the Kuomintang-controlled areas firmly supported the War of Resistance Against Japan and the cause of democracy. Many of them produced works of high quality. The conditions at the time, however, were still extraordinarily harsh. Understandably, some of them betrayed many of the deep-rooted weaknesses of the petty-bourgeois intellectuals in their works which gave vent to the feelings of frustration, anxiety, disillusionment and even pessimism. They tended to dwell on the trivialities of life and the conflicts of love, as their attention was diverted from the significant political issues and struggles. Some of them pandered to low tastes in their stories which were meant to give light sketches of urban life. Worse still, others entertained unrealistic hopes in the Kuomintang, primarily because of their insufficient understanding of class viewpoints. In the works of these writers, one finds shallow content and low-spirited "apolitical tendency," both reflecting the weak and gloomy spiritual state of the petty-bourgeois intellectuals. How could this dire situation be changed and the unhealthy trend arrested? Different proposals were put forward in the literary and art circles. Some emphasized that it was a matter of "attitude towards life." Some advocated the revival of "the subjective battling spirit." Others stressed wholehearted participation in practical struggles so that writers could get themselves out of their apolitical state of mind. Still others saw solutions in the improvement of literary and artistic techniques. Almost all of these issues were dealt with round about the year 1945 in the discussions on realism and on the two plays *Before and After the Qingming Festival* and *The Fragrant Grass*.

In June 1943 and March 1944, Yu Chao (Qiao Guanhua), who was then working for the *Xinhua Daily*, published two articles in the magazine *Cultural Plain*, namely "On Realism and the Attitude Towards Life" and "Between Birth and Death." These articles triggered debates among the staff members of the *Xinhua Daily*. He noted that some of the intellectuals had adopted a wait-and-see attitude and were in a state of apathy, listlessness and depression. However, the explanations of these phenomena were unsound and the solutions he offered were inappropriate. He had not analysed adequately the causes of the intellectuals' "spiritual crisis"; that is, the social factors and the weaknesses found in the intellectuals themselves. Neither did he point out that the only way for the intellectuals to solve these problems was to get involved in actual political struggles, through which they would undergo changes in outlook. Instead, he turned to bourgeois humanism for answer to all the questions.

Another view was expressed by Hu Feng in his article "To Throw Oneself into the Struggle for Democracy," published in the first number of *Hope*, January 1945, a magazine which he himself edited. He believed that only when writers took action, of their own free will, and "participate in the struggles with the harsh realities of life, can they begin to acquire strength of thought and demonstrate creative vigour in their works." Only thus, he went on, could the writers reject the "currently prevailing and ideologically lack-lustre literature and art" produced in the belief of objectivism. In the same number of *Hope*, he published Shu Wu's article "On Subjectivity" and gave it extremely high praise. However, some people disagreed with Hu Feng and criticized his ideas. This led to the controversy over the relation between realism and "subjectivity." The debate went on from the last stage of the War of Resistance Against Japan to the time of the War of Liberation. In 1945, mainly because of the appraisal of a few specific literary works, arguments developed over the relation between the political and the artistic nature of literature and art. Some of the works, for example had a very strong political content, but they were merely products of subjective formalism, with very little literary merit. On the other hand, there were also works of artistic distinction which were remote from political realities.

In order to help literary and art workers understand better the relation between the political and the artistic nature of literature and art, the *Xinhua Daily* held discussions, led by Zhou Enlai, on the two plays *Before and After the Qingming Festival* and *The Fragrant Grass*. Some of the articles written for the occasion oversimplified the issues, but they were also highly critical of the apolitical tendency shown in literature and works of criticism. The fusion of art and politics, it was reaffirmed, should be the guiding principle. Zhou Enlai was deeply concerned about the ideological progress of the literary and art workers. While pointing out undesirable tendencies found in literary theory and practice, he patiently helped the writers to avoid following the mistaken trends. "He suggested that the comrades and friends in the literary and art circles should earnestly study the thoughts of Mao Zedong, examine their past works accordingly and try to improve on what they are currently doing."*

Why did all these problems, mentioned above, appear in the Kuomintang-controlled areas during the last stage of the War of Resistance Against Japan? The causes could be attributed not only to the extremely harsh conditions at the time but also to the writers themselves. Most of the progressive writers in the Kuomintang-controlled areas were petty-bourgeois intellectuals. As such, they also belonged to the oppressed class and that was why they could integrate with the labouring masses. At the same time, however, a gap still existed in thinking and way of life between the masses and the petty-bourgeois intellectuals who had not undergone fundamental changes in outlook. These intellectuals could not endure the hardships of life for too long. Mao Dun well noted: "Two tendencies are obvious in their literary and artistic creations: despondency and impatience in whatever they want to pursue. The latter tendency is particularly noticeable in their theories on literature and art, which are, in truth, petty-bourgeois revolutionary theories."** History has borne out that there are essential differences in thinking on literature and art between the petty-bourgeoisie and the proletariat. Unless this fact is recognized, no Marxist solutions can be found to the problems which arise in any literature and art movement. That was why Zhou Enlai suggested that those in the literary and art circles should study the thoughts of Mao Zedong.

Mao Zedong's "Talks at the Yan'an Forum on Literature and Art" provided the guiding principles for the development of literature and art not only in the liberated areas but also in the Kuomintang-controlled areas. Inspired by the "Talks," for example, the *Xinhua Daily* in Chongqing published an editorial for the issue of November 11, 1943, entitled "The Prerequisites for Cultural Construction," which provided guidelines for the literature and art movement in the Kuomintang-controlled areas. On New Year's

---

* He Qifang, "Recollections of Comrade Zhou Enlai," *Literary Review*, No. I, 1978.

** Mao Dun, "The Development of Revolutionary Literature and Art in the Struggle Against the Oppressive Reactionary Forces," *Essays in Celebration of the National Congress of Literature and Art Workers.*

Day 1944 excerpts from the "Talks" appeared in the same newspaper under the title "Views of Comrade Mao Zedong on Literature and Art." That was the first time the "Talks" was openly and extensively introduced to the readers in the Kuomintang-controlled areas. In April of the same year, the Party's Central Committee sent He Qifang and Liu Baiyu to Chongqing from Yan'an. They were active in the progressive cultural circles introducing the "Talks" and they also studied the literature and art movement in the Kuomintang-ruled areas. During this period, Zhou Enlai regularly arranged meetings for writers and artists to study the "Talks" and explained to them in detail the Party's policy on literature and art. In the gathering on the evening of October 21, 1945, organized by the National Federation of Anti-Japanese Writers and Artists, he gave an account of the new and vigorous life and spirit in the Yan'an literary and art circles consequent upon the publication of the "Talks." He called on the writers in Chongqing to learn from their counterparts in the liberated areas so that they could achieve even greater results. Of course, the conditions in the two areas were different; so too, the missions of their writers. All the same, the writers in the Kuomintang-ruled areas were inspired by the "Talks" and encouraged by what their counterparts had done in the liberated areas. Accordingly, they became more active in the literary and art movement. As Guo Moruo observed, "they have begun to make an effort to integrate with the masses, under the influence of Mao Zedong's views on literature and art, which have given them a new direction."*

After the victory of the War of Resistance Against Japan, the literary and art workers, who had originally come from Yan'an and the Shaanxi-Chahar-Hebei Border Region but later gone to Northeast China, began to move southwards. At the same time, writers and artists from the cities such as Chongqing and Guilin also returned to their former homes. Once again Shanghai, Beijing and Guangzhou became centres of literary activities. Many periodicals resumed publication or were founded such as *Chinese Writers, Federation of Writers, Human World* and *Poetry Creation*. Among the

* See Guo Moruo, "Struggle for the Construction of the Chinese People's Literature and Art."

large-scale periodicals which also enjoyed a longer life were: *The Renaissance*, edited by Zheng Zhenduo and Li Jianwu, *Literary Magazine* by Zhu Guangqian and *Cultural Life* by Sima Wensen. Works of literary distinction which came out of this period included Ba Jin's *Bitter Cold Nights*, Qian Zhongshu's *A Beleaguered City* and Shi Tuo's *The Orchard Town*.

This happy scene, however, was soon to change. As part of the strategy designed for their attack on the liberated areas, thus launching the civil war, the Kuomintang increased its suppression of the democratic movement in areas under its control. Time and again, for instant results, it resorted to assassination. In July 1946, its secret agents murdered Li Gongpu and the famous poet Wen Yiduo. The following year, through reactionary publications such as the *Vanguards of Culture*, it openly advocated the "anti-Communist literature and art." They used whatever means available in their effort to stamp out democratic culture. Thus, newspapers were closed down, books and periodicals were banned, and writers persecuted. Consequently, the Communist Party had to make arrangements, difficult as they were, so that some of the writers could move to the liberated areas. It also helped a large number of cultural workers to get to Hong Kong, where they took full advantage of the political environment and established a new revolutionary cultural base. Their chief publications in Hong Kong were: *Popular Literature Series*, *Short Stories*, the overseas edition of *Cultural Life* and the Hong Kong edition of *The Masses*. *The Chinese Merchant*, a local newspaper, carried special pages devoted to literature and art, under the titles of "The Hot Wind" and "Tea Pavilion." In many different ways the writers and artists spread Marxist theories on literature and art. They followed the guidelines derived from Mao Zedong's theories, and put forward their own suggestions in promoting the literary and art movement. All these theories were studied in greater earnest than in the last stage of the anti-Japanese war, and much attention was paid to the union of theory and practice. In 1946 and 1947, the progressive cultural circles in Hong Kong published Mao Zedong's "Talks" as an offprint entitled, respectively, "Problems of Literature and Art" and "On the Problems of Literature and Art." Excerpts from the "Talks" and "On New Democracy" also appeared in the weekly *The Masses* in May 1947, under the title "Mao Zedong on People's Culture and People's Literature and Art."

The serious study of the "Talks" yielded significant articles such as Quanlin's "Views on the Present Literary and Art Movement," Lin Mohan's "On a Few Questions Concerning People's Literature and Art" and Feng Naichao's "The Remoulding of Literary and Art Workers." These articles mainly dealt with the following topics: the nature of the new literature; the direction of literature and art in serving the workers, peasants and soldiers; the popularization of literature and art and the raising of standards; the remoulding of the writers' ideology and the united front. There were also discussions on "dialect literature" in response to the practice, in the Kuomintang-controlled areas, of creating literature and art which could be easily understood by the local people. All these articles and discussions came at the right time because some intellectuals had appeared on the scene, who, following democratic individualism, identified themselves neither with the Communist Party nor the Kuomintang. In politics, they advocated "the middle road" or "the third road"; in literature and art, they promoted bourgeois liberalism. Their starting-point was, of course, bourgeois humanism. Not only did they negate the achievements of the people's liberation war, the people's democratic movement and land reform; they also misled people by conjuring up illusions about imperialism. The progressive cultural workers recognized the imminent danger of their ideology and promptly exposed its true character. In addition, the cultural workers did much in opening the eyes of the readers to the harmful nature of feudal and pornographic literature and art.

The works that came out in the last stage of the anti-Japanese war and in the liberation war inherited the militant, anti-imperialist and anti-feudal tradition of the new literature originated in the May Fourth Movement. The writers followed Mao Zedong's suggestion that "all the dark forces harming the masses of the people must be exposed and all the revolutionary struggles of the masses of the people must be extolled." They laid bare the corruption of the Kuomintang and depicted the people's struggles against oppression as they fought for the cause of democracy. Meanwhile, the political situation was changing. Mao Zedong's theories on literature and art spread; the influence of the new literature and art extended well beyond the liberated areas. Consequently, there were new developments in the Kuomintang-controlled areas as well. In content and thought, many of the works exposed the dark forces and extolled the people's struggles. Satirical works were particularly popular. In literary and artistic creation, there was also a new tendency, as Mao Dun observed, "to break out of the limitation of the May Fourth traditional forms in search of national and popular forms which appeal to the masses."*

A major feature of the literary creation of this period was the rapid development of satirical poetry. Many poems written in the early days of the anti-Japanese war were prompted by strong feelings that came with the fervent desire for national liberation. After the rise of the democratic movement in 1944, the new poetry turned to the exposure of the corruption and evils of the day. Mass recitation poetry became popular and a new poetic trend was set. The best known works of the period were Yuan Shuipai's *Ma Fantuo's Rustic Songs* and Zang Kejia's *My Precious One*. In the anti-starvation and anti-civil war demonstrations, these satirical poems were publicly recited or written on the banners of the marchers. Sometimes they were adapted for dramatic performances in the streets. Together with the satirical songs such as *Tunes from a Teahouse* and *Eccentric Songs*, they were extremely effective in moving the audience. "The satirical poems have grown in number," so Zang Kejia noted, "not because of the passing whims of the poets. They have seen enough of what hurt their eyes and their hearts. The poets have been pained into writing."** The poems written for public recitation were mainly works of young amateur writers who were involved in the democratic movement. Strong in political content, these poems were often written collec-

* Mao Dun, "The Development of Revolutionary Literature and Art in the Struggle Against the Oppressive Reactionary Forces," *Essays in Celebration of the National Congress of Literature and Art Workers*.

** Zang Kejia, "Piercing the Heart of Darkness" (Preface to *My Precious One*). This essay first appeared in *Xinhua Daily*, under a slightly different title, on June 14, 1945.

tively.

In drama, instead of historical plays produced when the political situation was unfavourable, plays written during this period directly attacked the evils of reactionary rule and voiced the people's demand for democracy. The masterpieces included Mao Dun's *Before and After the Qingming Festival*, Chen Baichen's *Promotion in Officialdom*, Tian Han's *Song of Beautiful Women* and Wu Zuguang's *Catching Ghosts*. These plays brought to light how the bureaucrat-capital exploited people who were working in minor enterprises. Imbued with a powerful combating spirit, they also exposed the corruption of the Kuomintang officials and depicted the painful lives of the people and their struggles against oppression. The strong satirical comic elements in the plays effectively drove home the very fact that the people's strength was increasing and the force of the reactionaries was declining.

After the victory of the anti-Japanese war, many dramatists turned to film production because of the Kuomintang's suppression of the progressive drama movement. They followed their unchanged goals still, though they now found themselves in a new artistic field. As Yang Hansheng observed, they "take the stand of the people, expose and condemn the crimes of the Kuomintang reactionary rule, which is the cause of the sufferings of the masses. At the same time they point out, through subtle hints, the direction that people should follow in their struggles."* Many films of high quality were made and they produced a great impact on the public. Among these were: *The Spring Waters of the River Flowing East*, *A Journey of Eight Thousand Li's* and *Ten Thousand Family Lights*.

The novels of this period, portraying many themes and characters, realistically reflected social life. Novels such as Mao Dun's *Discipline*, Lao She's *Four Generations under One Roof*, Sha Ting's *Return to Hometown*, Ai Wu's *A Mountain Region* and Yao Xueyin's *Long Night* not only laid bare the evils of reactionary rule, but also directly or indirectly depicted the people's rebellions and struggles. Other distinguished novels included Lu Ling's *Sons and Daughters of the Rich*, Huang Guliu's *The Story of Xia Qiu (The Story of*

* Yang Hansheng, "Progressive Drama and Film Movements in the Kuomintang-Controlled Areas."

Prawnball) and Xu Xu's *The Bitter Wind*. In response to the intense class struggles, many pungent essays were written and they also made their impact. Through their different but lively styles, writers of these essays such as Guo Moruo, Mao Dun, Feng Xuefeng, Zhu Ziqing, He Qifang and Lin Mohan attacked "the spectre of the old society" while they were welcoming the "morning star of a new age."*

All in all, in the last stage of the anti-Japanese war and throughout the War of Liberation after that, the progressive literary and art workers in the Kuomintang-controlled areas continued their revolutionary cultural activities in spite of severe persecutions by their enemies, Chinese or foreign. Against all odds, they achieved extraordinary results and produced fine literary works which also had deep political significance in the struggle against the Kuomintang reactionaries. Appropriately, Mao Dun reported at the first conference of writers:

> In pursuing the ultimate goal of struggle [for liberation], the literary and art movements in the Kuomintang-controlled and the liberated areas are in unison. The thinking behind each movement is basically the same; so, too, the way in which each has developed. In fact, for the past eight years the trend in the Kuomintang-controlled areas has been the advancement of the revolutionary literary and art movement in the direction pointed out by Chairman Mao. The movements have been trying to keep close to the people. Against political, economic and culture oppression, the literary and art workers in these areas continued their struggles against Japanese imperialism, American imperialism and the forces of the Kuomintang reactionaries. They have remained firm in their stand. Their contribution has been great in the national liberation war against Japan, in the democratic movement in defiance of the Kuomintang reactionary rule, and in the people's Liberation War. Indeed, the attempts of the reactionaries to cripple the new literature and art movement have never met with any success.

---

* Guo Moruo, "Impressions of Nanjing."

Chapter 1

Lu Xun: Father of Modern Chinese Literature

I. Life and Thought

Lu Xun (1881-1936), the pen-name of Zhou Shuren, alias Zhou Yucai, was born into a declining literati family in Shaoxing, Zhejiang Province. Early in life he was taught the classics including poetry. He loved folk art and drawing as a young child. When he was a little older, he began reading "unofficial histories," a type of literature consisting mainly of short sketches. As the range of his reading widened, his understanding of Chinese literature and history also deepened.

Lu Xun's maternal grandmother lived in the countryside. In his childhood he often accompanied his mother on her home visits, and these visits brought him into the midst of the peasants. As close links were formed, his rapport with them opened his eyes to their sufferings caused by oppression. When he was still in his teens, his paternal grandfather somehow got involved in a court examination scandal and was sent to gaol. Then came the long illness of his father, which further aggravated the financial situation at home. As a result, Lu Xun was regularly seen in pawnshops and pharmacies. The contempt and discrimination he encountered taught him a great deal about the hypocrisy and heartlessness of people living in a cruel society.

Lu Xun left home for Nanjing in 1898, when the bourgeois constitutional Reform Movement was approaching its height subsequent to the Westernization movement. He had abandoned what was generally considered the normal route to officialdom through examinations at different levels. Instead, he enrolled in the Jiangnan Naval Academy founded by the advocates of the Westernization movement. Later, he was transferred to the School of Railways and Mines attached to the Jiangnan Army Academy. There he first came across the reformist periodical *Contemporary Gazette* and the magazine *Selected Translations*, which sought to introduce to the reader Western politics, philosophy, economics and law. He kept himself up to date in his reading of the translations of foreign works in the fields of science, literature and art. The book which had a great impact on him was T.H. Huxley's *Evolution and Ethics*, translated by Yan Fu. Inspired by the theory of natural selection, he began to see the fate of China in evolutionary terms, namely "the survival of the fittest" in the bitter international struggle. He was burning with the desire to see a strong and dignified China.

In 1902, Lu Xun was awarded a government scholarship to study in Japan, first in the preparatory school in Tokyo. At the time, Tokyo was the centre of activities of the overseas Chinese revolutionaries. The Chinese students were fully committed to the patriotic, anti-Qing government movement and Lu Xun was an active participant. In a short poem written when he had just turned twenty-one, he expressed his patriotic aspirations:

The tower cannot avoid the god's sharp arrows;
Dark is the ancient garden crushed beneath the storm.
Unrecognized, I put my hope in an ice-cold star
*While offering my blood to the Yellow Emperor.**

The ideas of Darwin were widespread in Japan in the late nineteenth century. Anarchism and the philosophy of Nietzsche were also much welcomed by the Japanese intellectuals. During his early stay in Japan Lu Xun's interest was mainly in science. His translations, apart from the adaptation of the patriotic story "The Soul of Sparta," included science fiction through which he hoped to introduce scientific knowledge to the Chinese reader. He did research on Chinese geology and mineral resources and wrote an article on radium, which had been recently discovered by Madam

* Lu Xun, *Selected Poems*, translated by W.J.F. Jenner, Foreign Languages Press, Beijing, 1982, p. 31.

Curie. Guided by the belief that the practice of medicine could relieve his people of physical pain, he entered Sendai Medical School. "If war broke out," he wrote later in his Preface to *Call to Arms* (1923), "I would serve as an army doctor, at the same time promoting my countrymen's faith in reform."*

Lu Xun stayed in Sendai for two years. As fate would have it, one day in the lecture room he was watching documentary lantern slides of the Russo-Japanese War. On the screen suddenly appeared a Chinese, alleged to have been a spy for the Czarist army, now caught by the Japanese soldiers and was about to be executed. Among the spectators of this horrible scene were many Chinese with their expressionless faces. Lu Xun was deeply disturbed. He had hoped to find in the Japanese reform movement a frame of reference for the future of his own people. He had been seeking a proper understanding of "national character." Now he was awakened to the very truth that "the people of a weak and backward country, however, strong and healthy that might be, could only serve to be made examples of or as witnesses of such futile spectacles."** Consequently, he decided to give up his studies in medicine and devote himself to literature and art, fully convinced that these were the best cure for the illnesses of the human spirit.

In 1906, when he was back in Tokyo, Lu Xun began his literary activities. He planned to start a magazine to be entitled *New Life*, but the project fell through because of insufficient financial and human resources. His energy was then directed to the translation of works by writers of the oppressed nations of northern and eastern Europe. He published, in co-operation with his younger brother Zhou Zuoren, two volumes of *Stories from Other Lands* (1909). At the same time, he wrote articles such as "Cultural Trends" and "On the Demoniac Poets" for the magazine *Henan*, published by the Chinese students. These articles are characterized by his spirit of rebellion and independence. He had a particular liking for realist writers Gogol, Chekov and Sienkiewicz. But he was also attracted to romantic poets Byron, Shelley, Hug, Heine,

* Lu Xun, "Preface to *Call to Arms*," Foreign Languages Press, Beijing, 1981, p. ii.

** *Ibid.*, p. iii.

Pushkin, Lermontov, Mickiewicz and Petöfi and accordingly introduced to readers their works which express sympathy for the weak who rebel against the oppression of the strong.

Politically, he was opposed to the move towards militarism advocated by the Westernization group of aristocratic landlords. Neither could he accept the proposals for the creation of a constitutional parliament as conceived by the bourgeois reformists. Equally, the political representatives of the rising bureaucrat-comprador bourgeoisie aroused in him only mistrust and disgust, for he believed that in reality what they tried to establish was false democracy. As he put it, "they preach the idea of rule by the people, but their oppression will be worse than that of a tyrant." Lu Xun's mission was to bring about national revolution and the liberation of the people. That provided the basis for all his political convictions and theories. It also guided his approach to Western thought as he extracted from foreign ideas what would most benefit his cause. The theory of evolution sustained his faith in the demand for social change. It gave him unwavering hope for a better future and encouraged him to expose the evils of capitalism, which killed the human soul, and criticize the conservative masses as well as the crippling restraint imposed by customary beliefs. He upheld the dignity of the individual and was determined to break the shackles of feudalism, which enslaved the mind. Unfailingly, he supported any new sign of life. It can be said that the theory of evolution and the belief in dignity of the individual together formed a solid base of Lu Xun's early thought.

In 1909, Lu Xun returned to China and taught first in Hangzhou and then in Shaoxing. He began compiling pre-Tang Dynasty fiction and ancient records related to the history and geography of Huiji County (Shaoxing). These were later published in *A Collection of Ancient Chinese Fiction* (1926) and *A Miscellany of Ancient Books on Shaoxing Prefecture* (1915) respectively. When the Revolution of 1911 broke out, he became fully involved in the political activities which promoted its noble cause. About this time he wrote the story "Reminiscences of the Past" in classical prose, depicting the reactions of the feudal forces in a small town during the storm of revolution. After the formation of the provisional government, he was invited by Cai Yuanpei, then Minister of Education, to join his Ministry in Nanjing. Before long, he moved with the government to Beijing.

The Qing government had been overthrown. However, the revolution led by the bourgeoisie had failed to complete its historical mission. The economic foundation of feudal rule and the ideological system of feudalism remained as firm as ever. What was more, the imperial powers were still eagerly watching their prey, ready to pounce at the first opportunity available. Lu Xun went through the whole gamut of feeling, from excitement to dejection. During this period, from 1912 to 1917, he was occasionally driven by indignation to take part in various revolutionary activities, but more often his time was spent in deep reflection and silent thought. He analysed Chinese history and society, pondering over in particular the historical lessons of the 1911 Revolution. In his spare hours, he copied out classical texts, compiled inscriptions engraved on ancient bronze and stone tablets and verified the texts from the *Book of the Later Han Dynasty* and the *Works of Jikang*. All the work done so far fully prepared him for his academic research and literary creation later.

After the October Revolution of 1917 in Russia, China gradually awoke from her deep slumber. The country was ready for action. In 1918, Lu Xun together with Li Dazhao and others joined the *New Youth* magazine and began contributing short stories, articles and essays. "A Madman's Diary," in which he exposes the crimes of the "cannibalism of feudal ethics," appeared first in the May number of that year. It is the first short story written in the vernacular and marked a new epoch in the history of Chinese literature. Other masterpieces followed such as "Kong Yiji" and "Medicine." Through literature, Lu Xun fiercely attacked feudal traditions from different angles and his works greatly inspired young readers during the May Fourth Movement, attracting wide attention of the society. He also wrote many critical essays—"My Views on Chastity" and "What Is Required of Us as Fathers Today," to name only two—in which he shrewdly analyses the problems of the family, women and young people. His ideas were in tune with the spirit of the times. They lent invaluable support to the May Fourth

Movement and gave depth to the ideological and cultural revolution. Lu Xun was the most persistent fighter and the most influential writer throughout the movement.

The basis of Lu Xun's thought during this period was still the theory of evolution as he understood it. His ideas, however, grew out of the demands of practical struggle. From the standpoint of revolutionary democracy, he expanded what lies at the centre of the dialectics of Darwinism: the concepts of development and change. He was opposed to feudal ethics and attacked what was considered "the quintessence of Chinese culture." He cursed the "butchers of the present day" and vehemently criticized the social distortions. His analysis of Chinese society was accurate and precise and it provided welcomed guidance for the young people. He clearly saw the conflicts between the old ways and the new and pleaded that the latter should be given the respect they deserved. Above all, he realized that there were two kinds of people in the world: the oppressors and the oppressed.

A certain degree of complexity in Lu Xun's thought during this period is also noticeable. In 1919 he hailed "the first glimmer of dawn, the dawn of a new era,"* given out by the people. But in 1923, he could still underestimate the strength of the people, thus showing his judgment was at fault, when he wrote that "the masses, especially in China, are always spectators at a drama."** He spread the ideals of collectivism, urging people to emit "a small amount of heat" and "small amount of light," for each contribution would add to "the mighty flame" and "the light of the sun."*** At the same time, he could not as yet completely free himself from the chains of individualism. He turned to Neitzsche for support and was apprehensive that "in future if there were no mighty flame, I would then be the only light."† However, these apparent discrepancies cannot alter the fact that he was uncompromising in his demand for fundamental change, based on the ideals of revolution-

* Lu Xun, "Random Thoughts (59)—'Martial and Sagacious'," *Selected Works*, Foreign Languages Press, Beijing, 1985, Vol. II, p. 51.

** Lu Xun, "What Happens After Nora Leaves Home?", *Selected Works*, Foreign Languages Press, Beijing, 1985, Vol. II, p. 91.

*** Lu Xun "Random Thoughts 41," *Hot Air* (1925).

† *Ibid.*

ary democracy. He understood extremely well the forces of feudalism and imperialism and never wavered in the face of harsh realities. All his practical involvements gave deep meaning to the cause of social struggle.

During this period, Lu Xun wrote more than twenty short stories, collected in *Call to Arms* (1923) and *Wandering* (1926), and the characters portrayed fall into two categories: peasants and intellectuals. A significant theme in these early works is the lot of the peasants. As a compassionate supporter of revolutionary democracy, he was deeply concerned about their problems and in "The True Story of Ah Q," "My Old Home" and "The New-Year Sacrifice," for example, he vividly depicts the plight of the peasants at the time. The traditional characteristics of the intellectuals, too, are fully described, as in the stories "In the Tavern," "The Misanthrope" and "Regret for the Past." His stories are true reflections of the Chinese society from the 1911 Revolution to the First Revolutionary Civil War (1921-27). In addition to short stories, he wrote prose poems and essays, collected respectively in *Wild Grass* (1927) and the two volumes of *Bad Luck* (1926-27). The prose poems gracefully convey his feelings of uncertainty when he was in low spirits during the ebb of the May Fourth Movement and they distinguish themselves in modern Chinese literature by their unique style.

While working for the Ministry of Education, Lu Xun also taught at Beijing University and the Beijing Advanced Normal School. He lectured on Chinese fiction and published *A Brief History of Chinese Fiction* (1923-24) in two volumes, based on his lecture notes. In addition, he played an active part in establishing and organizing the literary societies The Tattler and The Unnamed and published periodicals such as *The Tattler*, *The Wilderness* and *The Unnamed*. He served as chief editor for the literary supplement of the *National Daily* and edited the *Unnamed Series*, designed mainly for translations of foreign literary works, the *Motley Series* and the *Unnamed New Series*, both of which were devoted mainly to creative writings.

In 1925, when he was teaching at the Beijing Women's Normal College, Lu Xun strongly supported the student movement and found himself in direct confrontation with the Beiyang (Northern warlords) government. The following year, came the March 18th Incident and he joined the masses in their struggle. In the process he broke through some of the constrictions of the theory of evolution and the philosophy of enlightenment. Somehow, he felt an even more fearful storm was brewing. As it turned out, it was a large-scale, spectacular class struggle.

After the March 18th Incident of 1926, Lu Xun was put on the arrest list by the Beiyang government. In August he went south and accepted the post of professor of Chinese literature at Xiaman (Amoy) University. There he finished writing the essays, begun in Beijing, for the book *Dawn Blossoms Plucked at Dusk* (1928) and wrote the first ten chapters of the unpublished *A History of Chinese Literature*. He also worked with young people in publishing literary magazines. Meanwhile, the great revolution was gaining momentum and the Northern Expedition against the warlords was winning one victory after another. The peasant movement was also spreading far and wide. In his letter to Xu Guangping, Lu Xun wrote with great excitement about the revolutionary situation. As he looked forward to the success of the revolution in the south, he accepted the offer of Zhongshan University (formerly Guangdong University) and took up the appointment in January 1927 as head of the Department of Chinese Literature and, concurrently, dean. He intended to form "a united front with the Creation Society and step up their attack on the old society."*

In Guangzhou, Lu Xun had more contacts with the Communists and more opportunities to study Marxism. These and his bitter struggle with the Rightists of the Kuomintang provided the background to his internal questionings which eventually led to a big leap in his thought. The thinking behind his essay "The Other Side of Celebrating the Recovery of Shanghai and Nanjing" already indicates that this leap in ideology was about to take place. On April 12, 1927, Chiang Kai-shek launched a counterrevolutionary coup d'état. Three days later came the April 15th Massacre in Guangzhou. Lu Xun demanded that the university should take

* Lu Xun, *In Two Places*, (1933), No. 69.

action to save the students who had been arrested by the government, but to no avail. In indignation, he resigned and disassociated himself completely from the university. Now he had witnessed slaughter which was more brutal, and sacrifice more heroic, than before. He saw "young people divided into two great camps —some of them acting as informers or helping the authorities to make arrests."* The internal disturbance exploded his old way of thinking, which had been guided by the belief in evolution.** He realized that the real revolutionary strength came from the masses of the workers and peasants and that he should move closer to them. After years of search through practical struggle, he had finally reached the conclusion that "the future belongs solely to the rising proletariat."*** He had gone "from the theory of evolution to that of class and changed from an unfilial son of the gentry to a real friend and a fighter of the proletariat and the laboring masses."† Indeed, Lu Xun had completely transformed his class origin.

Lu Xun left Guangzhou in September 1927 and in the following month settled down in Shanghai. In 1928 he edited the weekly *The Tattler* and, with Yu Dafu, the monthly *Torrent*. A year later, with Rou Shi and others he formed the Dawn Blossoms Press and translated and edited *Modern Short Stories of the World*. The publications they put out included the *Dawn Blossoms Weekly*, the *Dawn Blossoms Ten-Daily* and *Garden of Art* introducing Russian and European woodcuts. In the meantime, he was involved in controversies with the Creation Society and Sun Society over the issue of revolutionary literature. As the controversies covered a wide area related to the theories of literature and art, he turned to a more systematic study of Marxism. He translated Marxist theories on literature and art and introduced Russian novels to his readers. All these involvements led to self-criticism and self-education. Consequently, he consolidated his knowledge of actual revolutionary struggle and gained a deeper understanding of Marxism. He was

* Lu Xun, "Preface to *Three Leisures*," *Selected Works*, Foreign Languages Press, Beijing, 1985, Vol. III, p. 174.

** *Ibid.*

*** Lu Xun, "Preface to *Two Hearts*" (1932).

† Qu Qiubai, "Preface to *A Collection of Random Thoughts of Lu Xun*," *The Works of Qu Qiubai*, Vol. II, p. 997.

moving firmly ahead on the Marxist path.

In March 1930, the Chinese League of Left-Wing Writers was formed. The organization was initiated and led directly by the Communist Party. Serving as one of its founders, Lu Xun provided leadership. Outside the League, he also played a significant role in organizations such as the Communist-initiated Revolutionary Mutual Aid Society, the League for Freedom in China, the China League for the Defence of Civil Rights and the League for Anti-Imperialism and Anti-Foreign Aggression. In protest against the oppression of the Kuomintang and the atrocious crimes of imperialism, he made joint declarations with members of the progressive cultural circles. Notable among these are: the declaration made in 1931 exposing the Kuomintang's cruel murder of young writers; the letter of protest against fascist rule handed personally to the German Consulate in Shanghai in 1933 with Soong Ching Ling, Cai Yuanpei, Yang Xingfo and Lin Yutang; and the joint declaration made in 1936 with colleagues in the cultural circles calling for unity against foreign aggression and demanding freedom of speech. The Kuomintang put him on the arrest list and made many threats. His books were forbidden publication, and many passages of his essays were either edited out or completely changed. In spite of all this, however, Lu Xun remained uncompromising. He carried on his literary activities, editing magazines which were in either open or secret circulation such as *Sprouts*, *Outpost*, *Crossroads* and *Translations*. He was also involved in the editorial work for the periodicals *Literature* and *Taibai* and in promoting the popular art of woodcut.

As the struggle intensified, the urgency of the situation often required his instant counterattack. Consequently, he had to put aside the writing projects he had contemplated, including a once-planned long novel. Instead, he used the essay as a weapon in his close combat against the cultural "encirclement campaigns" launched by the Kuomintang. From 1930 on, he published eight collection of essays and *Old Tales Retold* (1936). The latter contains stories which are based on myths and legends—three of these tales were written before 1927. All these works were the products of the ideological as well as political struggles that he had gone through.

Not only do they have extraordinary artistic appeal, they also contain the thoughts of a brilliant Marxist fighter. Pervading the works is the optimistic spirit of revolution. Even in the most difficult times and the most dangerous conditions under Kuomintang rule, he fought the enemy tenaciously and served the people conscientiously. Always clear was the line he drew between love and hate. The poem "Self-Mockery," written in 1932, well sums up his state of mind:

There's nothing you can do about a hostile fate:
You bump your head before you even turn.
When in the street I pull my old hat down;
My leaky wine-boat drifts along the torrent.
Coolly I face a thousand pointing fingers,
Then bow to be an infant's willing ox.
Hiding in our little house, sufficient to ourselves,
*I care not what the season is outside.**

The thought of Lu Xun during this period had gained greater depth and his views of literature and art, which were formed through his practice in writing, developed more systematically than before. From the contents of his works, it is clear that he was not an ordinary revolutionary writer; rather, he was a Marxist revolutionary writer who was also a thinker. Everything he wrote amply revealed the spirit of collectivism and internationalism.

Through his participation in political and cultural activities, a close revolutionary friendship was formed between Lu Xun and the Communists. In July 1932 he had a cordial meeting with General Chen Geng, who had come to Shanghai from the revolutionary base to recuperate his health. At one time he planned to write a long novel about the hardships borne by the Red Army in their military campaigns. After the underground organization of the Communist Party had been broken up by the Kuomintang agents, Qu Qiubai took refuge in Lu Xun's home, where he stayed for some time and was most warmly treated. To express how he felt towards Qu Qiubai and the Communist Party, Lu Xun gave him

* Lu Xun, *Selected Poems*, translated by W.J.F. Jenner, Foreign Languages Press, Beijing, 1982, p. 57.

a couplet which he had copied out from the calligraphy book of He Waqin of the Qing Dynasty:*

It is enough to have one genuine friend;
I will treat him much like myself till life's end.

They also discussed many problems related to literary creation, translation, essay-writing, the history of literature and the popularization of literature and art. These discussions found expression in their writings, which contributed significantly to the application of Marxist theories in literature and art. In October 1935, when the Central Red Army, under the leadership of the Party Central Committee and Mao Zedong, finally arrived in the north of Shaanxi Province after the Long March of 25,000 *li*, Lu Xun and Mao Dun together sent them a congratulatory telegram, which read: "On you rest the future of China and mankind." When the Communist Party put forward the policy of the national united front against the Japanese aggression, Lu Xun, after studying the deep meaning of the policy with the greatest care, promised to give his unflinching support. He felt strong indignation against the Trotskyites and refuted arguments they made in their attempt to vilify the united front. In a reply letter to them he again declared openly: "I count it an honour to have as my comrades those who are now doing solid work, treading firmly on the ground, fighting and shedding their blood for the survival of this generation of Chinese."** In following the path from revolutionary democracy to communism, Lu Xun had picked the only way left for the intellectuals in semi-colonial and semi-feudal China. As it turned out, that was also the only right path.

On October 19, 1936, Lu Xun passed away in Shanghai. A fighter throughout his life, he devoted himself totally to the cause of revolutionary literature and the revolution of the Chinese people. When the revolution suffered a setback, he immediately moved to the very front of struggle and demonstrated his convic-

* That is, He Zhen, also named He Fanggu, from Qiantang, Zhejiang Province. He was famous for his seal-carving.

** Lu Xun, "Reply to a Letter from the Trotskyites," *Selected Works*, Foreign Languages Press, Beijing 1985, Vol. IV, p. 282.

tions with practical action. When those of the upper stratum of the petty bourgeoisie betrayed or deserted the revolution, he publicly declared his faithfulness to the communist cause. The more perilous the situation became, the harder he fought. He gave his all to the last. He was the embodiment of the noble qualities of the Chinese people: undauntedness in face of the utmost danger and readiness to step forward bravely in dire moments. In his essay "On New Democracy" Mao Zedong gives a most accurate evaluation of Lu Xun:

> The chief commander of China's cultural revolution, Lu Xun was not only a great man of letters but a great thinker and revolutionary. He was a man of unyielding integrity, free from all sycophancy or obsequiousness; this quality is invaluable among colonial and semi-colonial peoples. Representing the great majority of the nation, Lu Xun breached and stormed the enemy citadel; on the cultural front he was the bravest and most correct, the firmest, the most loyal and the most ardent national hero, a hero without parallel in our history. The road he took was the very road of China's new national culture.*

II. *Call to Arms* and *Wandering*

In the fierce "May Fourth Battle of the Languages" fought over the choice between *bai hua* (the vernacular) and *wen yan* (classical Chinese), Lu Xun sided with the former. He was the first writer to use the vernacular to write fiction. Later when he looked back upon his literary activities of this period, he explained, "In China then fiction was not considered as literature, and its writers could not rank as men of letters. Thus nobody thought of making a name in this way. I had no thought, either, of elevating short stories to the level of literature. I simply wanted to use them to reform society."** In his short stories he exposes the crimes of feudalism and describes the plight of the peasants, who have been both economically exploited and spiritually enslaved. He also depicts the

* Mao Zedong, "On New Democracy," *Selected Works*, Foreign Languages Press, Beijing, 1975, Vol. II, p. 372.

** Lu Xun, "How I Came to Write Stories," *Selected Works*, Foreign Languages Press, Beijing, 1985, Vol. III, p. 262.

lot of the intellectuals who struggle in the midst of intense social contradictions. The artistic excellence of his works spoke volumes for the potential of the vernacular and proved beyond any doubt that it should be adopted as the new language for a national literature. Furthermore, from the very beginning of his writing career, literature and the fate of the masses were linked together as he portrayed the life and thoughts of the oppressed people. Through specific creations in his short stories he drew people's attention to the deep-rooted social problems. The works themselves also provided excellent models in the development of modern Chinese literature.

Call to Arms comprises fourteen stories, written between 1918 and 1922.* Lu Xun chose the title in order to boost the morale of the revolutionaries, urging them to go forward without the slightest fear. The stories themselves are full of anti-feudal feelings. Both in the general thrust and specific descriptions, they are in complete harmony with the May Fourth spirit. In short, they embody the characteristics of the cultural and ideological revolution that was going on at the time.

"A Madman's Diary," which takes its title from one of Gogol's stories, is the first short story in modern Chinese literature. In the story, Lu Xun makes use of the medical knowledge acquired during his student days in Japan to portray the mental state and inner feelings of someone who is suffering from a "persecution complex." In the manner of a realist, he blends specific descriptions of social life with those of the feelings of a mentally deranged person. Lu Xun's serious approach and artistic excellence are noticeable throughout the story. The words of the protagonist may be those of an insane person, yet they contain many profound truths.

At the beginning of the story, the madman's fear of persecution is aroused when he senses that people are watching him, observing

---

* *Call to Arms* was published by Xinchao Press in August 1923 in its *Literary Series*. From 1926 on, it was published by the Beixin Bookstore in its *Motley Series*. In the thirteenth printing of the book in January 1930, Lu Xun took out the last story "Buzhou Mountain." The number of stories in *Call to Arms* since then has remained fourteen.

and discussing his behaviour. Gradually Lu Xun draws out the theme of the story—"exposing the evils of the clan system and feudal ethics."* The madman notices the strange look in the wealthy Mr Zhao's eyes and the ghastly pale faces of the children. The people he passes in the street are whispering to each other and the woman spanking her son is saying, "I'm so angry I could eat you!" All these remind him of the stories told by the tenant from the Wolf Cub Village, of how people resort to cannibalism in times of famine. The madman thinks of his elder brother's words and begins to suspect that there is something sinister behind the present arrangements made for him. He interprets the doctor's feeling his pulse as "simply a pretext for him to see how fat I was." To him, the instructions on taking the prescribed medicine—"To be eaten at once!"—mean that the doctor cannot wait to eat him. Accordingly he concludes that it is cannibalistic society and the history of that society is a long history of cannibalism. In his diary he writes: "I tried to look this up, but my history has no chronology and scrawled all over each page are the words: 'Confucian Virtue and Morality.' Since I could not sleep anyway, I read intently half the night until I began to see words between the lines. The whole book was filled with the two words—'Eat people.' " He believes that "there will be no place for man-eaters in the world in future" and cries out, "Save the children!"

The choice of a madman as the central character of the story shows Lu Xun's ingenuity as a writer. Through the feelings of the madman, the wild words he utters in his state of mental derangement and the specific references to cannibalism, Lu Xun intends to reveal the true nature of cannibalism which is practised even more widely in the spiritual realm. This will then enable him to make disturbing remarks on the historically-rooted evils of feudal society. In working out the plot, Lu Xun fully demonstrates his artistic talent as he uses the concrete and the abstract to reinforce each other. No wonder many readers at the time felt that they were reading something entirely new. In November 1919, a year and a half after the story was published in the *New Youth*, appeared Wu

* Lu Xun, "Preface to *The Short Stories,*" Vol. II, *Major Works of New Chinese Literature, Essays of Qiejieting (II)* (1937).

Yu's essay "Cannibalism and Feudal Ethics" in the same magazine. The story made a great impact on the readers and its influence was far-reaching.

After "A Madman's Diary," Lu Xun wrote "Kong Yiji" and "Medicine." The setting of "Kong Yiji" is Prosperity Tavern, presented in the story as the society then in miniature with much of its local colour. Facing the street is "a bar in the shape of a carpenter's square." High-class customers, who wear long gowns, use the inner room where they can order wine and dishes and sit drinking at their leisure. The short-coated labourers stand by the bar and drink their wine instead. Kong Yiji, the central character, is the only long-gowned customer who drinks his wine standing. Poverty-stricken, he is still trying desperately to keep his status as "scholar." He will not put aside his shabby and dirty long gown. Worse still, he resorts to stealing and defends himself by saying that "taking books can't be counted as stealing." In the story, all the details contribute to the portrayal of Kong Yiji as a tragic character and to the attack on the incurable harm done to the intellectuals by the feudal examination system. To a certain extent, Lu Xun also indirectly censures the kind of mentality that Kong Yiji represents.

"Medicine" is the story of Old Shuan, the proprietor of a teahouse, who buys a roll of steamed bread dipped in human blood in the hope of curing the illness of his son Little Shuan. However, it fails to cure the boy's consumption. Xia Yu, the revolutionary, devotes himself to the cause of liberating the masses, but he is executed as a criminal. Even to the end, the masses do not realize that he suffers and finally lays down his life for their cause. Worse still, driven by superstition they taste his blood, which is being used for the steamed rolls. The fate of Little Shuan is tragic enough, but even more so is that of Xia Yu. Lu Xun was aggrieved that the souls of the slumbering masses had been poisoned by feudalism. He also lamented the very fact that the bourgeois revolution was out of touch with the people. Hence the double tragedy in the story. Based on personal experience and feelings, he makes it clear in the story that if revolutionary ideas fail to catch hold of the masses, the blood of the pioneers will be good only for the making of steamed rolls. And even then it cannot cure consumption. "Medicine" may give one a feeling of gloom. However, the appearance of a wreath on the revolutionary's grave near the end implies that the story does "hold out some rays of hope."* It symbolizes people's hope in the revolution, which is indeed a distinct characteristic of the period.

Prominent among Lu Xun's works of fiction is "The True Story of Ah Q."** In the story he creates a typical peasant of the 1911 Revolution period and paints an accurate picture of the society then. In other stories such as "Storm in a Teacup," "My Old Home," "The New-Year Sacrifice" and "The Divorce," he also uses a peasant as the central character. All these stories reveal the exploitation and oppression of the peasants by feudalism.

"Storm in a Teacup" begins with the description of a pleasant evening scene in the countryside. However, in this tranquil setting the rumbling political storm can be heard. Nervousness grips the family of Sevenpounder, the boatman, when they hear the rumour that the deposed emperor will soon be restored. They fear that he will be in trouble because his queue has been cut off by people in town. The other characters such as Seventh Master Zhao and Old Mrs Ninepounder, with their different traits, are also vividly presented. The story ends on a calm note after the storm has blown over. But it is hinted that just as the restoration of the deposed emperor has failed and that life will go on exactly as before, the awakening of the peasants will not come about until they have been further enlightened.

"My Old Home" depicts the impoverished peasantry. In a lyrical vein Lu Xun writes about the happy days of childhood, which come back to him with all their splendour. He recalls how Runtu appears as a young hero in the watermelon fields on the seashore, holding pitchfork. Before his very eyes now is an entirely different person, albeit with the same name, one who has been crushed by the sufferings of a peasant's lot. "Many children, famines, taxes, soldiers, bandits, officials and landed gentry, all had squeezed him as dry as a mummy." A typical peasant, Runtu is

* Lu Xun, "Preface to My Selected Works," *Selected Works*, Foreign Languages Press, Beijing, 1985, Vol. III, p. 201.

** See the next section of this chapter.

simple and honest, industrious and taciturn and, much like the grand earth itself, endures all kinds of hardships and pain. Excessive suffering has bereft him of all feeling and consciousness of ranks has firmly gripped his mind. He bows to the "god" who controls his destiny. At the end of the story the narrator hopes the next generation will have "a new life, a life we have never experienced." This indicates that the emphasis of the story is not that one should cherish memories of the past. On the contrary, one should challenge the present reality and believe in the future. As Lu Xun puts it, "the earth had no roads to begin with, but when many men pass one way, a road is made."

"The New-Year Sacrifice" is different from "Storm in a Teacup" and "My Old Home" in that it places the characters in even more complex social relationships and voices strong accusations on behalf of the peasants. The protagonist, Xianglin's Wife, is a simple and good-natured woman in the village. She is hard-working and efficient; her only hope is that she can exchange her labour for the basic rights of life. Even so, her life is fraught with misery. After she is newly widowed, she runs away to the small town Luzhen to work as a servant. But she is soon dragged home by members of the family of her mother-in-law and "married off into the mountains" for their monetary gain. Just as she has had a taste of happiness in life, her second husband dies of typhoid. This is followed by the loss of her child, who is snatched away by a wolf. When, deeply grieved, she is back working once again for the Lu family, she has to put up with the jeers and jibes of the people she meets in town. The moralistic Fourth Master Lu regards her as someone who has corrupted public morals, indeed as a symbol of ill-fortune, and she is therefore not allowed to touch anything used for ancestral sacrifices. The superstitious Amah Liu terrifies her with the chatter about punishment in "the lower world" and persuades her to buy a threshold for the local temple, "to be trampled on instead of you by thousands of people." That, she is told, will enable her to atone for her sins. All these mental tortures eventually break the poor woman. She donates a threshold to the temple with her accumulated wages for a whole year's labour, thinking that she has fully paid her debts of sin and can henceforth live a new life. Alas, the feudal society still will not forgive her. Fourth Master Lu still will not allow her to touch the winecups and chopsticks used for the ancestral sacrifice. Driven to distraction, she is frightened "trembling like a mouse that had strayed out its hole in broad daylight." Finally, the Lu family decides to get rid of her and she becomes a beggar. When people are happily celebrating the New Year, she is tortured by the thought of hell and gripped by fear and suspicion. In the end she is swept away like dust. Throughout her life she cannot free herself from the four different ropes tied round her neck: that is, the four authorities in the feudal society—politics, superstition, the clan and the husband. The deep meaning of the story also lies in the fact that not only Fourth Master Lu, but even Amah Liu, who is in same social position as Xianglin's Wife, and those who "savoured" her misfortunes have all been poisoned by feudal ideas and conventions. Utterly insensitive, they inflict mental suffering on her and unknowingly contribute to the creation of this ordinary yet tragic drama in the old society.

Lu Xun's stories well portray the complex class relationships in the peasant community of his day and indeed in the Chinese society at large. He lays bare the root causes of the miserable lives of the peasants and writes about their physical sufferings brought on by economic exploitation. Significantly, he attends even more to the delineation of their mental state after they have been long poisoned by feudal ideas. He points out the contradiction between their inevitable move towards revolution, because of their social position, and their lack of democratic revolutionary awareness. No writer before Lu Xun has shown the same feeling of equality in the portrayal of the peasants. Neither is there a single piece of writing about the peasants which fundamentally negates the feudal system as Lu Xun has done, presenting the reader at the same time with a wide and perceptive historical view.

The intellectuals, too, are given prime attention in Lu Xun's stories. As he lived through the ideological changes in the cultural circles, Lu Xun observed closely the different types of intellectuals of his day. The stories "In the Tavern" and "The Misanthrope" describe how these types drift from anxiety and restlessness to dejection and decadence after the 1911 Revolution. In the story "In the Tavern," Lü Weifu is originally an extremely capable and energetic young man who passionately believes in the possibility of reforming China. After moving from place to place, however, he feels that none of the dreams of his youth has been fulfilled. Now he is teaching the Confucian classics, but doing it only as a perfunctory job. He drifts along and from time to time attends to "trivial matters" to amuse himself and please other people. He sums up his life thus: like a fly which makes a small circle and comes back to stop in the same place.

Compared with the dispirited and demoralized Lü Weifu, Wei Lianshu in "The Misanthrope" has a more gloomy outlook and is uncaring. Because he thinks it is beneath his dignity to mix with the crowd, he confines himself in a self-created cocoon. But the truth remains that he cannot isolate himself completely from society. Dogged by rumours and harassed by unemployment, eventually he has to cast aside his ideals and kowtow to reality. He becomes an adviser to one of the generals of the warlords and is now doing what he formerly detested and opposed. He is flattered and lauded by the people around him. It seems that he has won, but in truth he has been defeated. In the end, he dies a lonely man's death with deep scars in his heart. These two stories show the conflict between expectations and the reality, the clash between the force of revolution and the force of customs. They are shrouded in a stifling atmosphere, that of the failed Revolution of 1911, and also contain criticism of the weakness of character found in both Lü Weifu and Wei Lianshu.

Both Zijun and Juansheng in "Regret for the Past," no doubt people of the May Fourth period, are younger than Lü Weifu and Wei Lianshu. In fighting for the freedom of choice in marriage, Zijun courageously leaves her family against all kinds of reproach and derision. "I'm my own mistress," she remarks. "None of them has any right to interfere with me." She is firm in her demand for the liberation of self. However, the liberation of self cannot be achieved without the liberation of society and, in the absence of ideals, the trailing glory of love will also fade away. Living a peaceful and happy life, she occupies herself with the daily chores.

Soon her life and hopes both vanish into thin air. To Juansheng, these daily chores are a nuisance. When their days of living together are being threatened by unemployment, he realizes that "during the last half year, for love—blind love—I had neglected all the other important things in life." But he is too weak to cope with the even greater social pressure and can only put the blame for his failure on Zijun and on the fact that he is no longer free. Desperately, he tries to "save" himself. In the end the frailty of Juansheng in his personal struggle becomes all too obvious. The story is written in the form of Juansheng's "notes." His state of mind is described in poetic language and much of Lu Xun's criticism is contained in the detailed narration of events.

In describing the conflict between the individual and society, Lu Xun does more than extending sympathy to the intellectuals. He gives a piercing analysis of the individual and society as well. When he cannot see any force in life which is strong enough to alter the tragic fate of the intellectuals of the old society, Lu Xun the realist, most sincerely places his hope in the newcomers. This is evident in "A Small Incident," when the narrator of the story extols the rickshaw man. It is also evident in "The Lamp That Was Kept Alight," when the cry of the lunatic "I'll set the place on fire" is echoed in the song sung by the children at the end of the story. Sparkling in Lu Xun's works are the ideals which inspire people to move forward. These ideals are the indispensable elements of his realism in his exposure of the corrupt society.

Lu Xun's stories are full of originality. They are written in a most distinctive style. Rich but not gaudy, it flows smoothly and carries profound thoughts, blending humour with seriousness. In the formation of this highly personal style, works of classical literature both Chinese and foreign have played their part. Lu Xun admired the profundity and simplicity of the Chinese artistic tradition and he was also much influenced by the realism of Russian, Polish and Balkan writers. In discussing the art of the Chinese and foreign writers, he observed that "the best way to convey a man's character with a minimum of strokes is to draw his eyes."* A writer, he believed, should portray sharply the chief traits of a person's character without wasting words. "If you draw all the hairs of his head, no matter how accurately, it will not be of very much use."** By this he did not mean that the physical appearance of a character was not important. He thought that in portraying a character the artist should ensure that the object of artistic creation will bear resemblance to the original "in appearance and spirit."*** In his view, a writer of a higher order "almost does not need to describe the physical appearance of the characters. Their manner of speaking and their voice alone will not only express their thoughts and feelings but also give shape to their face and body."† Lu Xun was adept in the art of what is called, in Chinese, "bringing the painted dragon to life by putting in the pupils of its eyes." In a few words he could convey the thoughts and feelings of a character, who now appears before the reader and makes a strong impression on him. Many of the characters in his stories have a gloomy fate and the reader is deeply moved, finding it hard to forget what he or she has read. Willingly, the reader wants to change the paths of life trodden by these unfortunate characters. Lu Xun's technique of "drawing the eyes" and "catching the soul" of a character is highly effective. It strengthens the affective power of art, touching not only the reader's heart but also his very soul.

Concerning his techniques, Lu Xun explained: "I did my best to avoid all wordiness. If I felt I had made my meaning sufficiently clear, I was glad to dispense with frills. The old Chinese theatre has no scenery, and the New Year pictures sold to children show a few main figures only (though nowadays most of them have a background too). Convinced that such method suited my purpose, I did not indulge in irrelevant details and kept the dialogue down to a

* Lu Xun, "How I Came to Write Stories," *Selected Works*, Foreign Languages Press, Beijing, 1985, Vol. III, p. 265.

** *Ibid.*

*** See "The Translator's Postscript to *The Bad Child and Other Strange Tales*," *The Translations of Lu Xun*, Vol. IV, p. 466.

† Lu Xun, Preface to "Poor Folk," *Outside the Collections* (1935).

minimum."* It should be noted that Lu Xun was against wordiness and the use of frills but not totally against the inclusion of supportive background details. In some of his stories, occasionally he describes the setting. For example, the rural evening scene in "Storm in a Teacup" and the night scene of the river village in "Village Opera" are fresh and crisp, much like a beautiful sketch in Chinese ink. The dialogue in the stories suits the action and subtly reveals, through the economical use of words, the background and mood of the characters. These characteristics of his style can be traced back to the traditional techniques of Chinese classical art. In other stories, however, the construction of plot and narrative technique show traces of foreign influence. For example, what goes on in "Kong Yiji" is seen through the eyes of a pot-boy in a tavern. "Tomorrow" begins with a question from Red-nosed Gong: "Not a sound—what's wrong with the kid?" In "A Public Example," Lu Xun relies on the use of quick sketches throughout in the construction of its plot. These stories well indicate that he has adapted the technique of foreign writers in a Chinese artistic context.

Lu Xun was also skilled in condensing material from common daily life to a high degree in his portrayal of uncommon themes. He demanded that artistic creations should give the reader fresh impressions of things. This does not mean, however, that a writer should deliberately try to achieve the effect of novelty. Rather, he should delve into life itself. That is why he suggested that "the choice of material should be strict; the treatment should aim at depth."** Before he embarked on writing, he had analysed Chinese history and society and acquired a profound knowledge and deep insight. He had also accumulated a good deal of life experience. Furthermore, he faithfully adhered to his own principles of artistic creation, taking an interest in everything he saw but refraining from writing after he had seen only a little."*** The fundamental revolutionary democratic ideas which he held sharpened his pow-

* Lu Xun, "How I Came to Write Stories," *Selected Works*, Foreign Languages Press, Beijing, 1985, Vol. III, p. 263.

** Lu Xun, "Correspondence on the Materials for Stories," *Two Hearts* (1932).

*** For these principles, see his "Reply to the Magazine *The Dipper*," *Selected Works*, Foreign Languages Press, Beijing, 1985, Vol. III, pp. 162-3.

er of observation and enabled him to see the truths behind familiar external phenomena from the viewpoint of historical development, itself based on a high-degree condensation of the realities of life. He could therefore say what had not been said by others before and this lent depth to his works, making people think. Some of his stories may have given the reader an oppressive feeling.* They show traces of his thought, of course, during this difficult period of internal search before he turned to Marxism. At the same time, however, they accurately reflect the pain which an old country experienced when it was going through the process of transformation. This "oppressive feeling" did not lead his contemporary reader to despair. On the contrary, it touched the right chord in the reader's heart. In his works Lu Xun always comes to grips with the social problems of his day whether he is lashing out, giving encouragement, spurning the despicable elements or waiting for better times to come. Precisely because of this, his realism, compared with that in works of the past, is of a much higher order. His works are unequalled in freshness, depth and clarity. Above all, they are much powerful as a force in combat.

III. "The True Story of Ah Q"

"The True Story of Ah Q" was written between December 1921 and February 1922. The best known of his short stories, it is set in a remote and backward village called Weizhuang about the time of the 1911 Revolution. In this masterpiece, Lu Xun has created a typical peasant of his day, one who has been seriously maimed both mentally and materially. Without a home or an inch of ground that he can call his own, Ah Q takes up his abode in the Tutelary God's Temple. Nor does he have permanent employment. "When there was wheat to be cut he would cut it, when there was rice to be hulled, he would hull it, when there was a boat to be punted he would punt it." Cruelly exploited, he has lost his land and his means of independent livelihood. Even his name has gone.

* See Lu Xun's remarks in "Preface to My *Selected Works*, " *Selected Works*, Foreign Languages Press, Beijing, 1985, Vol. III, p. 202.

Once, after he has gulped down two bowls of yellow wine, he announces that he belongs to the clan of Mr Zhao. He is duly summoned by the bailiff to Mr Zhao's house. In a fury, Mr Zhao slaps him on the face and forbids him to use the same surname.

Ah Q's lot is truly miserable. But that is not how he sees it, for he feels that he is "always gaining victories." The first two chapters of the story contain some accounts of how he gains his "victories," focussing on the delineation of this trait of his character. He often brags of his past, saying, "We used to be much better off than you! Who do you think you are?" In truth, however, he cannot be certain even about his own surname. He has no wife, and yet he dreams of the future "thinking to himself, 'My sons may be much greater.' " The ringworm scars on his scalp are taboo to him, but he can also say that other people "don't even deserve" to have them. When he is defeated in a fight, he will think to himself: "It is as if I were beaten by my son. What the world is coming to nowadays!..." So he feels that he has won. When people force him to admit that is a case of "a man beating a beast," he more than complies pleading with self-contempt, "Beating an insect—how about that?" Then, immediately after the humiliation, he thinks that he is the "Number One self-belittler." When "self-belittler" is removed, what remains is "Number One." So he thinks, "Was not the highest successful candidate in the official examination also 'Number One'?" With this thought, then, Ah Q believes he has won again. When all the "means of winning a psychological victory" have failed to produce the desired result, he will slap his own face hard, twice. This will make him feel that he has given the slaps himself and that the one slapped is somebody else. Once again, he is satisfied with his victory. Sometimes, he derives satisfaction from bullying those who are not socially strong enough to protect themselves. For instance, after he has been beaten by Bogus Foreign Devil, he paws that newly shaved scalp of the little nun, regarding this act as his "feat" and wallows in the appreciation and laughter of the onlookers. However, this so-called "feat," his psychological victories, his self-denigration, self-contempt and self-justification—all of them are equally pathetic. "The means of winning a psychological victory" have made it possible for him not to face the very fact that he is being miserably oppressed.

The story highlights Ah Q's "means of winning a psychological victory." It also reveals the many complex elements found in his character. Indeed, Ah Q is full of contradictions. An exploited peasant who is good-natured, simple and gullible, he has long been poisoned by feudal thinking. He holds on to some of the ideas which are approved by "the teachings of the saints and sages" and in him one can trace the narrow-mindedness and the conservative outlook of the small producers. He believes in the strict segregation of the sexes and equates revolution with rebellion. He is contemptuous of the townspeople because they call a long bench, that is known to the Weizhuang villagers as a straight bench. In fact, he regards as "heretic" anything which is different from the customs in Weizhuang, but then Ah Q is also an impoverished peasant who has lost his land, one who moves from place to place. He is driven by circumstances to become a petty thief and has picked up the tricks of the layabouts. He does not think much of Mr Zhao or Mr Qian, and dares to look at Bogus Foreign Devil "with a furious glare." Still more, he thinks it is ridiculous that the villagers of Weizhuang have never seen fish fried in town or witnessed a public execution. Understandably, some of the traits of Ah Q's character cannot be found in the ordinary peasants of the feudal Chinese village. He looks down both on the townspeople and the villagers. Moving back and forth from the feeling of self-importance to that of self-debasement, he betrays the typical mentality produced by the environment of a semi-feudal and semi-colonial society. His "means of winning a psychological victory" well indicate the complexity of the social contradictions found in the Chinese village as a result of the invasion of foreign capitalism. However, these "means" are also the products of his personal experience. In presenting Ah Q, Lu Xun follows his own methods of artistic creation; that is, not choosing definite models for his characters, but creating them out of all that he has seen.* In accordance with the requirements of art in maintaining the general movement of the story, he makes the narration highly condensed.

* See "A Reply to the Magazine *The Dipper*," *Selected Works*, Foreign Languages Press, Beijing, 1985, Vol. III, pp. 162-3.

While concentrating on the refinement of thoughts, he also highlights one of the complex traits found in the central character. In this manner Lu Xun has created the unforgettable farmhand Ah Q. What he does or what happens to him carries profound meaning.

As the tides of imperialism continued to rise in China, the rule of the feudal class was ebbing away. Members of that class felt there was not much they could do about their plight and the "means of winning a psychological victory" which came into use truly signified their helpless state. As Marx and Engels put it, "in any era, the ideas of the ruling class will dominate the thinking of that era."* The truth is plain, for the class which controls what is needed for material production also controls what is needed for spiritual creation. Generally speaking, therefore, people who have been spiritually deprived will inevitably be controlled in their way of thinking as well. In the circumstances, it was natural that the peasants of Lu Xun's day were influenced by the ideas of the ruling class. Furthermore, the different classes were caught in the same environment and as they were people of the same nation, some of their experiences, in material terms, were bound to be the same or at least similar. Opportunities were thus created for the spread of the morbid mentality identified by Lu Xun. The class weaknesses of the peasants and the economic position of the small producers which had been long maintained in the system of private ownership of means of production, equally favoured the birth of the "means of winning a psychological victory." No wonder it was readily adopted by peasants like Ah Q, who could not as yet rid themselves of the inherent weaknesses of their class and who had also somewhat assimilated the mentality of the loafers.

Lu Xun wrote the story "with the intention of exposing the national failings."** As he explained, his "method is to make the reader unable to tell who this character can be apart from himself, so that he cannot back away to become a bystander but is bound to suspect that this may be a portrait of himself if not of every man,

---

* "German Ideology," *The Complete Works of Marx and Engels* [in Chinese translation], Vol. III, p. 52.

** "More Mental Reservations," *Selected Works*, Foreign Languages Press, Beijing, 1985, Vol. III, p. 286.

and that may start him thinking."* While making his points of general criticism, Lu Xun presents Ah Q as a typical farmhand, based on his close observation of the lives of the peasants. He faithfully follows the principles of typification in realism. Ah Q's "means of winning a psychological victory" are exclusively his. They may of course bear resemblance to other people's means of scoring their victories and there may also be fundamental differences. As Lu Xun says, "when you put a round skull-cap on his head he ceases to be Ah Q."** In his artistic vision, a character appears in a definite shape. Thus he recalls, "When I was writing 'The True Story of Ah Q,' some petty politicians and bureaucrats were infuriated. They insisted that they had been satirized, not realizing that the model for Ah Q at the time was in another small town. As a matter of fact, he was then husking rice for people."*** To Lu Xun, there is no contradiction between criticizing the phenomenon which he describes as the "means of winning a psychological victory" and creating a highly distinctive character such as Ah Q. The general is best reflected in the particular; the more deeply a typical character is portrayed, the more he will represent his kind. Accordingly, the more Ah Q's "means of winning a psychological victory" reflect the traits of his character as a peasant, the more they will contribute to the social satire in the story.

The story, from Chapter 7 on, tells of the changes in Ah Q after the arrival of the revolution. These changes, however, are not deviations from his characteristic behaviour. In fact, they further demonstrate the unchangeable nature of Ah Q as a typical peasant who has long been accustomed to using the "means of winning a psychological victory." When the end of the road for him is in sight, comes the rumour that the revolutionaries are about to enter the town. Ah Q has always thought that revolution means rebellion and that rebellion will get him into trouble. That is why he has

---

* Lu Xun, "A Reply to the Editor of *The Theatre*," *Selected Works*, Foreign Languages Press, Beijing, 1985, Vol. IV, p. 141.

** Lu Xun, "To the Editor of *The Theatre*," *Ibid*., p. 145.

*** Lu Xun, "The Pass in the Story 'Leaving the Pass,' " *Essays of Qiejieting (III)* (1937).

always detested it, not wanting to have anything to do with it. Now he sees that it has put such great fear in the widely-renowned successful provincial candidate. It has also struck terror into the villagers of Weizhuang. He cannot help "feeling rather fascinated." So he thinks to himself, "Revolution is not a bad thing. Finish off the whole lot of them ... curse them!... I'd like to go over to the revolutionaries myself." Ah Q welcomes the revolution with the earnestness of someone who has been exploited and Lu Xun has not overlooked this aspect of the revolution. Neither has he exaggerated it. Then, too, Ah Q feels that rebellion is something of an excitement. It seems to him that he is already one of the revolutionaries, who, in his imagination, are "all in white helmets and white armour, with swords, steel maces, bombs, foreign guns, sharp-pointed double-edged knives, and spears with hooks." He dreams that after the revolution the silver ingots, foreign coins, foreign calico jackets of the Zhao family, the Ningbo bed of the successful county candidate's wife, not forgetting that tables and chairs of the Qian family—indeed, all these will be moved to his abode, the Tutelary God's Temple. The first to die will be Young D and Mr Zhao, and then the successful county candidate and the Bogus Foreign Devil. Of course, Ah Q is extremely naive and muddle-headed in his understanding of revolution. However, as his dreams are filled with the peasants' feeling of revenge and the idea of equal distribution of possessions, they clearly indicate his urgent desire to change his social status. He sincerely places his hopes in the revolution and in him can always be found the potential support for its cause.

"The national revolution," Mao Zedong once observed, "requires a great change in the countryside. The Revolution of 1911 did not bring about this change, hence its failure."* The democratic revolution led by the bourgeoisie overlooked the demands of the peasants. True, it had overthrown the emperor, but in practical terms it had not brought the people any gain. In the story, Lu Xun has given a realistic account of what may be called "handing out the same medicine, only differently prepared." Indeed, the revolu-

* Mao Zedong, "Report on An Investigation of the Peasant Movement in Hunan," *Selected Works*, Foreign Languages Press, Beijing, 1965, Vol. I, p. 27.

tionaries have entered the town. But that has not brought about any basic change: the magistrate is still the highest official, the successful provincial candidate has now become the assistant civil administrator, and the head of the military is still the same old captain. In Weizhuang, the successful candidate in the Zhao family acts in collusion with the Bogus Foreign Devil, who has now assumed the pose of a bourgeois landlord's son. They move ahead of other people and eagerly pledge themselves to make revolution, letting it be known that this is "a time for all to work for reforms." However, when Ah Q, who genuinely wants to join the revolution, plucks up enough courage to go and see the Bogus Foreign Devil, he is given the sight of the "mourner's stick" and is not allowed to have anything to do with the revolution. After the Zhao family has been robbed, the captain, who has been a member of the revolutionary party for less than twenty days, feels that his prestige as a military man has to be maintained. Consequently, Ah Q has to be arrested, tried and executed in public as a crime-deterrent according to the saying "Punish one to awe one hundred." Thus the scene of public execution shown by the lantern slides which Lu Xun saw fifteen years before in Sendai, Japan, now made its appearance at the end of "The True Story of Ah Q" and is given specific descriptions. It is clear enough that the apathy of the people always deeply pains Lu Xun. "The grand finale" of the story is the tragic end of Ah Q. It is also the tragic end of the 1911 Revolution.

Against a vast historical background, "The True Story of Ah Q" lays bare the social contradiction and class relationships in the Chinese countryside of Lu Xun's day. It also brings to light the peasants' demand for liberation. Through his artistic creation, Lu Xun invited the reader to go over the historical lessons learned from the 1911 Revolution. He may have dwelt too much on the backwardness of the masses. However, that provided the context in which he could raise the question of how to bring about their democratic awakening, a question which carried significant meaning at the time. As yet Lu Xun had not found the answer. Neither could he indicate the way which would lead people to a happy life. But as always he stood by the oppressed. He sided with the peasants, strongly believing that they had the right to live a better life and, therefore, the right to join the revolutionaries if necessary. That was why he explained that "as long as there was no revolution in China, Ah Q would not turn revolutionary; but once there was one, he would."* In the midst of Lu Xun's realism one can see the optimism that comes with his sense of history.

After his appearance in Lu Xun's story, Ah Q has become a household word for the description of people who show much the same mentality. In 1926, the translation of the story by the French writer Romain Rolland was published in the magazine *L'Europe*. Since then, it has been translated into nearly forty different languages. "The True Story of Ah Q" is an immortal masterpiece not only in Chinese literature but in world literature.

IV. The Essays

As used by Lu Xun, the essay is a sharp instrument in his anatomy of society and a powerful weapon in his attack on the enemy. Essays occupy an extremely important place in his works. Especially in the later period of his career, he devoted his time and energy mainly to the writing of essays. As a result of his introduction and use of this literary form, the artistic and combative character of the essay rapidly gained a wide appeal.

The modern essay is a product of the May Fourth Movement of 1919, "grounded as it was in the 'literary revolution' and the 'ideological revolution.' "** In form and manner of approach it is distinct from the traditional prose works of this literary genre. Lu Xun's essays first appeared in the *New Youth* for the year 1918 under the title "Random Thoughts" and the works of his early period are collected in *Hot Air* (1925), *Bad Luck* (1926), *Bad Luck (II)* (1927) and *The Grave* (1927).*** In all of them one finds the inextinguishable fire of anti-imperialism and anti-feudalism. Through these essays, Lu Xun was able to tackle the issues which

* Lu Xun, "How 'The True Story of Ah Q' Was Written," *Selected Works*, Foreign Languages Press, Beijing, 1985, Vol. II, p. 317.

** Lu Xun, "The Crisis of the Essay," *Ibid.*, p. 342.

*** Lu Xun once called *The Grave* a collection of treatises. Some of these resemble his long essays in which he expresses his random thoughts.

he did not or could not deal with in his short stories.

The early essays of Lu Xun are characterized by their social criticism and they cover a wide range of topics. Of the essays published under "Random Thoughts" in the *New Youth* alone, "some are aimed at the practice of planchette writing, therapeutic quiet-sitting and martial arts; some are aimed at 'the preservation of national characteristics'; some are aimed at the bureaucrats of the day who take pride in the experiences; some are aimed at the satirical cartoons published in the Shanghai newspaper *The Times*."* Almost anything can be discussed in his essays; from nihilistic philosophy to slave mentality; from blind, inflated "patriotic writings" to bizarre social phenomena; from things past to things present and so on. Pervading the discussions of the numerous topics is the May Fourth spirit, that Mr De and Mr Sai.** For example, in "My Views on Chastity," "What Is Required of Us as Fathers Today," "What Happens After Nora Leaves Home?", "The Collapse of Leifeng Pagoda" and "Some Notions Jotted Down by Lamplight," he fiercely attacks the Confucian ethical code and feudal ethics. He is against "widowism" and "the tactic of strengthening the defences by clearing the fields." He advocates "family revolution" and urges young people to disrupt and destroy the feudal system. He calls upon them to wipe out "the era in which one is temporarily allowed to be a slave" and create, instead, "a third era, hitherto unknown in Chinese history." Through his use of vivid images and humorous language, Lu Xun pursues his points closely. The short essays in *Hot Air* are sharp and concise, crisp and clear, each containing his incisive criticism. Those collected in *The Grave*, on the other hand, are longer and are characterized by the free play of the writer's mind upon ideas as step by step he works out his argument.

After the split in the new culture united front, Lu Xun continued his battle against feudalism. He may have been in low spirits at times, but there is no trace of that in his essays which contain, as those written before, spirited attacks on the blind worship of Confucianism, the classics and the reversion to antiquated think-

---

* Lu Xun, Foreword to *Hot Air* (1925).

** Chinese terms used at the time for Democracy and Science.

ing. Before and after the May 30th Incident of 1925, the anti-imperialist feelings of the masses were running high. Headed by Hu Shi, the Right-wing of the bourgeoisie, which represented the interests of the imperialists, collaborated with the feudal forces in their attempts to frustrate the struggles of the masses. Consequently, in his writings Lu Xun changed the emphasis from social criticism to intense political struggle. The essays in the second half of *Bad Luck*, those in *Bad Luck (II)*, and the last pieces in *The Grave* are all related to the May 30th Incident, the student movement at the Beijing Women's Normal College and the March 18th Massacre of 1926. Lu Xun focussed his attack on the Europeanized gentry and the literary opportunists, pointing out clearly the new goals to be achieved in the democratic revolutionary struggle when the feudal forces were acting in collusion with the Right-wing elements of the bourgeoisie.

In his well-known essay "In Memory of Miss Liu Hezhen," for instance, he states, "True fighters dare face the sorrows of humanity, and look unflinchingly at bloodshed." He feels that the eve of a major battle has arrived and goes on to say, "Silence, silence! Unless we burst out, we shall perish in this silence!" He also announces in "More Roses Without Blooms," written on the day of the March 18th Massacre, that "this is not the conclusion of an incident, but a new beginning." The gentlemen and scholars, the "sheep leaders," will reveal more and more their true selves once they have completed their mission, "for these sheep are at the same time wild beasts. When they meet beasts wilder than they are, they behave like sheep; when they meet sheep weaker than they are, they behave like wild beasts."*

Not only do these essays contain Lu Xun's penetrating analysis, they often present typical images which accurately reflect that true nature of the lackeys of imperialism. Thus, in his essay "On Deferring 'Fair Play' " he puts forward his famous theory of "beating a dog in the water," arguing against tolerance. At the time Duan Qirui, a Northern warlord, was under attack from all sides. The workers and students in Beijing were holding demonstrations,

* Lu Xun, "Sudden Notions (7)," *Selected Works*, Foreign Languages Press, Beijing, 1985, Vol. II, p. 161.

demanding that he should relinquish all his power. Some people, however, preached "fair play," saying that "a brave prize-fighter never hits his opponent when he is down."* Lu Xun refutes their argument in his essay. Referring to historical facts, he explains, " 'To be wronged but to seek revenge' is forgiving. 'An eye for an eye and a tooth for a tooth' is just. In China, however, most things are topsy-turvy; instead of beating dogs in the water, we let ourselves be bitten by them." He continues, "The simple souls go on making the mistake of confusing forgiveness with giving free rein to evil, and continue pardoning wicked men." They are against "beating a dog in the water," not realizing that a dog cannot change its nature. Once it has crawled ashore, it will again bite people to death. "If we think it looks pathetic in the water," he goes on to say, "so do many other pests. And though cholera germs breed so fast, they look very tame; yet doctors show them no mercy." In the essay, he severely criticizes bourgeois liberalism, and the "Doctrine of the Mean" in traditional Chinese thought, fully demonstrating his firm stand as a follower of revolutionary democracy. The essay is specially mentioned in his Postscript to *The Grave*: "The last piece in this collection, 'On Deferring Fair Play,' " may be worth reading. Though not written in my own blood, it was written after I had witnessed the bloodshed by people of my generation and by the younger generation." Indeed, the essay is a painful summing up of the experiences of his long struggle. It is also another landmark in the development of his thought.

Lu Xun arrived in Shanghai from Guangzhou in October 1927. From then until he passed away, he wrote more essays. In the Postscript to the *Essays of Qiejieting (II)* (1937), written at the end of 1935, he looks back on the history of his essay-writing and notes, "Eighteen years have separated the first essay, written under the title 'Random Thoughts' for the *New Youth*, from the last piece in this collection. These essays total about 800,000 words. In the last nine years I have written twice as much as in the first nine. And in the last three years I have written as much as in the preceding six years." In the Preface to the *Selected Essays of Lu Xun*

* Lu Xun, "On Deferring 'Fair Play,' " *Selected Works*, Foreign Languages Press, Beijing, 1985, Vol. II, p. 229.

(1933), Qu Qiubai analyses the historical background of these essays. He remarks, "In fact, Lu Xun's essays are 'treatises on society,' a kind of combative 'feuilleton.' Anyone who has given any thought to what has happened in the past twenty years or so will understand the appeal of the essay as a literary form. The intense social struggles have made it impossible for a writer to create at his leisure and weave his thoughts and feelings into his works thereby giving them specific artistic shape. Neither can he express his opinions in the same way as before because of the ruthless oppression. That is why a writer who has a talent for humour can safely make his political stand clear through art, give his shrewd observations on social activities and express his warm sympathy for the struggles of the masses." Lu Xun's essays are a record of his times.

The essays written between 1927 and 1929 show that Lu Xun was definitely consolidating his ideas after the breakthrough in his ideological development. Most of these essays are collected in *And That's That* (1928) and *Three Leisures* (1932). In the former collection, some of those written in Guangzhou continue the tenacious attack of *Bad Luck (II)* on the feudal compactor. Of the others, some are about colonial Hong Kong, the imperialist oppression there and the characteristics of its culture under the aegis of imperialist rule. Most of them, however, carry his strong condemnation of Chiang Kai-shek's betrayal of the revolution and his massacres of the people. *Three Leisures* contains essays related to the controversy on revolutionary literature which arose in 1928. Some of these give a clear and rigorous analysis of the revolutionary situation; some discuss in a more comprehensive manner the relation between art and society, art and ideology. The focal point of the controversy at the time was the writer's world outlook, and Lu Xun had a full grasp of the key issues.

From about 1930 on, Lu Xun appeared in the literary circles as a mature Marxist thinker. He fought under the banner of the Communist Party, and the traces of his former internal questionings and struggles had completely gone. He had solved the problem which had plagued him for a long time, the problem, as he put it, of "looking forward to the rise of a new society, without knowing, however, what form the 'new' would take."* Replacing anticipation and search in his later essays is the desire to safeguard the ideals. This is evident in his defence of proletarian literature, the people's revolutionary cause and communism. The belief in collectivism gave him a certain calmness and easiness as he carried out his combative mission through art. A more relaxed style of writing can be seen in the two collections *Two Hearts* (1932) and *Mixed Dialects* (1934). In the essay "Thoughts on the League of Left-Wing Writers" and those written after the execution of the five martyrs of the League, Lu Xun makes his stand absolutely clear. Proletarian literature, he explains, "should be an intrinsic part of the proletarian struggle for liberation" and, through his vivid recounting of facts, he predicts that it will develop and grow in strength.

As terror and darkness reigned over China and as Lu Xun was on the government's arrest list, any writing which carried the tone of combat could have cost him his life. When, at the request of Agnes Smedley, he gave the essay "The Present Condition of Literature and Art in Darkest China" to the American magazine *New Masses*, some of his friends advised him to think of his own safety. He replied, unflinchingly, "That's all right. Someone should speak out. Someone should tell the truth."** In the polemics with the New Moon Society over fascist "nationalist literature" and the "Third Category," he uses class viewpoints to expose the hypocrisy of what the bourgeoisie advocates as "the theory of human nature," "the eternal themes," "the essence of the nation" and "the freedom of artistic creation." He explains clearly what some of the fundamental problems of literature really mean. On other occasions, he offers advice to the revolutionary writers by analysing the relation between literature and politics, writers and revolution, as in the essays "Unrevolutionary Eagerness for Revolution," "A Glance at Shanghai Literature" and in the talk given at the inaugural meeting

---

* Lu Xun, "A Reply to the *International Literature*," *Selected Works*, Foreign Languages Press, Beijing, 1985, Vol. IV, p. 35.

** Lu Xun's words were recorded by Agnes Smedley. See the Chinese translation of her article in the first number of *Knife and Pen*, published by Jinhua, December 1, 1939.

of the League.

In performing the function of social criticism and political combat, the essays published in the collections after *Two Hearts*, compared with those of his early period, reflect even more deeply and comprehensively the drastic social changes and the explosive political events of the day. The September 18th Incident of 1931 had intensified national contradictions. Accordingly, the Chinese Communist Party made many declarations, proposing national solidarity against the Japanese. However, Chiang Kai-shek was bent on pursuing the policy of non-resistance to foreign aggression as he continued his attacks on the revolutionary bases. Lu Xun analysed the various moves of the Kuomintang government, and exposed those who displayed their "patriotism" with a view to gaining promotion in office as well as those who pretended to "fight the Japanese" while secretly working out compromises with the enemy. These people, he made it clear, were the "dregs" of a society which had reached a historical turning-point. The genuine anti-imperialist patriots were the awakening masses under the leadership of the progressive class.

In January 1933, Lu Xun began writing for the supplement "Free Talk" of the newspaper *Shen Bao*, using different pennames. These essays are collected in *False Liberty* (1933), *Semi-Frivolous Talk* (1934) and *Fringed Literature* (1935).* Those collected in *False Liberty*, written between January and mid-May, 1933, are mainly short commentaries on current events. In pieces such as "An Apology for Flight," "The Fact of the Matter" and "A Mental Reservation," Lu Xun expresses his staunch support for the patriotic cause and defends the struggles of the youths and the masses, in much the same way as he does in the other essays written during this period which are included in *Mixed Dialects*. Based on the difference in background, social status, responsibilities and their intrinsic nature, he makes a sharp distinction between the

* The essays written in 1933 but not collected in *False Liberty* were included in *Mixed Dialects*. Some of the essays in *Fringed Literature* first appeared in *Taibai*, a half-monthly collection of essays edited by Chen Wangdao, and in the supplement "Trends" of the *Zhonghua Daily*, which was published by the Kuomintang reformists. The editorial board of the newspaper included revolutionary writers such as Nie Gannu and Ye Zi.

rulers and the ruled, the traitors and the patriots. He gives a clear and penetrating class analysis of the intense national contradictions. In his essays such as "Using Foreigners to Control Other Foreigners," "The Chinese People's 'Lifebelt,' " "On Writing and the Choice of a Subject" and "Above and Below," he points out that Chiang Kai-shek's slogan "Pacify internal foes and resist external ones," adopted to justify his policies, is utterly misleading. What it means, in truth, is: "Pacify the interior and stop resisting foreign aggression." To put it more plainly, it means: "Invite the foreign foe to pacify the interior."* Chiang Kai-shek was hoping that the Kuomintang and the foreign powers would wholeheartedly take military action together against the Chinese Communist Party. His policies, if carried out successfully, would mean not only the Chinese fighting the Chinese; they would also be the first move towards what the imperialists, including the Japanese, called "joint protection against communism." This, however, did not escape the observation of Lu Xun, who as usual, got to the root of a problem before he came up with an unexpected but convincing analysis.

As a result of increasing political oppression, the supplement "Free Talk" of *Shen Bao* published an announcement on May 25, 1933, "imploring writers to turn more to frivolous talk than to their grumbles." The scope of writing was to be narrowed. But, as Lu Xun says, "it is impossible to restrain a writer by dictating themes to him" and "those who talk about serious issues can of course turn to frivolous talk also."** Indeed, tackling serious contemporary issues in the manner of frivolous talk characterizes many of the essays collected in *Semi-Frivolous Talk*. In these essays, whether he draws material from Chinese history or the history of foreign countries, Lu Xun effectively indicates, through hints and implications, that the more savage the massacres become, the more easily one can see that the days of the rulers are numbered. It is a society in which "the animals have become the hunters and men, the

* "On Writing and the Choice of a Subject," *Selected Works*, Foreign Languages Press, Beijing, 1985, Vol. III, p. 272.

** See, respectively, "Foreword," "Poetry and Prophecy," "Free Thoughts in the Morning" and "Agreement and Explanation," *Semi-Frivolous Talk* (1934).

hunted."* In going against the tide of history the rulers are in fact showing the defeatist's psychology that "Only one road is left and that road leads to ruin."**

A new feature of these essays is Lu Xun's direct challenge to fascism. After the fall of Northeast China, Chiang Kai-shek pathetically turned to Britain and America for help. At the same time, however, he followed Mussolini and Hitler and hastened the introduction of the fascist reign of terror in China. As he saw it, Hitler was doing extremely well in Germany and he believed that fascism would take over the world. Lu Xun duly exposed the falsified interpretations of "world political trends" and satirized the slave mentality brought about by "compulsory submission."*** He pointed out clearly that Hitler's plans were being thwarted and that before long his adopted yellow-faced sons would turn out to be the objects of life's merciless "big laugh." And that has been borne out by later historical events.

The essays in *Semi-Frivolous Talk* also contain a good deal of social criticism and analysis of what was going on in the literary circles. Lu Xun's method remains the same throughout: frivolous talk masking the treatment of serious matters, trivial talk conveying profound thoughts. He lashed out at the decadent practices of the degenerate urban petty bourgeoisie such as "scrounging," hanging on to the rich and mighty, building dreams on lotteries, "saving the moon," indulgence in meaningless talk and "living by one's wits." Essentially, the attack was aimed at the deep-rooted poisonous elements found in the traditional spiritual realm. In writing about the trivia of daily life, he revealed the sharp social contradictions and by drawing parallel situations he made people think. Enlightened, they would rebel against the unreasonable system. In his observations on the activities in literary circles, he ridiculed the despicable bourgeois literati: the fawning writers, those "playing the fool," the so-called poets who bought their fame with money, the "scholars" who gained recognition by arrange-

* See, respectively, "Foreword," "Poetry and Prophecy," "Free Thoughts in the Morning" and "Agreement and Explanation," *Semi-Frivolous Talk* (1934).

** *Ibid.*

*** *Ibid.*

ment, gossip writers of inside stories about the rich, and those who practised social climbing. He exposed the true nature of the reactionary propaganda put out by traitors and opportunists and was totally against the topsy-turvy literary world in which one could find no distinction between right and wrong. Above all, he fought for every righteous cause, thus not only defending but extending the combatant tradition of art.

Almost all the essays collected in *Fringed Literature* are short commentaries and they take Lu Xun's social criticism one stage further. The range of topics covered is even wider. In addition to discussing the problems of women, children, superstition and suicide, they give invaluable suggestions on clothing, advertisement and even punctuation. Lu Xun is quick to notice the internal links in ordinary matters and, through dialectic analysis, he can explain their deep meaning. Sometimes, he confronts the problem directly, as in the essay " 'Beijing Types' and 'Shanghai Types,' " in which he analyses the nature of the two groups of literati on the basis of economic dependence. The facts, he points out, are clear enough. "The old capital swarms with officials, the concessions with businessmen. Thus the literati in Beijing are akin to officials, those in Shanghai to merchants. Those akin to officials help the officials to win fame, those akin to merchants help the merchants to make money." In another essay, "Destiny," he notes that some people of the ruling class want to use eugenics to prove that they are born superior. But it is all to no avail, for "history is an embarrassment to them. The father of the first emperor of the Han Dynasty was not an emperor and the son of Li Bai was not a poet. Without an objective base, therefore, they will fail to persuade the poor people to accept their destiny and be submissive. Essays such as these go deep into the matter under discussion. His analysis is crystal clear and his views are original.

Sometimes, Lu Xun resorts to indirect satire. For example, in "The Decline of Foreign Clothing" the muddle-headed conservatives are the objects of his satire. At the same time, he sarcastically explains how their savage legal system can be related to physiological features: "The neck is narrow, so beheading is invented; the knee-joint can bend, so kneeling is invented; the buttocks are fleshy and, since the crime is not too serious, beating is invented." Familiar observations thus enable him to put across deep messages. The essay "Sudden Notions" attacks mainly the opportunists who make their fortune by cheating. In exposing them, Lu Xun also satirizes people who use scientific inventions to uphold decadence. "Beside the mahjong table," he notes, "the electric lights have replaced the candles; in the Buddhist rituals the monks are shinning in the magnesium light. Every day what is the radio blaring out, if not *The Leopard Cat as a Changeling for the Prince*, *The Wronged Courtesan* and *Thank You, Drizzle*"? These incidents, aptly chosen from ordinary life, feature vividly in Lu Xun's biting satire, which was most effective at the time. The essays in *Fringed Literature* are lively and pungent. Instead of making direct political attacks, they paint a true picture of a society in spiritual decline, thereby cutting deeper in their criticism of the corruption of Kuomintang rule.

The three volumes of Lu Xun's *Essays of Qiejieting* were published in July 1937. He edited the first two and his wife Xu Guangping, the last after his death. These essays are rich in technique and content. They also show that the writer was well versed in Marxism and adept in its application. He let Marxist ideas run their course, as required in his pursuit of a certain theme, while keeping the characteristic features of the essay intact. The union of content and style, then, takes his achievement to a greater height. These essays well demonstrate the artistic virtues of a simple, concise and penetrating style.

The first volume of the *Essays of Qiejieting* contains Lu Xun's essays written in 1934 other than the short critiques collected in *Fringed Literature*. In form, there is more variety than in the latter collection; in content they are not limited to social criticism. At the time, Pu Yi had already been put on the throne as Emperor. Following Amo's declaration of exclusive claim on China, the Japanese aggressors penetrated the north of the country. The Red Army, after its failure to counter the Kuomintang's fifth encirclement campaign, moved north and fought against the Japanese. Enormously proud of his recent internal success, Chiang Kai-shek planned to yield further to the foreign aggressors. At this instigation, his subordinates wrote the essay "Friend or Foe?—A Review of Sino-Japanese Relations," begging for peace. The idea of acceptance began to take root in the minds of people who had got used to what was going on. Accordingly, Lu Xun attacked the aggressors and their lackeys. In his essay "Two or Three Things Chinese," he reveals the truth about the "Kingly Way" preached by the Japanese imperialists. The invaders in Chinese history, he reminds the reader, were always prattling about the "Kingly Way" while they plundered the people. They were in fact the "Fire God" masquerading as a "Saviour." Those who rose in rebellion were "dubbed 'perverse' and outlawed from under the jurisdiction of the Kingly Way."*

In "Random Talk After Sickness" and "More Random Talk After Sickness" he tells vivid stories and describes the fate of the enslaved. Behind the romantic affairs lie suffering and pain; behind the love stories lie humiliation and shame. Thus he shows clearly that "from the beginning of history, the Chinese have been slaughtered, enslaved, intimidated and tortured by their own people and foreign people alike. Under oppression, they have suffered more than is humanly tolerable. Every check on the records makes one feel that one is not living in the human world. Lu Xun urges people to learn lessons from history, face the bitter reality and rebel against the oppressors, native or foreign. As he sees it, the only way to survive is to take up arms against them. The Chinese people have a heroic tradition characterized by their indomitable will and courage, and in the essay "Have the Chinese Lost Their Self-Confidence?" he notes: "Since ancient times we have men who worked doggedly in silence, men who worked stubbornly at the risk of their lives, who strove to save others, who braved death to seek the truth." They and they alone are the true strength of the nation. Even if, in the 1930s, men of such calibre had been "trampled on, kept out of the news, smothered in darkness" or forced to go underground, the battle would be continued at any cost.

In the *Essays of Qiejieting (II)*, those written in 1935 focus their

* Lu Xun, "Two or Three Things Chinese," *Selected Works*, Foreign Languages Press, Beijing, 1985, Vol. IV, p. 30.

criticism on cultural affairs and the literary activities at the time. Lu Xun writes in the Preface: "This year, because of the calmness within and the oppressive forces without, I have almost given up talking about national matters. Occasionally I touched on these matters, as in 'What Is Satire?' and 'From Help to Twaddle.' They have been banned." In fact, he touches on "national matters" in more than these two essays since politics has always been his concern. For example, he says that the essay "About Dostoyevsky," written in Japanese, is intended to explain that "to the oppressors, those oppressed are either slaves or enemies and they can never become friends. Therefore their morality is not the same." And that is Lu Xun's direct answer to the proposals of the Japanese aggressors such as "Sino-Japanese mutual help" and "co-existence and mutual prosperity." The oppressed people and the aggressors, he explains, can never live together in peace. In the last part of the essay "Notes Without Titles(9)" he praises the citizens of Beijing for their support of the students who are attacked by the police in a demonstration connected with the December 9th Movement of 1935. He asks, "Who says the ordinary Chinese are fools? Despite all the dust thrown into their eyes and all the oppression, they can still see clearly." In his analysis he states, "It is true that the common people do not read the Confucian classics, do not understand the laws of history, do not know how to pick faults or analyse mistakes; but in general they are far better than those lofty, erudite literati at distinguishing between right and wrong." They are the flint of revolution, and "as long as the flint remains, the sparks will not die out altogether." Here is his reply to the Kuomintang reactionaries, expressing the writer's faith in the strength of the people and in the future of the revolution. True, in the turbulent days of the 1930s, most of the writers supported the revolution and stood by the people. But no one could equal Lu Xun, who openly confronted every issue, relentlessly continued his battle against the reactionaries, whom he utterly despised, and defiantly bore the brunt of numerous attacks.

The essays in the last *Qiejieting* collection were written when Lu Xun was in extremely poor health. In 1936 he was seriously ill twice but he refused to leave Shanghai for medical treatment because he feared the situation could change any time.* On both occasions, when his health showed signs of improvement he resumed writing. It was in these circumstances that he wrote "A Preface to Bai Mang's *The Children's Pagoda*" and "More Notes" and later, "Jottings in Mid-Summer," "That Too Is Life" and "Death." In these essays he reminisces about his comrades in arms or gives vent to his feelings as they strike him. The effect of illness on his state of mind is noticeable, his expression of indignation and excitement being occasionally accompanied by a touch of melancholy and anxiety. The style of writing is also different from that in most of the pieces in the *Essays of Qiejieting (II)*. It does not give the sense of ease found in other pieces such as "Leaving the Pass" and "My First Master" included in the same collection. His fighting spirit, however, remains unchanged. "Written in Deep Night" contains his grief and rage over the secret trials and murders conducted by the Kuomintang reactionaries. The folktales and other incidents in the essay are narrated in a plain but solemn tones similar to that in "Written for the Sake of Forgetting" collected in *Mixed Dialects*. These two essays profoundly stirred the hearts of the progressive youths in the 1930s. There are also essays written in support of the Communist Party's proposal for the formation of a national anti-Japanese united front. He refutes the slanderous arguments of the Trotskyites aimed at the Communist Party and also sharply denounces the savage invasion of the Japanese imperialists. After "Some Recollections of Zhang Taiyan," Lu Xun went on to write "A Few Matters Connected with Zhang Taiyan." It was unfinished when he passed away.

Lu Xun used the assay as a weapon in all his battles until the very end of his life. Each of the historical periods that he lived through had its own central struggle. In the May Fourth period it was the demolition of the feudal forces and customs. This was followed by the long and fierce battle against the warlords and the Rightists of the bourgeoisie. Especially bloody were the battles fought in the cultural "encirclement campaigns" mounted by the Kuomintang during the ten years of civil war. The essay was most

* Xu Guangping, "Lu Xun's Diary in Sickness and the Letters from Soong Ching Ling," *Wind of the Universe*, November 1937, No. 50.

effective in all Lu Xun's attacks and counterattacks. It was a means of immediate response to any challenge and it gave him room to cover a wide range of topics as he freely propagated his ideas. In "The Crisis of the Essay" he stresses that "the essays which live on must be daggers and javelins which, with their readers, can hew out a blood-stained path to a new life. Undoubtedly they may also bring pleasure and relaxation." While "keeping close" to real life, the essay should be "lively, pungent, enlightening and able to prevail on one's sentiment."* To Lu Xun, the life of the essay lies in combat and its content must be closely related to realistic life experience. It must also give the reader artistic pleasure while performing its affective function.

The essays of Lu Xun are an artistic record of the social life and thought of his time. What is written may "often be about a nose, a mouth, a single thread of hair. But together, they form a body, a complete image."** Indeed, through his essays Lu Xun has painted a portrait of his age. Engels praised Balzac's *The Human Comedy* saying that "it is an outstanding realistic history of French society, especially the high society of Paris." In the words of Engels, Balzac "uses the methods of chronicle and describes, almost year by year from 1816 to 1848, the increasing assault of the rising bourgeoisie on the aristocratic society."*** Lu Xun, through his essays, has completed the same mission in portraying the complex struggles in society and the growth and decline of different class forces in the period from the May Fourth Movement of 1919 to the eve of the anti-Japanese war. Underlying his essays is his intense love and hate: love for the people and hate for the enemy. They give full accounts of the sufferings and struggles of the people, their aspirations and ideals. The theoretical content is rich and profound. Lu Xun was different from the writers before him who followed realism not simply because, living in a different period, they wrote about the threat of the bourgeoisie to the aristocratic society while he wrote about the proletariat's replacement of the bourgeoisie as

* Lu Xun, "Preface to *Odd Jobs* (1935) by Xu Maoyong," *Essays of Qiejieting (II)* (1937).

** Lu Xun, Postscript to *Semi-Frivolous Talk* (1934).

*** Engels, "Letter to Margaret Harkness, London," early April 1888.

the leading force of the revolution. The fundamental difference lies in the standpoint from which the two opposing forces in each different era are viewed. The works of Balzac, for example, show that he wrote with regret about the degeneration and decline of "what he considers a model society."* Lu Xun's essays, on the other hand, are a record of his ideological progress as he gradually became the spokesman for the rising class, "representing the great majority of the nation."** His works, especially his essays, are instrumental in hastening the arrival of a new society. Lu Xun's spirit will continue to inspire people to move forward, into the future.

Lu Xun was a master of style. His language is precise and his vocabulary, rich. He observed closely the language used by the people and refined it for his works. He also advocated the proper adoption of foreign grammar and, if necessary, the use of classical Chinese. Thus, sometimes one finds in his prose parallel sentences and symmetrical phrases, which add variety and strength to his style. His essays display a wide range of knowledge, ancient and modern, national and foreign, knowledge that is related to sociology, history, science and culture. Accordingly, each special language finds its way into his essays. In general, however, the basic language is still the vernacular, which he had refined so that it is unmistakably concise, disciplined and forceful. His exact and lively language not only facilitates the development of logical argument, it gives full flesh to the concepts contained. Above all, it makes an unforgettable impression on the reader. His talent for humour, his techniques of satire, his passionate nature behind frosty looks —these also give his essays a highly distinctive personal style.

The influence of Lu Xun on young writers of his day cannot be overstated. "As writers of essays increase in number, so do the readers."*** In the late 1930s, appeared different schools of the "Lu Xun style," each making its invaluable contribution, in the midst of intense struggle, to the education of the people and the attack

* Engels, "Letter to Margaret Harkness, London," early April 1888.

** Mao Zedong, "On New Democracy," *Selected Works*, Foreign Languages Press, Beijing, 1975, Vol. II, p. 372.

*** Lu Xun, Preface to the *Essays of Qiejieting* (1937).

on the enemy. Thanks to his introduction and practice, the essay, which began to develop as a literary form during the May Fourth Movement, eventually established itself in modern Chinese literature, characterized by its ability to answer immediate demands and produce far-reaching influences.

V. Other Prose Works and *Old Tales Retold*

Lu Xun's other works of prose include *Wild Grass* (1927) and *Dawn Blossoms Plucked at Dusk* (1928). The former is a collection of prose poems and the latter contains recollections of his past. Each of these two books occupies an important place in his works.

The prose poems in *Wild Grass* were written between 1924 and 1926. Apart from the last two pieces, they belong to the same periods as the stories collected in *Wandering* and the mood of the writer is the same. Indeed, the lines from Qu Yuan's poem *Li Sao* which he quoted on the frontispiece of *Wandering* could have also been used for *Wild Grass*:

> *The way stretches endless ahead,*
> *I shall search through heaven and earth.**

These prose poems serve mainly as an outlet for his inner feelings, which are woven into his earnest self-analysis and his expression of unfailing devotion to the cause of struggle. The feelings are deep and the search is painful, both also being the hallmarks of the turbulent times. As things stood then, the united front of the new literature was about to break up and most of the intellectuals, unable to see a clear direction ahead, were caught in the same spiritual depression. Since Lu Xun's responsibilities were greater, and the hopes he cherished higher, he was understandably more vexed in spirit than the others.

Quite a number of the prose poems dwell on the clash between the ideal and the real, reflecting the conflicts in the writer's mind. Lu Xun felt that the dark forces were overwhelming and he gave

* Lu Xun, "Preface to My *Selected Works*," *Selected Works*, Foreign Languages Press, Beijing, 1985, Vol. III, p. 202.

them prominent attention in the poems. However, he also believed that he should not be slack in his struggle and that, indeed, he should firmly maintain his fighting spirit. "Such a Fighter" and "The Passer-by" both express his mixed feelings most vividly. After travelling a long way, the "passer-by" is worn out, but the voice of life is calling him and he wants to push on. Nothing can change his decision, whether it is worldly-wise and sincere advice or genuine concern. He does not know exactly what lies ahead; neither is he certain that he can reach the end of the journey. Still, he refuses to accept any "compassion" or "alms" and, with dignity, moves on. In "Such a Fighter," the fighter finds himself "in the lines of nothingness where all that meet him nod to him in the same manner." Together they swear an oath. Hanging above their heads are "all sorts of flags and banners, embroidered with all manner of titles: philanthropist, scholar, writer, elder, youth, dilettante, gentleman." They are wearing "all sorts of surcoats, embroidered with all manner of fine names: scholarship, morality, national culture, public opinion, logic, justice, oriental civilization." Facing these changing illusions and the enemy's weapons which can "kill without bloodshed," the fighter "raises his javelin." When all have crumbled and fallen to the ground, he discovers that there is nothing in their surcoats. In the end, even "the nothingness" has escaped. But he still "raises his javelin." It makes no difference to him whether he is called a "fighter" or a "criminal," whether it is victory or defeat. In a place where "no war-cry is heard," he "raises his javelin" as he has done in the past. The prose poem conveys the feelings of a lone fighter who, imbued with the self-spurring spirit, carries on the good fight. He never slacks off in his duties, neither will he ever retreat.

Written in a lyrical vein, "Autumn Night" describes a heavily frosted courtyard. The shivering little pink flowers are dreaming of spring. With all their leaves gone, the boughs of the date trees, "rigid as iron, silently pierce the strange, high sky." The insects, in pursuit of light, make every effort to get into the room and bravely dash themselves against the lamp. Infused with the thoughts and feelings of the writer, these accounts of the flowers, trees and insects convey a deep meaning. The social implications are also clear. "Amid Pale Bloodstains" was written after the March 18th Incident of 1926. Here, Lu Xun expresses his contempt for the might of the enemy. He laughs at the weakness of the creator and rejoices that "a rebellious fighter has risen from mankind," in whose eyes "heaven and earth change colour." In "The Awakening," written during the period of war between the northern warlords of the Feng and Zhi cliques, Lu Xun embraces with great joy the souls of young people who have been "roughened by the onslaught of wind and dust." As he puts it, they are much like the wild thistle, virtually crushed but still bearing one tiny flower to give joy to the travellers.

Wild Grass also contains some obscure pieces which convey in general the feeling of emptiness and loneliness. In "The Shadow's Leave-Taking," for example, the shadow is presented as a very lonely figure. Darkness will swallow him up and light will also cause him to vanish. He can only "wander between light and shade." But upon his leave-taking, the shadow feels a sense of mission, that of self-sacrifice. He wants to "go far away alone," hoping that from now on nobody will be found in darkness, not even "other shadows." In "The Epitaph," the reader can see the sullen character of a dead person from the inscriptions on the tablet which is "crumbling away and overgrown with moss." Thus the reader is told: "I tore out my heart to eat it, wanting to know its true taste." But he never knows its true taste and can only wait for the occasion when he can smile, that is, when he turns to "ashes." In this prose poem, the dead and the living represent the opposing thoughts in the writer's mind. The narrator, representing the living, manages to free himself from the hold of the dead and hurries away, "not daring to look back, for fear I should see it coming after me."

"The Beggars," "Revenge" and "Hope" are aimed at the hypocrites, the bystanders and the despondent. Lu Xun wanted to write about the pain in the depth of his heart and soul but because "at the time it was difficult to speak outright"* he could only express himself implicitly. He uses familiar talk and internal monologue in

---

* Lu Xun, "Preface, Written in 1931, for an English Edition of *Wild Grass*," *Wild Grass*, Foreign Languages Press, Beijing, 1974, p. 1.

"The Blighted Leaf" to convey the feeling of gratitude, and in "The Kite" the burden of repentance. "Dead Fire" and the next six pieces begin with "I dreamed I was ..."—only in that state can his feelings most appropriately find expression. The new technique of artistic presentation used in "The Shadow's Leave-Taking" is developed further in "After Death." On the assumption that death simply means the paralysis a person's motor nerves while sensation still remains, Lu Xun, in his satire, observes the behaviour of the human pests of gossip-mongers, empty talkers and swindlers—the flies and ants in the prose poem. Thus, even after his death, he is asked to sell books such as *Commentaries on "The Spring and Autumn Annals."* In "The Wise Man, the Fool and the Slave" and "On Expressing an Opinion," Lu Xun satirizes respectively the slave mentality and philistinism manifested in people's behaviour. The style of writing inclines more towards prose than poetry, and the meaning is quite plain. Other pieces in the collection such as "Snow" and "The Good Story" are marked by their freshness and the description of scene, elegant style and extensive meaning. The thoughts and feelings of Lu Xun in *Wild Grass* are conveyed in the spirit of poetry and they should be approached by the reader in the same spirit.

In form and style, *Wild Grass* shows foreign literary influence. At the time, the writing of prose poems was a novel attempt. Many young writers were attracted by this new literary form with its variations, and their works continually appeared in the weekly *The Wilderness* and in the literary supplement of the *Morning News.* This literary form developed further in the 1930s and quite a few distinguished works were produced. In the history of modern Chinese literature, Lu Xun's *Wild Grass* is the work which sets the trend for the writing of prose poems.

Shortly after writing prose poems, Lu Xun began the series under the title "Recollections of the Past" for the half-monthly magazine *The Wilderness.* As he put it, these ten pieces, published from February to November 1926, are "records transcribed from memory."* They were collected in May 1927 under the title *Dawn Blossoms Plucked at Dusk*. In these recollections of the days of his childhood and youth, this criticism and narration are interwoven. Movingly, he recounts his life in the village and in town, in the family and outside, in China and abroad. In "Dogs, Cats, and Mice," *The Picture-Book of Twenty-Four Acts of Filial Piety* and "Wu Chang or Life-Is-Transient," equal emphasis is put on recollection of his past and criticism of society. The writer moves freely in his prose, blending humour with seriousness. In "Ah Chang and the *Book of Hills and Seas*," "The Fair of the Five Fierce Gods," "From Hundred-Plant Garden to Three-Flavour Study," "Father's Illness" and "Fragmentary Recollections," with light and serious touches interlaced, he paints a vivid picture of social customs and human behaviour. "Mr Fujino" "Fan Ainong" are his recollections respectively of a former teacher and an old friend. But they also contain accounts of life abroad and the activities of the revolutionary movement beyond Chinese shores.

As in his stories, Lu Xun has created many unforgettable characters in these works of prose. The talkative Mama Chang is frank and open. She follows strictly many irksome conventions but she can do what other people cannot or will not do. Mr Fujino is honest and sincere, a scholar who is easy to approach and not punctilious. On the other hand, the high-minded Fan Ainong, cherishing his ideals, is eccentric and has very little to do with other people. These characters come to life even though Lu Xun has given only a few sketches of them. Distinctly presented, too, are others such as the teacher in "From Hundred-Plant Garden to Three-Favour Study," who reads the texts aloud, "threw back his head a little and shook it, bending his head further and further back"; Mrs Yan in "Fragmentary Recollections" who encourages the children to spin round but will say, when the child suddenly falls down as his aunt is coming into the room, "See, didn't I say you'd fall? You wouldn't listen to me. I told you not to do it, not to spin...."; the arrogant university students who "even when empty-handed would walk with arms akimbo like crabs, making it

---

* Preface to *Dawn Blossoms Plucked at Dusk*, Foreign Languages Press, Beijing, 1976, p. 2.

impossible for a student of a lower grade to get past." Lu Xun's art is amply demonstrated in the vivid descriptions, in a few strokes, of the mannerisms of his characters.

What is written about the people and the incidents in *Dawn Blossoms Plucked at Dusk* is often steeped in the writer's intense love and hate and carries pungent social criticism. In his plain narrative, one finds much that is praised or censured; in his concise recollections, one sees the clear distinction made by the writer between right and wrong. Reminiscences and thoughts, satire and lyrical expression of personal feelings—they blend well in the writing. Sometimes, of course, his criticism may be direct, as in "Dogs, Cats, and Mice" when he objects to elaborate wedding rites or in *The Picture-Book of Twenty-Four Acts of Filial Piety* when he exposes the absurdity of some of these acts. However, more often his criticism lies deep in the content of the work itself. "Father's Illness" exposes two self-exalted doctors whose medical knowledge is shallow. "Fragmentary Recollections" presents Mrs Yan as a rumourmonger and an instigator of mischief. In both pieces, Lu Xun recounts the facts in such a way that in the process his criticism is conveyed. Sometimes, he may in a passing statement indicate his disapproval of what is generally accepted as customary practice. For example, in "The Fair of the Five Fierce Gods," just as he is about to go to the fair his father suddenly asks him to memorize lines from the primer *Rhymed History*. At the end of his recounting of the incident Lu Xun adds a brief note: "Even now, when I think of it, I still wonder why my father made me learn a lesson by heart at a time like that." Equally effective is the way he ends "Father's Illness" after he has followed Mrs Yan's order to call his father loudly, as is the custom, when he is breathing his last: "I can still hear my voice as it sounded then. And each time I hear those cries, I feel this was the greatest wrong I ever did my father." A seemingly calm statement, it nevertheless conveys deep emotion. This kind of prose has an air of ease and familiarity. The achievement of that effect, however, calls for a high degree of craftsmanship and a profound knowledge of society and a rich experience of life.

Lu Xun also broke new ground in literary creation with his *Old Tales Retold*, published in January 1936. As he says in the "Preface to My *Selected Works*" (1933), edited by himself, they are 'stories based on myths and history.'"* These eight stories were written at different times in a span of thirteen years, during which Lu Xun's world view underwent changes. Thus, compared with the first three stories, the remaining five show a striking development in his thought and in the way he distils life experiences when retelling an old tale. In the preface to the collection, he explains how the historical material is used in his stories: "In some places the narrative is based on passages in old books, elsewhere I gave free rein to my imagination." He boldly incorporates modern events, so as to give his criticism a sharp focus. The eight stories equally display his fighting spirit and artistic excellence in literary creation.

"Mending Heaven," the first tale was written in 1922 and included in the first edition of *Call to Arms* under the title "Buzhou Mountain." It takes its origin from the legend of Nü Wa kneading mud to create human beings and melting colourful stones to mend heaven.** As stated in the Preface to *Old Tales Retold*, Lu Xun originally had the intention of "simply using Freudian theories to explain the origin of creation—the creation of men as well as of literature." The setting of the story is the primeval universe, and the magnificent scenes are painted in rich colours. Nü Wa, the mother of mankind, appears as a simple and honest woman. She is filled with the joy of creation as she kneads mud, and in her arduous task of mending heaven one can see the majestic beauty of labour. The specific descriptions of the wide range of activities in the story show that he has in fact gone beyond Freud's theory of psychoanalysis. While he was working on the story, Lu Xun read an article by a moralist attacking some love poems written in the new poetic form. In disgust, he turned away from legend to reality. "When I returned to my story," he recalls in the preface,*** "try as I might, I could not prevent a little man in antique dress from appearing between the legs of the goddess." The moralist is pre-

* Lu Xun, "Preface to My *Selected Works*," *Selected Works*, Foreign Languages Press, Beijing, 1985, Vol. III, p. 202.

** See *The Imperial Encyclopaedia of the Taiping Era*, compiled by Li Fang (925-996) and others in 977, and *Huai Nan Zi* respectively.

*** Lu Xun, "Preface to *Old Tales Retold*," Foreign Languages Press, Beijing, 1961, pp. 1-2.

sented as a diminutive, laughable character. At this point, the theme of the story is extended to include the anti-feudalism significance of practical struggles. From then on, the narration is more restrained compared with the flow before and the ending is somewhat abrupt. Lu Xun refers to the inclusion of incidents from modern life in his story as a lapse "from seriousness to facetiousness."* This method, however, repeats itself in the other stories that follow, a fact which indicates, no doubt, the writer's intention of using his talent for humour to embody social criticism in a new artistic form.

"The Flight to the Moon" is taken from *Huai Nan Zi.* According to this legend, the master archer Hou Yi shot down nine suns, killed the giant boar, the huge python as well as all other animals big and small. In Lu Xun's story, having done all these, Hou Yi finds that he and his wife Chang E have nothing else to eat except noodles and crow sauce. Unhappy with her lot, she swallows the elixir and flies to the moon. In the meantime, Hou Yi's former pupil Feng Meng appears, a fraud who is unscrupulously hankering after fame. In an attempt on Hou Yi's life he applies the art learned from the master and shoots at him from hiding. Lu Xun puts Hou Yi in all these typical situations, thereby portraying the righteous character of the hero and the loneliness of a brave fighter.

"Forging the Swords" was first published under the title "Mei Jian Chi," the son of Gan Jiang. It is based on the story from *Tales of Marvels* and *Records of Spirits* about Gan Jiang, the master of sword-forging and Mei Jian Chi, who avenges his death. Lu Xun concentrates on the second half of this legend and, in particular, the delineation of the "dark man" as if he were a born avenger who took up the cause for other people. His passionate nature has paradoxically turned him into an icy character, and he is sharp in whatever he says or does, rather like the swords forged by Gan Jiang which the son Mei Jian Chi carries on his back. Mei Jian Chi entrusts the dark man with the mission of avenging his father's death, offering him both his head and his sword. The dark man disguises himself as a performer of tricks and manages to get into

* Lu Xun, "Preface to *Old Tales Retold,*" Foreign Languages Press, Beijing, 1961, pp. 1-2.

the palace. Then, leaping at the opportunity which presents itself, he cuts off the king's head. After this, he cuts off his own head to repay Mei Jian Chi in kind for his trust, now that the mission of avenging his father's death has been completed. The reader can readily identify in real life the likes of Feng Meng, the ruthless king and his muddle-headed councillors, as delineated by Lu Xun in "The Flight to the Moon" and "Forging the Swords."

In the stories "Curbing the Flood" and "Opposing Aggression" Lu Xun presents two characters in a positive light, Yu and Mo Di respectively, in the midst of his criticism directed against the society of his day. Legend has it that four days after his marriage Yu left home and for eight years—thirteen, according to another version of the legend—he attended to his duties in curbing the flood. Thrice he passed by his home but did not stop to go in. To the people, he was an ideal leader, who came from the lower social order and who dedicated himself entirely to public good. As portrayed by Lu Xun, Yu looks like a typical labouring peasant: "a hulk of a man with huge hands and feet, a swarthy face and brownish beard" and "rather bow-legs." In him are found the fine qualities of the peasants, simple people who are hardworking and whose quiet ways speak well for their power of endurance. The noble character of Yu is distinctly contrasted with the scholars on the Mount of Culture who indulge in empty talk, the officials from the Bureau of Water Conservancy who conduct their all-important inspection and the petty people all around carry on with their petty ways. In their midst, Yu stands out as a hero representing the masses.

Mo Di was an intellectual in ancient times who did manual labour himself and practised what he preached. He advocated self-sacrifice, anti-aggression, extension of love beyond one's self to other people, readiness to help those in need, and a strong sense of justice. In Lu Xun's story "Opposing Aggression," Mo Di is shabbily dressed and his rough hands and feet bear witness to the hard manual work that he has done. Brave, intelligent and always alert, he follows his philosophy of self-denial. When he hears that the King of the State of Chu is planning to attack the State of Song, he travels day and night to see the king hoping that he can dissuade him from going to war. Before he sets out on the journey, however, he instructs his disciple Guan Qian'ao to get fully prepared for battle, saying that nobody should count too much on his venture. But he does win the king over to his sense of righteousness and, relying on his practical knowledge, also puts Gongshu Ban in his place. Both Yu and Mo Di are highlighted as positive figures and portrayed as "the backbone of China."

In the two stories, Lu Xun has also created with deep feeling Mo Di's disciples Qin Huali and Guan Qian'ao as well as Yu's unnamed fellow-workers, the "black, gaunt, beggarly-looking figures which neither moved, spoke nor smiled, as if cast in iron." Then there are the people from the countryside who dare argue with Mr Bird-Head. Through their specific actions, these characters demonstrate the positive aspects of morality. They are far superior to Gongshu Ban, Cao Gong Zi, the scholars on the Mount of Culture and the officials from the Bureau of Water Conservancy. Lu Xun downgrades all of them and lashes out at the social rats and city foxes. To him, the masses have certainly become a powerful force.

The three stories "Gathering Vetch," "Leaving the Pass" and "Resurrecting the Dead," through the writer's re-creation of historical figures, criticize the negative thinking of the day. "Gathering Vetch" is about the brothers Boyi and Shuqi, who willingly die of starvation in the Shouyang Mountain. They choose to die "refusing to touch the grains of Zhou" because King Wu has decided to start a punitive war against King Zhou of the State of Shang, where they are from originally. Lu Xun expatiates upon what happens to the brothers after they have moved out of the Old People's Home and gone into Shouyang Mountain, fully describing their poverty-stricken and panic-stricken state. He attacks the shameful behaviour of the rumourmongers, those who make capital of other people's misfortunes, and those who will sell even their souls to get what they want. At the same time, however, he also shows the reader that the brothers are full of contradictions and that their feeble and ineffectual passive resistance leads them inevitably to their tragic end.

"Leaving the Pass" contains dialogues between Lao Zi and

Confucius and what happens to the former at the Hangu Pass. In his narration, by giving significance to the ordinary incidents in daily life, Lu Xun criticizes the forlorn philosopher Lao Zi, who tends to give in. "Resurrecting the Dead" is based mainly on a fable in the chapter "Supreme Joy" of the book *Zhuang Zi*. The story takes the form of a one-act play. In his *Theory on the Equality of Things*, Zhuang Zi preaches nihilism, beginning with the assumption that "this may be right, but the reverse may not be wrong." He advocates the essential non-distinction between matter and self, thus obliterating any difference between life and death, past and present, things large and small, wealth and poverty. In the story, Lu Xun puts Zhuang Zi at the very point when the dead man comes back to life after five hundred years and now in the flesh, pester Zhuang Zi for clothes and other things. Out of necessity the philosopher has to abandon his philosophy. Now he garrulously talks about the differences between life and death, past and present, things large and small, wealth and poverty. He wants to draw a distinction between matter and self, right and wrong. Through the use of lively and amusing dialogue, Lu Xun exposes the absurdity of Zhuang Zi's theory and makes it plain that alas, nihilism itself will be eventually annihilated! Such revelation came at the right time, for after the September 18th Incident of 1931, national defeatism prevailed and intellectuals turned to passive resistance and nihilism avoiding involvement in struggle. With his eyes set on the future, Lu Xun fought for the present and his work of prose, like his essays, greatly enlightened his readers.

In the "Preface to *Old Tales Retold*," Lu Xun says that the stories are mainly "hasty sketches." This is true particularly of the last five tales. Whether in the portrayal of character or in the narration of events, they are different from the stories in *Call to Arms* and *Wandering*. His basic technique is bold outlining. In addition, he often practises the art of caricature when he incorporates scenes from modern life. Their modern colour is well preserved and his special treatment of the familiar daily matters contributes greatly to the delineation of character and development of plot. The modern ideas contained in these stories stand out from the historical facts, and the reader will comprehend their true meaning as the embodiment of material or spiritual phenomena. In this way then, they make a deep impression on the reader. Some of Lu Xun's literary techniques in *Old Tales Retold* remind one of those in Gogol's *Nose*. His comment on that work is revealing: "Strange indeed, the writer may be talking about bizarre things, but the technique is that of realism."* By introducing the concerns of modern life into the stories, he has not made the ancients out as even more dead than they are.** On the contrary, he succinctly portrays the essence of their character and without distorting historical facts, uses them to mirror the people in the post-May Fourth Movement period, particularly those in the 1930s.

Like many other great writers, Lu Xun was constantly searching in the realm of literary creation. He responded to the demands of his age for revolution, followed his own instinct for battle and devoted himself to creative work in various areas of literature and art. What he wrote provided examples and standards for each period. In the history of modern Chinese literature, his works are literary pointers: *Call to Arms* and *Wandering* for the short story, *Dawn Blossoms Plucked at Dusk* and *Wild Grass* for prose and prose poems respectively, and his essays for a literary form which is flexible and lively enough to serve the various purposes of the writer. In *Old Tales Retold* he recreates the myths and anecdotes from history, well demonstrating the potential of these "hasty sketches" as a verbal weapon. The work is inventive both in theme and technique, fully revealing a great writer's spirit of exploration in art.

---

* Lu Xun, "Postcript to *Nose*," *The Translation of Lu Xun*, Vol. X, p. 660.

** Lu Xun, "Preface to *Old Tales Retold*."

Chapter 2
Guo Moruo

I. Life and Literary Activities

Guo Moruo (1892-1978) was born in Shawan, Leshan County of Sichuan Province. In his childhood, he was taught the *Book of Odes, Three Hundred Poems of the Tang Dynasty, Poetry of a Thousand Schools* and *The Essence of Poetry.* To the story of these works he owed his love of poetry at an early age. After the Qing Dynasty, rulers began introducing measures of superficial reform, books and magazines appeared which sought to inform the reader of current world events and spread democratic ideas. Reading such publications widened his intellectuals horizon.

In school, Guo Moruo extensively studied the Chinese classical literary works such as *Zhuang Zi*, *Elegies of Chu*, *Records of the Historian* and *Selections of Literary Prose.* He also read the political essays of Liang Qichao and Zhang Taiyan and the foreign literary masterpieces translated by Lin Shu. As he was enlightened by democratic ideas, he became dissatisfied with the corrupt educational system. He opposed the authorities, thus revealing early his rebellious character, and was dismissed from school three times. The 1911 Revolution gave him many great expectations, but his excitement was short-lived because of the political confusion at the time. Disappointed and in low spirits, he was anxious to leave Sichuan for a much bigger world outside.

At the end of 1913 he left home and arrived in Japan via Korea early the following year. He was accepted by the First High School in Tokyo, where he studied in the preparatory class. In 1915, he enrolled in the Sixth High School in Okayama. Three years later, after graduation, he entered the Imperial University in Fukuoka,

Kiyushou and chose medicine, hoping that "It would be of practical use to China and her people." In Japan he felt the scourge of Japanese militarism. When the Japanese militarists dictated the "Twenty-one Demands" to China in 1915, he was filled with patriotic indignation. In "a fury that reached the skies," he left Japan and went back to Shanghai.

During his first four years of study in Japan, Guo Moruo read many well-known foreign literary works. In particular, the works of Tagore, Goethe, Heine and Whitman enriched his mind. His interest in Tagore, Goethe and the Dutch philosopher Spinoza accounted for his subjection to the influence of pantheism, and he once stated plainly that "pantheism is really atheism."* He "tended somewhat towards pantheism,"** because pantheistic thinking chimed in with his contempt for both authority and idols. It was also in accord with his advocacy of self-expression and individualism. Furthermore, the idea of "non-separation of object from self" as preached by pantheism gave free rein to the poet's powerful imagination through which he could transform things in the universe into poetic beings that served as animated objects of his emotional response. It is therefore understandable that Guo Moruo mistakenly believed that "pantheism suits best the poet's concept of the universe."***

The October Revolution and the May Fourth Movement profoundly inspired Guo Moruo and he was attracted by the different new trends of European thought then prevalent in Japan. He began his literary activities with great enthusiasm and entertained ideas, though rather hazy, of reforming society and vitalizing his people. Together with some of the patriotic Chinese students in Japan, he formed the Summer Society and was engaged in propaganda work against Japanese imperialism. In February and March 1919 he wrote the story "The Shepherd's Lament,"† in which he expressed

* Preface to the Chinese translation of Goethe's *The Sorrows of Young Werther*, *The Collected Works of Guo Moruo*, Vol. X, p. 178.

** *Ten Years of Creation*, *Ibid.*, Vol. VII, p. 58.

*** "Three Notes on Poetry," *Three Leaves*, *Ibid.*, Vol. X.

† Published in *New China*, Vol. I, No. 7, November 15, 1919. The date of publication has been wrongly given as 1918 in *Starry Skies* (Tai Dong Press, 1923) and in *The Collected Works of Guo Moruo*, Vol. V.

his patriotic thoughts. Before long, his poems began to appear in the supplement "Lantern on Learning" of *The New Daily of Current Affairs*, edited by Zong Baihua. His most productive period was the stretch from the second half of 1919 to the first half of 1920. *The Goddesses* published in 1921, not only established him as an outstanding poet, but also ushered in a new epoch in modern Chinese poetry.

In July 1921 Guo Moruo founded the Creation Society and played a leading role in its activities. He was back in China three times in 1921 and 1922. What he saw shattered his vision of the country, which he expected to have been transformed after the May Fourth Movement of 1919. Shattered, too, was his hope that a progressive society could be created through individual endeavours. Nature, which had given him many songs of praise, now became the haven for his melancholy feelings of loneliness. His state of mind is well reflected in some of the poems in *Starry Skies* (1923) which are depressed in tone in which the poet turns to nature for relief.

In 1923 Guo Moruo graduated from the Imperial University and returned to China. After establishing *Creation*, a quarterly, he founded the *Creation Weekly* and the *Creation Daily* with Yu Dafu and Cheng Fangwu. His works regularly appeared in these publications. This was the most productive period of the Creation Society in its early days, and Guo Moruo's political thinking went through fairly significant changes. The revolutionary zeal after the February 7th Movement of 1923 aroused him from grief and pain. True, as yet he had not been able to free himself completely from the influence of individualism; from time to time, he still felt that the power which came from self-awakening could remove the heavy burden of tradition and bring about the liberation of society. However, he also began to understand "the trammels of private ownership." He called for "an attack on the venomous dragon of capitalism,"* and pointed out that historical materialism was "the only solution to the existing problems." As he put it, "until the economic system has been reformed, whatever dream of reality,

* "The New Movement of Our Literature," *Creation Weekly*, No. 3, May 1923.

dignity of the self and gospel of love will remain only the morphine or coconut wine of the leisured class."* His ideas of course are not specific enough, but they nevertheless have their value as thoughts which emerge in the process of his poetic creation. In the poems written after *Starry Skies*, gone are the traces of the poet's expression of personal feelings through his descriptions of nature. Instead, the praise of workers and peasants, previously found in *The Goddesses*, is even more passionate. In one of the poems Guo Moruo declares that he is no longer infatuated with the "story face" of nature, marked by "its multifarious contradictions."** Rather, he will "tightly hold the hands extended by the labouring masses."*** The poems in *Vanguard* (1928) sharply reveal the change in the poet's themes.

In 1924 the *Creation*, a quarterly, and the *Creation Weekly* ceased publication. This was followed by the departure of the leading writers of the Creation Society, Yu Dafu and Cheng Fangwu. The activities of the Society thus came to an end. These setbacks together with personal financial problems put Guo Moruo in a state of depression, and he "did not know whether it was wise to go forward or not."† In April of the same year he went to Japan and began translating the Japanese Marxist economist Kawakame Hagima's book *Social Organization and Social Revolution*. In spite of its flaws, the book played a significant part in Guo Moruo's ideological development, for the task of translation gave him the opportunity to study Marxism more systematically. "The translation of the book," he admitted, "marked the turning point in my life. It woke me up from my drowsy state and pointed out the way when I was at the crossroads, not knowing where to go."†† Hitherto, he had been filled with hate for the capitalist society. Kawakame Hagima's book made him "understand the internal contradic-

* "My View on Tagore's Visit to China," *Ibid.*, No. 23. October 14, 1923. It is dated October 11 at the end of the essay. The date is wrongly given as October 11, 1922 in Vol. X, *The Collected Works of Guo Moruo*.

** "The Troubled Grapes," *Vanguard* (1928).

*** "Early Morning in Shanghai," *Ibid.*

† "Ten Years of Creation," *The Collected Works of Guo Moruo*, Vol. VII, pp. 165, 183.

†† "The Lone Swan—A Letter to Cheng Fangwu," *Ibid.*, Vol. X, p. 289.

tions of capitalism and the historical inevitability of its transformation."* He was now "deeply "convinced that society will definitely move towards communism. That is the natural route, as natural as the course followed by the rivers and streams flowing into the sea."** In the same year he visited Yixing for he wanted to study the battles previously fought by the warlords. The crimes of the war-mongers and the sufferings of the people deepened his understanding of the many class contradictions which made up the realities of life.

The May 30th Movements of 1925 brought in the high tide of revolution. Guo Moruo was actively involved in the current revolutionary activities; consequently, his world view and concepts of literature and art began to change drastically. He further criticized individualism. In the Preface to *Essays on Literature and Art*, written at the end of 1925, he stated: "Formerly, I respected individualism and worshipped freedom. For the past year or so, however, I have made some contact with those from the miserable, low social order. I realized that, against their will, the vast majority of people have lost their freedom. Now, small numbers of people want to preach individualism and freedom. They are really expecting too much." He also emphasized that "to practise individualism, there should be equal opportunity for everybody to practise individualism. To live in freedom, there should be equal opportunity for everybody to live in freedom." In the course of battle with the nationalist group, he published a series of essays including "A Pauper's Empty Talk," "Communism and Common Control" and "The Creation of a New Country" in the half-monthly *Flood*. These essays, with their strong revolutionary inclinations and distinct class viewpoints, forcefully struck back at the nationalists' distortions and vilifications of communism. He exposed their reactionary nature and pointed out that "when they urged people to build a wealthy and militarily strong country upon the old system, they were really trying to

* "Ten Years of Creation," *The Collected Works of Guo Moruo*, Vol. VII, pp. 165, 183.

** From his unpublished letter to He Gonggan written in 1924. The passage is quoted in "A Leap into the Kingdom of Freedom," written in 1926. *The Collected Works of Guo Moruo*, Vol. X, p. 434.

maintain the prosperity of the minority privileged class." He advocated "pursuing the course of proletarian revolution" and "building a new country which adopts the system of public ownership in order to bring about the material and spiritual liberation of the people."* The impact of the May 30th Incident of 1925 on him was such that he also wrote the historical play *Nie Ying*. The play, which faithfully reflects the anti-imperialist mood of the people at the time, amply shows the poet's strong sense of political responsibility.

In March 1926 Guo Moruo went to Guangzhou to take up the appointment as Dean of the Faculty of Arts at Guangdong University. Before he left Shanghai, he wrote "The Awakening of Writers and Artists," "Revolution and Literature" and other essays. His views on literature and art had developed further. In these essays he criticized the aimlessness of literature and its non-utilitarian tendency. His positive theory was built on class viewpoints, which guided his analysis of the relation between literature and revolution as he considered its social function. In "Revolution and Literature," for example, he was "in sympathy with the proletarian socialist literature of realism" and made concrete suggestions about the contents of revolutionary literature. He also pointed out in "The Awakening of the Writers and Artists" that "the literature we need is that which speaks for the fourth class. This literature follows realism and it has a socialist content." These two essays may contain simplistic and sweeping statements, thus still showing the unavoidable flaws found in the early theories of revolutionary literature. However, they do indicate the progress made by the petty-bourgeois writers who had been awakened by the Great Revolution of 1927.

At the start of the Northern Expedition in July 1926, in answer to the call of war duty, Guo Moruo served first as the chief secretary of the Political Department of the Northern Expedition Revolutionary Army, then as deputy director and finally acting director of the Department. When Chiang Kai-shek betrayed the revolution and began the massacre of the revolutionary masses, he

---

* "Too Lazy to Read, Too Inquisitive to Find Out," *Appendix*, *The Collected Works of Guo Moruo*, Vol. X, pp. 427, 425.

published "Let Us Look at Chiang Kai-shek Now" in the *Central Daily*. In the article he exposed the crimes of Chiang Kai-shek, pointing out that "he is an even more brutal, vicious and cunning executioner than Wu Peifu, Sun Chuanfang, Zhang Zuolin and Zhang Zongchang." In the same year, he took part in the Nanchang Uprising of August 1.* Then he moved with the revolutionary army to the south and en route joined the Communist Party. After the failure of the army's military campaigns in Guangdong, he went back to Shanghai via Hong Kong. The poems of this period, collected in *Restoration* (1928), responded to Chiang Kai-shek's massacre with "tempestuous music" of battle and the "vigorous beats of war drums." When the proletarian revolutionary literature movement began in Shanghai, he was one of its active supporters.

After 1928, Guo Moruo spent ten years in exile in Japan, where he studied Chinese palaeography and ancient social history. From the standpoint of historical materialism he proved that a slave society existed in ancient China. Forcefully, too, he refuted the absurd argument that "historical materialism is not a suitable approach to Chinese affairs." These were his outstanding achievements in scholarship and research while he was strongly supporting the activities of the Tokyo branch of the League of Left-Wing Writers. His literary works of this period included the autobiography "My Childhood," "Before and After the Rectification," "Ten Years of Creation"—its sequel was written in 1946—and "The Northern Expedition." Of Guo Moruo's ten years abroad, Zhou Enlai once said that during this period, when the tide of revolution was on the ebb, he "conserved his energies, devoted himself to studies for the sake of self-enrichment so that he could make new contribution to the revolution with new strength."**

When the anti-Japanese war broke out, Guo Moruo returned to China, leaving wife and children behind.*** Under the direct

---

* On August 1, 1927, over thirty thousand men of the Northern Expeditionary Army staged an armed uprising in Nanchang, Jiangxi Province. The Nanchang Uprising marked the beginning of armed struggle led independently by the Chinese Communist Party, and the day of August 1, from then on, has been known as China's Army Day.

** "What I Want to Say," *Xihua Daily*, Chongqing, November 16, 1941.

*** "Mingled Songs of Homecoming," *War Cry*.

leadership of Zhou Enlai, he took part in the national salvation movement. He was one of the main leaders of the National Federation of Anti-Japanese Writers and Artists, serving at the same time in the anti-Japanese united front as director of the Third Office of the Military Council's Political Department responsible for wartime cultural propaganda work. His poems of this period were collected in *War Cry* and *Cicada*. He also wrote historical plays, among them *Qu Yuan* and *The Tiger Tally*. After the capitulation of the Japanese, he staunchly supported the anti-civil war democratic struggle. Once again he was in the forefront of action. In literary creation, he produced many works of distinction.

After the founding of New China, Guo Moruo continued his literary activities. At the same time, he bore a heavy load in his service to the country and the people, providing leadership in the fields of science, culture and education. He made new contributions to socialism in the interests of China and her people. On June 12, 1978, he passed away.

Guo Moruo was not only an outstanding poet, writer and playwright, but also a Marxist historican and scholar of paleography. He is another bulwark, next to Lu Xun, on the Chinese cultural front.

II. *The Goddesses*

The Goddesses was published in August 1921 as one of the items in the Creation Society Series. The first collection of Guo Moruo's poems, it is also a distinguished and highly influential collection of new poetry in modern Chinese literature. Apart from the prefatory poem, it contains fifty-six poems. The earliest poem was written about 1916; most of the others were written in 1919-20, and a small number in 1921.

The October Revolution shook China, and as the May Fourth Movement gathered momentum, people began to see rays of hope in the long night. The old moral code, the autocratic political system and feudal idols were all under severe attack. Science, democracy, socialism and everything new were enthusiastically pursued. Vitality filled the air. It was an epoch marked by the spirit of rebellion, reform and creation. In expressing the desire to break out of the confines of feudalism, in voicing strong demands for social reform and in emitting boundless enthusiasm for the commendation and pursuit of high ideals, *The Goddesses* distinctly reflects the characteristics of the May Fourth Movement. Indeed, in poetic terms it is the strongest voice of this period.

The most representative poems in the collection are "The Nirvana of the Feng and Huang" and "Rebirth of the Goddesses." In the former, which draws on the legend of the phoenix, the male Feng and the female Huang gather fragrant wood, commit themselves to the flames and rise from the ashes young again. The process symbolizes the death of old China as well the poet's old self to be followed by the birth of a new China and the poet's new self. On the eve of the new year, above the Danxue Mountain the plane trees are withered and the spring is parched. "The frozen sky" is "traversed by icy winds."* A pair of phoenixes are flying to and from making arrangements for their cremation. They dance high and low, the male Feng crying "jig-jig" and the female Huang "jug-jug," answering each other's call. They curse the cruel realities; they curse the dark and rank old universe, comparing it to "a slaughter-house," "a prison," "a grave" and "a hell." They express their doubts and ask, "Universe, O universe!/Why do you exist?" Tortured by grief, they prefer to die and begin gathering fragrant wood. In their condemnation of the realities can be seen the poet's pent-up grief and indignation as he reflects on the state of the country and the sufferings of the people. The process of self-sacrifice and rebirth of the phoenixes creates a solemn and stirring atmosphere. Together they sing, "My time has now come,/ my hour of death has come." Then the conflagration reaches the skies and burns up the old self and the old world, with all its corruption and injustice. Reborn in the flames are not only phoenixes but also the poet himself.

Two days before he wrote the poem, Guo Moruo had already

* Quotations from the poem are taken from "The Nirvana of the Feng and Huang," *Selected Poems from "The Goddesses,"* translated by John Lester and A.C. Barnes, Foreign Languages Press, Beijing, 1958.

expressed his wish to be like the phoenix. He wanted to make a pyre of fragrant wood and "burn up the present human body ... so as to give birth to a new self."* To throw everything into the flames, to make a clean break with the old world, to destroy the old self completely, and to experience pain and then joy in the process of creating a new self—all these well portray the people's spirit of anti-imperialism and anti-feudalism during the May Fourth Movement. The shallowness and the vulgarity of the ordinary birds in the poem, while meant to show up the repulsiveness and baseness of reality, set off the deep pain and the magnificent beauty of the phoenixes' self-burning. Their rebirth is sung by the poet in lines which flow freely and naturally. The use of repetition adds to the poetic effect as he glorifies the scene of grand harmony and joy, giving free rein to the passionate yearning for light and the pursuit of ideals. This is indeed creation and new birth after the trying process of struggle. Through poetry, the poet expresses his hope in the future that is to be shaped by the May Fourth Movement, and the poem is a symbol of the awakening of China and that of the poet himself. According to Guo Moruo, the poem was written in one day, at two sittings. In the poem the outpourings of the heart and the rapid tempo of poetic melody fully demonstrate the poet's hurricane-like creative power at work.

In "Rebirth of the Goddesses," as in "The Nirvana of the Feng and Huang," Guo Moruo uses myths to portray the theme of rebellion, destruction and creation. Here, it is the legend of Nü Wa melting coloured stones to mend heaven. As presented at the beginning of the dramatic sketch, the universe is in darkness, filled with gloom. The "harsh clamour from the waves in the sea, from wind in space" is "the counterpoint of evil cries." Listening to the "wafted life-music," the goddesses have a premonition of impending catastrophe yet again. They all step down from their niches and sing in unison:

We will create a new sun,
No longer will we remain mere statues in niches.

In the scene of battle between Zhuan Xu and Gong Gong, the poet,

* Letter to Zong Baihua, January 18, 1920, *Three Leaves.*

through his poetic language, hints at the sufferings of the people brought on by fighting among the warlords. After the pillar of heaven cracks, Zhuan Xu and Gong Gong fall dead—both events indicate the poet's intense hate for the reactionary rulers in history. Eventually, in the darkness come voices uttering the will of the people. The goddesses do not think it is worth picking up the pieces. Instead, they will create a new sun, prophesying that it will "shine through all the inner world and the outer."

In many other poems in *The Goddesses*, Guo Moruo writes enthusiastically about warmth, light and the sun, all of which symbolize the needs of the times as well as the objects of his own pursuit. These poems vividly mirror the grand awakening of an old nation as the May Fourth Movement reached its peak. The spirit of the times blessed the poet with powerful emotions, which in turn found an appropriate outlet in his poetry.

Quite a number of poems in *The Goddesses* are imbued with the poet's thoughts of China and his eulogy of the newborn. These poems are also tributes to the May Fourth Movement, which had aroused his deep patriotic feelings when he was living in a foreign land. In these poems of intense emotion, one can see the shadows of the reborn goddesses and the phoenixes in the flames. "The Good Morning" and "Ode to Bandits," for example, have much in common. The tone in both poems is majestic and the style, vigorous. In the former, the setting is "a golden morning." In one breath the poet says "Good morning" altogether twenty-seven times: to "Young China," "the newborn fellow-countrymen," the pioneer of the revolution, the art masters, the magnificent mountains and rivers and all the good things in the world. "Ode to Bandits" was written in protest as an answer to the Japanese journalists who used the smear-label "scholar-bandits" to vilify the Chinese students after the May Fourth Movement. The poet's anger permeates this well-known poem, in which he warmly praises "the true bandits, ancient and modern, native and foreign," who have made their respective contribution to the initiation of reform.

"Coal in the Grate" best conveys Guo Moruo's deep thoughts of China when he was living abroad. In "Ten years of Creation" he wrote: "To me, China after May Fourth is like a young and beautiful girl who is full of initiative, hoping to do better all the time. She is just like my lover.... The poem 'Coal in the Grate' with its 'nostalgic feelings for one's homeland' is my love song for her. I sing her praises in both 'Good Morning' and 'Ode to Bandits.' " Compared with these two songs of praise, his love song "Coal in the Grate" is not as bold or free. But it has its own subtle beauty. The poet compares himself to the burning coal, and his country to "a fair young maiden."

Ah, my fair young maiden,
I shall not betray your care,
Let you not disappoint my hopes.
For her my heart's delight
*I burn to such a heat.**

In a similar vein, some of the poems in *The Goddesses* express the poet's faith in the future of China and her people, a faith which is inseparable from his determination to dedicate himself totally to China's development. However, as China entered a new revolutionary period after May Fourth, the dark forces refused to be overcome easily. Guo Moruo, back in China, was greeted with sorrowful and desolate scenes—"Human skulls meet the eye, coffins fill the streets." At last, he felt that this maiden had shattered his hopes. He wrote: "I have woken up from my dream! Oh, the sadness of disillusion!"**

Another significant theme treated in the collection is the celebration of the self which is full of the spirit of rebellion, demonstrating the strength which comes from its union with all things in the universe. Whether in dealing with rebellion, destruction or creation, the poet writes about the distinctive characteristics of the self in a lyrical vein. Some of the poems even sing of the rebel's self in a passionate tone. This self can subdue the sun and the moon and it can move the whole world. It is "the sum total of the energy of the universe." It "burns like raging flames," "roars like

* *Selected Poems from the Goddesses*, translated by John Lester and A.C. Barnes, Foreign Languages Press, Beijing, 1958, p. 17.

** "Impressions of Shanghai," *The Goddesses* (1921).

the waves of the sea" and "races like electricity."* It defies all idols and feudal authorities openly declaring, "I am also an iconoclast!"** It possesses creative power:

> *The creative forces of man can rival those of the gods.*
> *If you will not believe, look upon us, we grandiose structures!*
> *Even the sun in the sky must bow his head to us!****

This self also fuses with the whole universe, inspiring the poet to "sing the praises of the self-expressive universe."† As presented in Guo Moruo's poems, this is not the self which is imprisoned in a small personal world, not the self which is marked by loneliness, arrogance, sorrow and decadence. It is the self which embodies the spirit of the times and which demands national liberation. In the midst of the poet's admiration and worship of this self, sometimes he also expresses his thoughts on how it can be reformed.

Many poems in *The Goddesses* convey the poet's affection for labour and the labouring masses. In "Three Pantheists," he praises the three pantheists as people who earn their living by manual labour. In "O Earth, My Mother," he believes that the peasants in the fields are the nurses of mankind and that the workers in coal-pits are the Prometheus of mankind. In "A Visit to the West Lake" he even wants to kneel before the old man who is hoeing the fields under the Leifeng Pagoda and lick the brown earth on his feet.

There are also poems in the collection which sing of nature, such as "Sea of Light" and "Drunken Song Under a Flowering Plum Tree." The poet, influenced by pantheism, believes that "the being of the whole universe" is only "the self-expression" of all things therein and that man is a part of the natural world. He loves nature, melting himself into it so as to achieve the state of "non-separation of object from self." These poems are songs of celebration: "Sunrise," "Stirrings of Spring," "Hymn to the Sun" and "Morning Snow."

---

* "The Hound of Heaven," *The Goddesses* (1921).

** Quotations from "I Am an Idolater," "Pyramids" and "Drunken Song Under a Flowering Plum Tree" respectively. See *Selected Poems from "The Goddesses,"* Foreign Languages Press, Beijing, 1958, pp. 36, 40, 34.

*** *Ibid.*

† *Ibid.*

In "unbounded nature" he senses that

> *Everywhere is life in pulsing light-waves,*
> *Everywhere a new spirit in the air.*[*]

The "majestic eagle" flying above his head makes him think of "the phoenix soaring in his heart."[**] Some of the poems are written in a magnificent and unrestrained style; others are marked by their delicacy and grace. He may be lauding the "glaucous ocean, clamorous breakers," "the newborn sun" and the "cloud-islands in the sea of the sky."[***] He may be captivated by the natural scene:

> *Over the pool are young willows,*
> *Under the willows a long shelter.*†

He may be writing about the "drunken-red new leaves," "the tender grass" and "the tall trees" which are "soaked in the soft music of dreams."†† Whatever theme pursued, the poems have a freshness about them, carrying as they do a joyful, optimistic and invigorating tone. These poems are full of the daring May Fourth spirit and the vitality of the poet.

The Goddesses is steeped in revolutionary romanticism. Throughout the collection, the poet expresses his commitment to total rebellion against the dark realities and the decaying corrupt tradition, his yearning for freedom and liberation, his earnest hope in the search for light and a new life, his firm belief in the future of the revolution and his optimistic views on the creation of ideals. All these strongly reflect the revolutionary hopes, demands and ideals of the Chinese people, especially the young intellectuals. These revolutionary aspirations provide the base for their revolutionary romanticism. The poems, artistically characterized by their strong colours, passionate tone and quick tempo, amply reveal the poet's galloping imagination, boldness of expression and great powers of conception. He uses Chinese myths and legends ingen-

* "Sea of Light," *Selected Poems from "The Goddesses,"* Foreign Languages Press, Beijing, 1958, p.31.

** "Light in My Heart," *The Goddesses* (1921).

*** "Hymn to the Sun," *Selected Poems from "The Goddesses,"* Foreign Languages Press, Beijing, 1958, p. 37.

† "Bright Morning," *Ibid.*, p. 54.

†† "A Visit to the West Lake," *The Goddesses* (1921).

iously to suit his poetic purposes; indeed, whatever he does serves extremely well his "emotional outbursts, which are like volcanic eruptions."* His techniques are distinctly those of romanticism. He once remarked that "poetry is 'written' not 'made,' "** and in most of the poems in *The Goddesses* his feelings flow spontaneously. Poems such as "The Nirvana of the Feng and Huang" and "O Earth, My Mother!" were written when he was seized by a poetic mood. The lines run freely in the poet's creative process, and he did not stop to attend meticulously to the polishing of his art. However, the overflow of feelings and his poetic craft together create the impression that the lines are written with ease whether they are marked by ruggedness or gracefulness of tone and style. This artistic harmony of matter and manner, for example, is noticeable in the poem "The Burden of Xiang," in which the smooth flow of verse matches the natural flow of the poet's feelings:

> *Above the Jiuyi Mountains the white clouds come together and part;*
> *The waters of the Dongting Lake ebb and flow.*
> *O the clouds of sorrow in our hearts!*
> *O the floods of tears in our eyes!*
> *Never will they depart!*
> *Never will they ebb away!*

Guo Moruo's extensive reading ranges from classical Chinese poetry to the works of well-known foreign poets. In different ways and degrees, he was influenced by these works. He once said, "The poetic drive behind Whitman's effort to free himself from all old restraints is in accord with the vigorous spirit of the May Fourth Movement. I am completely overwhelmed by his majestic and unrestrained tone."*** He had a special liking for Qu Yuan, whose character is accurately portrayed in the dramatic sketch "The Burden of Xiang." In presenting the ancient poet's indomitable spirit of rebellion against the dark realities and his desire to pursue high ideals, Guo Moruo also found full expression for his own

* "Preface to My Poetry," *Boiling Soup*.
** Letter to Zong Baihua, January 18, 1920, *Three Leaves*.
*** "My Poetical Career," *The Collected Works of Guo Moruo*, Vol. XI, p. 143.

conditions and feelings during the May Fourth Movement period. The same spirit and desire pervade many of the poems in *The Goddesses.* Li Bai was of course one of his favourite poets. He rewrote the Tang poet's "Sunrise" in the form of free verse, sharing in the grand spirit and tone of the original poem.

In style, the most distinctive characteristic of *The Goddesses* is the poet's bold and forceful free verse, and the poems which stir the readers' hearts most are those written in that poetic form. By freeing himself from the fetters of the old poetry, Guo Moruo has created a new world for the post-May Fourth free verse. He does not follow any fixed poetic form with its strict tonal patterns; neither does he use rhyme. The melody is in harmony with the rhythm of his feelings, which are often expressed through the repetition of words or lines. These poems, the products of the poet's powerful imagination, found strong echoes in the hearts of the readers. Just as he anticipated in the prefatory poem to the collection, *The Goddesses* made a great impact on the young people at the time, "touching the chords in their hearts, lighting the lamps in their hearts."

Some of the poems in *The Goddesses* are not written in free verse; instead they follow fairly strict rules of poetic form and prosody. The songs in the dramatic sketch "The Twin Flowers." for instance, are written in the traditional five-character form. "Bright Morning" and "Estuary of the Whampoa" have a regular line pattern and rhyme scheme. Parts of the poem "A Visit to the West Lake" are written in the manner of the old poetry *ci*, which can also be sung. Guo Moruo is adept at using different poetic forms to convey his different moods and feelings.

The Goddesses is the poetic expression of the spirit of the times. Its artistic magnificence and unique style have both enriched Chinese poetry. Its influence too, cannot be overstated, in paving the way for poets of the new poetry. Shortly after the publication of the collection, Wen Yiduo wrote in his essay "The Spirit of the Age in *The Goddesses*": "As to the new poetry, the works of Guo Moruo truly deserve to be called new. Artistically, they are the furthest removed from the old poetry. More important, his spirit is the spirit of the times, the spirit of the twentieth century. People say that literary works are the products of the age. True enough, *The Goddesses* is a worthy product of its age." Wen Yiduo believed that *The Goddesses* "voices not only the fervent but also the noblest feelings which are lying deep in everybody's heart."* In his essay "Guo Moruo and *The Goddesses*" written in celebration of the poet's fiftieth birthday, Zhou Yang noted that Guo Moruo was "the representative poet of the great May Fourth period of enlightenment, the prophet-poet of new China." He hailed *The Goddesses* as "the bugle, the war-drums, which woke us up, gave us courage and led us in our struggle."** The poetry of Guo Moruo with its overflowing revolutionary romanticism has indeed opened a new chapter in the history of modern Chinese poetry.

III. *Vanguard, Restoration* and Other Collections

After *The Goddesses,* Guo Moruo published *Starry Skies* in 1923, a collection of poetry and prose written in Japan and Shanghai between 1921 and 1922. The May Fourth Movement was then on the ebb, the political situation was confusing and the new revolutionary movement was still in its early stage of development. Guo Moruo returned to China several times and saw a disaster-ridden country. His "cup of bitterness" was full as he found himself in sharp internal conflict. On the one hand, he now hated all the more the realities of the times and, nourishing strong patriotic thoughts and rebellious feelings, demanded fundamental social reform. On the other, under the influence of individualism and pantheism, he was looking for temporary escape in nature or in a surrealist world of fantasy. The poems in *Starry Skies* reflect clearly the state of his mind, plagued by contradictions. Lacking in these poems is the spontaneous overflow of revolutionary romanticism which characterizes *The Goddesses.*

However, the two collections *The Goddesses* and *Starry Skies* do share common themes. In both the poet expresses his wrath as he surveys the "sea of blood," that is the old world. He praises the

* *The Works of Wen Yiduo,* Vol. III, No. IV, pp. 185, 194.

** *Liberation Daily,* Yan'an, November 16, 1941.

ancient heroes who made self-sacrifices in serving the masses and he places hope in the modern labourers, whom he hails as the pioneers of the future in his poem "The Times of the Deluge." *Starry Skies* also contains poems which are fresh in tone, smooth in rhythm and rich in connotation. In "The Streets in Heaven," for instance, the poet observes:

The street lights in the distance are shining,
Like numerous stars twinkling.
The bright stars have appeared in the sky,
Like the numerous shining street lights.

I think in the vault of heaven,
Surely, there are some beautiful streets and markets.
There will be merchandise put on display.
Surely, they are rarities not to be found in the world.

See the narrow Milk Way,
Surely, it cannot be that wide.
I think the girl tending the herd on the other side
Can cross over easily on a cow's back.

I think at this very moment
They are loitering in the streets of heaven.
No? Look at that shooting star,
It is their lantern shining on their way.

Published in 1928, *Vanguard* contains twenty-three poems, most of which were written in 1923, when the revolutionary mass movement was gaining momentum under the leadership of the Communist Party. As the influence of Marxism was growing, Guo Moruo underwent marked changes in his thoughts and feelings. He lifted himself out of the deep depression and the slow, fluctuating sentiments as described in *Starry Skies*. Once again, he confronted the harsh realities and wrote about revolution. He realized that unless it followed "the Russian style of proletarian dictatorship/ Destroying completely the old roots and branches/ Emitting new light in the history of mankind," China "can never hope to rise again."* He prophesied that "In the middle of Jing'an Boulevard/ Eventually will be violent volcanic eruptions."** He wanted to join "the workers and peasants of the world," "liberate people from their sufferings" and "bring about the birth of a new world."***

"We'll Meet in Red Light" conveys profound thoughts through its echoing melody. The poet predicts final victory of the revolution: it is as inevitable as the retreat of night and the coming of dawn. He writes:

In the midst of this lacquer-like darkness
The sun is still moving.
He is sharpening his golden arrows,
Intending to shoot all the demons.

The image of a brave revolutionary fighter is thus presented and the poet's optimism inspires the readers with hope.

Another significant poem in *Vanguard* is "The Sun Has Gone," written in memory of Lenin's death. In the poem he first describes the deep grief of the people of the world at the loss of the great revolutionary leader. Then in a vigorous vein, he extols the grand achievements of Lenin:

His scorching rays have parched the demons in heaven,
His burning currents have melted the iceberg.
The poverty-stricken people, without clothes, without work,
Have been blessed with the holy fire he has stolen from the gods.

Guo Moruo fully understood the irreparable loss of Lenin and its effect on world revolution. That was why he wanted to join the labouring masses of the world, continue the work of "driving away darkness and annihilating the demons." The poem gave the contemporary readers hope in the revolution "when the waves of the four seas are sending out sounds of grief."

---

* Quotations are respectively from the poems "Dialogue Between the Yellow River and the Yangtse River," "Morning in Shanghai" and "The March Song" in *Vanguard* (1928).

** *Ibid.*

*** *Ibid.*

Vase is a collection of love poems written in the early spring of 1925. In addition to the dedicatory poem, it has forty-two short poems which convey the romantic yearnings of the poet. The lines are heavily charged with emotion, "the volcanic eruptions in the heart," and they reflect another aspect of the May Fourth spirit. Some of the poems, however, are sentimental in tone, conveying the melancholy feeling that life is but a dreamy existence.

The collection *Restoration*, published in 1928, contains twenty-four poems, which were written when the reign of white terror had reached its peak after the failure of the Great Revolution. During this period, Guo Moruo had taken seriously ill. But neither the bloody massacres by the reactionary rulers nor his ill health could dampen his revolutionary spirit. On the contrary, in a stronger and more determined voice, he gave a sonorous reply to the oppressive forces. These poems too, are richer in content.

In "I Think of Chen Sheng and Wu Guang," for example, his mind goes back to the first peasant uprising in Chinese history. He thinks of what Chen Sheng and Wu Guang did: "chopping wood for weapons, holding up poles for banners." He reflects on the miserable state of the peasants of his day and on the inevitability of their rebellion. In the poem, Guo Moruo makes strong accusations on behalf of the suffering peasants. He also writes that the root cause of their pathetic existence is the presence of "numerous tyrants like Emperor Qin"; that is, the "foreign imperialists" and the "running dogs they keep, warlords, the comprador class, the landlords and bureaucrats." At the end of the poem, he lauds, "the peasant rebellion led by the workers" as "our salvation, the force that will change the whole world." In another poem, "Dialogue Between the Yellow River and the Yangtse River (II)," he also extols the real strength of the Chinese revolution, predicting that "over 320 million poor peasants" and "five million rising industrial workers" can transform themselves into "the largest, the most powerful, and the most dangerous bomb," a bomb which can "break up the whole world."

Most of the poems in the collection express revolutionary thoughts and feelings, accompanied by what the poet calls the "tempestuous music" of battle and the "vigorous beats of war-drums." He notes that "half of our huge blood-stained banner has turned white." Countless revolutionaries are being slaughtered by the enemy and Guo Moruo can no longer control his grief or suppress his rage. However, he is never pessimistic; neither does he lose courage. "Before my eyes, everything is white," but he firmly believes the sparks of revolutionary fire can never be smothered. He writes:

Go for the kill, if that is your will!
You kill one, then you have to kill a hundred:
On our bodies are the fine hairs of the Monkey King;
Give each hair a puff, and we shall have many new selves.

He also understands clearly that victory of the revolution is not a gift from heaven or from anyone. It can be achieved only through struggle:

I have already prepared a glass of red, birthday wine.
My friends, this wine is from my blood-filled heart.
Let it brew this night: bloody rain, murderous wind!
We will win the new sun and the new universe!

Restoration is solid evidence of poetic achievement in the early period of proletarian revolutionary literature. It is also Guo Moruo's further contribution to China's new poetry after *The Goddesses*. After the outbreak of the War of Resistance Against Japan, he continued to write poems, which were later collected in *War Cry* and *Cicada*. His style in these two collections may not be as vigorous as that in *The Goddesses*. But the overflow of warm feelings once again reveals the poet's revolutionary romanticism. "Salvoes of national Revival," "Ode to War of Resistance" and "War Cry," for instance, sing of the just cause of the war against the Japanese aggression. Other poems such as "Sins of the Pyramids," "In Praise of Progress" and "Crying for the Suffering People" express the poet's hatred of darkness, his yearning for light and his high regard for revolution.

IV. *Qu Yuan* and Other Works

An outstanding poet, Guo Moruo is also a versatile writer of stories, plays and essays. Particularly significant is his achievement in historical drama, in which he "uses the past to explain the present."

In November 1919, he published the story "The Shepherd's Lament," in which he expressed his own patriotic feelings through the narration of the tragic lot of a Korean woman. The stories written after this were collected respectively in *Pagoda*, *Below the Horizon*, *Olives* and *Fallen Leaves*. Most of them contain elements of autobiography of his youth, portraying and analysing his life and thought in the early days. These works also fully reflect the mood of the period, even though in literary achievement and influence they cannot be compared with his poetry.

Guo Moruo began writing historical plays after the May Fourth Movement. In the ideological liberation movement of the time, the trend of anti-feudal culture had already been firmly set. He wanted to use drama, a newly-developed literary form, to give new interpretations of history "in the spirit of the May Fourth Movement." As he saw it, this would be his contribution to practical struggle. Accordingly, he wrote *Zhuo Wenjun*, *Wang Zhaojun* and *Nie Ying*.

Zhuo Wenjun was written in February 1923. As recorded in history, Zhuo Wenjun was a widow who defied the authority of her father and eloped with Sima Xiangru. That was rebellion against the feudal ethic whereby a woman must remain with one man her whole life and never remarry even if her husband dies. However, for generations the feudal moralists condemned it as "an elopement of lust." The hack writers and scholars too, treated it as a scandalous romantic escapade. In the play, Guo Moruo gives a new interpretation of Zhuo Wenjun's character from the standpoint of a defender of freedom and justice. She defies her father's wishes and openly joins Sima Xiangru. Guo Moruo's treatment of plot is such that her rebellion against "paternal authority" in matrimonial matters is presented in the most favourable light. Upon publication, *Zhuo Wenjun* was instantly popular with young people and, consequently, its performance was banned by the feudal-minded rulers at the time. The play with its strong emphasis on rebellion and taking fate into one's own hands thoroughly expresses the young people's demand of liberation during the May Fourth period.

Wang Zhaojun, written in July 1923, shows that the playwright has made even greater use of his imagination and creative talent. There are more characters, and in rejecting the traditional explanation of Wang Zhaojun's sufferings Guo Moruo has created not "a tragedy of fate" but "a tragedy of character." He underplays the feeling of helplessness, which is intensified by the appearance of Wang Zhaojun holding a *pipa*, a Chinese musical instrument, on her way to the distant land of despair, set against the background of graveyards visible in a sombre evening. Highlighted instead is her uncompromising, rebellious character. Coming from a poverty-stricken family, Wang Zhaojun has an even greater share of suffering than Zhuo Wenjun. In the play, she is not intimidated by the authority of the emperor; neither is she tempted by the promise of wealth. She defies Emperor Yuan of the Han Dynasty and chooses to go to "the desolate northern lands" of the Huns, where she will be married off. Both in theme and in central thought, the play is different from *Zhuo Wenjun*. It defends human dignity and integrity, well illustrating the truth of the saying "It is better to be piece of shattered jade than to be an undamaged tile."

Nie Ying was written after the May 30th Movement of 1925. The play is set in the period of the Warring States (475-221 B.C.) and it dramatizes the part played by Nie Zheng in Yan Sui's assassination of Xia Lei, the prime minister of the State of Han. In the play Nie Zheng and his sister Nie Ying sacrifice their lives in the interests of the people. They are thus different from the chivalrous characters that historical records have made them out to be, who performed acts of heroism in the spirit of individualism. Pervading the play are the ideas of equal distribution of wealth, elimination of tyrannical powers and brotherhood among people who have come from different states. The message of rebellion in the play is clear: "We should all take up our swords and spears, go and kill our emperors and prime ministers." Guo Moruo's ideas greatly enlightened the Chinese people before and after the May

30th Incident of 1925 as they opposed the rule of the warlords and struggled against imperialism. The three plays *Zhuo Wenjun*, *Wang Zhaojun* and *Nie Ying* were collected in one edition, published in 1926 under the title *Three Rebellious Women*.

During the period of war against the Japanese aggression, the policy of the Kuomintang was to offer passive resistance to the enemy but conduct active campaigns against the Communists. After the shocking Southern Anhui Incident of 1941, the Kuomintang intensified its fascist rule, further suppressing freedom of expression and the progressive forces. Consequently, writers had to resort to subtle and even obscure ways in their attempts to expose the perversion of the reactionaries. In the circumstances, the writing of historical plays became the trend and Guo Moruo's achievement is outstanding. Through his involvement in practical struggle during wartime, he deeply understood the outcries of the people and the mission set for the period. His reflections on history gave him strength and sustained his fighting spirit. From December 1941 to April 1943, he wrote six plays: *The Twin Flowers*, *Qu Yuan*, *The Tiger Tally* and *Gao Jianli* (all in five acts), *The Gall Bladder of the Peacock* (in four acts) and *The Grass of Nan Guan* (in five acts). These plays were performed in Chongqing, Guilin and other cities with remarkable political and artistic results. Most effectively, the performances accelerated the development of progressive drama. In the plays, through different historical figures and intricate plots Guo Moruo presents the themes of anti-aggression, anti-capitulation, anti-autocratic tyranny, anti-submission and anti-political recantation. He advocates love of China and her people, national solidarity against foreign invasion and firm upholding of principles. He fiercely attacks the people who embody greed, deceit, imperiousness, cruelty, meanness and selfishness. Heartily, he extols those who take up a noble cause with great courage and people who show the virtues of loyalty and uprightness, thereby educating and inspiring others by setting personal examples. Against the tide of anti-communism at the time, Guo Moruo moved to the forefront of the counter forces. His contribution led to the breakthrough in progressive drama.

Compared with his early works, these historical plays are

marked by a greater degree of realism while they still amply show the characteristics of revolutionary romanticism. As much as he could, Guo Moruo collected all the historical materials related to each play. Meticulously, he studied these historical figures, their psychology and personality, along with the customs, the social and political system and the prevailing ideology of their day. The deep understanding he gained in his research gave him the freedom of using facts in his own way in the process of artistic creation. He grasped the essence of history and, in accordance with the laws of art and the development of plot, incorporated his own hopes and ideals in what he wrote. Boldly he experimented, aiming to achieve "resemblance through omission of certain facts."* In each of these plays, the delineation of character, the development of plot and the ingenious use of language together create an artistic masterpiece, producing remarkable dramatic effects. Inserted in the plays are lyrical poems and songs which add to the atmosphere as required by the plot, thus heightening the feelings expressed and enriching the poetic colour of the scenes.

Of all his historical plays of this period, the best as well as the most influential is *Qu Yuan*, a dramatization of the life of the ancient poet of the State of Chu in the period of the Warring States. The play highlights the clash between Qu Yuan, who represents the patriotic front, and Queen Zheng Xiu and others who are willing to sell the country. In the portrayal of Qu Yuan's character, Guo Moruo presented the theme of undaunted courage in the hero's struggle against oppression while serving the country and the people.

Qu Yuan appears in the play as a great statesman and poet. In "an age of war and confusion," he has never stopped thinking of the future of his country and the destiny of his people. He sees through the political game played by the State of Qin, which is bent on swallowing up the other six states. That is why he strongly advocates the formation of a united front with the State of Qi against the State of Qin. Forthright and full of integrity, Qu Yuan can never imagine that people like Queen Zheng Xiu will ever

* Guo Moruo, "History, Plays and Facts," *Boiling Soup*.

demean themselves to do him any harm. Even when he is wrongfully accused of having "behaved disgracefully at court," he still cannot tear himself away from the thoughts of his country and his people. With deep pain in his heart, he tries to persuade King Huai of Chu not to spurn the proposal of alliance with the State of Qi against Qin. He pleads: "You should think more of our people, more of the people of China." He reprimands the Queen: "You have plotted not against me, but against our entire kingdom! I have done nothing to be ashamed of! I can look on death without flinching! Which of us is right and which wrong, which loyal and which treacherous, future generations will decide. What you have plotted against is not me but yourself, our king, our country and all China!" The fatuous King Huai of Chu, however, turns a deaf ear to Qu Yuan's sincere words. He tears up the alliance treaty signed between the States of Chu and Qi, as he turns to Qin treading the path of compromise and surrender. Qu Yuan is accordingly put in gaol. As he sees his own country being swallowed up by darkness, the poet, who has now lost his freedom, is filled with grief and indignation. He lets out his violent emotions, appealing to the might of the elements. In his "Ode to Thunder and Lightning" he calls on the roaring wind to "blow away the darkness which weighs heavier than iron upon our eyes"; he calls on the rumbling thunder to carry him to a place "where there is no intrigue, no filth, no selfishness"; he calls on lightning, wishing that it would be the invisible sword of his heart which he could use to "pierce, pierce, pierce through the darkness which is heavier than iron." He calls on everything which is roaring, or sparkling in the darkness: "Vent your boundless wrath and smash to atoms this dark universe, this gloomy universe!"

In the play Guo Moruo has created two contrasting female characters: Chan Juan and Queen Zheng Xiu. He points out: "It can be said that Chan Juan is the symbol of Qu Yuan's poems. She represents the beauty of morality and justice."* Chan Juan is utterly devoted to Qu Yuan. She has a great respect for his integrity and his works, knowing deep in her heart that he is "the pillar of the

* Guo Moruo, "Qu Yuan and King Liya," *Catkin Sword Past and Present.*

State of Chu, a pillar that can hold the heavens." She may appear to be a simple, innocent and modest girl who is eager to learn. In times of crisis, however, when true character is submitted to the severest test, her high ideals and fine qualities are brought out. Then one sees her noble character, "exquisite as the orange trees," as she becomes the embodiment of the moral spirit of the masses. Totally unlike Chan Juan, Queen Zheng Xiu is full of self-seeking. She fawns on foreign powers and in collusion with the State of Qin, plots against Qu Yuan. Without the slightest sense of shame, she betrays her country and her people. She is portrayed effectively as the very opposite of Qu Yuan.

Song Yu is presented in the play as "a shameless, spineless writer." A sycophant, a man without any principles, he is selfish, hypocritical and is willing to sell his soul to get what he wants. He is another foil to Qu Yuan, whose virtues are set off even more for being upright, uncompromising, frank and highly principled. Equally, he is a strong contrast to the character of Chan Juan.

Interspersed in *Qu Yuan* are lyrics and songs. The play begins with the poet reading aloud his poem, "Ode to the Orange." Through his descriptions of the orange trees in the poem, Qu Yuan explains his personal beliefs and convictions: "During these troubled times, character is of paramount importance. It is easy to act like a man in peaceful times, for then a man is born in peace and dies in peace. But, during a time of great changes and upheavals, to act like a man is a very difficult thing.... We should live honourably and die honourably." After the death of Chan Juan at the end of the play, the "Ode to the Orange" is chanted, thus harking back to the beginning of the play. Like the main theme in a symphony, it reverberates echoing the theme of the play: "Fight dauntlessly for truth till the very end." Set at the climax of the play is Qu Yuan's dramatic monologue "Ode to Thunder and Lightning." Not only is the "Ode" the most significant revelation of his character, it also most strikingly brings out the theme of the play. As Zhou Enlai said, "It is Guo Moruo's intense hatred of the Kuomintang reactionary rule uttered through the words of Qu Yuan. 'Ode to Thunder and Lightning' is an accusation made against the Kuomintang reactionaries by Guo Moruo on behalf of the people under their rule."*

The Twin Flowers and *The Tiger Tally*, his two other historical plays of this period, also had a great deal of influence. *The Twin Flowers* is an expansion of the two-act play *Nie Ying*. In this new version, the protagonist Nie Zheng no longer appears as "a gallant fighter who is willing to die for a true friend." Instead, he has been given the virtues of one who loves justice passionately and hates evil intensely, willing to sacrifice his life for the people. He is asked by Yan Zhongzi to kill Xia Lei and Marquis Ai of the State of Han. True, the two of them have done him no wrong, but he accepts the assignment because he detests them for what they are doing: actively engaged in intrigues, but afraid to take state revenge," "fawning on foreign powers in pursuit of personal gain" and "enabling the aggressive State of Qin to become even more aggressive." Through the play, Guo Moruo expresses his hope that the oppressed people will, like Nie Zheng, "spill their blood for the growth of the flower of freedom."

The Tiger Tally was written a month after the completion of *Qu Yuan*. Guo Moruo used the historical tale of "the stealing of the tiger tally to save the State of Zhao" to present the character Lord Xinling as a defender of justice, devoted to the cause of anti-aggression. In the play, Ruji appears as a virtuous and courageous woman who has a strong sense of honour. The Consort of Wei is given the role of a sagacious mother who is sympathetic towards Lord Xinling and Ruji, fully supporting their just cause.

From the outbreak of the War of Resistance Against Japan to the victory of the people's War of Liberation, Guo Moruo continued to write. Those were the years "when the defiant ghost of the old era was seen everywhere. But everywhere also appeared glittering morning stars, chaste and holy, heralding a new age."** His works of this period included not only historical plays but also poetry, prose and literary reportage. The poems were collected in *War Cry* and *Cicada*, and the essays and other works of prose in *Feather Letters, Catkin Sword, Past and Present, Boiling Soup* and *The*

* Xu Dixin, "The Firm Grass Against the Strong Wind — In Memory of Guo Moruo," *People's Daily*, June 22, 1978.

** "Impression of Nanjing," *The Collected Works of Guo Moruo*, Vol. IX, p. 576.

Beginning of the Universe. His works of literary reportage were published in two collections, *Travels in the Soviet Union* and *Impressions of Nanjing.* He also wrote about his own wartime experience in *Mighty Waves.* These works are all imbued with his warm feelings for democratic struggles. His thinking is clear, and his style sharp. Whether in commenting on current affairs or in expressing his random thoughts and feelings, they had a considerable influence at the time.

Guo Moruo lived through the different period of the Chinese new democratic revolution after the May Fourth Movement of 1919. His literary career also spanned the different stages of development in the history of modern Chinese literature. On the revolutionary cultural front his records are most impressive; so too, are his literary achievements.

Chapter 3
Works of the Literary Societies During and After the May Fourth Movement Period

I. Works of Hu Shi, Liu Bannong and Other Writers of the Early Period of the Literary Revolution

The May Fourth literary revolution of 1919, which aimed at creating a new literature to replace the old, hastened the reform of both literary language and content. In the early period of the revolution, the *New Youth*, while advocating new literary theories and a realist literature, continually published literary works written in the vernacular. Lu Xun, Li Dazhao, Hu Shi, Shen Yinmo and Liu Bannong, who were all leading members of the magazine, devoted themselves to vernacular creative writing and their works demonstrated the achievement of the literary revolution. Later in the same year, periodicals such as *New Tides*, *Young China*, *Morning Post*, *Lantern of Learning* and *Weekly Review* also began publishing vernacular works. Between 1921 and 1922 appeared numerous works which were anti-feudal in spirit as they voiced the demand for national awakening. In form and style, these writers introduced innovation. After repulsing the attempts made by the literary revisionists, the new literature eventually established itself as the mainstream of modern Chinese literature.

In the early days of the literary revolution, the first writer to publish vernacular poems in the *New Youth* was Hu Shi (1891-1962). His *Attempts*, published in two volumes in March 1920, is also the first collection of poems written in the vernacular in the history of modern Chinese literature. The title comes from the line "Attempts since days of old have never led to success" by

Lu You, a poet of the Southern Song Dynasty. Hu Shi rewrites the lines as: "Success since days of old have always come from attempts." He chose the title because he wanted to "offer 'the spirit of experimentation,' embodied by the collection, to all the writers in China, inviting them to make their own attempts."*

The first volume of *Attempts* contains twenty-one poems, all written in 1916 and 1917 when Hu Shi was studying in America. Some of them first appeared in the *New Youth*. Though written in the vernacular, the poems still follow the classical poetic form of five or seven characters a line. As Qian Xuantong observes, "He has not yet rid himself of classical influences."** Hu Shi himself also admits that he "still has not been able to move beyond the confines of the old poetry" and that his "is merely old poetry somewhat touched up."*** The twenty-five poems collected in the second volume were written between September 1917, after Hu Shi had returned to Beijing, and the end of 1919. These poems, which had been published in different numbers of the *New Youth* since January 1918, show that he began to free himself from the prosody of the old poetry. In form and diction, they also show greater innovation. Not only are they written in the vernacular, the number of characters used for each line is irregular. The tonal patterns in classical Chinese poetry are not followed; instead, the lines produce a natural cadence of their own. For example, the language of "Going Up the Hill" which contains no trace of the old poetry, is full of colloquial vernacular rhythm. In the poem, Hu Shi describes an ordinary activity most poetically as he portrays the theme of striving for high achievement. The poem had a great influence in the early period of the literary revolution. Later, it was set to music and became a popular song.

A great number of the poems in *Attempts* express the writer's feelings through the objects he presents. The loneliness of the butterfly in "Butterfly," the contentment of the pigeon in "Pigeon" and the arrogance of the crow in "Old Crow" reflect the poet's own state of mind. Hu Shi was involved in the new culture movement

---

* Hu Shi, "My Preface," *Attempts*, Shanghai: Yadong Library Press, March 1920.
** Qian Xuantong, "Preface to *Attempts*."
*** Hu Shi, "My Preface," *Attempts*, Shanghai: Yadong Library Press, March 1920.

led by the *New Youth*. Some of the poems, therefore, naturally convey his desire to shatter feudal thinking in order to achieve the ideals of freedom and democracy. The poem "Authority" shows his contempt for feudal power. His condemnation of feudal corruption and his leaning towards bourgeois democracy are both evident in poems such as "First Birthday," written for the *Morning News* on the occasion of its first anniversary; "Optimism" and "A Plundered Star," upon the close down of the *Daily Review* and the *National Daily* by the authorities respectively. Some poems reveal that he did not have a clear concept of China as a nation. The poem "You Must Not Forget," for example, exposes the crimes of the plundering warlords and soldiers. In conclusion, however, he writes: "How can such a country deserve to be loved?"* He goes on to say:

> *You must not forget, your old man upon dying, only wished*
> *China would be conquered as soon as possible --*
> *By the Cossacks, by the Prussians. Any would do!*
> *The country could not be any worse than it is now!*

In his indignation, Hu Shi had obliterated national distinctions and strayed far from his love of China, betraying the essential May Fourth Movement spirit.

The ideas contained in *Attempts* are not particularly profound. However, the innovations in form and language in the poems had much influence in the early stage of the literary revolution. Thus, Qian Xuantong writes in the preface to Hu Shi's collection: "I am also one of the promoters of vernacular literature. Now that I have read *Attempts*, I am overjoyed."** *Attempts* went through many editions, in which poems were added and omitted—Lu Xun, Yu Pingbo and Zhou Zuoren had a hand in making some of the omissions.*** After the appearance of Hu Shi's vernacular poems, the *New Youth* and many other magazines continued publishing the new poetry. In particular, the publication of Guo Moruo's *Goddesses* opened up a new world in poetic creation.

---

* First published in the *New Youth*, Vol. V, No. 3. There are revisions in *Attempts*.

** Hu Shi, *Attempts*, 1st edition, p. 17.

*** See Hu Shi, Preface to the 4th Edition of *Attempts*, Shanghai, Yadong Library Press, October 1922.

In addition to vernacular poetry, Hu Shi also wrote *An Important Event in One's Life* (1919), a play which propagates the idea of personal choice in marriage, encouraging women to break the shackles of feudal conventions and follow the same path chosen by Ibsen's Nora. The play had a positive effect on the anti-feudal, new culture movement as well as the early development of new drama. After the peak of the May Fourth Movement, Hui Shi abandoned the cause of new literature. In 1922 he left the *New Youth* and set up his own weekly, *Endeavour*, preaching "good government" and urging people to "put the Chinese cultural heritage in order." Later, in both political and literary pursuits, more and more he went counter to the Chinese people's struggles against imperialism and feudalism.

Of the members of the *New Youth*, apart from Hu Shi, Liu Bannong and Shen Yinmo also published their poems early. In his essays, Liu Bannong (1891-1934) fiercely attacks the forces of feudalism, ignorance and folly. His major literary achievement, however, lies in poetry. He studied and experimented with the form and cadence of the new verse. The long and short poems in his *Waving the Whip*, which are written in different poetic forms, deal with a wide range of social realities. His prose poem "Carrot Seller"* and the short poem "Separated by a Sheet of Paper" expose the abominable crimes of the heartless rich and speak out for the silent oppressed poor. "The Sorrows of an Apprentice," written in the classical *yuefu* form, and "Rickshaw Blanket" in free verse, describe the sufferings of the apprentices and the rickshaw men. In other poems such as "Imitation of Children's Songs" and "Imitation of Songs" he uses folk songs or local expressions to make sketches of the life of the poor. All these poems, written in plain language, clearly indicate the poet's concern about the current state of affairs, his sympathy for the labouring masses and his inclination towards democratic thinking. In "The Blacksmith," "The Old Ox" and "The Old Carpenter," he portrays the labourers, extolling their creative spirit and honest character. The long poem "Breaking the

* Published in *New Youth*, Vol. IV, No. 5, May 1918.

Ice"* focuses on united effort and unceasing endeavour in striving, with optimism, for the achievement of goals. The May Fourth stamp on these poems is obvious enough. In artistic terms, Liu Bannong's poems are rather plain. However, some of them are well known for their harmony of rhythm and movement, for example, his poems "How Can I Not Think of Her?" and 'The Evening of a Small Peasant Family." He also used Jiangyin dialect to write many "four-line mountain ballads," which were collected in *Clay Pot.*

Shen Yinmo (1883-1971) published his poems in the *New Youth,* volumes 4-7. In "The Rickshaw Man" and "Slaughtering Sheep," he writes about the unfairness in life and extends his sympathy to those who suffer on that account. "Pigeon" expresses the author's demand for independence and individualism, which can protect a person from being manipulated by others. In "Moonlit Night," the image of the self is set in the scene of moonlight and frosty wind. The poem spoke for the disciples of individualism at the time. Shen Yinmo blends in the cadence of classical poetry with that of the new poetry and his artistic subtleties have their own special appeal. "Three Strings" was particularly admired by the contemporary readers for its poetic style and for the cadence created through his ingenious use of alliteration and double vowel rhyme.

After the *New Youth* ceased publication in July 1922, the poems of Kang Baiqing, Yu Pingbo and Liu Dabai appeared in *Young China, New Tides, Weekly Review* and other periodicals. Kang Baiqing's poems were collected in *Grass.* Many of these are about "the sweet sorrows of parting" or his travels, and the poems are noted for their detailed description of scene and their crisp tone, demonstrating the freshness of vernacular poetry. But in general his poems lack polish. Quite a few of them give the impression that they are merely prose arranged in the form of verse.

Yu Pingbo's first collection was *Winter Night.* In the poems, his feelings are conveyed through the description of scenes. The tone is clear but melancholy. The poems written after 1922 were collected in *Return to the West* and *Recollections.* In the former, the tone

* Published in *New Youth,* Vol. VII, No. 5, April 1920.

of melancholy deepens, as the poet reflects on the sufferings in life; in the latter, he turns from his pursuit of eternal love to the recollection of childhood. The influence of classical poetry is visible in Yu Pingbo's poetry in diction, cadence and manner of presentation.

Compared with the other practioners of the new poetry, Liu Dabai (1880-1932) reflects the thinking of the May Fourth Movement more distinctly in his works. "The Red New Year," "Song of the Labour Day" and "Song of the May First Movement" are the first poems which hail the tide of revolution brought in by the October Revolution in Russia. "Come, Landlords" and "Ballad of Cloth-Selling" tell of the greed and cruelty of wealthy landlords, while "Chenghu Never Dies" and "Recalled at Every Meal" pay tribute to the young peasants who have sacrificed their lives for the revolution. In these poems, the class viewpoints are clear and definite. Liu Dabai's style is simple and its smooth rhythm is often similar to that of folk songs. However, in many of the poems in *Old Dreams*, except "Ballad of Cloth-Selling," one can still find derivations from the old poetry. The poems written after 1921, such as those in *Kissing the Post*, show more and more the dispiritedness of the poet as he surrendered himself to the feeling of loneliness.

In the realm of fiction, Lu Xun's achievement was outstanding during the early period of the literary revolution. His works and those of other literary pioneers inspired Wang Jingxi, Yang Zhensheng and Ye Shaojun, who gradually came to the fore as their publications appeared in the literary magazine *New Tides*. Wang Jingxi's short stories were collected in *Snowy Night*. His aim was to describe as faithfully as possible what he had seen and experienced. Though his art could have been more polished, his works give a sense of the writer's realistic understanding of life. For example, in the story "Snowy Night" he depicts the hardships borne by a poor family, showing compassion for the ill-fated women and children, while in "A Diligent Student" he gives a detailed study of the mentality of someone who hankers after high office and fame.

The short stories of Yang Zhensheng (1890-1956) such as "The

Fisherman's Home," "A Soldier's Home" and "The Virgin" are quick sketches of life. They show the progressive thinking of the writer who "tries his best to describe the sufferings of the common people."* His principle of literary creation, as borne out in the delineation of character and life in the novella *Yujun*, written in 1925, was "faithfulness to subjective views." He may have gone too far in "imposing art on nature."** But the plot has many twists, the style is highly disciplined, the presentation is well controlled, and the novella from beginning to end never ceases to interest the reader. It made a definite impact at the time. Like Yang Zhensheng, Ye Shaojun began publishing his works of fiction in the early period of the literary revolution. His works underwent even greater development later.

As a literary genre, the vernacular essay came into being at the same time as the new poetry and fiction. Within that genre, in quantity and achievement, the most prominent are the essays which express the writers' various thoughts as they respond to the immediate needs of the struggle. The popularity of the essay owed its origin to the creation of special columns such as "Random Thoughts" and "Free Talk" in the *New Youth*, the *Weekly Review*, and the *Morning News*. Later, through the persistent practice of Lu Xun and other writers, it became "synonymous with the literary feuilleton."***

Besides Lu Xun, Li Dazhao (1889-1927) also wrote short essays criticizing the social ills of the day. In his attack on the old society, the combative tone is strong. "New Era" predicts that the fate of feudalism and militarism after the October Revolution will be just like that of "dry leaves against the autumn wind." In the essay, he calls on all the people in "dark China" to march forward and welcome "the light of dawn." Through his brilliant use of symbols in "False Trademark" and "Radish Party," he reminds people that they should beware of the various types of "socialism." Many things have "a red peel," he notices. But, who knows, they "may

---

* Lu Xun, Preface to *The Short Stories*, Vol. II, *Major Works of New Chinese Literature, Essays of Qiejieting (II)*.

** Yang Zhensheng, Preface to *Yujin* (1925).

*** Qu Qiubai, Preface to the *Selected Essays of Lu Xun* (1933).

turn out to be slices of a radish," red outside and white inside. These essays show the sensitivity of an enlightened Marxist. In "Politicians" and "Politics, Slaughter-House Style," he uses logical argument and, ingeniously and succinctly, gives an anatomy of the warlord's politics. The manner of approach is different in "Supreme Government" and "How Do You Feel Now, Mr Wei?" It is direct confrontation and outright expression of indignation and anger.

After the rise of vernacular prose and the essay, literary reportage also came into being. The earliest works of this genre in modern Chinese literature are Qu Qiubai's "A Journey to Famine Country" and "Red Capital and Records in the Heart."

II. Works of Bing Xin, Zhu Ziqing, Wang Tongzhao and Other Writers of the Literary Research Society

The first literary society devoted to the promotion of the new literature was the Literary Research Society, founded when the novels of the "Saturday School" were in vogue. While opposing feudal literature, the Literary Research Society also made a firm stand against the cheap writings of the "Saturday School." In its declaration, the Society announced that "the time is well past when literature and art were to provide amusement in happy hours or to become a means of idling away the time in moments of disappointment. We believe that literature is a kind of work which is very important to life." Based on the belief that literature can benefit life, the Literary Research Society stressed that "literature should reflect social realities, point out and discuss the various problems of life."* That, to put in a nutshell, was the basic assumption of the members of the Literary Research Society. They affirmed the "literature is the mirror of life" and rejected the principle of the aesthetic school that "literature is a pure art for the sake of art." Their works deal mainly with the realities of life. Hence the publication of much of their so-called "problem fiction."

* Mao Dun, "Preface to *The Short Stories*," Vol. I, *Major Works of New Chinese Literature*.

However, as to the specific ways of constructing a new literature, the views of the members of the Literary Research Society differed. Some of them emphasized the beauty and truth of literature. For example, Zheng Zhenduo, who advocated "a literature of blood and tears"* and rejected the feudal concept of using literature "to serve feudal teachings," argued that "not with any intention does the writer create; not with any intention does the reader read."** On the other hand, Shen Yanbing, who devoted himself at the time mainly to the writing of critical essays, spread the progressive idea that "true literature is that which reflects life in society." He pointed out that in an oppressed country, writers should observe and depict the evils in society, the sufferings of the people and the ideological clash between the old generation and the new.*** Precisely because these beliefs provided a starting point, some of the members, inspired by the May 30th Movement of 1925, went further to accept the idea of constructing a proletarian literature and art.

In methods of literary creation, the Literary Research Society, after the *New Youth*, advocated realism. It emphasized that "in the pursuit of realism in the new literature, the material must be chosen with the utmost care and the depiction must be faithful. For instance, the writer has to go to Sheshan Mountain at least once before he starts writing about it. One should not shoot an arrow without a target."† However, many people at the time failed to see distinction between realism and naturalism and they even promoted the latter as the latest extension of the former. Hence the essays such as "Literature and Life" and "Naturalism and Modern Chinese Fiction."

To further the development of the new literature, the Literary Research Society seriously turned to the introduction of

---

* Xi Di (Zheng Zhenduo), "A Literature of Blood and Tears," *Literary Xunkan (Ten Days)*, No. 6, June 30, 1921.

** "On the Construction of a New Concept of Literature" *Ibid.*, No. 37. May 11, 1922.

*** Lang Sun, "Literary Creation and Social Background," *Short Story Monthly*, Vol. XII, No. 7, July 1921.

† Shen Yanbing, "What Is Literature?" *Literary Theories, Major Works of New Chinese Literature.*

foreign literature. The main task was the translation of works of realism from Russia (and Soviet Union), France, Northern Europe and Eastern Europe. Through translation, works of foreign writers were introduced, writers such as Pushkin, Tolstoy, Turgenev, Chekov, Gorky, Maupassant, Romain Rolland, Ibsen and Sienkiewicz. At the same time, based on the vague ideas of "literature for life's sake," the works of decadent and even reactionary-inclined writers were introduced such as Artsybashev. The *Short Story Monthly*, for its part, published special numbers: "Studies on Russian Literature," "Studies on French Literature" and "Literature of the Injured Nations." It also put out "The Tagore Number," "The Byron Number" and "The Anderson Number." All the efforts of the Literary Research Society bore fruit, as new writers and new works continued to appear. In style, Ye Shaojun, Bing Xin, Zhu Ziqing, Wang Tongzhao, Xu Dishan and Lu Yin may differ. But these early writers of the new literature followed the same trend in literary creation as advocated by the Literary Research Society.

Bing Xin (Xie Wanying, 1900-) was one of the members of the Literary Research Society who began writing early. Most of her early works published in the *Morning News* are "problem fiction." In "Two Families," she uses the art of comparison and contrast to point out the need for the reformation of the old family and the creation of a new life. "This Man Alone Is Off Colour" lays bare the oppressive, feudal patriarchal system through her depiction of the conflicts between father and son created by the student anti-imperalist movement. In "Leaving the Country," the returning scholar with all his patriotic aspiration cannot put his talent to use. His heart-breaking experience confirms the fact that the dark forces of the warlords' rule have strangled all forms of life. "The Sister of Zhuang Hong" and "The Last Rest" are about the tragic lot of oppressed and ill-treated women, to whom the writer is sympathetic. These stories, collected later in *Leaving the County*, show clearly that the patriotic May Fourth Movement and the tide of new thinking had strongly affected Bing Xin. Passionately concerned about the realities of her day, she was utterly dissatisfied with the feudal authorities. However, the protagonists in her works, such as

Ying Ming and Ying Shi, are rather weak. The pressure put on them are really not all that great and, instead of staging any outright rebellion, they let the feudal forces "gain a victory without putting up a good fight." In fact, to the oppressed women, these stories can only mildly suggest that the solution is to strive for "opportunities for education."

After the high tide of the May Fourth Movement, some contradictions became apparent in Bing Xin's thought. Under the influence of Christian doctrines and the philosophy of Tagore, she "retreated into the small world of the family, describing and lauding the kind of 'human love' which cannot exist in a society that is bedeviled by class distinctions."* Her stories "Superman" from the collection *Superman* and "Awakening" from *The Past*, as well as the volumes of poetry *The Stars* and *Spring Waters* belonged to this period. In these works, she dwells on maternal love, childlike innocence and purity, spreading the empty belief that "the world is love." In a society long under feudal autocratic rule, human relationship had become a matter of heartless social interaction. Not surprisingly, for her young readers who did not have much experience of life the illusion that "the world is love" had its appeal, for it gave them a kind of spiritual solace. As a writer, she is good at using her literary style to create a rich lyrical atmosphere in her works, which also accounts for their influence at the time.

Compared with her early stories and poetry, Bing Xin's essays brought her greater recognition for their achievement. As she puts it, "The way I write, essays suit me, not poetry. That I do know."** "Laugh," one of her earlier works, is a fine piece of vernacular prose in the early period of the new literature movement. Later essays such as "Dream," "The Past (II)," "Letters to My Young Readers" and "Thoughts in the Mountains" also give the reader a sense of beauty close to that conveyed by lyrical poetry or landscape paintings. Most of these essays were written abroad, as she thought of her family, her hometown and her country. Maternal love and

* Bing Xin, Preface to *The Selected Stories and Essays of Bing Xin.*

** Bing Xin, Preface to *The Collected Works of Bing Xin*, published by Beixin Press.

childlike innocence still feature prominently in these works, but the tone is somewhat changed. There is also disappointment upon the shattering of empty dreams, frustration upon the failure to find answers in her search for the meaning of life, and melancholy upon recollection of childhood. She also praises the labouring masses in her writings. The style of her prose is light; the feelings expressed are transparent and delicate. She takes full advantage of the easy flow of the vernacular as well as the disciplined simplicity of the classical language. Bing Xin is a talented writer with a very personal style.

Another member of the Literary Research Society who distinguished himself in poetry and prose was Zhu Ziqing (1898-1948). He began writing poetry in the early days of the May Fourth Movement and was one of the editors of *Poetry*, the first magazine devoted to the publication of verse in the history of modern Chinese literature. His poems were collected in *Traces* (prose and verse) and the first volume of *Snowy Morning*. In the poem "Seeing Han Bohua Off to Russia," he uses the red clouds as a symbol for the Soviet Union. The enthusiasm with which he faces reality can also be seen at the end of the poem "Light," as he writes: "If you want light, you have to create it yourself." However, Zhu Ziqing did not really know how to create this light and often in his poems (for example, "In a Rush") one finds the poet's "gossamer-like" sense of loss and the pain that comes after illusions have vanished. The long poem "Destruction," written in 1922, is also steeped in the feeling of loneliness and emptiness. But the speaker in the poem is not dispirited; neither does he sink into pessimism. Instead, he still spurs on. Putting behind him all his empty dreams, he exclaims, "Let me again be my ordinary self!" He promises:

From now on I will not set my eyes on the blue sky,
Or bow my head to stare to the pure water.
I will only watch my footsteps carefully.
Step by step, I will tread on the earth
And deeply implant my footprints.

The poem is over two hundred lines long and through the modulation in tone, from restraint to light movement and reverberation,

Zhu Ziqing writes about the contradictions in his thoughts and feelings and describes the process in which these contradictions are resolved. "Destruction" is far superior to most of the poems written by other poets at the time.

As a progressive, patriotic writer with a sense of righteousness, Zhu Ziqing more and more expressed his strong anti-imperialist and anti-feudal feelings during the May 30th Movement of 1925, when the tide of revolution was running high. Traces of these feelings are already clearly noticeable in some of his poems and prose written since 1924. For instance, in the poem "For A.S." he praises the "torch-like hands" and the "billow-like eyes" of the revolutionaries who "want to build a red paradise on earth." After the May 30th Massacre, created by the imperialist reactionaries, he wrote "The Song of Blood,"* in which his outbursts of indignation are like "volcanic eruptions." In the essay "The Massacre by the Government," he makes strong accusations against the atrocities of the warlords and produces forceful accounts as someone who has participated in the struggle against the March 18th Massacre of 1926 in Beijing. Some of the other essays indirectly deal with significant social problems: for example, "White Men — God's Chosen People," "The Prince of Life—Seventy Cents" ("Traces of Wenzhou (IV)") and "Civilization in a Boat."

Artistically, Zhu Ziqing's achievement in prose is better represented by his essay such as "A Glimpse of Father's Back," "The Moon of the Lotus Pond" and "For My Dead Wife," collected in *A Glimpse of Father's Back* and *You and I.* In "A Glimpse of Father's Back," he writes about a father seeing his son off, who is leaving home for a faraway place because of the change of fortune in the family. Through his simple and honest narration, the writer expresses his loving thoughts for his old father. The feeling of sadness also illustrates the plight of the petty-bourgeoisie, whose decline was inevitable in spite of their repeated efforts to save themselves. In the essay, Zhu Ziqing's style is simple, precise and sincere; the language is colloquial but refined. Essays like this and those written later and collected in *Random Accounts of a European Journey* and

* Published in *Short Story Monthly*, Vol. XVI, No. 7, July 1925.

Random Accounts of London, with their moving power that comes from art, "show that the special strength of the old literature, self-assumed of course, are not beyond the achievements of vernacular literature." Zhu Ziqing's essays had a great influence on the devotees of the new literature, significantly contributing to the development of vernacular prose.

During the War of Resistance Against Japan and the Liberation War, Zhu Ziqing continued to write, and his essays were included in collections such as *On Refined and Popular Taste* and *Standards and Yardsticks*. He faced the ruthless realities and through practical action supported the progressive student movements. He would rather "suffer the pains of illness, even die of starvation, than receive 'relief food' from America." Understandably, in some of the essays, he voices his indignation against the dark realities at the time.

Wang Tongzhao (1897-1957) began publishing his stories and poems in the May Fourth Movement period in *Short Story Monthly*, *Light of Dawn* and *New Tides*. In the early 1930s, his short stories appeared in collections, *The Night of the Spring Rain* and *Marks on the Frost*; his poems, in *The Heart of a Child* and *This Age*. He also wrote two medium-length novels, *A Leaf* and *Evening*. In his early career as a writer, he shared the idea of "literature for life's sake," held by members of the Literary Research Society. But he tended more to indulge in fantasy than give objective descriptions. Often his "scenes and characters are set in a world of illusion." He valued "vivid, artistic expression of meaning,"* and looked upon abstract love and beauty as prescriptions for the cure of life's ills. "Deep Meditation" and "Smile," among others, hail the magic power of this "love" and "beauty."

As he continued his writing career, however, Wang Tongzhao gradually realized the sharp conflicts between his ideals and reality. In *After the Snow* and *The Night of the Spring Rain* he portrays with disappointment and frustration the theme of the destruction of beautiful dreams. The poems in *The Heart of a Child* and the medium-length novel *A Leaf* contain a certain sadness as the writer

* Preface to *The Selected Short Stories of Wang Tongzhao*.

continued his exploration in life. As changes occurred in his thinking, Wang Tongzhao gradually turned to the exposure and denunciation of any phenomenon which deviated from reason. In "The Child's Words by the Lake," through the reply of a street urchin he describes the predicament of a poor family. "The Rank of Life and Death" draws attention to the injustice done to the labourers who have been reduced to destitution, while "The Sinking Boat" protests against the crime of foreign merchants who, for their own greed, overload a boat thus resulting in the drowning of peasants when it sinks. In "Shadow of the Ghost," "The Commander" and other short stories, he satirizes and attacks debauchery and disorderliness, both products of the feudal system. These stories are fairly close to actual events, but his abstract thinking about beauty, love and the philosophy of life found in his works of the early days of May Fourth period is noticeably absent. Noticeable too, is that he had turned more to realism. Similar changes, through the use of obscure imagery and fairly difficult language, are also seen in different degrees in the poems written after 1924 and later collected in *This Age* such as "Strong Wind, Thunder and Rain" and "Words of the Sedan-Chair Carrier."

The work which shows, more than any other, the changes in Wang Tongzhao as a writer is the full-length novel *Mountain Storm*, published in 1933. Set against the background of a village in northern China under the rule of the warlords, the novel depicts vividly the economic decline in the countryside caused by the economic invasion of the imperialists, heavy taxes and levies, natural disasters and the havoc of war. In these circumstances, the peasants try desperately to find a way out of their plight. The novel shows the process of change that Xi Dayou goes through, from "dependence on the land for a living," "living and working in peace and contentment," eventually to "looking for a way out." At first, because of a dispute over the selling of vegetables, he is unjustly arrested by the soldiers. To pay off what he owes for redeeming himself, he is forced to sell his land and property. This blow hastens the death of his ailing father. Now Xi Dayou begins to change and becomes irritable, often flying into a temper. "His simple and sincere heart can no longer accommodate his former total trust in all things." Then numerous disasters fall on him and the other peasants of the village: advanced taxes, forced levies, drought, the bandits' plundering, conscription, and the starving soldiers' harassment. Gradually Xi Dayou loses his close attachment to the land. The harsh realities of life have made it impossible for him to accept Uncle Chen's advice based on "the doctrine of predestination." With his family he leaves the "dilapidated, poverty-stricken, disease-ridden and deeply-frightened village," heading for the town in the hope of finding a new life.

In the novel, the description of the process of change in Xi Dayou is "detailed and specific," thus creating "before our eyes a frightening picture of the pillage of the peasants."* Related to the main theme are the destinies of various characters: the father of Xi Dayou; Second Uncle Xi, who is honest and hardworking but conservative and narrow-minded; Idiot Song, a vagrant hired-hand; Xu Li, who takes risks out of desperation; Village Head Chen, who is full of complaints; Wei Er, who is contented with his lot; and the old Scholar Xu, who spends all day in his small room nourishing his last, faint hopes. All these characters, with their own individual traits, set off the protagonist Xi Dayou. In addition, their different life experiences together form a realistic picture, which, with its tone of tragic indignation, most effectively portrays the condition of the peasants at a time of "the oncoming of rain in the mountains and gale in the house." Among the novels of the 1930s which depict the economic collapse of the villages, *Mountain Rain* is both solid and vigorous. Its shortcoming, however, is that Wang Tongzhao often allows narration to replace description with the result that at times it makes rather lengthy and difficult reading.

Wang Tongzhao had also written about the young intellectuals of the post-May Fourth Movement in another full-length novel, *Spring Cream*. His other works include volumes of poetry and collections of short stories.

Xu Dishan (Luo Huasheng, 1893-1941) was another prominent writer of the Literary Research Society. In his early years he was influenced by the Buddhist thought. This influence and his precar-

* Dong Fang Wei Ming (Mao Dun), "Wang Tongzhao's *Mountain Rain*," *Literature*, December 1933, Vol. I, No. 6.

ious living as he moved from Taiwan to the mainland have both left their marks in his works. His first short story, "The Bird of Destiny," describes the tragedy of a pair of young lovers who are driven to suicide, and the writer raises objections to the feudal marriage system. In the story, the heroine's pious religious sentiment and the calm with which she and her lover throw themselves into the river distinctly reflect the Buddhist idea of nirvana. *The Diligent Spider Weaving Its Web* depicts the life and experience of Shang Jie, and brings to light the ruthless oppression of women in a feudal society where male authority is not to be challenged. Shang Jie compares life to the fragile "spider's web"; she believes that the meaning of life lies in the continual mending of this broken web, just as what the spider does. Many of the short stories, collected in *The Diligent Spider Weaving Its Web*, his early works, have their settings in Fujian, Guangdong, South Asia and India. They are rich in local colour. The plot is full of twists, and the language is clear and smooth. The characters are strong and tenacious, all blessed with the spirit and energy of life. Their pious religious thinking is often noted; so, too, their belief in predestination. Seldom do they openly oppose the unjust realities.

In his early essays collected in *Magic Rain in Bare Mountains*, which Xu Dishan himself describes as "diverse and mixed,"* elements of the positive and the negative are found together. His well-known essay "Peanuts" is rich in plain and honest sentiments, revealing much about the writer's personality and his attitude towards life. "Woods in the Spring," with its light tone, suggests a return to simple nature. The mixed and complicated elements in Xu Dishan's works gradually disappeared as changes occurred in his literary creations. The short story "Spring Peach" may at times convey the wish that it is possible to transform grief into joy. But the writer has written vividly about the noble character of the suffering masses and the simple and sincere friendship which exists among them. In the story, he has created a woman labourer who is kind, strong, forthright and unyielding; in short, someone who is entirely different from Shang Jie. This is a significant sign

* Preface to *Magic Rain in Bare Mountains.*

of progress in Xu Dishan's writings. After the outbreak of the anti-Japanese war, as he had closer political contacts with the people, he wrote many fine pieces of work: for example, "The Gills of the Iron Fish," which is about the lives of the intellectuals.

Lu Yin (Huang Ying, 1898-1934), a woman writer, also began her writing career by exploring the problems of life. Her early short stories published in the *Short Story Monthly* deal with certain aspects of social realities. For instance, "A Letter" is about the tragic death of a poor peasant's daughter who has been tricked by a local tyrant into becoming his concubine. "Two Primary School Pupils" exposes the crime of the warlord government in its massacre of the petitioning young pupils, while "Can the Soul Be Sold?" tells of the misfortunes of the cotton-mill workers. From her short story "Or, Man's Sorrow" on, as Mao Dun pointed out, "the anxious question 'What is life?' has become the main theme of her works."* If through her works Bing Xin intended to guide her readers out of the miseries and pains of life into the world of love, then Lu Yin, as she herself said, strove to "shatter the empty dreams cherished by people and throw off the mask of joy."** She persuaded the readers to hate and weary of the world. In the story "Or, Man's Sorrow," Ya Xia commits suicide for he can no longer stand the disappointments in life and the pains of illness. Li Shi in "The Diary of Li Shi" dies of grief, "the illness of the heart," after the illusion of her homosexual love has vanished. In *The Old Companions on the Seashore*, Lu Sha and her girl friends enjoy their happy times together. But soon they are to part and the sorrows of departure leave them with only empty sights. Behind the love problems in the stories collected in *The Old Companions on the Seashore* are the writer's curses on "the evil society," "the terrible life" and "the selfishness of mankind."

In her later stories collected in *Mary* and *The Morning and Evening Tides of the Soul* such as "Father" and "The Failure of Professor Qin," Lu Yin unveils the bad characters of the old family. The writer's indignation against the feudal authorities is well

* Mao Dun, Preface to *The Short Stories*, Vol. I, *Major Works of New Chinese Literature*.

** *The Autobiography of Lu Yin*.

expressed and her stories have much social significance. In her works, Lu Yin often uses the autobiographical style or diary form. Her language is simple, direct, rigorous and natural. She is not interested in displaying her art, which could have been more refined. The plot is rather loose and slow-moving. In the novelle published after 1929 such as *The Returning Wild Geese*, *Ivory Ring* and *The Heart of a Woman*, the plot is better constructed than before, the style is brisk and the pessimistic tone is less often used. But because there was nothing new in her choice of subject matter or in the portrayal of life, these works did not receive much attention from contemporary readers.

III. Works of Ye Shaojun

Among the works of the Literary Research Society, those by Ye Shaojun (Ye Shengtao) best demonstrate the characteristics of realism. As early as 1911, he began writing short stories, and they were published mainly in *Short Stories Series*, *Saturday* and *The Sea of Short Stories*, all run by the writers of the Mandarin Duck and Butterfly School. These stories, as he said, were the products of his encounter with foreign literature and the influence of Washington Irving's *Tales of a Traveller* was particularly strong. They are written in classical Chinese and the treatment of subject matter is not deep enough. The approach, however, is honest and serious. These stories are mainly about "the ordinary happenings in life,"* exploding the dark realities and expressing the writer's sympathy for the poor. His tendency towards realism, already obvious, was carried further in his later works, and this accounts for some of their special features. In certain aspects, one can find in his early works traces of transition in the modern movement, from an old democratic literature to a new democratic literature.

When Ye Shaojun began writing stories in the vernacular in 1919, he had already been deeply influenced by the new thinking at the time. The early collections *Lack of Mutual Understanding*,

* "A Few Words About the Past," *Home of the Not Yet Bored* (a collection of essays).

Conflagration and *Below the Line* distinctly show his democratic leanings. Some of the stories describe the humiliation and harm done to the lower class people: for example, the exploited peasants in "Bitter Vegetables" and "Morning Journey" who have to pay exorbitant rents and heavy taxes, the boy in "The Little Coppersmith" whose parents are too poor to send him to school. In presenting these characters, the writer uses a plain style to convey his sympathy for the oppressed. In other stories such as "A Friend," "Lack of Mutual Understanding," "Foreign Flags" and "Posthumous Child" (a later work), he focuses on what was then generally considered outdated, laughable social behaviour as he satirizes ordinary urban people living under the semi-feudal and semi-colonial system: their gloomy existence, vulgarity, self-contentment, selfishness, indifference, hypocrisy, craftiness and conservatism. Many of these works have a certain coldness about them. There are also stories, however, which are characterized not by cold description of objective realities, but by the writer's fervent display of his subjective ideals. He was dissatisfied with the ugly scenes he witnessed, but realized that there was nothing he could do about it. Empty dreams of love and beauty helped him to retreat from unpleasant reality. Stories such as "An Outing in the Spring" and "Hidden Love" have an air of illusion, both containing weaknesses in art and in the ideas conveyed.

For a long time in his early career, Ye Shaojun was involved in primary and secondary school education. He knew full well the goings-on as well as the lives and outlook of people in educational circles. It is not surprising, therefore, that more of his works including the most successful ones, draw on this particular area of his knowledge. The representative stories are *Meals*, *The Headmaster* and *Mr Pan in the Mire*. Although the protagonists in these stories may have the same weakness, in that they bend their principles to suit the circumstances, they do have entirely different personalities. *Meals* describes how a village teacher is constantly threatened by starvation because he is in the clutches of hooligans. In the story, the writer expresses much sympathy for "the nonentities" while he criticizes their cowardice for they are willing to accept any kind of humiliation in order to continue their existence.

The *Headmaster* is about an intellectual who cherishes ideals. But because he burdens himself with far too many worries, he dares not confront the feudal forces. The story accurately reveals the inner conflicts of someone who knows the right direction to follow, but lacks the courage to move forward. In a few sentences at the end of the story, the writer brings out the true character of the headmaster. *Mr Pan in the Mire* is a fine story, well known to the contemporary readers. It vividly portrays a mean and feeble intellectual during the confusing period of fighting among the warlords. In order to escape the scourge of war and the threat of unemployment, Mr Pan uses all his wits to adapt himself to the changing circumstances. He panics at the slightest sign of danger. Once momentary security is assured, however, he flatters the warlord rulers. He wallows in vulgarity and disgrace, with no principles whatsoever. To him it is nothing but self-preservation. In the story the writer has penetrated the character's soul, fully revealing his traits. The achievement is a clear indication of his deep understanding of the precarious lives of the intellectuals, their meanness, selfishness and contentment with momentary security in old China, a country then afflicted with confusion and internal strife.

The May 30th Movement of 1925 galvanized Ye Shaojun and brought about changes in the thinking behind his works. Some of the short stories in the two collections *In the City* and *Not Yet Bored* show that he had begun to observe the actual struggles that were going on. He strove to portray new characters who were different from the weak and compromising intellectuals in his early works such as *Meals* and *The Headmaster*. Thus, in Mr Guo, the primary school teacher in the story "Resistance," one already finds early signs of the idea of collective struggle. *In the City* is about Ding Yusheng, a strong character, who goes back to his hometown to start a secondary school. Baptized in the new thinking, he has enough courage to go against feudalism. "Among the People" describes what happens to some petty-bourgeois intellectuals who, inspired by the revolution, go to the countryside in order to be with the people. The story is a true record of the times and the trends of thinking among the intellectuals. In "Night," written in the winter of 1927, he exposes the crimes of the reactionaries in their massacres of the people who took part in the revolution. This he does through describing the feelings of an old woman who has lost her daughter and son-in-law. At the end of the story, as she faces the orphans of the martyrs, "she boldly decided that once again she would take on the responsibilities of a mother." In this way, the writer hints at the awakening of the people to the revolutionary cause. If the early works of Ye Shaojun sought mainly to criticize the gloomy lives of ordinary city people and intellectuals, then his work after 1925 (for example, *A Package*) carried even stronger criticism. The writer had encountered new historical realities. He portrayed significant themes related to the struggles of the times, delineating new characters who were of necessity more determined in their combative mission.

In 1928, Ye Shaojun wrote *Ni Huanzhi*, a novel published in serial form in the *Education Magazine*. The novel describes the lives and thinking of some petty-bourgeois intellectuals during the period from the 1911 Revolution to the First Revolutionary Civil War. It mirrors the tremendous impact made on the young people by the gigantic May Fourth and May 30th revolutionary movements. Ni Huanzhi, the protagonist, is a young man who passionately pursues whatever is new. Like many progressive intellectuals after the failure of the 1911 Revolution, at first he places every hope in education as a means to save the country. Most sincerely, he expects that this "ideal education" will create a better society. He also dreams of a marriage which is built on the pursuit of the same goals by husband and wife, a marriage blessed with mutual help and love. He falls in love with Jin Peizhang, who has the same interests and outlook. But the cruel realities begin to shatter his dreams. Not only does he suffer many rebuffs in his devotion to education, his family life also falls short of his original expectations. Now, he feels the loneliness and pain of "having gained a wife, but lost forever a comrade, someone he loved." Then comes the May Fourth Movement. Under the influence of Comrade Wang Leshan, Ni Huanzhi broadens his vision, which goes beyond the school to include the masses. Eventually he devotes himself to the cause of social reform. At the height of the May 30th Movement and the

Great Revolution, Ni Huanzhi participates in the intense revolutionary activities. Thus he has changed from the reformist who "believed in education as a saviour of China" to someone who is dedicated to the cause of revolution.

What Ni Huanzhi has gone through so far is fairly representative of the experience of the contemporary progressive youths. He is carried forward by the current of the times, but does not dissolve himself into that current. Once the revolutionary situation changes for the worse, he easily feels that everything is over. Thus, after the April 12th Massacre by the reactionaries, unlike Wang Leshan he does not persist in heroic struggles. Instead, he feels helpless because "things have changed all too easily." He becomes disappointed and pessimistic, shedding tears over his drinks. In the end he passes away in the midst of doubts and hopes, wondering "when light can be seen." The writer's limited life experience and the weakness in his thinking inevitably affected his writing. There is not enough direct and specific portrayal of Ni Huanzhi after he has turned to the revolution. Neither is the delineation of the revolutionary Wang Leshan all that clear. The novel from Chapter 20 on, compared with what is written before, is loose and lacking in force. However, all things considered, *Ni Huanzhi* is still a comparatively good piece of work.

Besides Ni Huanzhi, the other characters in the novel with their own special traits are easily recognizable. Jin Peizhang, for instance, carries the hallmark of the traditional Chinese women. The educationist Jiang Bingru is liberal in his views while the local tyrant Tiger Jiang is greedy and insidious. That *Ni Huanzhi* is regarded as a significant full-length novel of its period has everything to do with the writer's seriousness in his approach to writing. Upon its publication, Mao Dun pointed out: "There is no question that this is the first novel which has its setting in the historical events of the past ten years. There is no question that *Ni Huanzhi* is also the first novel which deliberately shows how a petty-bourgeois intellectual with revolutionary zeal has been affected by the mighty events over a period of ten years, how he moves from the countryside to the city, from devotion to education to participation in mass movements, from liberalism to collectivism."* Mao Dun's evaluation of the novel has proved valid.

Ye Shaojun's later short stories were collected in *Four and Three*. These stories reflect from different angles the corruption in the Kuomintang-ruled areas during the Second Revolutionary Civil War. "More by a Few Bushels" describes how a bumper harvest is turned into a disaster. "A Declaration" tells the public that it is a crime to love one's own country. "Fleeing from Calamity" proves that deposits in a bank are like gambling. "Grateful for a Personal Favour" points out that to graduate means to be unemployed. "Investment" exposes schools which are run like business enterprises. "Raising a Spirit" is about scholars who having been educated abroad, now turn themselves into sorcerers. The sources of material for these bizarre stories are much wider than before; the satire is also more pungent. Though some of them are rather like quick sketches, they nevertheless possess the same distinctive characteristics as found in his other stories.

The works of Ye Shaojun are simple, serene and natural. They do not have an intricate plot; nor does the writer deliberately experiment with startling new techniques and forms. Instead, he strived to recreate life itself, revealing the inner world of the characters and their mental state. His descriptions are detailed and vivid. He seldom expresses his views and feelings directly; rather, they "find their home between the lines."** The short stories are compact in structure, illustrating the careful treatment of theme and development of plot, and their natural ending leaves the reader with further thoughts. The language is polished. It is not ornate; neither does the writer use local dialect and slang without special intent. Ye Shaojun's style is both precise and expressive, itself an achievement which was beyond the reach of his contemporary writers who believed that "how you talk is how you write."

Most of Ye Shaojun's essays were collected in *Home of the Not Yet Bored*. "A Place Without Autumn Insects" and "Lotus Roots and Water Shield" convey his nostalgic thoughts, but they also describe

* Mao Dun, "On Reading *Ni Huanzhi*," *Literary Weekly*, Vol. VIII, No. 20.

** Ye Shengtao, "Preface to *The Selected Works of Ye Shengtao*," 1st edition, Kaiming Press, July 1951, p. 8.

the hesitance of some of the intellectuals after the May Fourth Movement and their sense of loss while they are still serious in their pursuit of goals. "The Morning Glory" gives the reader a fresh and invigorating feeling that the "life-force" is forever spiralling upwards. "In the Midst of the Rainstorm on May 31st" is denunciation of the atrocious crimes committed by the Chinese and foreign reactionaries. Ye Shaojun's essays were praised by Ah Ying, who found that "each piece is much like a well-written, exquisite poem of life."* The style of his prose is characterized by its clear language and honest feelings.

In his early career as a writer, Ye Shaojun also wrote poems, some of which were collected in *Snowy Morning*, volume 6. Most of the poems tend to be rather plain. The long poem "Battlefields in the River Liu Region," published in the *Short Story Monthly* (Vol. 15, No. 11), describes the sufferings of the people caused by the fighting among the warlords. Artistically, it may give the reader the impression of prose appearing in verse form. Nevertheless, it is one of the early attempts at writing long poems made by modern Chinese poets.

Ye Shaojun was also the first writer of children's stories in the history of modern Chinese literature. In some of the stories in his early collection *The Scarecrow* such as "The Little White Boat" and "The Dream of Little Fang," he creates for children a surrealistic "paradise of innocence." Many of the other stories, however, deal with social realities seriously. In *The Stone Statues of Ancient Heroes*, a later collection, the ideas of collectivism and the spirit of optimism prompting people to forge ahead pervade some of the stories. Ye Shaojun wrote the continuation to Anderson's tale *The Emperor's New Clothes*, satirizing the ruthlessness and ignorance of the rulers."The Silkworm and the Ant" raises the question of labouring for whom, "The Words of the Birds and the Animals" and "The Experiences of the Locomotive" in the collection *Four and Three*, subtly reflect the political struggles of the masses at the time.

In the early 1920s, Ye Shaojun was already involved in editing

---

* *The Essays of Sixteen Modern Writers.*

the works of other writers. For instance he edited and published Ding Ling's *An Uneventful Dream*, Ba Jin's *Destruction* and works of Shi Zhecun and Dai Wangshu, all of which immediately brought them recognition as writers of merit. From the mid-1930s on, he devoted his energy more and more to the editing and publication of books and magazines. Indefatigably he did much good work in the education of the young and in language teaching. During the War of Resistance Against Japan and the War of Liberation, he continued to write essays, old style poems, literary criticism and provided language teaching materials. Though he did not manage to write many short stories, throughout those years he remained in the literary forefront. In spring 1946, he began serving as director of the General Department of the Federation of Chinese Writers and Artists. He attended to the daily work of the Federation and made valuable contributions to unity and progress in literary and art circles.

IV. Works of Yu Dafu and Other Writers of the Creation Society

Following the Literary Research Society, also founded in 1921 was the Creation Society, another literary group for the promotion of new literature. Membership of the society grew to nearly thirty in 1924. Together with the Literary Research Society, it had a most significant influence on the development of modern Chinese literature.

Although the ideological inclinations of the members of the Creation Society differed, their literary assumptions were generally similar. They glorified genius, valued divine inspiration and strove for the perfection and beauty of literature. In the poem "The Creator," for example, Guo Moruo writes:

Blow, blow, you autumnal wind,
Rush, rush, my pointed brush,
I know divine inspiration has arrived;
I will create with all my might.

It is also stated in the "Afterword" of the *Creation* quarterly (Vol. 1, No. 2): "Our isms, our ideologies are not the same. Neither do we insist they should be the same. The view that we all share is that we should follow the demands from the bottom of the heart and get on with our activities in literature and art." In his essay "The Mission of the New Literature," Cheng Fangwu states: "At least I feel that giving up the thought of fame and fortune in order to pursue perfection and beauty in literature is well worth our life-long devotion." While emphasizing the response to the "demands from the bottom of the heart" and "the mission of literature itself," members of the Creation Society also stressed literature's "mission for the time." They believed that "fierce artillery fire should be turned mercilessly on the old society."* Through literature, they wanted to "release the spirit of the proletariat and reveal the naked and uncorrupted human nature."**

These literary assumptions differ from those which advocated "art for art's sake" and "the supremacy of art." In truth, however, they were inclinations towards romanticism with emphasis on the significance of subjectivity and the role of the self. Many members of the Creation Society admired the works of Goethe, Heine, Byron, Keats, Whitman, Hugo, Romain Rolland, Tagroe and Wilde. In translation they chose Germen romantic literature and they also introduced works by writers of the symbolist, expressionist and futurist schools. Members of the Creation Society were different from those of the Literary Research Society in creative writing. While the latter stressed realism, they tended towards self-expression, which distinctly characterized their poetry, essays, fiction and plays. In the works which expressed their dissatisfaction with the then corrupt society, they did not emphasize detailed description and deep analysis of the dark realities. Instead, they directly and boldly voiced their strong protest and condemnation. In poetry, Guo Moruo best represented the Creation Society; in fiction and essays, the best known and most prolific writer was Yu

* Cheng Fangwu, "The Mission of the New Literature," *Creation Weekly*, No. 2, May 1923.

** Guo Moruo, "Our New Literature Movement," *Creation Weekly*, No. 3, May 1923.

Dafu.

Born in Fuyang, Zhejiang Province, Yu Dafu (1896-1945) studied classical poetry at an early age. He also loved classical fiction and drama. In 1913 he went to Japan with his elder brother. After several years of high school education, he enrolled in the Economics Department of Tokyo Imperial University. His interest, however, lay in literature. During his stay in Japan he read foreign literary works extensively, especially those by modern European and Japanese writers. Living abroad for almost ten years, Yu Dafu, like many other Chinese students and residents in a foreign land, encountered different kinds of discrimination and humiliation. These experiences gave him a passionate love for China. They also deepened his hate for the world and its ways. All this gradually shaped his melancholy character and gloomy outlook. In 1921, upon the forming of the Creation Society, he began writing fiction. The following year, he returned to China and participated in the literary activities of the Society, editing its periodicals. Later, he taught at different universities in Anhui, Beijing, Wuchang and Guangzhou. Throughout these years, however, his energy was directed mainly towards writing.

Sinking, the first collection of Yu Dafu's short stories, records his life and thoughts during his stay in Japan. Together with Guo Moruo's *The Goddesses*, it was the first publication in the Creation Society Book Series. The collection included, among others, "Sinking," "The Silvery Grey Death" and "Moving South." The most representative of these early stories is "Sinking," which describes a Chinese student in Japan suffering from melancholia. He yearns for genuine friendship and tender love. But in a foreign country, he encounters only contempt and humiliation. Driven by despair, he treads the path leading to his downfall. The despondency of the protagonist in this piece, well reflects the psychological state of young people of the May Fourth period who were awakened in spite of heavy oppression, but did not know how to change the current situation. Deeply grieved, the protagonist cries out: "China, oh, China, why can't you become strong?" "So, let me love my country, let my country be my lover!" "China, oh, China! You are the cause of my death. Be prosperous soon! Be strong soon! Many of your sons and daughters are still in pain!" The story greatly moved the young people at the time and was censored by the feudal conservatives. As Guo Moruo said about the early works of Yu Dafu, "His fresh style is like a spring breeze sweeping over the barren Chinese society, instantly arousing numerous youths from their sleep. His forceful self-expression is a blitz on the age-old, deeply-hidden hypocrisy of the feudal literati and officialdom. The hypocritical moralists and scholars have been shocked into fury. Why? It is because his utter honesty has made it difficult for them to carry on with their hypocrisy."*

From the beginning of his writing career, Yu Dafu was known in the literary circles for the striking characteristics of his romanticism. He subscribed to the view that "all literary works are the autobiographies of the writers."** He was different from Lu Xun, who following the realist tradition used the protagonist "I" in his fiction. In Yu Dafu's fiction, the protagonist "I" often frankly and boldly reveals himself through the writer's rich, emotive styles so that "the voice of rebellion is heard in the groans uttered under heavy oppression."*** In the collection *Sinking*, short stories such as "Wind Bell," "The Homesick Man," "Journey Through the Vineyard," "Homecoming," "Homecoming (II)" and "Before Separation" are all autobiographical in nature, even though sometimes he does not use the protagonist "I" as the narrator. "Journey Through the Vineyard," written in 1923 in the form of a series of letters to his wife, records the life of the writer shortly after his return to China. These letters vividly describe the life of a poverty-stricken intellectual who is troubled by his financial problems and his painfully confused state of mind. The emotion is strong and the tone of his writing, mournful. The story spoke well for the people who were under heavy economic pressure. *Caishiji*, a historical novel, was written as an answer to the attack from Hu Shi and others. In the novel, through the portrayal of the poet Huang Zhongze of the

* Guo Moruo, "On Yu Dafu," *The Collected Works of Guo Moruo*, Vol. XII, p. 547.

** Yu Dafu, "Looking Back on Five or Six Years of Literary Creation," *The Past*, *The Collected Works of Yu Dafu*, Vol. III.

*** Zheng Boqi, "Preface to *Short Stories*," Vol. III, *Major Works of New Chinese Literature*.

Qing Dynasty, Yu Dafu expresses his anger as he protests against evil forces. The tone is different from that of Guo Moruo's poetry, which is crisp, indignant and optimistic. His fiction is often solemn and mournful. This, of course, had much to do with the personality and life experience of the writer. But it also shows how he had been influenced by the sombre literary works, Chinese and foreign, especially those of the Qing poet Huang Zhongze, Rousseau, Dostoyevsky as well as the "end-of-the-century" literature.

Although the works of Yu Dafu are characterized mainly by their strong romanticism with a sombre tone, elements of realism increased as his experience and observation of social realities gradually gained depth. This is noticeable in some of his short stories in the collection *Cold Ashes*, "The Spring Night of Intoxication," written in 1923, contrasts the down-and-out protagonist "I," who ekes out a meaningless livelihood by selling his writings, with the strong-willed and honest cigarette-factory worker Chen Ermei, who is unflinching in her struggle against difficulties. In the story Yu Dafu commends the good heart of the woman worker and her simple rebellious spirit. He also exposes the existing evils and sneers at the weakness and incompetence of "the pitiful unknown men of letters." "A Humble Sacrifice," written in 1924, is an elegy for a good-natured and dutiful rickshaw man who works extremely hard every day. He dreams that one day he will be able to buy himself a rickshaw. But this remains an empty dream, for heavy stress eventually kills him. The narrator, the "I" in the story, is full of sympathy for the rickshawman, but also feels that he cannot help. All he can do is to give him "a humble sacrifice" of a paper rickshaw. "A Mild Snowy Morning," written in 1927, is a tragic story about a university student who comes from the countryside. These stories, which delineate people who are oppressed and wronged, condemn the crimes of the old society and Yu Dafu himself believes that they "are somewhat coloured by socialist thought."* They also indicate that he was further inclined towards socialism as he gradually matured as a writer. Although "The Past," written before "A Mild Snowy Morning," already shows his artistic

* Yu Dafu, "Preface to *Works Selected by Dafu*."

maturity and basic realist approach, it nevertheless cannot be compared with the three aforementioned stories, containing as it does laments of the passing of youth and love. In the stories written in the early 1930s such as "The Late Osmanth Flowers," "The Alms-Begging Monk" and "Late Evening," the style is serene and transparent and the characters have an endearing freshness about them. However, these stories glorify seclusion and resignation, reflecting a person's state of mind in the late evening. They are far removed from the realities of the turbulent society of that time.

In his stories, Yu Dafu often unreservedly describes "abnormal sex psychology" and highlights the significance of sexual love. The sentimental romanticism of these works is thus given a certain colour of decadence. The short story "The Bleak Night" and the novella *Stray Sheep* described the sexual frustrations of young men and their encounters with prostitutes. Even in *She Is a Weak Woman*, a novella which is mainly about the life of women workers, there are descriptions of abnormal sex. Of course, such descriptions are linked to the protagonist's grudge against the world and the pursuit of liberation of individuality. But by resorting to the techniques of naturalism in these descriptions of sexual love and carnal desires the writer inevitably weakens or even does harm to the positive content of thought in his work. Thus, in *Stray Sheep* the writer's original intention is to depict the unbending character of a young actress, which shows itself as she lives her miserable life. But in the novel, prominence is given to the descriptions of a woman when she gains sexual love and sadness when she loses it. Consequently, much of the positive social meaning of the novel is lost.

In addition to fiction, Yu Dafu wrote many essays and his achievement in that genre has also been well recognized. The style in many of his works of fiction is delicate and charming, much like the exquisite style of his essays. In expressing true feelings elegantly, these essays "well reveal the frustration of a gifted intellectual living in times of turmoil."* "An Open Letter to Literary Youths," in *Cold Ashes*, is a passionate call on the young people to rebel against the old social order. The more than twenty short essays collected under "Trivial Words" in *Broken Pieces* discuss current affairs and satirize political events. Still more attractive is his book of travels, *Footprints Everywhere*, in which he describes gracefully the landscape: its vast expanse, the mountains and streams, the light and shade. Through these descriptions, he reveals his thoughts and feelings. Sometimes what he wants to say is only hinted at. Occasionally, he includes poems written in the classical style, thus enriching the artistic content of the piece. "Spring Day at Fishing Terrace," for example, is a fine piece of writing. He visits Tongjun at night and leaves for Fuchun in the morning. The scenes on the journey are vividly described and the poem included in his prose further conveys his deep feelings:

> *It is not that I treasure my health before the wine,*
> *Alas, feigned madness will be mistaken for the truth!*
> *Overtaken by drink, I once whipped my famous horse.*
> *I dread that my excessive love may break a beauty's heart.*
> *Predestined doom surely is the sin of heaven.*
> *Cocks crowing, storms raging, the waves churn up dregs of the sea.*
> *Bitter tears and laments — what is their ultimate use?*
> *Righteous men are all talking about Emperor Qin.*

A striking characteristic of his travel accounts, then, is the weaving of thoughts and feelings, which come from his concerns about China and her people, into the descriptions of scenes. Yu Dafu has thus given the literary traveloque, which has a long tradition in Chinese literature, the colour of his times.

Among writers of the Creation Society, the course of Yu Dafu's life and literary career was the most tortuous. Following in the footsteps of the Chinese people in their anti-imperialist and anti-feudal struggles since May Fourth Movement, he continued to make progress in his political thinking. Sometimes, however, there

* Ah Ying, "Preface to *The Essays of Yu Dafu*," *The Essays of Sixteen Modern Writers*, Guangming Press, March 1935.

were deviations and relapses. He hated the rule of the warlords, old and new. In "Nine Diaries," he condemns Chiang Kai-shek's betrayal of the revolution. He also joined the League for Freedom in China and the China League for the Defence of Civil Rights. But in the midst of intense struggle, he often held back. For a few years, too, he lived in seclusion. Then in his last novella *Flight*, written in 1935, he pointedly deals with the theme of class struggle in the countryside.

In spite the twists and contradictions in Yu Dafu's life and literary career, he "remained faithful to May Fourth, not once betraying May Fourth."* To the very end he did not lose a progressive intellectual's virtues of loyalty and dedication to noble ideals. In 1938, at the invitation of Guo Moruo, he went to Wuhan and took part in the anti-Japanese work organized there. Later, he moved first to Singapore and then to Sumatra and other places, where he was actively involved in the anti-Japanese activities of the overseas Chinese, editing progressive newspapers and periodicals. In September 1945 he was assassinated by the Japanese imperialists in Sumatra.

Zhang Ziping (1895-1959), a prolific writer, was for some time a prominent member of the Creation Society. He began writing full-length novels early. Like Yu Dafu, he wrote about his life in Japan. But he did not use a strong and subjective romantic style. Instead, he turned to the techniques of realism, concentrating more on the objective delineation of people and events. But as revealed in his works, "his realism is rather superficial and he has not touched the hearts of the matter."** Most of his novels deal with the tragedy of love. In his early works, such as the short story "She Gazes Sadly at Her Native Land" and "Spring in the Mei Mountains" as well in his full-length novel "Fossils in the Alluvion," he raises certain social issues. Artistically, they also have their merits. Later, however, he was more and more occupied with the portrayal of the eternal triangle of love, even resorting to pornographic writing

---

* Hu Yuzhi, "The Exile of Yu Dafu and His Disappearance," *The New Literature: Historical Materials*, 1978, Vol. I.

** Zheng Boqi, Preface to *The Short Stories*, Vol. III, *Major Works of New Chinese Literature*.

and the exploitation of sex in his works, which are naturally, further and further removed from the anti-imperialist and anti-feudal spirit of the May Fourth new literature.

The early Creation Society writers also included Zheng Boqi and Cheng Fangwu. Though Zheng Boqi (1895-1979) did not write much, his stories and plays collected in *Resistance* have definite social meaning. The short story "The First Lesson," written in 1922, describes the experiences and feelings of a Chinese student in Japan, thereby exposing the imperialist nature of Japanese militarist education. Though it is more like a sketch than a story, it is among the first works which treat the theme of anti-imperialism. At the time, it was most valuable. The one-act play *Resistance* dramatizes how the patriotic youth fight the imperialist soldiers who try to harass Chinese women. It reflects the ever-rising patriotic, anti-imperialist feelings of the masses after the May 30th Incident of 1925. These works have a definite combative hallmark. Simple and direct in the treatment of theme, they contain rather special features among the works of the Creation Society members.

Cheng Fangwu (1897-1984) was engaged mainly in the work of literary theory and criticism. However, his collection *Wandering* also includes graceful poems and sketch-like short stories. In some respects, his works resemble those of Guo Moruo. His one-act play *The Welcome Party*, published in 1923, dramatizes the clash between the old and the new generations in a feudal family. The play removes the hypocritical masks of the ruling forces, as it presents the righteous revolt of the young generation. It was also one of the early plays which denounce the decadent American bourgeois culture.

Another influential writer was Feng Yuanjun (1900-74), who was the first to publish short stories in the quarterly *Creation* and *Creation Weekly*, under the penname of Miss Gan. In the stories, "Separation," "Journey" and "After Separation" collected in *Juanshi*, which together loosely form a sequence, she writes about the courageous rebellion of two young lovers against feudal conventions as they passionately pursue the happiness of love and the freedom of choice in marriage. The use of confessional monologue fully reveals the goings-on in the character's mind. Though in these works, as Lu Xun observes, "the writer is trying to reason out something, he does not let this affect his writing, which is natural."* Her story "Traces of Spring," written in letter form a little later, is not much more than fragments of prose. Feng Yuanjun eventually turned to the study of history of literature.

Younger writers of the Creation Society were influenced in different ways by the two leading writers of the Society, Guo Moruo and Yu Dafu. The short stories of Ni Yide were collected in *Autumn in Lake Xuan Wu, The Shores of the Eastern Sea* and *Lilies.* In these works, he tells of his life story, sometimes sighing over his misfortunes and sometimes expressing the feeling of loss as he recalls his bygone love. Through these narrations and recollections, he shows his dissatisfaction with and indignation against the social conventions and the out-dated marriage customs. Some of these works carry the Yu Dafu-type of deep melancholy tone. Feng Naichao's early poems, collected in *The Red Gauze Lantern*, are rhythmic and colourful, but they celebrate only "Heavy smoke in the wilderness; heavy dejection."** After 1927, however, his thinking and style changed drastically as the Creation Society went through dramatic changes. In "Move Along, Fast" and "Songs of Today," the feeling of emptiness is completely gone from his poems published in the *Creation Monthly.* Instead, one finds his denunciation of the idle landlords' exploitation of the peasants. He also fiercely satirizes the rule of the Kuomintang warlords in his three-act comedy *A County Magistrate.*

Significant changes took place in the Creation Society after the May 30th Movement of 1925 and the First Revolutionary Civil War from 1921 to 1927. Leading members of the Society including Guo Moruo and Cheng Fangwu had been given the baptism of practical revolutionary struggle. Many young writers had also joined the Society after their study in Japan and they were pushing for a change of direction, towards revolution. In 1928 the Creation Society and the newly-formed Sun Society jointly advocated a proletarian revolutionary literature. They were actively engaged in

---

* Lu Xun, Preface to *The Short Stories*, Vol. II, *Major Works of New Chinese Literature.*

** "The Forlorn, Ancient Moon," *The Red Gauze Lantern.*

the introduction of Marxist literary theories through translation. Some of the members left the Society either because of differences in personal opinion (Yu Dafu), or the change of political direction (Zhang Ziping and Wang Duqing). In its later years, the Creation Society was influenced by Leftist dogmatism and published articles containing erroneous views. However, even so, the truth remains that the Society did play a very important role in bringing the new literature and the revolutionary movement closely together.

V. The Tattler, the New Moon and Other Literary Societies; Works of Zhou Zuoren, Xu Zhimo, Wen Yiduo, Ding Xilin and Others

In addition to the two major literary societies discussed above, there were other active and influential ones such as the Tattler, the Unnamed, the Sunken Bell and the New Moon.

The Tattler Society was named after its weekly, first published in November 1924. Its leading members and contributors were Lu Xun, Zhou Zuoren, Qian Xuantong, Sun Fuyuan, Chuan Dao, Feng Wenbing, Xu Qinwen and Lin Yutang. Originally, they were all closely associated with the supplement of the *Morning News*. After the paper came under the control of the Literary Research Society, they found the weekly *The Tattler*. Unlike the Literary Research Society and the Creation Society, which had definite literary viewpoints of their own, the Tattler Society merely announced in the first issue of the weekly that it "seeks to promote liberal thinking, independent judgment and their richness of life."* From its start the weekly showed progressive tendencies, for it wanted to "voice protests against dogmatic arbitrariness and despicable meanness."** It published "mainly articles containing precise thoughts and criticisms, although there is also room for creative writing and articles on literature, art and ideas."*** Special columns were also created such as "Random Thoughts" and "Causal Talk" which were aimed

* See "Foreword" to the first number of *The Tattler*.

** *Ibid.*

*** *Ibid.*

at the vices of the day. The continued publication of this kind of prose brought into being what was then known as "the Tattler style." Lu Xun, the "General of the Tattler School," published not only his short stories in the weekly such as "Master Gao" and "Divorce," but also many essays. These essays were later collected in *Bad Luck*, *Bad Luck (II)*, *And That's That* and *Three Leisures*; the prose poems, in the volume *Wild Grass*.

Under the support and influence of Lu Xun, *The Tattler* stressed criticism of society and culture. Its special combative stand was based on the members' belief in "free talk, the removal of inhibitions, hastening the introduction of the new and repelling anything of the old which may prove harmful to the new"* In all the significant political struggles of the day, *The Tattler* always stood firm in the progressive camp: in the battle with the remnants of feudalism, old and young, over the expulsion of Puyi from the Imperial Palace at the end of 1924; in the anti-Japanese and anti-British imperialism campaigns after the May 30th Incident of 1925 and in the exposure of the bloody massacre of March 18th of 1926 by the Duan Qirui government. Throughout these campaigns Lu Xun, Qian Xuantong, Zhou Zuoren and other leading members of the Tattler Society, together with other progressive writers such as Liu Bannong, Zheng Zhenduo and Zhu Ziqing, wrote against the reactionary forces. *The Tattler*'s attack was particularly fierce in exposing the *Modern Review*, which received financial support from the warlord government and accordingly fawned on the feudal forces and the imperialist powers. From the verbal attacks emerged a precise, critical and causal prose which is full of pungency and humour—"the Tattler style."

However, members of the Tattler Society did not have a uniform style. Zhou Zuoren and Lu Xun, for example, differed widely from each other as writers. A younger brother of Lu Xun by four years, Zhou Zuoren (1885-1968) received the same kind of education in his childhood and youth. They went to Japan together to study and participated in the same literary activities. Together, they translated *Stories from Other Lands* (1909). Together, they

* Lu Xun, "*The Tattler* and I," *Three Leisures*.

joined the *New Youth* and edited *The Tattler*, but later their literary paths diverged. During the May Fourth new culture movement, basically Zhou Zuoren still belonged to the new culture camp represented by Chen Duxiu, Li Dazhao and Lu Xun. Actively engaged in the translation and introduction of progressive foreign literature, he was one of the chief translators of *New Youth*. His article "The Literature of Man," published in the magazine at the end of 1918, was a significant piece of work after Hu Shi's "Modest Proposals for the Reform of Literature" and Chen Duxiu's "On the Literary Revolution." In this article on the literary revolution Zhou Zuoren suggests that "the literature of man is a written record and study of the problems of life based on humanism."* Although, essentially, in his viewpoints he could not go beyond the confines of European bourgeois progressive literary thought, his explorations in literary theories greatly enlightened the readers at the time. The influence was definitely positive. Shortly afterwards, Zhou Zuoren advocated "a people's literature," propagating his progressive literary ideas.

In early 1919, Zhou Zuoren began publishing vernacular poems in the *New Youth*. Poems such as "The Little Stream," "Two Snow Sweepers," "On the Road," "The North Wind" and "The Painter" express his thoughts and feelings in a fresh language. Although, as he himself said, "the language of these 'poems' is that of prose and the content is nothing extraordinary,"** his poems had a positive influence on the early development of the new poetry. They are entirely devoid of the tone of self-pity found in some of the old poetry and free from the control of thought imposed by the old prosody. These poems were later chosen by the Literary Research Society for the anthology *Snowy Morning* (Volume II). They were also collected in *My Past Life*, a selected volume edited by the writer himself. "The Little Stream," "The Painter" and "The Wrong Path" delicately convey the writer's quiet reflections on life, taking the reader into a refreshing new world.

After his early attempts at poetry, Zhou Zuoren turned to writing essays, which were published in the Supplement of the

---

* *New Youth*, Vol. V, No. 6.

** Zhou Zuoren, "Preface to *My Past Life*."

Morning News and in *The Tattler*. Gradually he found his own prose style. Yu Dafu once compared the styles of Lu Xun and Zhou Zuoren. "Lu Xun's style is sharp," he wrote. "It is like a dagger, a few inches of steel which can cut to the bone. He grasps the main points and they are expressed clearly in a few words.... By contrast, Zhou Zuoren's style is relaxed and facile. If read casually, his essays may give the impression that they are diffusive and overloaded with insignificant details. A closer reading, however, will make one feel that every sentence in his random talk has its strength and that it cannot be removed without seriously affecting the unity of the work. The same is true of each word, which cannot be changed.... The two writers also differ in their wit and humour. Lu Xun is a master of satire, which is pungent and incisive. Zhou Zuoren, on the other hand, inclines towards irony which is gentle and calm."* Yu Dafu's remarks accurately describe the essential differences between the two writers.

The early essays of Zhou Zuoren were collected in *A Garden of My Own*, *Books for a Rainy Day*, *The Dragon* and *The Tiger*. Some of the essays, sarcastic in tone, are about the vices of the day. "Wounded," for example, through the writer's use of irony, denounces the warlord government's suppression of the patriotic movement. In a similar style, the essay "Silence" criticizes the government's efforts to destroy freedom of speech. Through his humour, Zhou Zuoren makes plain his likes and dislikes to the reader. He deals with literary topics in essays such as "The Function of Poetry," "The Unity of Literature and Art," "Literature and Art and Morality" and "On Short Poems." There are also reviews on the works of other writers, for example, "Sinking," "The Tales of Oscar Wilde," "Where Are You Going?" and "Dreams." In all his literary discussions, the reasoning out of ideas is done through a casual style conveying his random thoughts. There are even more essays, which describe the familiar matters of daily life or which recall the past such as "Bitter Rain," "Recollections," "A Chapter of School Life," "Wild Herbs Edible from My Hometown," "Cakes and Sweetmeats in Beijing," "On Tea-Drinking" and "Letters from the Hills."

* Yu Dafu, Preface to *Essays*, Vol. II, *Major Works of New Chinese Literature*.

These essays do not contain any startlingly new ideas, but they make pleasant reading, as they naturally reveal the inner world of the writer. They are, as he put it, "his chats on paper."* Thus, in "Letters from the Hills," he calmly and plainly writes about his confused state of mind while he is convalescing in the Azure Cloud Temple in the Fragrant Hills, Beijing:

> The chiming of the Buddhist bells at dawn and in the evening seems to be urging us, who do not have any belief or sense of belonging, to choose a proper path. Recently, I have suffered from wavering and confusion of thought. To the highest degree, it may be said. Tolstoy's selfless love, Nietzsche's superman, the ideals of communal life, the belief that man is born good, the teachings of Christ, the Buddha and Confucius—all these have an equal appeal to me and I respect them all. But I cannot blend them to form a theory which can guide me through life. All these ideas are stored higgledy-piggledy in my mind. They are truly like the goods in the shops in my hometown.**

Indeed, the thoughts in Zhou Zuoren's essays are diffusive. However, his essays have the virtue of naturalness, and they are quite different from the artificial "eight-legged" prose of the old literature. Thus Hu Shi wrote in 1922: "The most noteworthy prose works for the past few years are those by Zhou Zuoren, among others.... Their achievement has completely shattered the myth that 'elegant prose cannot be written in the vernacular.'"*** In the Preface to *Prose*, Volume II, of *Major Works of New Chinese Literature*, Yu Dafu pointed out that "of the works of modern Chinese prose, those by Lu Xun and Zhou Zuoren are the richest and the most outstanding." These observations explain the influence of the early essays of Zhou Zuoren in his day.

After the April 12th Incident of 1927, Lu Xun, having learned "a lesson written in blood," gave up his belief in evolution and accepted the world outlook of Marxism. Consequently, his essays gained more lustre. By contrast, Zhou Zuoren moved out of "the

* Preface to *A Garden of My Own*.

** Zhou Zuoren, *A Garden of My Own*, p. 304. In the same essay published in *Book for a Rainy Day*, he changed the expression "ideals of communal life" to "communism."

*** Hu Shi, *Chinese Literature of the Past Fifty Years*.

tower at the crossroads" into the ivory tower. He first preached "the Doctrine of the Mean" and "tolerance," then advocated the writing of "essays for leisure reading," and later even attacked the "Left-wing literature and art movement." In the end he even supported "national capitulation." After the outbreak of the War of Resistance Against Japan, he remained in Beijing and eventually degenerated into traitor.

The Tattler did not publish many short stories. Among those which did get into print, occasionally, were the pieces by Feng Wenbing and Xu Qinwen. The short stories of Feng Wenbing (also known as Feiming, 1901-67) first appeared in the weekly *Endeavour*. He began to shine as a writer after "The Story of the Bamboo Grove" was published in *The Tattler*. His stories are mainly about villagers, old and young, and he chose to depict the charm of their simple daily life rather than try to look for social meaning in the treatment of theme. Though called short stories, they are really closer to essays. The content of his early pieces such as "Special Envelop" and "Women Clothes-Washers" may appear to be rather thin, but these stories do show progressive tendencies. In his later stories such as "Peach Garden," "Dates" and 'Bridge," he writes mainly about the familiar matters of daily life and local customs. These works are rich in artistic style and the characters presented are full of their own traits. In the stories written after these, however, he is obsessed with the treatment of obscure ideas. His language also becomes more and more involved and difficult. Commenting on the obscurity and ambiguity of Feng Wenbing's style, Lu Xun remarked that "it is deliberate meandering, a reflection of the self-pity of the writer."*

Xu Qinwen (1899-), by 1927, had already published the collections of short stories *Hometown* and *A Pair of Woollen Socks*, as well as three novella. Though he also wrote about the life of the villagers, he was quite different from Feng Wenbing. His early works, published in the Supplement of the *Morning News*, indicate that in technique he was not yet mature as a writer. Neither did he manage to clearly delineate his characters. However, in the stories

* Lu Xun, *Essays of Qiejieting (II)*, Preface to *The Short Stories*, Vol. II, *Major Works of New Chinese Literature*.

"An Insane Woman," "Shidang" and "The Death of Yuanzheng," he already focuses on the miserable state of the labourers in the village. In his novella *Ah'er and His Runny Nose*, written a little later, he tells of the life of a wronged woman Ju Hua, thereby exposing the injustice of feudal customs and the damaging traditional moral values of the villagers in the eastern Zhejiang Province. Many of his other works deal with the life of young intellectuals. In these, he either depicts their emotional conflicts with light-hearted humour or satirizes their selfish and unhealthy pursuit of love. "The Ideal Companion," "Verbal Promises" and "The Suspicions of a Younger Sister" were written in the writer's humorous and subtle style. But they lack depth. He had reservations in his satire, and the social meaning was not too strong. More deserving of mention is "My Cousin's Garden," which portrays how a young intellectual who wants to do something meaningful is eventually crushed by the surrounding forces. This sad story brought out the deeply-hidden grief of the young people at the time.

The Wilderness Society and the Unnamed Society shared much the same outlook, in general, as the Tattler Society. Founded in October 1925, the Wilderness Society published the weekly *The Wilderness*, edited by Lu Xun. Its aim was "to be direct and honest in expression its views, to recognize the present reality and hope for a better future."* In the attack on the old forces, it was more aggressive than *The Tattler*. It also had closer links with the student movements of the day. Its prominent members were Gao Changhong, Wei Suyuan, Li Jiye, Huang Pengji, Shang Yue, Tai Jingnong and Xiang Peiliang. However, soon Gao Changhong and others, who were deeply influenced by the philosophy of Nietzsche, broke away. They founded the Hurricane Society in Shanghai and promoted the so-called "hurricane movement" which stressed extreme individualism. Their publication was *Hurricane*. Later the Wilderness Society merged with the Unnamed Society and the weekly *The Wilderness* changed its name to *The Unnamed*. In addition to creative writing, the Unnamed Society introduced and translated

* From Lu Xun's announcement of the publication of *The Wilderness* weekly. See the advertisement column in *Beijing Daily*, April 21, 1925.

foreign literary works, especially literary works from Russia. The young writers of the Wilderness-Unnamed Society received support and guidance from Lu Xun, who edited for them the *Motley Series* and the *Unnamed Series,* which consisted mainly creative writing and translations respectively. The two series had a great deal of influence at the time.

Tai Jingnong was the leading writer of the Unnamed Society. The fourteen short stories in his collection *Sons of the Earth* drew their material from the lives of the people. In a simple but rather rugged style, each story gives a picture of "the pain and misery of the human world." In this world one finds: an old woman driven to insanity and death after all the members of her family have been killed during the war ("New Graves"); a young village girl, who is chosen to be an object of sacrifice because feudal beliefs have it that marrying her to a dying man can save his life—it does not, of course, and she is soon widowed ("Flames of the Candle"); poverty-stricken parents who are forced to sell their children ("Earthworms"); a much-wronged man whose wife is taken away from him because the local wealthy tyrant fancies her and he is duly thrown into gaol ("The Wounded"); desperate people who risk their lives trying to get out of their plight ("Red Lantern"). Though the portrayal of the goings-on may not be deep enough, these works are nevertheless truthful sketches of village life. Stories such as "Brother Tian" and "At the Wedding" vividly describe the customs observed in the village. "While writers vie with one another in writing about the joys and sorrows of love, the various aspects of life in the cities," Lu Xun pointed out, "Tai Jingnong, more than anybody else, concentrates on what goes on in the village and reproduces the country air in his works."* Indeed, these are the valuable features of the short stories in *Sons of the Earth.* In a later collection published in 1928, *The Pagoda Builders,* Tai Jingnong writes about the tyrannical rule of the new warlords and the revolutionary martyrs who firmly continued their struggle under white terrorism. But owing to his lack of practical experience, the characters tend to pale next to those in his former works.

* Lu Xun, *Essays of Qiejieting (II),* Preface to *The Short Stories,* Vol. II, *Major Works of New Chinese Literature.*

In its emphasis, the Sunken Bell Society was different from the Tattler and Unnamed societies. After its founding in 1925 in Beijing, the Society published *The Sunken Bell* weekly, which was later changed to a half-monthly magazine. In a period of almost ten years the Sunken Bell Society writers "look outwards for nourishment from foreign countries and inwards in search of their own souls. They want to discover the eyes and tongues of their minds, so that they can see the world clearly and sing songs of truth and beauty to the lonely souls."* Both in literary creation and in the translation of the foreign works, mainly works by German authors, these writers did a lot of solid work and contributed much to the development of the new literature. Thus Lu Xun praised them: "They are the most tenacious, most honest group in China. Their struggle is also the longest."**

The leading writers of fiction of the Sunken Bell Society were Chen Weimo (1903-55) and Chen Xianghe (1901-69). In Chen Weimo's short stories, collected in *By the Stove*, the characters are often "those who have not been cared for and loved." They "are born in loneliness and grow up in loneliness. They will pass away and be buried in loneliness."*** In the foreword to the collection, he stated that he wanted to "find out how much room there is in my small heart for the miseries coming from outside." This further accounts for the feeling of loneliness that pervades his works. Characters in Chen Xianghe's stories are often pessimistic, but nevertheless hard-struggling young intellectuals. They are not favoured by fortune and understandably they go against the opposing forces. In these characters, one can also see shades of the writer's own life and experience. Among the stories collected in *Restless Soul*, "Mourning for—" and "Restless Soul" contain truthful portraits of young people, even though these stories suffer from lack of artistic refinement.

There are also works in *The Sunken Bell* which directly deal with social realities. For example, Chen Weimo's "A Vicious Gener-

---

* Lu Xun, "Preface to *The Short Stories*," Vol. II, *Major Works of New Chinese Literature, Essays of Qiejieting (II)*.

** *Ibid.*

*** "People Who Look for Dreams," *By the Stove*.

al" and "Wailing over the Beacon-Fire" portray the sufferings of the people of central Sichuan Province during the fighting among the warlords. In "Sinking One's Own Boat," Gao Shihua goes beyond Chen Weimo, as he describes the fighting spirit of the boat people who choose to die so that their oppressors will also be drowned. Their attempt to "seek life in death" is an act of heroism, though not unaccompanied with grief.

Feng Zhi (1905-), prominent member of the Sunken Bell Society, was known mainly for his poetry. Most of early poems were collected in *Songs of Yesterday*. They are mainly love poems, although occasionally he expresses his sympathy for the suffering poor, as in "Evening Post" and other poems. His language is polished and natural; his sentiment, delicate and sincere. But the poems often have a melancholy tone, prompting the feeling of loss as one "witnesses a vanishing dream or a fading smoke." So one reads in the first stanza of "I Am a Small Stream":

I am a small stream.
Not by design do I flow by your side;
Not by design do you cast your shadow—
Much like a rosy cloud,
On my soft, gentle flow.

The feeling is sincere and in "The Silkworm" the same sincere yearning is expressed, this time by repeating the same two lines at the beginning of each of the three stanzas:

If you shed a few tears listening to my song;
No need to look out of the window and ask, "Who are You?"

The dispiritedness in much his poetry was of course his own, but it was also objective reflection of the spiritual depression of the period, when the young intellectuals who had been awakened after the May Fourth Movement felt that they were unable to get out of their individual private world. The most striking characteristic of Feng Zhi's poetry is his depth of feeling and warmth of expression. About his lonely state of mind, he wrote:

Loneliness is a long snake
Lying there, cold and wordless.

However, this snake is far from being cold as it may have appeared. It is being "burned by the thoughts of home" and it is "thinking of the lush meadows." It does something more:

> *Gently, like the moonlight,*
> *Surreptitiously it slips away from you,*
> *Bringing me, for my sake, your dream—*
> *Your dream like a flower, so bright, so red!*

The deep feeling of loneliness and the low spirits found in Feng Zhi's poetry, in fact, had to do with his yearning for a better life. That yearning is made clear in the poem "The Hurricane," in which the poet waits for the arrival of a goddess who "ladles out water from the Heavenly River and washes a dying planet" so as to "give it a good and different shine." In other poems such as "The Bamboo Flute Player" and "Curtains," he narrates legendary love tragedies, condemning the evils of the feudal marriage system as he writes about the young people's ideals of love.

A Northern Journey and Other Poems was the product of Feng Zhi's first contacts with social realities. In content, the poems have more realist substance. The range of emotion and thought is also wider than that in his previous works. However, the musical notes are still those flowing out of the flute, quiet and moving, rather than the sound coming from war-drums and bugles. He is meticulous in the choice of diction and the use of rhyme. The melody is gentle and soothing; the beauty of rhythm is hidden in the flow of his verse. No wonder Lu Xun hailed him as "the most outstanding lyrical poet."* After the 1930s, Feng Zhi was engaged mainly in research on foreign literature and his poetic output was relatively small. In *Sonnets*, written during the anti-Japanese war, he explored the fourteen-line poetic form and made a further contribution to the development of modern Chinese poetry.

Yang Hui, playwright of the Sunken Bell Society, was best known for his later work *Emperor Ling of Chu*. His first work was the four-act play *Visitor*, published in the Supplement of the *Morning News* in 1923. The mood of the play is gloomy. His

* Lu Xun, *Essays of Qiejieting (II)*, Preface to *The Short Stories*, Vol. II, *Major Works of New Chinese Literature*.

other plays published in *The Sunken Bell* shortly after show a change in tone and style. *New Year's Eve*, *Tears of Laughter* and *In the Shade of an Old Tree* draw material from the lives of the poor, whose deeply-hidden sorrows are brought out in their forced smiles. *Celebrating the Baby's First Month* presents sad events caused by the scramble for family property. The atmosphere of the play, in spite of its superficial gaiety, is gloomy and sinister. Yang Hui was able to portray depth of personality in his characterizations. While the works of most members of the Sunken Bell Society incline towards romanticism, his one-act plays contain more elements of realism.

In 1922 Ying Xiuren (1900-33), Pan Mohua (1902-34), Feng Xuefeng (1902-76) and Wang Jingzhi (1902-) founded in Hangzhou the Lakeside Poetry Society. It was then generally known as the society which "genuinely and wholeheartedly devotes itself to the writing of love poetry."* The society published two anthologies, *Lakeside* and *Songs of Spring*. In addition, Wang Jingzhi had two collections of his own, *Breeze of the Orchid* and *Lonely Country*. Most of them are short poems of a few lines, describing love of the fleeting feelings of the poets. One of them reads as follows:

I regret to have let him go out,
I regret not to have gone with him.
For hours I've been waiting for him,
Yet he's not back,
I've been to many places looking for him,
But he's not seen anywhere.

Another poem goes:

Your eyes are as sharp as scissors
Capable of untying any knot;
Otherwise, why my shackled soul gets free
As soon as your eyes fall upon me?

These poems, though specific, subjective in content, played a positive role after the May Fourth Movement in 1919, when young people wanted to try new literary forms reflecting their yearning

* Zhu Ziqing, "Preface to *Poetry*," *Major Works of New Chinese Literature*.

to break away from the old ethical conventions. Ying Xiuren and Pan Mohua broke with the limitation of expressing personal grief and happiness in their works and also reflected the social problems. Pan Mohua (Pan Xun) in particular vividly portrayed characters such as A'gui and Huochi and a desolate scene in China's countryside around 1919 in his stories such as "Heart Turning to the Countryside," "In the Human World" and "At the Night." They were later collected in *Raindrops.* Works on such themes as rural life and the peasants were rarely seen in China's literary circles in 1922 and 1923.

More prominent than of the Sunken Bell and the Lakeside Poetry societies was the New Moon Society, founded in Beijing in 1923. Its leading members were all students returned to China from England and America. At its inception, they did not make any declaration about their literary principles. However, from the essays written by its members, it can be deduced that their common belief was that art should be above everything. Some of their slogans are: "When beauty is seen in nature, that natural beauty will be seen as resembling art"; "Art does not serve life; on the contrary, life serves art"; "Absolute realism means the bankruptcy of art." Their object was to establish "a pure art."* Obviously, this topsy-turvy view of the relation between art and life, based on the ideology of idealism rather than materialism, was derived from decadent Western bourgeois literary thinking.

In 1926 the Supplement of the *Morning News* created a poetry section, edited by Xu Zhimo. In March 1928 the *New Moon* monthly made its first appearance in Shanghai. From the essays published in the magazine, such as Xu Zhimo's "The Attitude of the *New Moon*" and Liang Shiqiu's "Literature and Revolution," among others, it was clear that they had adopted an open stand against revolutionary literature. They tried to give the impression that in their viewpoints they transcended class, using as they did terms such as "healthiness," "dignity" and "general human nature." In truth, however, they were advocating bourgeois literary theories. The key members of the New Moon group, such as Hu Shi, had a

* Quotations are from Wen Yiduo's "Prosody," Zhao Taimou's "National Drama" and Yu Shangyuan's Preface to *National Drama Movement.*

strong political consciousness and their theory of "art for art's sake" was adopted merely as a red herring. The achievements and short-comings of Xu Zhimo, Wen Yiduo and other New Moon writers differed. Their careers also followed different courses later.

The most important representative of the New Moon Society was Xu Zhimo (1891-1931), generally known as the "chief" of the New Moon Poetry school. In 1922 he returned to China after a spell of academic study in England. He taught at Beijing University and at other universities in Shanghai. Teaching duties apart, he was actively engaged in the writing of poetry, essays and stories. In the ten creative years before his death in an air crash, he published several volumes of poetry: *Poems of Zhimo*, *A Night in Florence*, *Fierce Tiger* and *Wandering*, which was published after his death. In addition, there were essays collected in *Fallen Leaves*, *Analysis* and *Traces of Paris* as well as short stories in *The Wheel*. All these works amply demonstrate his superior artistic talent. They also reflect his rise and fall as a writer.

Most of Xun Zhimo's poems written in the early period after he returned to China were collected in *Poems of Zhimo*, published in 1925. Some of these poems such as "A Gentle Song for Fallen Leaves" and "Fragments of a Poem" overflow with the feeling of loss. Most of the others, however, are positive in content, fresh in tone, and lively and natural in form. In the terrible times of fighting among the warlords, the poet nourished his sympathy, based on humanism, for the suffering people. He wrote "A Strange World," "Master, Master," "Several Pieces of Oiled Paper for Cover," "Scenes of Peace and Prosperity" and "A Gloomy Life," among others, which are filled with sorrow and indignation. His manner of writing is close to the realist approach as he describes the rugged paths of life and the pains of mankind. He remarked, "The turbulent passions in my early works have gone, but my feelings still overflow in most of my poems."* As he surveyed the forlorn scene, he wrote:

By myself, by myself I meditate on this strange world—

---

* Xu Zhimo, Preface to *Fierce Tiger*.

*Who is singing the inharmonious, man-made musical notes?**

Xu Zhimo did not comprehend that the deep sufferings of the Chinese people originated from the invasion of the imperialists and the rule of feudalism. He placed hope in the British and American brand of democracy. In "Searching for a Star," "Baby" and other poems, he yearns for the pursuit and realization of bourgeois democracy. The tone is optimistic as he uses the image of a baby to symbolize British and American democracy. So he waits "in anticipation of the birth of a big, white baby."** Such a yearning found an echo in the hearts of many young people of the May Fourth Movement period. *Poems of Zhimo* chimes in with the voice of the May Fourth period and as such, it can be regarded as a product of contemporary thinking.

History has since proved that the British and American brand of democracy cannot save China. The "big, white baby" that Xu Zhimo was waiting for has not been born in China. As Mao Dun remarked, "that was why Xu Zhimo became disillusioned.... Evidence of his disillusionment is obvious in his works after *Poems of Zhimo*; that is, *A Night in Florence* and *Fierce Tiger*."*** In *A Night in Florence*, Xu Zhimo has not yet completely forgotten the woes of mankind. The poem "Marshall," for example, describes the sufferings brought about by the warlords. In "Songs of the Lushan Mountain Stone-Cutters," the poet still retains his sympathy for the labouring masses. However, many of the poems in the collection have a sense of loss and dispiritedness about them. In the poem "Dagu Harbour, Late Night, March 12," he writes:

Today's hopes are tomorrow's disappointments,
The stars are shining coldly far above.
Life is but the scum floating in the waves!

Fierce Tiger and his later poems are shrouded in the same gloom. Xu Zhimo described himself as "an incorrigible individualist." To him, "democracy simply means individualism in general." He confessed: "We do not want any hurricane, we want a soft

* Xu Zhimo, "Strange World."
** Xu Zhimo, *Fallen Leaves.*
*** Mao Dun, "On Xu Zhimo," collected in *On Writers*, Literary Press, 1936.

breeze; we do not want any tempest, we want a gentle rain."* The appeal of a leisurely life inevitably made him feel uneasy and scared about revolutionary struggle. In the tempests of the May 30th Movement of 1925 and the Great Revolution of 1927, he wrote essays such as "Blood," "The Anniversary of Lenin's Death —On Revolution," "Romain Rolland" and the poem "Western Window." He kept himself more and more distant from the people and the times.

Xu Zhimo's achievement as a poet is best represented by his lyric poems. The contents of these poems had little to do with the society of his time, but were descriptions of his own feelings, "the lines from the warm spot of my heart," as the poet himself put it. "Good-bye Cambridge" is a good example of Xu's talent and character. His deep love for his old school blended with the unique scene for departure: the sunset paints the willows golden and the ripples in the pond reflect the splendour of a rainbow. In his dream he became "a blade of waterweed in the gentle waves of the Cambridge River." The poet's warmhearted and romantic personality is shown by the poem's graceful and light tone.

In the poem "In the Mountain," Xu Zhimo wrote about how the protagonist "I" longed for his lover who was at a distant mountain.

I do not know
What it is like in the mountain tonight;
There must be moonlight, pine,
And a deeper serene night.

I want to mount the moonlight,
Change into a waft of breeze
Floating in the mountain,
Waking the drowsy pines in spring.

* * *

I'll blow away a new needle-leaf of green
That falls before your window,
As soft as a sigh,
I mustn't startle you from your dream.

---

* Xu Zhimo, "Anniversary of Lenin's Death—On Revolution," *Fallen Leaves.*

With rich imagination and precise language the poet expressed his longing and love for his beloved. The poetic mood was created by the metaphor of the poet as a breeze on the mountain. It conveys his subtle emotions and shows his high level of skill in writing poetry. Xu Zhimo was an important contributor to the development of China's new poetry.

Wen Yiduo was also a leading poet of the New Moon Society. An active promoter of the new poetry, he followed a poetic path which was enormously different from that of Xu Zhimo. In his early days, Wen Yiduo was already strongly attracted to classical poetry and art. He entered Qinghua School in 1913 and after graduation in 1922, went to America for further studies. The nine years of American-style of education at Qinghua School and the three years in America, during which he studied painting, literature and drama, brought him under the influence of aestheticism in literature and art. He adored Keats and Li Yishan, and was determined to be "a loyal devotee of art." In *Red Candles*, published in 1923, one can already see his leaning towards aestheticism and his fondness for an ornate style. Thus, in "The Death of Li Bai" he salutes those who perish in their pursuit of visionary beauty. The poem "Scabbard" expresses the yearning of someone who is so enraptured by the scabbard that he "will love to lose his life in its splendour." In "Colours," he glorifies the supreme beauty of colours.

But there are other aspects in the literary thinking and works of Wen Yiduo. He said in one of his letters that "practical life constantly drags me away from the world of poetry to the world of mundane affairs."* The racial discrimination he experienced abroad and the sinister warlord rule back home aroused his intense patriotic passions. In his letter home, January 1923, he wrote: "Words cannot describe the feelings of a thoughtful Chinese youth who finds himself staying in America.... I have my own country. I have inherited history and culture of five thousand years. In what respect am I not as good as the Americans? Can I not have my pride simply because we have not been able to produce guns and

* *The Works of Wen Yiduo*, Vol. III, pp. 17, 69.

rifles?"* He compared his emotional state to that of "a dormant volcano."** In truth, however, the eruption is obvious in many of his poems. "The Lonely Swan" depicts the power of "a ruthless tyrant" which enables him to rule the world, the power that comes to him after he "gets drunk on the blood of the weak." In the poem "Chrysanthemums, in Recollection," he writes with passionate feelings about "China's flower" and the "flower-like China." His poetry reflects his patriotic yearning to see China. In "Hymn to the Sun," he writes:

Oh Sun—speedy golden bird—Oh Sun!
Let me ride on your back and go round the earth
So that I can see my homeland once a day!

This passionate love for China is even more intense in Wen Yiduo's *Stagnant Water*, published in 1928. In language and metrical discipline, the poems are even more refined; in content, more substantial. "Prayers" and "Only One Sentence" loudly echo the solemn and dignified voices of the people. "Songs of the Launderers" is a righteous condemnation of racial discrimination and the evil power of money which is reigning everywhere in America. Wen Yiduo had high hopes in the future of China and her people. He firmly believed that once "the volcano cannot hold its silence," the imperialists and reactionaries would "tremble, sticking out their tongues and stamping their feet." But the higher his hopes, the greater the disappointment. When he stepped on Chinese soil again, after long years of waiting, he wrote "Discovery" with deep pain:

What I saw was a nightmare; how could it be you?
It was terror; it was a nightmare hanging on a cliff.
It was not you; it was not my love!
I questioned the heavens, pressed the four winds.
I questioned, thundering at the earth's naked chest.
No answer ever came; I cried and called for you.
I vomited; out came my heart—you were in my heart!

---

* *The Works of Wen Yiduo*, Vol. III, pp. 17, 69.
** "Letter to Zang Kejia," *Ibid.*, p. 54.

Not only is the poem steeped in the poetic tradition of classical romanticism, dated back to the ancient poet Qu Yuan; it also reveals the individualistic character of the poet himself.

As he faced the realities with utter honesty after his return to China, Wen Yiduo wrote about the lives of the suffering masses under the rule of the warlords. Accordingly came poems such as "Desolate Village," "Tiananmen" and "Fast Feet," among others. In "A Quiet Night," he shows his deep concern about the fate of China and her people. The scene is made up of brightly shining lamps, "virtuous tables," the aroma of old books, the snores of children —indeed, a scene of tranquillity and happiness. However, the poet's world exists outside this small room. He declares, "Quiet night! I cannot, cannot accept your bribes." He objected to the poets who sang exclusively of their "personal weal and woe." That itself speaks well for Wen Yiduo's convictions as a poet. He refused to associate himself with the foreign reactionary forces. Later, after long searchings of heart, he unreservedly chose the path of the democratic fighters.

In the 1920s, however, Wen Yiduo's narrow conception of "countryism" turned out to be an obstacle to his joining the people's revolutionary movement. His eulogy of national cultural tradition was somewhat tinged with nostalgia and the feeling of "family pride." The sympathy he extended to the suffering masses was still that which came from bourgeois humanism. These were Wen Yiduo's ideological limitations so that after he had cursed the "hopeless, stagnant water" the only thing he could say was: "Let evil cultivate the wasteland!"

As a poet, Wen Yiduo was one of the first to advocate a new prosody for Chinese verse. He experimented with many different poetic forms. Artistically, the poems in *Stagnant Water*, his representative work, are marked by a strong sense of structure, close observation of form, harmonious rhythm and precision in the use of metaphorical language. As expected, there are traces of Western poetic influences. But, to a large extent, the strength of the poems comes from classical Chinese poetry.

In Spring 1927, Wen Yiduo went to Wuhan to participate in the propaganda work for the Northern Expedition against the warlords. Shortly after, he came back to Nanjing, where he taught at the university and did research on Chinese classical literature. After the outbreak of the anti-Japanese war, he threw himself into the patriotic democratic movement and became a famous anti-fascist fighter. On July 15, 1946, he was assassinated by Kuomintang secret agents. The magnificent, unforgettable patriotic poems of Wen Yiduo are full of his life and blood.

Another influential poet who associated himself with the New Moon Society was Zhu Xiang (1904-33), whose poems were collected in *Summer*, *Wide Grassland* and *Eternal Words*. His representative work is *Wide Grassland*, a collection of short poems in which he writes about the zeal of youth, the melancholy feeling of someone who is away from home, or the aloofness of someone who has a grudge against the world. Other poems are of a philosophical nature. All of them have the characteristics of meticulous conceptions and a delicate style. His love poems and patriotic poems excel in clarity of expression and beauty of rhythm. The influence of classical poetry is obvious, but he also benefited from the lyricism of folk songs. Poems written in this vein include "Love Song," "Mourning for Sun Yat-sen," "Soul of the Nation" and "Wind from Outside the Great Wall"—the last two from the collection *Eternal Words*. Zhu Xiang's poems are written in many different forms and they have a natural metrical rhythm. His "Wang Jiao" is based on the tragic love story of "The Hundred Years' Sorrows of Wang Jiaoluan." It is the embodiment of the young intellectuals' ideals of love in the period after the May Fourth Movement. The poem, nine hundred lines long demonstrates the poet's control over metre and rhyme. It was an ambitious attempt at the time. Later, Zhu Xiang turned to teaching. In 1933, plagued by poverty as a result of unemployment, he drowned himself in the Yangtse River.

Another poetic school which appeared after the May Fourth Movement was the group of symbolists, best represented by Li Jinfa. Influenced by the French symbolist poets, members of this school went for the stimulation and the satisfaction of the senses. They valued the fleeting appearance of illusions. While the New Moon School emphasized the beauty of poetic rhythm, the symbolists negated any relationship between poetry and music. To them, poetry was purely visual art. Their works contain what they called "the strangeness consequent upon the linking together of concepts." Individual concepts, components of thought, they believed, were not too difficult to understand; put together, however, their meaning could become incomprehensible. Although like the poets of the New Moon School, they paid a good deal of attention to the use of metaphorical language, they often went beyond the limits of language. The abstruseness of their works, then, is a distinctive feature. Many of Li Jinfa's poems in *Gentle Rain*, *Singing for Happiness* and *Spongers and Famine*, collections published between 1925 and 1927, are a mere higgledy-piggledy assemblage of words and their meaning is extremely obscure. For example, in "Instant Thoughts," from *Singing for Happiness*, he could write:

> *Like withering leaves, spattering blood on our feet,*
> *Life is the smile hanging on the lips of the God of Death.*

In "Past and Present," from *Gentle Rain*, the poet wants to "seek the source of life/ And the cold, lonely feeling after death." Compared with the realists and the romanticists, the symbolists did not make much contribution to the development of modern Chinese poetry.

In the midst of all the activities of the different literary societies and schools, modern drama also began to come to the fore in the new culture movement. The history of Chinese drama and opera is long. Modern drama, however, took its origin in the early twentieth century, and the source of inspiration came from Western drama. The Chinese scholars in Japan founded the Spring Willow Society and in 1907 performed in Tokyo the third act of *La Dame aux Camelias* and *Uncle Tom's Cabin*, an adaptation from Lin Shu's translation of the novel. After the 1911 Revolution, some of the members of the Spring Willow Society returned to Shanghai. They worked with the local initiators of modern drama and performed *Drastic Turn-About*, *The Clock of Society*, *Warm Blood* and other plays. As these performances were well received by the audiences, local drama activities began to flourish elsewhere. Unfortunately, however, Yuan Shikai's warlord government soon suppressed the drama movement. Consequently, many of the drama groups were disbanded. Some of the members, pandering to the low tastes of the petty bourgeoisie, vulgarized modern drama into what was then known as "civilized new drama."

During the May Fourth new culture movement, modern drama was revived. The promotion of "the amateur stage" led to the formation of many drama groups. In 1921, Shen Yanbing, Ke Yicen, Chen Dabei and Wang Zhongxian founded the People's Drama Society; Chen Dabei and Li Jianwu, the Beijing Experimental Drama Society; Ying Yunwei and Gu Jianchen, the Shanghai Drama Association, which was later joined by Ouyang Yuqian and Hong Shen. Founded later but equally active in the promotion of modern drama, were the Southern China Society led by Tian Han and the Xinyou Society, by Zhu Rangcheng. Foreign plays were performed, such as *Lady Windermere's Fan* and *The Second Dream*, as well as plays written by members of the societies themselves. Among the forerunners as playwrights were: Tian Han, Hong Shen, Ouyang Yuqian, Ding Xilin, Xiong Foxi, Chen Dabei and Wang Zhongxian. The representative works of the time include the one-act play *A Night in a Cafe*, by Tain Han; the three-act play *Zhao, the Emperor of Hell*, by Hong Shen; the five-act play *Pan Jinlian*, by Ouyang Yuqian; and the one-act comedy *A Wasp*, by Ding Xilin.

Ding Xilin (1893-1974) was best known for his portrayal of the lives and anecdotes of the middle and upper class intellectuals. Old Lady Ji in *A Wasp* gives people an impression that she believes in her children's freedom of choice in marriage. In truth, however, she makes sure that her decisions will be carried out. But Mr Ji and Miss Yu outwit her and win out in their choice of love. In the play, the comic effect is created through the use of double talk and lying words. The language is witty and humorous; the construction of the plot, ingenious. In another play, *Oppression*, Ding Xilin deals with a trivial and yet very common social problem. The old landlady does not want to let her room to any bachelor. But then her daughter gives it to a bachelor engineer. Through a series of conflicts related to the letting and the forced relinquishing of the room, the playwright has created a comedy which conveys his sympathy for the homeless people who experience "mental oppression" from landlords. In that sense, the play is also a criticism of the current social prejudices. During the anti-Japanese war, Ding Xilin wrote *Three Chinese Dollars*, *Waiting for the Wife to Come Home* and *Miaofeng Mountain*. The one-act play *Three Chinese Dollars* satirizes the high-ranking Kuomintang officials who value money as much as their life and the fawning policemen who are involved in petty crimes. It is one of the best one-act plays after the May Fourth Movement characterized by its lively atmosphere, skillful construction of plot and humorous dialogue. The four-act plays *Waiting for the Wife to Come Home* and *Miaofeng Mountain* also have their own different charm. Ding Xilin's works, on the other hand, reflect the influence of British literature on Chinese modern literature after the May Fourth Movement.

Among the plays performed by the drama societies after the May Fourth Movement were Chen Dabei's *Conscience*, Wang Zhongxian's *A Good Son* and Xiong Foxi's *Top Scholar, Foreign Version* and *A Patriotic Heart*. These plays may have flaws, but they each made their contribution to the early development of Chinese modern drama.

Chapter 4
Mao Dun

I. Life and Early Works

Mao Dun was a Left-wing writer who had great influence during the Left-wing literature movement. Mao Dun is the pen-name of Shen Yanbing (1896-1981), a native of Wuzhen, a small town in Tongxiang County, Zhejiang Province. His father had reformist ideas, and was interested in natural sciences. He taught himself algebra and calculus, but died in his early thirties. Mao Dun grew up in an enlightened family atmosphere, although his mother was a strict disciplinarian. He read *Romance of the Three Kingdoms*, *Journey to the West* and other Chinese classics while he was still a young boy. When he was in middle school, the 1911 Revolution which toppled China's last imperial dynasty broke out, and like many of the educated youth at that time Mao Dun was elated.

However, Chinese society remained much the same as before. There was still no freedom in school and when Mao Dun rebelled against the heavy-handed ways of the authorities, he was expelled from his middle school for unruly behaviour and went to another school in Hangzhou. Many years later he said of his middle school education: "What did it give me? I recall that I was unhappy that no books written later than the Qin and Han dynasties were taught; we had to write in a rigid form of prose characterized by parallelism and ornateness, learn poetry of the famous seven poets who lived in the second century and write letters, modelling those written in the sixth century." Undoubtedly this education gave Mao Dun a good grounding in Chinese classical literature. But it was incompatible with his family education. Mao Dun commented: "My middle school life was grey and humdrum."*

Mao Dun was unable to continue studying after he finished preparatory courses at Beijing University in 1916 because of his family's limited financial resources. He took a job as an editor at the Shanghai Commercial Press and at the same time contributed articles to the *Students* and *Lantern of Learning* magazines.

Mao Dun participated in the New Literature Movement after the May Fourth Movement in 1919. In the article "Appraisal of 'Appraisal of the Old and New Literatures,' " Mao Dun wrote that the new literature should be able to "express and guide people's life." "It should serve the common people and not only the privileged classes." He stressed that in building a new literature "attention should be paid to ideology."

Mao Dun was one of the founders and key members of the Literary Research Society founded in 1921. In the same year he became editor-in-chief of the *Short Story Monthly*. As the chief editor he reformed the ten-year-old magazine, using it to criticize feudal literature and promote the new literature. He resigned one year later in the wake of opposition and slanderous attacks by feudal diehards.

As an important advocator and promoter of the new literature, Mao Dun was mainly occupied with theoretical criticism and the translation of foreign literature in the early 1920s and during the First Revolutionary Civil War (1921-27). Revolutionary democracy and realism were the mainstays of his political and literary thinking. Mao Dun was very serious about literature and viewed it as more than entertainment. He thought that "literature is a means of depicting life. It should take life as its subject, be it through objective description of things or subjective exposition of ideals."** He advocated realistic literature written for the good of mankind. In his article "Social Background and Creation" Mao Dun wrote: "Literature that depicts social life is genuine literature, one that is linked with mankind. Social background deserves particular atten-

---

* "My Middle School Years and Later," *Impressions, Reflections and Reminiscences*, Cultural Life Press, October 1936.

** "The Reason China's Literature Is Undeveloped" *Literary Xunkan* (*Literary Ten Days*) No. 1, May 10, 1921 written under the penname Xuan Zhu.

tion in oppressed countries." He further pointed out, "'grievance' literature is the orthodox literature of troubled times." Mao Dun thought it was a major defect of the new literature that China did not have a writer like Gorky who "had lived among the fourth class people"* and written about their sufferings. In the article "Naturalism and Modern Chinese Novels" he urged writers to study social problems, depict objectively real life and they should "go for a long period of training and on the spot observation."** "Literature and art should be able to inspire the people," he believed, and that "literature should bear the important responsibility of awakening the masses and giving them strength."*** These ideas of Mao Dun's conflicted with those who advocated going back to the ancients, the "Mandarin Duck and Butterfly" school writers and those who believed in aestheticism in literary and art circles. Mao Dun positively influenced the writers of the Literary Research Society. He promoted realism and become an important critic in the New Literature Movement.

From the very beginning of his literary career Mao Dun worked hard translating and introducing foreign literature to the Chinese people. He published "A Study on Russian Literature" and "The Literature of the Oppressed Nations" on the *Short Story Monthly* (Vol. 12, extra and No. 10) of which he was chief editor. His early work was mainly concerned with the introduction and translation of Russian progressive literature and the literature of the Soviet Union. He was also interested in the old literature of oppressed nations in eastern and northern Europe. Early European naturalist writers argued that they were writing about the reality, and China's new literati could not then tell the difference between naturalism and realism. So in his attempt to introduce realistic foreign literary works to China he also promoted Emile Zola's naturalism. He intended to use the naturalist "pure objective" descriptions to replace writings contrary to truth. Traces of naturalism are evident in Mao Dun's early works.

---

* *Short Story Monthly*, Vol. XII, No. 7, July 1921.

** *Ibid.*, Vol. XIII, No. 7, July 1922.

*** "When Will the 'Great Turning Period' Come?" *Literary Weekly*, No. 103, December 31, 1923.

Mao Dun began his revolutionary activities in 1921. In Shanghai he joined first a Communist group and then the Chinese Communist Party, becoming one of its earliest members. He took part in the preparations for the founding of the Party and its subsequent work. Later he taught at the Party-sponsored Shanghai University. He was active in the May 30th Movement of 1925. His writing matured as the revolution developed. In the article "On Proletarian Art," published in 1925, Mao Dun wrote about the nature, content and form of the new literature and art of that period. He not only confirmed the relationship between literature and the times and its impact on society, but also attempted to discuss proletarian art from the Marxist class viewpoint.

In early 1926 Mao Dun attended a conference held by revolutionary parties in Guangzhou to assess the current situation, returning to Shanghai after the "*SS Yat-sen* Incident"* in March that year. At the end of the year he went to Wuhan, then the centre of the revolution, and became the chief editor of the "Republic Daily." Recalling his life of that period, Mao Dun later said, "From 1925 to 1927, I had frequent contacts with the leaders of the revolutionary movement. At the same time my job enabled me to keep in touch with grassroots units and the masses."** The life experience of that period provided abundant material for his writing.

In April 1927 Chiang Kai-shek, representing the interests of the landlord and bourgeois classes, openly betrayed the revolution in Shanghai. In July the same year the Wang Ching-wei clique held an anti-Communist conference in Wuhan. The revolution, which was on the upsurge, came to a sudden end. This was a great shock to Mao Dun. He left Wuhan for Nanchang, but was stopped at Guling and in August, returned to Shanghai instead. He switched from literary theoretical criticism to writing.

---

* On March 18, 1926, Chiang Kai-shek conspired with his followers to order the cruiser *Chungshan* (*Yat-sen*), commanded by a Communist, to proceed from Guangzhou to Whampoa. After the ship had left Guangzhou upon his order, Chiang Kai-shek spread the rumour that it had left without authorization and that its departure was designed to start an insurrection. Two days later Chiang ordered his troops to arrest all the Communist Party members in the Whampoa Military Academy and in the First Army of the National Revolutionary Army.

** "Preface to *Selected Works of Mao Dun*," April 1952, Kaiming Press.

From the autumn of 1927 to the spring of 1928 Mao Dun wrote *The Canker*, including three loosely related novella: *Disillusion*, *Wavering* and *Search*. It deals with the life and ideological changes of a number of young petty-bourgeois intellectuals before and after the Great Revolution (1924-27). *Disillusion* is set in pre-revolutionary Shanghai and the revolutionary centre Wuhan. Zhang Jing, the heroine, has been raised in a tranquil family environment and spoiled by her mother. Given to fantasies and emotionally fragile she detests evil, but lacks the courage to fight it; she seeks progress but does not have any will of her own; she is easily excited by her hopes and ideals and just as easily gives them up; she lives alternately in excitement and disillusion. She is fed up with the noise of Shanghai and also its worship of money. Both school and love have failed her. Inspired by the rising revolution she comes to Wuhan with new aspirations. She makes up her mind to undergo training and endure hardships. She is deeply moved and inspired at the Northern Expedition's oath-taking ceremony at Nanhu. Three times she changes jobs, only to become disillusioned and sad. Her fragile emotions prevent her time and again from finding the solace and spiritual sustenance she sought, a common problem of some of the intellectuals swept up by the revolution.

Wavering is a story about events during the First Revolutionary Civil War set in a small county town. It describes class struggles and social developments. Descriptions of mass movements, speculation by the land-owning class and activities of other characters with varied political attitudes and personalities illustrate the panorama of recent history. The protagonist Fang Luolan, head of the Kuomintang county headquarters, who is supposed to be an alliance of the revolution, wavers and compromises with the reactionary forces at a crucial moment of the revolution. He does not have the courage to expose Hu Guoguang, who has strategically entered the revolutionary ranks to carry out sabotage. He is afraid of the strength of the people. When the revolution suffers a setback he deserts it for his personal safety. Li Ke, though superficially described in the story, is a resourceful, staunch revolutionary. As the crisis in the revolution becomes apparent, he arrives at the county town as special commissioner. He points out the root cause of the mistakes in the work of the county and risking his life, exposes Hu Guoguang and talks to the people who have been led astray by Hu Guoguang. After the revolution failed he leads the remaining armed forces to Nanxiang for new battles. The appearance of the character of Li Ke and the description of battle scenes make *Wavering* the least depressing in mood among the trilogy.

As the author himself says in his article "On Reading *Ni Huanzhi*," *Search* intended to "expose the morbid and perplexed state of intellectuals in the early spring of 1928." The characters in the book are zealous for revolution when it was in its high tide. However, when the revolution was suppressed and reactionary terror prevails the country they feel lost. Still holding high aspirations they do not want to join the reactionary side, but due to their class limitations they are unable to find the right direction.

Zhang Manqing gets nowhere with his idea of "saving the country through education," nor does Wang Zhongzhao with his ideas of "saving the country through journalism." Zhang Qiuliu indulges in the extravagant life of an official, ruining himself as well as others; another character, Shi Xun is suspicious and dispirited and tries to find a way to die. "Ideals do not match reality" is their conclusion after they fail to attain their ideals.

The Canker is Mao Dun's first work. Despite the fact that the main aspect of the revolution is thinly described and some of the details were not very well chosen, it broadly reflects life in those times and shows the attitudes that motivated people, so the novel attracted attention as soon as it was published.

He began using Mao Dun as penname when he published "Disillusion" in the *Short Story Monthly* in September 1927. The two characters "Mao Dun" mean contradiction in Chinese. And indeed, at that time he was full of contradictions. He described his state of mind at that time in an article "From Guling to Tokyo."

To escape arrest by the Kuomintang and hoping to boost his morale by a change of environment Mao Dun went to Japan for a short period of time. Having been tempered in the great storms of revolution Mao Dun was not depressed when the revolution suffered setbacks, although he still had some contradictions in his mind. These complex feelings and inner struggles are perceptible in his "Seven Essays Written at Leisure," which he wrote in Japan.

Mao Dun's ideological change can be perceived in his short story *Creation* published in February 1928. It was clear by then that he took a positive attitude towards social liberation. Pessimism is no longer pervasive in his work. His novel *Rainbow* published in 1929 is more optimistic. It is an incompleted novel, ending with the May 30th Movement in 1925. Although the ending of the finished part seems a bit too hasty, it is a complete story.

The protagonist Mei Xingsu is a rebellious woman who challenges the old moral values. She likes to go her own way. The novel begins with Mei Xingsu, sailing down the Yangtse River through the Kui Gate, the entrance to Sichuan Province on the river. The Yangtse gorge scenes reflect the turbulent feelings of the heroine. To Mei Xingsu, Sichuan Province inside the Kui Gate is a world apart. Chapters two to seven recall the life and thoughts of Mei before she leaves Sichuan. The author describes in great detail how the new ideas of the May Fourth Movement draw her: "Literature attacking conventional ideas stimulates her; that which advocates individual rights excites her; and previews of a better world intoxicate her." The book also tells about Mei's hesitations and frustrations, typical of many young intellectuals during the May Fourth Movement who were striving to understand their own value or seek the significance of life through individual struggle.

Unlike many others Mei refuses to retreat or become dispirited. She goes to Shanghai. The last three chapters describe Mei's confusion and disturbed state of mind when she first arrives in Shanghai. Later with the help of Liang Gangfu, a revolutionary, she studies Marxism and realizes that "she has to start learning from the very beginning." She joins the May 30th Movement, determined to "take up the historical obligation" of "burning away the iron chains forced upon us by imperialism and warlords." The description of Mei's mental change is not sufficiently developed. She treds the path which led many young intellectuals of old China from individualism to collectivism.

In the spring of 1930 Mao Dun returned from Japan and found the rural revolution and cultural changes going on and the

Left-wing literary movement spreading. He joined the Chinese League of Left-Wing Writers and was later its executive secretary. He was very close to Lu Xun and active in promoting Left-wing literature and art. His writing reached a new peak as his ideology changed and as he gained new experience in life and writing.

In the first year or so after his return from Japan Mao Dun wrote the medium-length novels *Road* and *Three Companions* and short stories on historical themes. With the Wuhan students' movement in 1930 as its setting, *Road* is about a college student, named Huo Xinchuan. At first suspicious about politics and society Huo Xinchuan gradually awakens in the course of the student movement with the help of a revolutionary called Lei.

Three Companions is about three young men of different types. Xu drifts from agnosticism to worship of chivalry and from there to his death. Hui is a nihilist, but his nihilism breaks down in the face of a harsh and indifferent reality. Yun, from a rich peasant family, is a realist. His family goes bankrupt under the oppression of big landowners and he is plunged into the reality of struggle. Like the revolutionary Lei in *Road*, the revolutionary Ke in *Three Companions* spreads revolutionary ideas. But because the author was not familiar with the life of the youth after the Great Revolution of 1927 the characters he described were not sufficiently developed or convincing. But Mao Dun's description of the disillusionment and vacillation of petty bourgeois youth in the revolution and their awakening and becoming more and more realistic under reactionary terror should be regarded as valuable insights.

The time around 1932 was the most vigorous and fruitful period in Mao Dun's writing career. His celebrated novel *Midnight* and short stories "The Shop of the Lin Family" and "Spring Silkworms" were all written during this time. These works manifest Mao Dun's artistic talent for depicting the complexities of society and historical trends. Thus Mao Dun established his position in modern Chinese literature as an outstanding writer of revolutionary realism.

Mao Dun continued to write literary criticism through the Second Revolutionary Civil War (1927-37). He wrote critiques on several famous Chinese writers including *On Lu Xun*, *Discourse on*

Peanuts, On Bing Xin and *On Xu Zhimo.* In these books he systematically analysed the writers since the May Fourth Movement. Critics praised these books for their solid reasoning and contents. His essays "China's Society Revolution and the Building of Proletarian Literature"* and "Literary Works We Must Create"** discussed the creation of a proletarian revolutionary literature. His essay "The Image of 'Nationalist Literature and Art' " was a rebuttal of the fascist "Movement for Nationalist Literature and Art." In the same article Mao Dun also repudiated the theories of the French bourgeois scholar Hippolyte A. Taine which had influenced Mao Dun in his youth.

In the War of Resistance Against Japan Mao Dun was chief editor of *Beacon-Fire*, a combined weekly put out by *Literature, Mid-Current, Literary Season* and *Translations* publications. After the fall of Shanghai to the Japanese, Mao Dun first went to Hong Kong and then to Changsha, Wuhan and Guangzhou. In March 1938 he was elected the executive committee member of the newly-founded National Federation of Anti-Japanese Writers and Artists. Although drifting from place to place Mao Dun kept active in literary work. He was chief editor of *Words' Forest* and the *Literary and Art Front*, supplements to the Hong Kong newspaper *Li Bao.* He wrote the novella *The Story of the First Stage.* Towards the end of 1938 Mao Dun was invited to teach at Xinjiang College and to take charge of the local cultural association.

Mao Dun left Xinjiang in May 1940 when Sheng Shicai, governor of Xinjiang, began to show his true colours, as a reactionary. On his way back to the coast Mao Dun stopped in Yan'an and lectured at the Lu Xun Art Academy. He was impressed by the militant spirit and vigorous life in the anti-Japanese base areas. He reminisced with affection about his short visit to Yan'an in his prose article "On Landscape" and "Tribute to the Poplar Tree." After the Southern Anhui Incident of 1941 Mao Dun wrote the novel *Corrosion* to expose the crimes of secret organizations on which the Kuomintang relied to maintain its fascist rule. Another

---

* *Literary Guide*, Vol. I, No. 8, November 15, 1931. Written under the penname of Shi Hualuo.

** *The Dipper*, Vol. II, No. 2, May 5, 1932.

novel *Frosted Leaves as Red as Flowers in Spring* and the play script *Before and After the Qingming Festival* came out soon after.

During the Third Revolutionary Civil War (1946-49) Mao Dun joined the democratic forces against civil war and suppression. He wrote the novel *Be Tempered* and many essays and prose articles. At the end of 1948 Mao Dun went to the liberated areas. In July 1949 he attended the first National Congress of Literature and Art Workers and was elected vice-chairman of the Chinese Federation of Writers and Artists and chairman of the Association of Chinese Literary Workers (the predecessor of the present Chinese Writers' Association).

Mao Dun became the first Minister of Culture of New China. He held other leading posts in the cultural field, wrote numerous literary reviews and did much to help young writers. He played an important part in the building up of socialist culture. At the Fourth National Congress of Literature and Art Workers held in November 1979 he was elected honorary chairman of the Chinese Federation of Writers and Artists and chairman of the Chinese Writers' Association.

Mao Dun died in Beijing on March 27, 1981. During the more than sixty years since 1916 Mao Dun had made valuable contributions to China's literature and was a pioneer in realistic writing. Together with Lu Xun and Guo Moruo, Mao Dun laid the foundation of modern Chinese literature. His contributions are indelible.

II. *Midnight*

Midnight, a milestone in Mao Dun's writing career, is representative of revolutionary realism in modern Chinese literature. After lengthy preparation Mao Dun began to write this book in October 1931 and finished it in December 1932.

Mao Dun profoundly understood Chinese society of the early 1930s. Among his friends and acquaintances were revolutionary activists as well as liberals, people from his hometown, entrepreneurs, civil servants, merchants and bankers. He was familiar with the situation in Shanghai's industrial and commercial circles.

For a period Mao Dun regarded it as his daily lesson to "watch people in the stock market frenziedly speculating and people soliciting share buyers to start some factory or other." At that time a debate was going on in academic circles as to the nature of Chinese society. The arguments raised in the debate and his own observations inspired Mao Dun to write this book. With plots revolving around vivid characterizations he refuted the view that "China has already become a capitalist society." He also drew upon his experiences from the First Revolutionary Civil War.

The story in *Midnight* revolves around the conflict between the national industrialist Wu Sunfu and the comprador capitalist Zhao Botao. It reflects Chinese society in the early 1930s when revolution was developing and spreading rapidly. Imperialist powers were fighting for influence in China and there were clashes of interest between China and foreign powers and among the foreign powers. As a result of these conflicts Chinese reactionary forces representing different interests started fighting among themselves. The heavy taxes they collected aggravated the conflict between the taxpayers and the reactionary rulers. As Chinese industrialists, who were under ever increasing pressure from imperialist powers, exploited the Chinese workers more brutally, they met stronger resistance from the workers. With foreign goods being dumped on the Chinese market, Chinese merchants raising prices and the government imposing heavier taxes, conflict between the landlord class and the peasants sharpened: rents and usury rates were raised, and the peasants hated the landlords all the more. Under such circumstances a revolutionary movement against imperialists, warlords and landlords was inevitable in China.

The characters in *Midnight* are developed against this historical background. Their different personalities and fates mirror the powerful trends of that era. The setting is Shanghai, but the whole of Chinese society is reflected. The events the book describes took place over a period of only two months from May to July of 1930, yet within these two months one can see China's past and future. *Midnight* is the product of Mao Dun's profound understanding of life and artistic ability.

The character Wu Sunfu, a national industrialist, is not depicted as a vulgar rich man. He intends to build an industry, starting with a power plant, in his native place Double Bridge Town and turn it into his "kingdom." But the town with a population of 100,000 is too small for him to fulfill his aspirations. His "aim is to build enterprises, increase the number of chimneys, and expand the market." His ambition is to "do away with those indolent so-called entrepreneurs" and "put all the enterprises under his iron hand." Besides watching out for the interests of his enterprises he has to "keep an eye on politics."

Wu Sunfu is ambitious and has learned to run a modern industry in Europe and the United States. With his piercing gaze he often inspires others to follow a cause and wins their cooperation. Unfortunately times are bad for him. In semi-feudal and semi-colonial China, Chinese industry is in the grip of imperialists. Wu Sunfu's ambition to develop China's own industry is a dream that can never come true. He spends his days battling on several fronts: struggling against comprador capitalist Zhao Botao, trying to put down strikes in his factories and buying smaller factories that later become burdens to him. The Yizhong Credit Company that he, Sun Jiren and Wang Hefu set up together goes bankrupt as a result of conflicts between warlords, the collapse of the rural economy, overproduction in industry and an all-out embargo by Zhao Botao. Wu Sunfu's grand plan explodes like a soap bubble as the Yizhong Credit Company collapses only two months after it was set up. The only way out for the ambitious, self-confident Wu Sunfu is to give up. Through Wu Sunfu's failure the novel shows that capitalism is difficult to establish in China and those who go against the people will get nowhere.

The author uses Wu Sunfu as a typical example of the Chinese national bourgeoisie in semi-colonial and semi-feudal China, and highlights his personality against the multi-sided, complex social relations of the times. Wu Sunfu wants to develop Chinese industry, but he is crushed by worries about his personal interests. He believes it is his duty to develop industry and objects to Du Zhuzhai's speculation in real estate, gold and on the stock market with his capital. However, he has to speculate on the stock market himself. He is intelligent and capable, but his weaknesses are also shown. Sometimes he is confident, arbitrary; at other times he is uncertain and suspicious. Sometimes high hopes and dejection follow each other. He appears to have well-thought-out plans for everything, but he is actually very unreasonable. All these contradictary traits are part of Wu Sunfu's character.

Wu Sunfu's personality and fate are described not only through the struggles between him and Zhao Botao over their interests in Wu's Yizhong Credit Company and the stock market under Zhao's control, but also through the relations of Wu Sunfu to the feudal rural economy. He is irreconcilably opposed to the peasants' armed uprisings. His brutal attitude towards the workers' movement and his hatred for the revolution reveal his reactionary nature.

Much of the novel is devoted to Wu Sunfu's family life and the people around him, revealing the indifference, greed and selfishness of the bourgeoisie. Wu Sunfu cannot escape the fate ordained for him by the laws of history. He hides his fear by feigning to be cool and calm. He never lets anyone, not even his wife, see his moments of dejection. He relies on strong stimuli to momentarily forget "the gloomy future and personal career crisis that send fear into his marrow." He tries to end his problems in an unsuccessful suicide attempt. Wu Sunfu, a characterization of great artistic quality, stands on a par with the character Ah Q in Lu Xun's book.

There are other successful characterizations in *Midnight*. The characters' outlooks bear the brand of the era and the class they belong to. Tu Weiyue is Wu Sunfu's lackey. As he describes Wu Sunfu's ability and ambition, the author depicts Tu Weiyue's alertness, calm and bravery. Just as Wu Sunfu cannot avert his own failure, Tu Weiyue with all of his schemes is unable to block the swelling tide of the workers' movement.

Zhao Botao is a comprador financier serving the imperialists. Backed by fascist power he enjoys political as well as a economic advantages over Wu Sunfu. Although little is written about his political relations, the descriptions expose him as cunning, brutal and licentious.

Feng Yunqing is a "land-eating country spider." He forces his daughter to become Zhao Botao's mistress to obtain information about the stock market. This vile trick shows the shamelessness of the feudal landlord class and the despicable character of Zhao Botao. Distinctive, too, are such characters as the professor, Li Yuting and the poet, Fan Bowen who live on the wealth of the rich and powerful. The author once said he intended to incorporate the underhand dealings of 1930 which he described as a new version of *The Scholars* into the general structure of this book. This intention was not entirely realized, although the degenerate mentality of some of the scholars of that time was reflected in the characters like Li Yuting, Fan Bowen and others.

Mao Dun was especially skilled at portraying the inner thoughts of his characters. He did not present them as static and isolated entities, but placed them in the context of the times, developing them with meticulous in-depth description in the midst of acute conflicts. The character Wu Sunfu, struggling on several fronts, is sometimes excited, then worried; sometimes calm and confident, at other times restless and apprehensive. His state of mind and personality are laid bare as he faces unpredictable successes and failures. Du Zhuzhai's greed is fully exposed when matters reach a head at the stock market; Li Yuting who lives by courting favour with the rich is shown as a double-dealer when the intense, but covert rivalry between the Wu and Zhao families comes into the open. In many places the writers enhances the atmosphere, the mood of the characters and their personalities through descriptions of landscape, using such descriptions to develop the characters, the mood and the atmosphere of the story.

The language Mao Dun uses in *Midnight* is refined, meticulous and vivid. The old proverbs and idioms he occasionally uses fit in perfectly. His narration and dialogue vary with the mood and the characters, enabling readers to see the characters of the book and hear them talk.

Midnight consists of nineteen chapters. The first and second chapters introduce the characters and provide background. Each of the multitude of intricate, but well-arranged events in the remaining chapters develop around a particular topic and serve the novel's central theme at the same time. Although the episode of the peasants' revolt in Double-Bridge Town is somewhat sketchy, it reflects rural China in the 1930s. This part also shows Wu Sunfu's close relations with the feudal rural economy and his hatred for the peasants' revolt. Although the main thread of the plot is woven around the conflict between Wu Sunfu and Zhao Botao, the author also writes about the growth of the revolutionary forces to indicate Wu Sunfu's inevitable defeat and to point out the only way for China's salvation.

That *Midnight* turned out a success is not due to chance. Like all accomplished writers, Mao Dun pays special attention to analysing people in the context of their society. He tried to explain society from the Marxist viewpoint and uses class relations as themes for his books. That was how *Midnight* was conceived.

Mao Dun had a special fondness for the Chinese classical novels *Outlaws of the Marsh* and *The Scholars*. He also read extensively such foreign writers as Charles Dickens, Walter Scott, Alexandre Dumas, Guy de Maupassant, Emile Zola, Leo Tolstoy and Chekov as well as writers from oppressed countries, digesting and assimilating their good points. The ability to "digest the essence of old literary works to create new methods," as he himself wrote in his "Preface to *Broad Plain*," is another important factor that has made *Midnight* a success.

Mao Dun tried to depict the movement of workers and peasants and create working-class characters, but he was not very successful. He later summarized the reasons: "This novel has portrayed people of three categories: the comprador financier, reactionary industrialists, and revolutionaries and the masses of workers. I have directly observed people of the first two categories, but I only have secondhand material about the third type—accounts by the people involved or even by a third person. Because of this the comprador financier and reactionary industrialists described in the novel are much more true to life and convincing than the revolutionaries and the workers."*

Soon after its publication the Kuomintang government listed *Midnight* as a forbidden book. But revolutionary literary circles and the general readership thought highly of it. In a letter to Cao

* Mao Dun, "Preface to *Selected Works of Mao Dun*."

Jinghua, Lu Xun wrote: "Now on our side there are quite a few new writers. Mao Dun has written a novel named *Midnight* ... which puts them far behind."* Lu Xun regarded *Midnight* as a great achievement of revolutionary literature, one that nothing in reactionary literature could compare with. Qu Qiubai commented on *Midnight* as "The first successful novel of Chinese realism." *Midnight* raised the level of Chinese realist literature. On a par with *The True Story of Ah Q*, *Midnight* is a brilliant addition to the history of China's modern literature. Translated into several languages, it has been well-received by foreign writers and readers.

III. "The Shop of the Lin Family," "Spring Silkworms" and Other Short Stories

From February 1928 to March 1929 Mao Dun wrote five short love stories: "Creation," "Poetry and Essays," "Suicide," "A Female" and "Overcast," which later were collected into an anthology entitled *Wild Roses*. The author's intention was to reveal class ideology of the characters in the course of their love affairs.**

Junshi, the protagonist in "Creation," wants to create a new image for his wife Xianxian by remolding her into a bourgeois woman. Xianxian, however, goes a step further than her husband's mediocre intention. "The day his creation succeeds, his ideal goes bankrupt."*** In "Poetry and Prose" the protagonist "C," bored with Gui, longs for his cousin, and in the end loses both. The author is critical of Junshi in "Creation" and "C" in "Poetry and Prose." His sympathy goes to Xianxian and Gui who, influenced by new ideas, dare to break free from conventional morality. Thus the two stories contain the themes of women's liberation and social liberation. In "Poetry and Prose," however, too much attention was given to sex, and this blurs the main theme.

"The Water Land" from the anthology *Broad Plain*, written

---

* "Letter to Cao Jinghua," *Letters of Lu Xun* (I), p. 352.

** "Preface to *Wild Roses*."

*** "Preface to *Collection of Mao Dun's Short Stories*," Peoples' Literature Publishing House, April 1980.

between 1929 and 1930, was based on historical facts. It tells how in the Qin Dynasty conscripts from a poor region kill the two officers from rich peasant families and start a revolt on their way to the frontier at Yuyang. The story describes the fear, self-pity and struggles of the officers and the fierce vengeance of the poor peasants fighting for their freedom. Although this short story is as Mao Dun said, "divorced from reality," it was significant because he had begun to feel dissatisfied with his previous works. Before he was certain to be able to write successfully about great current events, he drew his material from historical stories.

"The Shop of the Lin Family" and "Spring Silkworms," representative of Mao Dun's short stories, were written in the same year as *Midnight*. In a postscript to *Midnight* Mao Dun wrote: "According to my original plan this book should have been much longer. I intended to include the economic situation in the villages into this book and the ideology of small town people.... I also wanted to elaborate on some of the minor events mentioned in the book. I had to give up these ideas because the terrible heat of that summer damaged my health. So the book appeared as it is now—mainly about city life." "The Shop of the Lin Family" and "Spring Silkworms" were actually part of Mao Dun's greater plan to write about society in China. The rural and small-town life described in these two short stories, in addition to the city life described in the novel accurately reflect the Chinese society at that time.

On January 28, 1932 the Japanese invaded Shanghai. After the city fell Mao Dun returned to his hometown where he saw how imperialist economic aggression had pushed the rural economy to the brink of bankruptcy, a process accelerated by the Japanese invasion. Desolation prevailed in the once well-to-do villages and small towns south of the Yangtse River, which gave Mao Dun the framework for "The Shop of the Lin Family" and "Spring Silkworms."

Mr Lin, a merchant in a small town, industriously manages his family store with thrift. But the decreasing buying power of the impoverished villagers, with whom the store mainly does its business, forces him to lower prices again and again. Still he cannot sell much. He is driven to the limit of his resources at the end of the year when creditors come to collect debts and he has nowhere to turn to for the money because of the war in Shanghai. Furthermore, the Kuomintang reactionaries blackmail him for money and force his daughter to become a Kuomintang official's concubine. Taking advantage of Mr Lin's difficulties other merchants with more capital pressure him. Pressed from all sides Mr Lin closes down his shop. The tragedy of the Lin family is typical of the fragile Chinese industry and commerce. The story also shows that the bankruptcy of the Lin family's shop hits many others. Grandma Zhu San and Widow Zhang, two among many people who put all their life savings in the store and who live on the interest, suffer a severe blow. The story ends with these victims struggling desperately for existence. It is a powerful criticism against the system of the old society where "big fish swallow small ones and small fish eat shrimp." The writer both sympathizes with and criticizes Mr Lin. Mao Dun's skill as a realistic writer is fully displayed in this short story in which profound social content is written in a limited space—an important feature of Mao Dun's works.

"Spring Silkworms," written later than "The Shop of the Lin Family," is set in a village south of the Yangtse River. It is a story of the family of Old Tongbao. Instead of seeing their life improve after a good harvest of spring silkworms Old Tongbao's family becomes even poorer. Unable to feed themselves even in a good year, the peasants of old China had to seek other ways to survive. The writer shows the background that causes the suffering of the poor villagers: Shortly after the battle against the Japanese invasion in Shanghai in early 1932, foreign goods were dumped onto the Chinese market; the Chinese silk-weaving industry was going bankrupt; there was no market for silk, merchants keep lowering the purchasing price of silk cocoons and feudal landlord usurers become more brutal in their exploitation. Old Tongbao and other villagers have a good harvest of silk cocoons that they have rarely had for many years. Instead of enjoying the fruits of an entire month's labour, "the good harvest only brings the people in Old Tongbao's village more debts! Old Tongbao's family gets nothing back for the fifteen *dan* (1 *dan* = 50 kilogrammes) of leaves from their mulberry trees, but a debt of thirty dollars on top of it. All the hunger and sleepless nights they have suffered for a month are in vain!"

Like other peasants of his generation Old Tongbao is honest and hardworking but conservative. Having lived sixty years and seen many troubled ties, he trusts his experience to judge and deal with the present situation. Vaguely he senses that the "world is getting worse" because there are "foreign devils." He not only hates the "foreign devils," but also anything labeled with foreign lettering. He believes that life can improve only when the peasants get a better harvest from the fields and from silkworm-raising. He believes in fate and the gods, and demands that his son Ah Duo stick to the superstitious rules in silkworm-raising. Times have changed; things are different, but Old Tongbao remains unchanged. This is one of the chief reasons he is such a tragic figure. Ah Duo is different from his father. He does not believe that a bumper harvest can change their fate. Optimistic, he is not troubled by his father's worries. Although he begins to have a deeper understanding of the social phenomena taking place around him and feels there is a tension among people that cannot be resolved, he cannot figure out why. The story develops around the different attitudes of the older and younger generations in Chinese villages of the 1930s on how to get rid of poverty. The growth of Ah Duo's generation and awakening of Old Tongbao's generation is an inevitable trend in the progress of the rural regions in old China.

"Autumn Harvest" and "The Last Days of Winter," written after "Spring Silkworms," reflect this trend. "Autumn Harvest" tells about Old Tongbao's long-cherished hope for a good harvest, which is shattered like soap bubbles. The heavy blow took the old man's life. Only then do his eyes light up with awakening and understanding. "The Last Days of Winter" further describes the deteriorating rural economy and the rise of the peasant resistance. After their publication the three short stories were called "Trilogy of the Villages." They reflect the miseries of the poverty-stricken peasants, their awakening from conservatism and finally their struggle.

"The Shop of the Lin Family," "Spring Silkworms" and Mao Dun's other works focus on major real life issues. They present a picture of enterprises, big or small, in big cities or small towns, going out of business; and good harvests in the countryside, instead of bringing joy to the peasants, plunge them into despair because they cannot find market for their products. At a time when the Chinese economy was breaking down and people were fearful, these stories not only reflected the various social problems people were concerned about and the contradictions and conflicts that caused them, but also exposed the social roots of these problems. They played an important role in arousing the consciousness of the public.

During that period Mao Dun wrote quite a few short stories on divergent subjects. The themes of these short stories reflect society and class struggle from different angles. "The Minor Witch" describes an armed rebellion by the local people because the local landlord and the reactionary military police are trafficking in opium and the landlord and his son-in-law are fighting for control over the local military force. "The Death of the Gods," as Mao Dun put it in the foreword to *Collection of Mao Dun's Short Stories* (published by the People's Literature Publishing House, April 1980), "uses the tragic end of the gods in Scandinavian legends to allegorize the dissolute life and inevitable fall of the Chiang Kai-shek regime." "The First Morning at Work" is a bitter story about a young female employee who has to fawn over her superior in order to keep her job. "In Front of the Pawnshop" tells of the tragedy of Wang Ahda's family and the inhumane suffering of the working people under the oppression of imperialism, feudalism and bureaucratic capitalism. "Floating Algae" focuses on the family life and suffering of two peasants, Caixi and Xiusheng. It reveals the shocking poverty and budding rebellion in the rural areas.

Mao Dun was concerned about children in the old society and wrote stories about them. "The Story of Big Nose" is about young vagrants in Shanghai. Young as they are, they have acquired bad habits, but the author does not blame the children. "My Son Has Gone to a Meeting" is about a 13-year-old who joins a demonstration. It reflected the rising resistance against Japanese aggression. "A Young Printer" is a story about Zhao Yuansheng, a poor young man with high aspirations, who takes a job as a printer. These works show Mao Dun's support for the emerging children's literature at that time.

IV. *Corrosion* and Other Works

During the anti-Japanese and Liberation wars Mao Dun led an unsettled life, moving from place to place and working for the democratic movement against the dictatorship of the Kuomintang and the invasion of the Japanese. During these ten hard years Mao Dun managed to write four novels *The Story of the First Stage, Corrosion, Frosted Leaves as Red as Flowers in Spring* and *Be Tempered*, and the short story collections *The Death of Jesus, Be Wronged*, the play *Before and After the Qingming Festival* and many other essays and prose. Among these works *Corrosion* is the best and most influential.

The Story of the First Stage, was first published in 1938 as a series under the title of "Where Will You Go?" in "Words' Forest," a supplement to the Hong Kong paper *Li Bao*. It acquired its present name when it came out in book form in 1945. The story takes place against the background of the August 13 battle in Shanghai. From different angles the author depicts the drastic and complex social and ideological changes in the four months from the beginning of the anti-Japanese war to the fall of Shanghai to the Japanese. While revealing the different attitudes of people of different social strata towards the war the author also exposed the corrupt practices of the Kuomintang rule, pointing out the reasons for the fall of Shanghai. But the book was written in too much of a hurry, so that the characters and plots are sketchy and superficial.

Corrosion, written in the summer of 1941, first appeared as a series in Hong Kong's *Life of the Common People* magazine and then came out in book form. The story takes place in Chongqing, the wartime capital of the Kuomintang government around the time of the Southern Anhui Incident in 1941. It criticizes the Kuomintang's fascist rule.

Secret agent Zhao Huiming, the heroine, comes from a feudal bureaucratic family. Once active in the student movement and anti-Japanese activities, she cannot shake off the constraints of her class upbringing and social environment. She is egotistical and vain and lacks the ability to discriminate right from wrong. Unable to stand threats and enticements, she becomes a member of Kuomintang secret agent organization. Since she does not belong to one of the favoured factions in that organization, she is bullied and molested by high-ranking agents. However, she still has fragments of conscience. She still asks herself "What makes one a human being?" She experiences pain and contradiction, but there is no one she can turn to for solace and advice.

The story is written in the form of a diary, a convenient medium for revealing her private thoughts. The complexities of Zhao Huiming's inner world are meticulously described: her pangs of conscience after she has been deceived, her self-confession, self-derision and self-defence; and her painful struggle as she decides to break away from the secret agent organization. The detailed descriptions arouse the reader's hatred for the Kuomintang fascist rule which ruined China's youth spiritually and physically. The story also shows the inner workings of these secret organizations.

The author does not describe Zhao Huiming's thoughts in a static and isolated way. Major social events and the contradictions they engender are reflected in Zhao's thoughts and emotions. Although the limitations of the diary form prevent the author from presenting a broader social background, the book retains the features of Mao Dun's works which realistically portray the times and society.

According to the original framework the novel was to end with the murder of Zhao Huiming's former lover Young Zhao. But when it first appeared in serial form in the magazine *Life of the Common People*, many readers wrote to the editor and asked that Zhao Huiming be given a chance to turn over a new leaf—a demonstration of the powerful artistic attraction of this characterization. She had become a real person in those times which impelled readers to demand her development rather than her destruction. Zhao Huiming hates the Kuomintang rule where, she realizes that "demons are everywhere," and tries to free herself from the life of a secret agent. Her conscience tortures her as she is ordered to persuade Young Zhao to surrender. Young Zhao's love, trust and advice and the efforts of revolutionaries "K" and Ping to rescue Young Zhao help her to see light and hope. The death of Young Zhao strengthens her determination to break with the evil way of life that has ruined her ideals. The final scene in which Zhao Huiming rescues a girl student from the grip of secret agent is not an arbitrarily appended happy ending, but a logical outcome of the development of her character.

Corrosion summarizes the author's observations of the Kuomintang reactionaries over the many years since the outbreak of the anti-Japanese war and is the most important literary work exposing the nefarious politics under the Kuomintang government of that time. *Corrosion* is next only to *Midnight* in its ideological and artistic accomplishments.

The author originally planned *Frosted Leaves as Red as Flowers in Spring* as the first part of a novel about society from the May Fourth Movement to the First Revolutionary Civil War. In the rainy season, when the river is flooded, steam boats of the Huili Shipping Company cause the river to overflow and damage the fields along its banks. The landowners and peasants rise up in protest. With the three-sided quarrel between the company manager Wang Boshen, diehard landlord Zhao Shouyi and the young reformist landlord Qian Liangcai as the background, the novel describes customs and relationships in families of the landlord and capitalist classes before the May Fourth Movement. The story ends with the evil forces compromising with each other, reformist ideas coming to naught and the peasants becoming the real victims.

The author gave the book the present name because he intended to liken the pseudo-Leftists to frost-bitten leaves, which look "red" but are not genuinely so. The frosted leaves also implied the short-lived nature of the reactionary forces. But the author had only finished the first part of the book, and the content of this part has nothing to do with the implied meaning of the title.

The five-act play *Before and After the Qingming Festival*, written in the autumn of 1945, is about the lives of several "respectable people" and couple of miserable people. The main characters are

Lin Yongqing, the owner of the Gengxin Machinery Plant, and his wife Zhao Zifang. Lin is capable, confident and conceited, but is likely to vacillate in the face of difficulties; Zhao is decisive and strong-willed but impulsive. With the help of his wife, Lin moves his factory from Shanghai to Chongqing. Under very difficult conditions the plant develops fairly well, but it is short-lived. "The government controls are shackles and handcuffs; rocketing prices for food and raw materials are a dead weight on one's back." Things go from bad to worse for the factory. Tempted by visions of striking it rich, Lin starts to dabble in the stock market, but his dreams crumble in no time. His factory faces bankruptcy under the ever-increasing pressure from financial capitalists. Zhao Zifang, his wife, encourages him to carry out reforms, renovate technology and reduce costs. But their hopes are illusory. At last they come to see that "without democracy in politics there is no way out for industry," and that "the shackles and handcuffs that hold industry down must be smashed."

Many characters appear around the protagonists Lin Yongqing and Zhao Zifang: diminutive Yu Weimin, the opportunist scholar and rogue; Jin Tan'an, a bureaucrat, businessman and gentleman who can be both generous and vicious; the Machiavellian Yan Ganchen; and the petty politician Fang Yincai who "licks his superiors' boots and bullies his subordinates." The author gave a sarcastic twist to the names of these characters.

The author shows sympathy for two other characters in the play—Zhao Zifang's girlfriend Tang Wenjun and Tang's husband Li Weiqin, a small clerk. The couple lead a hard life. More than a year after their marriage they still do not have a place where they can live together. Persuaded by the sly Yan Ganchen, Li Weiqin embezzles public fund to speculate in gold. He is arrested when the gold case is exposed and he becomes the scapegoat for Yan who goes scot-free. His wife Tang goes out of her mind. Through her utterances the author vehemently condemns the old society.

Due to the author's lack of skill in playwriting there are obvious defects in the play: the play is depressing in mood, dialogues are too long and tedious, and the characterizations are not distinctive. But the play provided reflection on important historical events and pointed out the direction for the national bourgeoisie in the War of Resistance Against Japan.

Mao Dun's novella *Taking a Position* was first serialized in the *Vangard of Literature and Art* in Chongqing from August to December of 1943. It was rewritten as a full-length novel and again serialized in Hong Kong's *Wen Hui Bao* from September to December of 1948 with the new title *Be Tempered*. This is the first volume of the author's planned novel in five volumes about the anti-Japanese war. The story is set in Shanghai around the August 13th Incident in 1937. Through the activities of the story's main characters—capitalist Yan Zhongping, noted physician Su Zipei and country gentleman Zhao Puzhai and their families, the author describes the attitudes of people from all walks of life in the early days of the war. In spite of the intricate plot and many characters, the story line is clear and the characters are distinct from one another.

Su Zipei is honest and kindhearted and remains loyal to his calling; Yan Zhongping supports the anti-Japanese war, but tends to vacillate; his brother Yan Boqian, an official of the Nanjing government, is treacherous and ruthless; his daughter Yan Jiexiu, an activist in the anti-Japanese war, is lively and resourceful. The author vividly describes the simple, patriotic platoon commander Sun and the enthusiastic and progressive youths Su Xinjia and Zhao Kejiu. The story is rich in the atmosphere of the times and the language is succinct and unrestrained, demonstrating the many-sided accomplishments of Mao Dun as a writer.

Mao Dun also wrote essays (including sketches and notes), some of them were published before he began writing novels. After the May 30th Movement Mao Dun wrote "In the Afternoon of May 30," "Storm" and other essays, praising the revolutionary actions of the masses. In 1928 he published his long article "From Guling to Tokyo" in which, Mao Dun dissected his own ideological changes during the revolution. His articles "Knocking at the Door," "The Whistle of the Bean Curd Peddler" and "Fog," written during his sojourn in Japan, record his uncertainty and frustration and his yearning to dispel his melancholy.

As his political horizons broadened and his experience in life became more abundant Mao Dun began to deal with social topics of greater depth and scope in his essays. During China's deepening crisis after the September 18th and January 28th incidents, Mao Dun wrote "Anniversary of the Bloody War," "Anniversary of the 'September 18th Incident' " and "Beyond the Glossy Legs and Creamy Breasts," denouncing the Japanese aggression against China and attacking the Kuomintang's policy of "settling domestic affairs before resisting foreign aggression." His arguments and analyses were cogent and penetrating. "Casual Notes in My Hometown" records the author's impressions during a visit home in 1932. In the form of letters this essay describes the different attitudes of people in the town and the nearby countryside towards the January 28th Incident and the pathetic plight of the bankrupt villages and the declining town.

The essays Mao Dun wrote in those years were intended to expose and condemn the old order but the author's idealism occasionally shows between the lines. The articles "Winter Days," "Before a Storm" and "Footprints on the Beach," for example, expressed his ardent yearning for revolution and victory. Metaphorically these articles described the political and social conflicts in China in the 1930s and hinted that a bright new era would inevitably replace the old order. Referring to the politics of those times Mao Dun writes in "Winter Days," "When the winter is harshest it will soon come to an end and spring is already knocking at the door." Of the society at that time he says, "It seems to be wrapped in a gray airtight shroud" which should be "torn to pieces" to "let rainstorms wash clean the whole world!" (from "Before the Storm").

After visiting and giving lectures in Yan'an in 1940 Mao Dun wrote "On Landscape" and "Tribute to the Poplar Tree" in praise of the revolutionaries there. Both pieces are well-known, although "Tribute to the Poplar Tree" written later in March, 1941, is more popular. The author likens the lofty, steadfast poplar trees that stand erect against the wind on the northwestern loess plateau to the peasants of north China who fought staunchly for national liberation. At the same time the author directs biting sarcasm at those people who "hold the common people in contempt and stubbornly insist on going backward." The article leads the reader step by step through beautiful landscapes. One of the traditional methods in Chinese literature is to write about objects, although the real intention is to describe people. Mao Dun used successfully this method in the essay "Tribute to the Poplar Tree."

Mao Dun's essays have several distinct features. One is his knack for dealing with large themes in short articles. His essays about a minor aspect of daily life provoke the reader's reflections on events of major social significance. Another is his meticulous and true-to-life depictions of people. In his essays he cleverly combines acuity with vagueness and solemnity with humour, a trait which gives his writings great flexibility and proved necessary because of the political situation at that time. Sometimes without directly assailing the evils of the old society the author attacked them by innuendo, stimulating the reader to think and arousing anger in the reader. And finally Mao Dun's beautiful and poetic language has a strong artistic appeal.

Chapter 5
Lao She

I. Early Novels and Short Stories

Lao She (1899-1966) is the penname of Shu Qingchun, also known as She Yu, who was born into a poor family of Manchu nationality in Beijing. His father, a member of the imperial Manchu guards who had a wage of only three ounces of silver per month, was killed by the eight powers' allied army in 1900 when Lao She was not yet two years old. From then on, "the whole family was supported by my mother alone.... In order to feed and clothe us, my mother had to wash, mend and sew clothes for others. In my memory, her hands were scarlet and swollen all the year round."* Hardworking and kindhearted, Lao She's mother imparted to him pride and discipline. "It was my mother who had been my genuine teacher and who passed her character to me. She didn't known a single word, but what she taught me was the enlightenment of life."** The majority of the modern Chinese writers after the May Fourth Movement in 1919, including those who emerged in the twenties and thirties were all from the middle or upper class; they began their literary careers more often than not as "unfilial sons and rebellious subjects" of their class. Lao She was entirely different from them. He came from a poor family and from his childhood led a hard, strenuous life. Because of his own experiences, combined with the social problems he had heard about he was strongly against the oppression of the poor. His experiences exerted a deep and lasting influence of his choice of literary themes.

* "My Mother," *Half-Monthly Collection of Best Articles*, Vol. 1, No. 9-10, April 1943.
** *Ibid.*

After graduating from a normal school at nineteen, Lao She became successively a primary school headmaster, a secretary of an educational committee and a middle school teacher. By the time the May Fourth Movement broke out, Lao She had already begun his educational work; though he did not take part in the movement directly, "I bought and read all books published at the time."* The anti-imperialist and anti-feudalist slogans of the movement brought him to a higher level of social consciousness: "Opposing feudalism made me come to know the dignity of being a man and that one should not be the slave of the feudal ethics, while opposition to imperialism gave me the dignity of being a Chinese and that the Chinese people should no longer be the slaves of foreigners. It was this two-fold recognition that had become the fundamental thought and feelings which emerged in my creative writing later on."** Since the May Fourth Movement Lao She had discovered a new form of literature which aroused his interest and "which deeply engrossed me in this new literature and art."*** Lao She later said, "The May Fourth Movement had given me a new heart as well as a new literary language." "But for the May Fourth Movement, it would be impossible for me to become a writer. It had created for me the conditions of becoming a writer."† Although it was several years later that Lao She became a writer, it was the great changes brought about by the May Fourth Movement that motivated him to turn to writing.

Lao She's first work was the short story "Little Bell," written around 1922-23 and published in the school magazine of the Nankai Middle School in Tianjin. He said, however, that it was only "performing my duty in a prefunctory manner to meet the demand of the editor." †† Therefore, he did not include this work in his collection of short stories afterwards. The formal start of his

* "My Experiences of Literary Creation."

** "What the May Fourth Movement Gave Me," *Liberation Army Daily*, May 4, 1957.

*** "Twenty Years of Writing Practice," *Wartime Literature and Art*, Vol. 9, No. 3-4, September 1944.

† "What the May Fourth Movement Gave Me," *Liberation Army Daily*, May 4, 1957.

†† "How I Came to Write Short Stories."

literary career should be dated after he left for London in 1924 to teach Chinese in the School of Oriental Studies at the London University. He read a lot of English fiction after learning English. The loneliness of living in a strange land made him yearn for home. Recalling the scenes of the past made them appear in his mind just like a series of pictures. So, "whenever reading a novel, I often failed to know what I was reading and was lost entirely in recollection of my own past. What emerged in the novels were pictures which seemed the same as those in my memory; why don't I write down those pictures of my own?"* Thus he produced his first novel *The Philosophy of Old Zhang*. Immediately after this, he wrote the novels *Thus Spoke Master Zhao* and *Mr. Ma & Son*. As soon as these works were published in the magazine *Short Story Monthly*, they attracted attention among the literary public for their easy and fluent style of writing. *The Philosophy of Old Zhang* drew its material from life in Beijing and its suburbs under the rule of the Northern warlords. In this work, "the majority of its characters were people whom I had seen myself and its events were those I myself had taken part in."** The novel was a tragedy which depicted a rascal who broke up two young couples. Under his persecution, one of the partners died and the other was compelled to run away. Set in London, the novel *Mr. Ma & Son* was intended to show the difference between the Chinese and English people and to humorously reveal their differences and the misunderstandings caused by them. Through a series of jokes, the novel also shows the way in which Chinese living overseas suffered from racial discrimination. In exposing racism these novels touched a serious topic. However, at that time, due to his attitude of wanting to be humorous and "placing myself in the position of an onlooker"*** Lao She had no intention of tackling significant themes in his work. On the contrary, he wrote comedies about oppressive characters and the suffering of their victims. As a result, his criticism of the oppressors and his sympathy for the victims were weakened. In this manner, his satire, the strength of the works, was

* "How I Came to Write *Thus Spoke Master Zhao*."

** *Ibid.*

*** *Ibid.*

greatly weakened and his humour became almost unctuous; it also created the impression that these works were superficial and digressive at times. These defects were apparent in the novel *Thus Spoke Master Zhao* in which Lao She drew his material from the life of college students. About this work, Lao She once said, "I've left the student life for more than six or seven years, and now the situation of the students is quite different from when I myself was a student." Though deeply sympathizing with the zeal and activities of the students, he did not understand them, and he wrote the novels just as an onlooker. Therefore, he could not help trying to find jokes from their struggle for emancipation and freedom, from the serious but confused scenes.... As a matter of fact, what I've done is nothing but tickling those new personages."* So far as the description of students and the students' activities after the May Fourth Movement was concerned, some plots were not truthful and some satires were inappropriate. In spite of these defects in the above-mentioned novels, Lao She was a distinguished novelist all the same. Mao Dun once commented, "Behind the lines which Lao She wrote with laughs and curses in turn, I could still feel his serious attitude towards life, his sense of justice, his warm heart as well as his earnest loves and hope for his motherland."** His writing was reflective of the struggle against imperialism and feudalism and he advocated democracy and patriotism. These novels were humorous and satirical and rich in the Beijing local colour peculiar to Lao She. By emphasizing the principle of reflecting the society through detailed description of everyday life, Lao She proved himself a writer of realism in style. He was particularly good at portraying city people of middle and lower class background and using comical method to express tragic themes. With his unique style, Lao She occupied an important position as one of the earliest novelists in the new literature.

In 1930 Lao She returned from England and on his way home, he stayed in Singapore for half a year, working as a teacher in a middle school. It was in Singapore, then a British colony, that he

---

* "How I Came to Write *Thus Spoke Master Zhao*."

** "On Lao She's Brilliant Works Produced in the Last Twenty Years," *Wartime Literature and Art*, Vol, 9, No. 3-4.

saw more evidence of oppression and racial discrimination, and he was drawn by the student revolution sweeping the Orient. Although he did not fully understand the movement and still took the stance of an observer towards revolution, facts compelled him to pay more attention to China's fate and to treat life more seriously. Therefore he said, "shortly after arriving in Singapore, I made a big advance in my ideology."* He stopped writing a novel about a love affair entitled *It's Perhaps So*, although he had already finished more than forty thousand words, and set about to write a fairytale called *Xiao Po's Birthday*, depicting a group of innocent children in both a fictitious and realistic way. He attempted to express adult problems in this story and his sympathy for oppressed people and his wish "to unite together all the weak and small nations in the fight for a common cause." The implications of anti-imperialist ideas were further elaborated in this fairytale. At the end of the seventies, relating this work with the social development in Singapore, a Singaporean writer praised Lao She's book for its deep insight into Singapore's society at that time, concealed in a children's story." He concluded that Lao She "had revealed some important problems concerning the overseas Chinese in South Asia and the local society."** Obviously, this work was an expression of Lao She's constant consideration about the emancipation of oppressed nations. After returning from abroad, Lao She successively taught at the universities in Jinan and Qingdao. At that time, following the rapid advance of the Japanese invaders, social upheavals frequently occurred and the people lived in an abyss of misery. The situation urged Lao She to ponder anew many questions and this search for understanding and solutions in this period was evident in his writings.

The first work he produced after his return from abroad was the novel *Da Ming Lake*, reflecting the killing of more than five thousand Chinese people by the Japanese imperialists in Jinan on May 3, 1928. As it was said by Lao She himself that, "there was not a touch of humour in *Da Ming Lake* because the scenes of the May

---

* How I Came to Write *Xiao Po's Birthday*."

** Wang Runhua, "The Prophecy of Today's Singapore Expressed in Lao She's *Xiao Po's Birthday*," *Xingzhou Daily*, 4th and 6th of December 1979.

3rd Massacre were always in my mind."* Since the manuscript of this work was burnt during the Japanese invaders' sudden attack on Shanghai on the night of January 28, 1932, *Da Ming Lake* was not published. Some incidents from this novel were used when Lao She wrote the short story "Crescent Moon."

A Tale of the Cat Country, finished in 1932, was a novel in fable form. *A Tale of the Cat Country* was critical of the Kuomintang's rule. It mainly depicted "the weakness of the Chinese nation and the remoulding of national character."** In this respect, "the cat-man exposed those weak points that had been castigated by a series of writers from Wu Jingzi to Lu Xun."*** Without doubt, it was a serious theme. This novel lashed out at feudalism and reactionaries more than any of his other early works. At the same time, however, it also distorted the people's revolutionary movement. In the novel *Thus Spoke Master Zhao*, there was some scoffing at young students, but in this book, it developed into sneering at the revolutionaries. For a long time, Lao She took an ironic attitude and at times, he showed an abhorrence of politics. No matter how deeply he sensed the corruption and injustice of the society, Lao She still doubted the revolutionary movement that aimed at transforming society. Amidst his jokes one could still feel the heavy pessimism present because of his failure to see brighter prospects. This was very evident in his novel *A Tale of the Cat Country*. Immediately after the publication of this book, Lao She publicly said, "As I see it, *A Tale of the Cat Country* is a failure which proved what an ordinary head I have on my shoulder."†As he explained afterwards, the reason why he produced this novel "is my disappointment in national affairs and various military and diplomatic setbacks. For a sentimental man without any definite ideas like me, it is easy to become disappointed."†† From this comment it can be seen that this work was the product of his political hesitation. The

* "How I Came to Write *Da Ming Lake*."

** Wang Yao, "Random Remarks About the Research Work on Chinese Modern Literature," *Study of the Chinese Modern Literature Series*, No. 4, 1980.

*** Cyril Birch, "Lao She—the Humorist in His Humour," *The China Quarterly*, No. 4, 1961.

† "How I Came to Write *A Tale of the Cat Country*."

†† *Ibid.*

failure of *A Tale of the Cat Country* showed that in the process of his seeking a way out for his disaster-ridden country Lao She had taken a winding path.

Since the 1960s, however, this novel has been translated and published in the United Sates, the Soviet Union and other countries. Different editions of the novel in the same language have been published, because it was translated by different people. In 1980 it was translated and published in Japan as science fiction. Some people in China also think *A Tale of the Cat Country* is the earliest science fiction in China. In recent years opinions on how to understand and evaluate the ideological significance of the novel have differed markedly.

Divorce, written in 1933, was a comparatively satisfactory novel to Lao She himself.* Through the description of the gloomy and senseless life of a group of employees who served in the reactionary government, this novel indirectly exposed the corruption in the bureaucracy and the second half of this work also disclosed the crimes of the secret agent system. In this novel, Lao She had tried once again to use humour;** but here the humorous incidents were helpful in the development of the theme. Although the satire of the selfish, vulgar, and repellent characters in this novel was not sufficiently forceful, Lao She criticized them with humour. Lao She drew the material of this novel from ordinary life in Beijing (formerly known as Beiping). He said, "Beiping is my native place and when I thought about it, a lengthy picture scroll of 'the ancient capital' would at once unfold before my eyes."*** It was through the details of middle and lower class life that Lao She showed the joys and sorrows, partings and reunions of these people. He was good at such descriptions. A number of passages in this novel are like scrolls of paintings full of life. This work was also well-balanced, which overcame the lack of structure existing in his earlier novels. *Divorce* was a more realistic work and at the same time it was also a more mature product which demonstrated Lao

* "Twenty Years of Writing Practice," *Wartime Literature and Art*, Vol. 9, No. 3-4, September 1944.

** "How I Came to Write *Divorce*."

*** *Ibid.*

She's unique artistic style. Another of his novels, *The Biography of Niu Tianci*, finished after *Divorce*, had less ideological significance than *Divorce*. It was also a humorous satirical novel.

After 1932, while continuing to write novels, Lao She also began to write short stories. His stories written from 1932 to 1936 have been compiled into collections like *Going to a Fair*, *The Sea of Cherry Flowers*, *Frogs* and others. The earlier works were still humorous, such as "Hot Steamed Stuffed Buns," "The Little Devil of Love" and so on. Before long, however, he produced many works with serious themes. "The Lius' Compound" depicted the wretched life of the poor people in a shabby Beijing courtyard; "The Sacrifice" was about a comprador-bourgeois intellectual who had returned from the United States; "Liutun Village" portrayed a rural woman despot who savagely oppressed others by using her connections with foreigners; while "Caterpillars" and "Neighbours" emphasized the vulgar life of the townspeople and their petty and low psychology. The short story "Assuming Office" was about a bandit who kept contact with other bandits after becoming the inspector in charge of the local public security. "The Story Heard from Others" portrayed an incompetent official who had good luck in his career and enjoyed a meteoric rise. Both of these short stories criticized the corruption of the reactionary bureaucratic institutions. In "An Iron Bull and a Sick Duck" and "A New Type Hamlet" intellectuals were the principal characters; the former depicted how hope of saving China by developing science was finally shattered under the reactionary rule, while the latter reflected the decline of Chinese industry and commerce caused by the Japanese goods flooding China's market. In "The Black Li and the White Li," Lao She portrayed a revolutionary. By criticizing the abuse of power and the injustices suffered by the Chinese people, semi-feudal and semi-colonial China was realistically and colourfully depicted from different angles. These works show Lao She's ideological standpoint of anti-imperialism and anti-feudalism.

Of all Lao She's short stories "The Crescent Moon" was the most widely acclaimed by the reading public. It showed the miserable suffering of two generations of rural women, a mother and her daughter, who, were forced into prostitution because of poverty. The daughter was naive and knew nothing about crime, therefore, her downfall was all the more tragic. "The world is the place where wolves and tigers devour ravenously; so, evil doers gain advantages." This was the view that Lao She showed throughout the story. It unfolded itself through the daughter's recollection of her life. With a wealth of lyrical language and the repeated appearance of the symbolic "crescent moon," the story had a lonely and sad atmosphere.

Compared with the novels Lao She wrote in his earlier period, these short stories were not only broader in subject matter, but also much clearer in their ideology and more concise. Lao She said it was much more difficult to write a short story than to write a novel. In his opinion, short stories "call for technique to an utmost extent for it was an independent genre the success of which relies almost mainly on technique."* He deliberated more on the artistic technique in writing short stories than in writing novels. Quite different from novels which were usually written in a straightforward way, his short stories stressed both structure and balance; great attention was paid not only to the development of the story but also to the description of the environment and atmosphere. For instance, in the short stories like "The Man in Breeches," "Philanthropists" and others, the author satirized the ludicrous behaviour of sordid philistines and hypocrites. The short stories "Taking Grandsons in Arms" and "Reopening after a Cessation of Business," are full of comic dialogues which show the stupid and hypocritical aspects of life. In the hands of Lao She, humour became a powerful weapon. In works such as "Lao Zi Hao"** and "Fatal Spear Thrusts," Lao She depicted the thoughts of his characters and played up the realistic atmosphere to show the changing times. Contrary to the works written in flowery languages appearing at that time, they gave readers much food for thought. Lao She mainly wrote novels at the start of his literary career, and only after the fifties did he begin to be known for his plays. He also wrote many excellent

* Lao She, "How I Came to Write Short Stories" and "The Shorter the Story, the Harder to Write."

** Referring to stores, pharmacies, restaurants and other establishments with a long history and good reputation.

short stories.

Lao She was fond of humour, but he was aware of the fact that "laughter can't be forced."* One of his characters said, "My laughter bursts out always together with tears and I often fail to know which is which."** Considering the changes during the early and later period, the criticism in his earlier works was comparatively mild; as he himself said, "I want to mock and abuse, but did not do it to the utmost. So I lost satire but I got humour."*** In the mid-thirties, his writing became more serious and his social criticism became stronger. While compiling his collection *The Sea of Cherry Flowers* in May 1935, Lao She explained in its preface that the change of his writing style "is entirely in keeping with my mood at that time." With the increase of his understanding of the deep misery of China, the style and content of his works also changed correspondingly.

II. *Camel Xiangzi*

The novel *Camel Xiangzi* was written in 1936 by Lao She after he resigned his teaching post in Shandong University and realized his ambition of becoming a professional writer. He was motivated to write this novel by a story he had heard about a rickshaw puller who had bought and sold a rickshaw three times successively. Lao She, who had grown up in a slum of the poor was familiar with the miserable life of rickshaw pullers which he thought was good material for a novel. "From spring to summer in 1936, I was engrossed in collecting material" and working out how to portray the images of its characters and how to arrange the story and its plot.† *Camel Xiangzi* marked the turning point of his work upon a new stage of development. At this point Lao She's work became more serious than humorous.

Camel Xiangzi describes the sad life of a young rickshaw puller

---

* "Preface to *The Sea of Cherry Flowers*."

** *My Whole Life*.

*** "How I Came to Write *The Philosophy of Old Zhang*."

† "How I Came to Write the Novel *Camel Xiangzi*."

in Beijing called Xiangzi. After pulling a rented rickshaw, Xiangzi, who was from the countryside wanted to buy a rickshaw of his own in the hope of becoming an independent labourer. In the prime of his life, he was energetic, diligent and hardworking; he did his utmost to achieve his goal. With his firm conviction and through persistent effort for three years, Xiangzi finally got a rickshaw for his hard work. But, shortly after, defeated soldiers of a warlord robbed him of the newly bought rickshaw. He further suffered more blows of fate one after the other. Continuing to struggle, Xiangzi stuck to the idea that he could realize his long-cherished dream by trying harder. However, his efforts were all in vain: the rickshaw he bought with his wife, Tigress' savings had soon to be sold to pay her burial expenses. This ideal of his "had caught him all along just like devil's shadow and made him suffer a lot of bitterness and grievances in vain"; and then, after having experienced a series of setbacks, his ideal was crushed in the end. His neighbour Joy's suicide blew out the last spark of his hope, and then he gave up his attempt and his faith in life, sinking gradually from a progressive and energetic young man into despair and depression. Xiangzi, who was originally upright and kindhearted, had become despondent. This tragedy shows how pre-Liberation society broke down people's spirit.

Xiangzi was an ordinary rickshaw puller with a strong character and the fine qualities of the working people. He was honest, kindhearted, hardworking, full of vigour and had a persistent spirit just like a camel. Though he tolerated hardships in everyday life, Xiangzi also had a spirit of revolt, which could be seen in his angry resignation from the Yang family and his thoughts of revenge on Fourth Master Liu, the owner of the rickshaw yard. His tenacity and determination was manifested in his refusal to accept his low social status. He was honest and refused to accept Gao Ma's advice to become a money-lender and he did not want to take over Fourth Master Liu's estate of sixty rickshaws. His idea that "he would have everything once having had a rickshaw of his own"—was not an ambition to climb the social ladder and become a master of a rickshaw yard to exploit others. He dreamed of nothing but to achieve an independent life through his own labour. Xiangzi's concern for Old Horse and his grandson Little Horse showed his kindheartedness. The reason why Xiangzi's tragedy aroused such strong sympathy from readers was that, apart from his low social status and his unjust suffering, his good character was appealing.

Diligent and tenacious he then went downhill. This was evidence of how an unjust society corroded the hearts of the people. Lao She wrote in the novel, "Among the poor, sloth is the natural result of hard work that goes unrewarded and they have some reason for their irascibility." He also said, "Human beings struggled to get above the wild beasts, and now, they have driven their fellow men to a life of animals again. Though living in a civilized city, Xiangzi has become a beast. It is by no means his own fault." With sympathy for the humiliated poor, Lao She wrote this tragedy which was a severe criticism of the cruelty of the society at the time.

The novel described how Xiangzi painstakingly tried to make his ambition come true. In spite of a pressing desire to improve his life and social status, Xiangzi stuck to his plan of attaining his goal by individual effort, without an idea of how he could emancipate himself. As a result of his independent thinking he kept away from his friends which put him in a helpless position, unable to cope with the blows that hit him one after the other. He confined himself to the hope of buying a rickshaw of his own as the only way to improve life. Therefore, no sooner had he understood that it was impossible for him to realize his dream, than Xiangzi was completely demoralized, because he had lost not only his ideal, but the whole significance of his life. Like the simile made in the novel, it looked like taking a short cut while pulling his rickshaw, but Xiangzi "lost his way in the circled alley and found himself in the original spot after having finished a round of pulling." This added to the pathos of his bad luck and thus gave the readers an impression of an even more unbearable failure. At the end of the novel, the author pointed out that the road Xiangzi had taken was an "individualistic alley"* which was, in fact, a criticism of his hero, as well as against the brutality of society. The novel declared the failure of those who tried to emancipate themselves by individual struggle. This individual story was more socially significant than literary works which exposed the dark side of society in a general way.

As well as the description of Xiangzi's experiences, the novel also touched upon a number of other characters and their difficulties such as the cruel rickshaw yard owner Fourth Master Liu; the political persecution of Professor Cao, Er Qiangzi's rise and fall; the miserable encounters of both Old Horse and his grandson Little Horse; Joy's slow destruction. Woven together these personal histories comprise the social environment in which the whole story took place. Tigress, a character closely associated with Xiangzi, was a bold and shrewish woman in her thirties. As the only daughter of Fourth Master Liu, she dealt with the rickshaw pullers on behalf of her father. Although she was exploitive, Tigress had her own worries and longing for happiness. Having settled her heart on Xiangzi, she was forced to break with her father. Although he did not love Tigress, Xiangzi had no choice but to accept her love at last. Their union turned out to be a blow to Xiangzi in the process of his individual struggle. The vivid description of such a complicated heroine like Tigress and the entanglements caused by their relationship made the plot of the novel more interesting and moving. Lao She showed deep understanding of the life and psychology of his characters.

Written in a bright and fresh style, the novel was filled with the scenes of life typical in Beijing at that time. However, the description was comparatively weak when it came to the historical background and the whole story had little connection with the important social changes happened at that time. Besides, the ending of the story seemed somewhat pessimistic. According to Lao She's own recollection, soon after the publication of this novel, "a worker asked me: 'If Xiangzi died like this, what hope could we

* After Liberation, the original conclusion of *Camel Xiangzi* was cut out in the reprinted edition, and so were these words.

have after all?' I was at a loss for words to answer."* The book revealed, the miserable conditions widespread in that epoch and reflected the futility of individual struggle in the face of oppression. With concise and simple Beijing dialect, Lao She narrated the scenes full of local colour and portrayed all his characters with distinct individual personalities. Lao She was very successful both in applying the realistic method of writing and refining his literary language.

From the outset of his creative writing Lao She had used the realism of the revolutionary literature which had sprung up during the May Fourth Movement and by the time he had finished the novel *Camel Xiangzi*, realism was all the more evident in his work. In the history of modern Chinese literature Lao She was one of the outstanding writers who wrote about the poor. *Camel Xiangzi* is a good example. When the novel was finished, Lao She said, "I am more satisfied with this novel than any other of my previous works."**

Camel Xiangzi is one of the works responsible for Lao She's important position in the history of modern Chinese literature. Before the publication of the novel in installments in the magazine *Wind of the Universe* was finished, the War of Resistance Against Japan broke out resulting in great social changes. Although the publication of the book met with many difficulties, that did not affect its wide circulation. Lao She was often invited to read some chapters of his popular novel at gatherings held at the time. In the mid-forties, the novel was translated into English and published in the United States and was well-received by foreign readers.

Among his works published in the same period with *Camel Xiangzi*, was the novel *Dph Wen* (published in series in the magazine *Analects*, originally entitled *The Voters*) and the novella *My Whole Life*. *My Whole Life* is a policeman's autobiographical account in which Lao She depicted the miserable conditions of the urban poor. The hero of this novella remained in a hopeless state for decades and finally his family broke up. The plot of this work turned out to be more undulating, and it reflected a broader range

* "Preface to *Selected Works of Lao She*."

** "How I Came to Write the Novel *Camel Xiangzi*."

of society than *Camel Xiangzi*.

Throughout the work Lao She wrote about the cruelty of society and the frustration in failing to find a solution to problems. "The lot of the poor people—far from what had been imagined by those philanthropists who give them some thin gruel in charity—could not be saved merely by some bowls of gruel. To give them some gruel to eat is nothing but to let them suffer a bit longer; they will die of hunger sooner or later. The only way out for the poor consists in a complete change of this world." Thus Lao She declares his opposition to the old society.

According to Lao She's own account, soon after finishing *Camel Xiangzi* and *My Whole Life*, he "set about to write two novels simultaneously in the first half of 1937 before the War of Resistance Against Japan broke out on the 7th of July. When the sound of gunfire came from the Marco Polo Bridge on July 7, I stopped writing when I had just finished about thirty thousand words for each of them."* Later on, the manuscripts of these novels were lost.

III. Popular Art and Literature, Drama, and *Four Generations Under One Roof*

Since the outbreak of the War of Resistance Against Japan, there was a great change in both the life and the writings of Chinese writers; this was particularly evident with Lao She. Among the new writers emerged after the May Fourth Movement in 1919, Lao She was the most prominent one noted for the patriotic spirit and anti-imperialism in his works. He regarded all kinds of the imperialists' servants and the slaves of foreign masters as the objects of his sarcasm, because he detested China's subjection to imperialist powers. On the eve of the anti-Japanese war, he wrote a number of short stories about the Japanese imperialists, as well as many essays lashing out at the Kuomintang government for its non-resistance policy. After the July 7th Incident, China's crisis further aroused his patriotism. In November 1937 he left Jinan

* "How I Came to Write *Cremation*."

which was soon to fall into Japanese hands, arriving at Wuhan after passing through many places to join the literary activities for the resistance against Japanese aggression. At that time, the new situation brought about by the cooperation between the Communist Party and the Kuomintang, as well as the unity among the literary and artistic circles offered him the opportunity to have direct contact with the Chinese Communist Party and the revolutionary writers who later supported his work. In March 1938, the National Federation of Anti-Japanese Writers and Artists was established; Lao She was elected head of its general affairs section. As the Federation had no chairman, he was responsible for all of its work. During the eight years of the War of Resistance Against Japan, Lao She did a lot of useful work under the leadership of the Communist Party in consolidating and expanding the united front of the literary and artistic circles against the Japanese aggressors. In the summer and autumn of 1939, on behalf of his organization Lao She joined the group sent to comfort and encourage the soldiers on various battlefronts. This trip took him five months in total and covered more than twenty thousand *li* (1 *li* = 0.5 km.), including Shaanxi, Gansu, Qinghai, Suiyuan and Ningxia.* While passing through Yan'an, he visited the bases of resistance against the Japanese aggression and was received by Mao Zedong and other leaders of the revolution. All these experiences exposed him to the social realities and broadened his political horizon, which helped him to understand the Communist Party of China and the Chinese revolution, and at the same time, to see new prospects for the poor. Because of these experiences a change occurred in his writing.

Having wanted for a long time to try different forms of literature and art,** Lao She began to experiment more. Consequently, he became known among Chinese writers for the variety of his writing. His writing was even more outstanding during this period.

He said, "The storm of war has blown to the front all those who held a sword in his hand; I sincerely hope that, though my

---

* "Back from the Northwest," *Da Gong Bao*, December 17, 1939.

** "How I Came to Write *Swing the Sword Towards the North.*"

unqualified poems and plays are as insignificant as two eggs, I could dedicate them to the anti-Japanese war together with those who had ten thousand *dan* (1 *dan* = 1 hectolitre) of grains to offer. In this manner, apart from short stories and essays, I've learned to write *guci*,* old-fashioned opera, folk songs, plays and new-style poetry."** Early from his childhood Lao She was familiar with and fond of various forms of traditional popular literature and art and knew that these forms influenced the Chinese people. At the outset of the war while he was still living in Jinan, Lao She had considered how to make use of these literary forms to write anti-Japanese propaganda. He discussed with the well-known artists Bai Yunpeng and Zhang Xiaoxuan how to improve the writing of versified stories sung to the accompaniment of a small drum. When he arrived in Wuhan and Chongqing, he began to work with Fu Shaofang, Fu Guihua, Dong Lianzhi and other famous artists. He not only strove to learn from them, but also composed for their performances. As a result, Lao She successively produced a series of versified stories, such as "A Newborn Baby," "The Lament of an Illiterate," "Little Wang Drives a Donkey" and so on. He also wrote some stories about the war in the form of the old-fashioned opera, such as "The Heroic Deeds of a Royal Fighter," "Wangjia Town," etc. These work were later compiled into a collection in 1934. About his long poem *Swing the Sword Towards the North*, which he wrote on the basis of his contact with soldiers at the front, he said, "While writing this poem, there was a heated discussion on 'national form' in the literary and art circles. In order to experiment combining the old with the new, I composed my lines by following the example of the old form."***

On the eve of the anti-Japanese war, the question of how to use traditional literary forms to create the wartime literature and art was considered by writers and with their efforts and experiments, many writers were active in popularizing the new literature. Lao She was one of the most diligent and fruitful writers in this

* Versified stories sung to the accompaniment of a drum or other instruments.

** "A Self-Account of My Writing Over the Three Years," in the magazine *Wartime Literature and Art*, Vol. 7, No. 1, January 1941.

*** "How I Came to Write *Swing the Sword Towards the North*."

field.

During the Resistance War, Lao She mostly wrote plays, a new medium for him. He wrote *The Remnant Fog*, *Nation Above All* (in collaboration with Song Zhidi), *Zhang Zizhong*, *The Question of Maintaining Face*, *The Dragon and the Snake on the Land*, *Go Back Home!*, *Who Arrives in Chongqing First*, *The Roar of a Tiger* (in collaboration with Zhao Qingge and Xiao Yiwu) and *Peaches and Plums in the Spring Breeze* (in collaboration with Zhao Qingge). Apart from praising the anti-Japanese fighters, some of his works also exposed the reactionary rule of the Kuomintang while others satirized human weaknesses. His characters were generally well-defined and the dialogue was quick-witted and lifelike. With the exception of a few plays, such as *Zhang Zizhong*, which belong to the category of serious dramas, most of his plays were also humorous. However, he failed to explore the main themes of these works deep enough and the dramatic conflicts were sometimes too loose and vague.

His first play, *The Remnant Fog*, was the story of a corrupt and greedy official who was used by a Japanese woman spy. At the end of the play, the official was arrested. But when the chief detective was about to arrest the woman spy as ordered, a guard sent by the wife of a higher official set her free and took her to join a dinner party. The play not only revealed the insidious activities of the enemy, but also exposed the corrupt rule of the reactionaries. With its disclosure of insidious activities in an administrative department, *The Question of Maintaining Face*, another of his plays, was very influential. Secretary Tong, the leading character from an aristocratic family and an official for many years was removed from his post because of his tyrannical behaviour, but still tried to maintain face. His servant Zhao Qin, a kindhearted and simple man, unexpectedly inherited a large sum. Among the characters, some managed to curry favour with the people in power, while others struck at people when they were down. In this play, Lao She satirized the vulgarity of these people, criticizing the reactionary officials.

Set against different social backgrounds during the war, Lao She's plays also portrayed positive characters who were immersed in hard work. The purpose of these characters was to serve as foils to those characters who were corrupt and evil doing. When performed on the stage, these plays aroused sympathetic responses from the audience. Nevertheless, they usually fell short of being inspiring. There were traces which showed that Lao She was still in the process of learning his craft. It was through these plays that Lao She accumulated useful experience which led to a series of excellent plays like *Dragon Beard Ditch* and *Teahouse* in the fifties.

While writing popular short stories and plays, Lao She also wrote novels. During the later period of the War of Resistance Against Japan and the War of Liberation he produced two collections of short stories *The Passenger Train* and *Anaemia*; and the novels *Cremation*, *Four Generations Under One Roof*, *The Drum Singers* as well as others.* Among them, the most important were *Four Generations Under One Roof* and *The Drum Singers*. The former, consisting of three parts: "Frustration," "Ignoble Existence" and "Famine," showed that having undergone bitter experiences, the people in the enemy-occupied area began to wake up, gradually realizing that only by persistent efforts would they be able to save themselves. So, with struggle and suffering, they finally won a victory.** The novel revealed the cruelty of the enemy rule, the treachery of traitors and collaborators, the cowardice and suffering of kindhearted intellectuals as well as the strong will of the poor. Among these characters there were some who fled Beijing and joined the fight against the Japanese and others who remained in the city, engaging themselves in the anti-Japanese activities. Con-

* Lao She had once published his novel *Transformation* in installments in the fortnightly *Resistance to the End*. But the magazine closed after the sixteenth chapter, and the book left unfinished.

** See "Famine," the third part of *Four Generations Under One Roof*. When published in installments in *Short Story Monthly* from May 1950 to January 1951, the novel ended at the twentieth chapter on the outbreak of the Pacific War. It was thirteen chapters less than what Lao She had originally planned to write. Therefore, for a long time it was generally assumed that the book was incomplete. The abbreviated English version, translated by Ida Pruitt and published in New York in 1952 under the title of *The Yellow Storm*, contained the content of the remaining thirteen chapters, which shows that the novel was finished. The book ends with the Qi family of four generations and their neighbours celebrating the final victory of the War of Resistance Against Japan.

centrating on the Qi family's four generations including the neighbours who lived in the same small alley, the novel had a complicated plot. Lao She expressed sympathy for those who were patriotic and exposed the evil of the traitors. At the outset of writing the novel, Lao She said, "While designing this work, I've been ambitious, but when I put it into practice, at once I ache mentally and physically. I'm not sure that I'll finish this novel or not."* It is said that this is the novel on which "Lao She had spent his biggest effort and the longest time and therefore he himself felt comparatively satisfied with it."**

Through its vivid descriptions of the customs and scenes of ordinary life on the streets in Beijing, the novel has drawn a picture of the misery of the people who lived in the enemy-occupied area. The small alley used as the arena in which the main plot of the novel unfolded is where Lao She was brought up. This novel is filled with the author's anxiety and righteous anger about the Japanese invasion. However, as the background of this work is limited merely to Beijing and the story concentrates on only one family, it fails to describe the masses and their struggle against the Japanese aggressors. Lao She had not experienced the life described in this work, he relied mainly on second-hand material. This could not help affecting the depth of his understanding of the society described in the novel.

At the beginning of 1946, Lao She was invited to lecture in the United State and not until the founding of the People's Republic in 1949 did he return to China. During this period, apart from finishing "Famine," the third part of his novel *Four Generations Under One Roof*, he also produced a new novel, *The Drum Singers*. Though the English version of this work was published in the United States in 1952, it was unavailable for Chinese readers for a long time because the original manuscript was lost. The novel was translated from the English version into Chinese and published only in 1980. This long-neglected work is another excellent realistic novel. Taking place during the war against the Japanese aggression, the novel relates the partings and reunions of a group of

---

* "Preface to *Four Generations Under One Roof*."
** Wang Xingzhi, "Madam Lao She Talks About Her Husband."

storytellers. In old China, poor artists were always subjected to humiliation and exploitation without any protection. As depicted in the novel, the life of artists was very miserable: among them three young women were cheated and ruined, while some others resigned themselves and finally became destitute. Instead of stressing their degeneration, Lao She emphasized their growing consciousness. Cherishing a dream, Fang Baoqing took a very serious attitude towards his art while his daughter, Xiulian, longed for an independent life. In order to take part in the anti-Japanese activities, they were enthusiastic in reforming their art. But, no matter what painstaking efforts they made, they were struck down time and again by the cruel society. Their low social position became unbearable and they longed for the emancipation of both art and artists. Under Lao She's pen, the initiative of his characters to grasp and change their own fate emerged. This initiative was rarely seen in earlier characters.

In this novel, the revolutionary writer Meng Liang is a character Lao She created with great success. Kind and warmhearted Meng Liang encouraged and helped the father and the daughter of Fang's family. Although the old society still dominated the novel, the sunlight of a new time had begun. The novel came to an optimistic close: "Just as the waves push forward incessantly in the Yangtse River, the man of a new generation has taken the place of the old one." This proverb shows precisely what the novel reflected; the artists had started to march towards a new life.

The Drum Singers was completed at the historical turning point when the Liberation War was about to win a nation-wide victory. Lao She mirrored the social changes taking place at that time, which revealed in turn a change in the author's own ideology.

In early 1949, Lao She wrote in his letter to a friend that "it is not comfortable" to stay in the United States as a visitor. He also said, "I've just finished *Four Generations Under One Roof*, which is now being translated into English. That explains why I haven't returned. It's a big book and the translator is not very good. It'll take some time to translate the whole book. I should have been back long ago if not for the book."* In October the same year Lao She left San Francisco and returned to China in December. Since then he had worked with unprecedented vigour and enthusiasm and turned out many good books. He was awarded honorary titles of "People's Artist" and "Model Worker in Literature and Art Circles." Lao She was a good representative of China's writers and intellectuals in their ideological development.

In conclusion, the majority of Lao She's works were drawn from the life of the poor in cities. Plot development was important to his work and he used the Beijing dialect skillfully. It is obvious that some of his works were influenced by English novels, from which he learned to relate his stories with humour and the use of witty language. He tried to popularize literature and art. His works have always had a great number of readers at home, including not only students and intellectuals, but also broad masses of city people. *Camel Xiangzi* and *Teahouse* have been praised abroad. These works have become the pride of China as well as part of modern Chinese literature.

---

* "Letters of the Writers," supplement of *Hua Shang Bao* (*The Chinese Merchant*) in Hong Kong, February 26, 1949.

Chapter 6

Ba Jin

I. Early Works

Ba Jin, whose real name was Li Yaotang, was born in 1904 in a bureaucrat-landlord family in Sichuan Province. As a child he saw the corruption and intrigues of big feudal families and the suppression of young people by the feudal autocracy. In his father's office he saw how feudal officials persecuted the people. These experiences aroused revulsion in him against the feudal system. On the other hand, he recalls: "I loved to be with the servants. I grew up among them. The honesty of the working people and their bitter lot stirred up thoughts of rebellion in me. I said I didn't want to be a young master. I wanted to stand on their side and help them."* Already then Ba Jin was a budding rebel against the feudal social system and family.

When he was fifteen the New Culture Movement born of the May Fourth Movement began. Various democratic and socialist trends of thought gave rise to anti-imperialism and anti-feudalism. Ba Jin closely followed the events taking place in this new movement. He had never felt so inspired and enlightened.

The *New Youth, Weekly Review* and other new publications became Ba Jin's textbooks in which he sought explanations for his growing dislike of the old order. His personal explorations gradually merged into the struggle of society as a whole. This period was a decisive turning point in Ba Jin's life and ideology. "I often say I was the product of the May Fourth Movement. Like a clap of spring thunder the May Fourth Movement woke me up from my

* "Brief Notes: My Childhood."

sleep and opened my eyes to a brand new world." It was this movement that plunged him into the battle against the feudal system and for a new society.

In 1932 Ba Jin left his family and the isolation of Sichuan Province. He wanted to go to Beijing University where the New Culture Movement originated, but ended up in school in Shanghai and Nanjing. In 1927 Ba Jin went to France in his quest for ideas about social liberation.

Of the multitude of radical ideas that sprang up around the May Fourth Movement anarchism appealed most to Ba Jin. Kropotkin's political essay "To the Young" and Liao Kangfu's play *Before the Dawn*, both anarchist works, played a large part in the formation of the young Ba Jin's philosophy and political outlook. His first piece of writing entitled "How to Build a Society of Real Equality and Freedom" was a political essay advocating anarchism. During the 1920s Ba Jin translated works on anarchism and wrote about anarchism himself.

The New Culture Movement brought in its wake modern science, and democratic and socialist trends of thought. In the eagerness to learn foreign ideas, socialism, anarchism, individualism and collectivism were all studied. Chinese intellectuals read Nietzsche, Kropotkin and Marx. It was only later that Marxism-Leninism was recognized as the genuine truth for the emancipation of mankind. Ba Jin is one of the modern Chinese writers who traversed this intellectual zig-zag path. New ideas that held all authority and restrictions in contempt launched Ba Jin onto the path of democratic revolution. They became his ideological weapons in the fight against imperialism and feudalism. His works were tinged with the radical thinking of making a clear break with the old world.

Ba Jin's concern for the liberation of the masses and for the real problems of the Chinese people enabled him to guide his thinking and actions in the light of China's social realities. Eventually he parted with anarchism some ten years after he first embraced it.

Ba Jin's first literary works were poems and essays written in a modern style. Published in the July to November 1922 issues of

Literary Ten Days, a supplement to *The New Daily of Current Affairs*, and in the 1923 October issue of *Women's Magazine*, these works showed the plight of the maltreated. He wrote about orphaned children being sold in the marketplace, about sedan chair carriers and beggars. Ba Jin wrote that nowhere in the world are the rich willing to give their wealth to the poor, and that "there is no way to bring about a better world other than to create it oneself." These essays drew little attention at that time and later, but they indicated the fundamental tendencies in Ba Jin's work over the next few decades: through the exposure of social oppression and class contradiction to arouse the poor to rise up in resistance and opposition to the unfair social system.

Ba Jin began to write seriously when he was in France in 1927. Nostalgia frequently overtook him during these lonely days in a foreign country. Old memories were relived. "To console my lonely young heart," Ba Jin wrote later, "I began to write my experiences in life."

On April 12, 1927, the Kuomintang reactionaries betrayed the revolution. New warlords replaced the old ones. The Chinese people who had been anticipating the victory of the revolution were plunged into new misery. At that time a worldwide protest campaign had been launched to rescue two condemned anarchists —the Italian-born political activists Sacco and Vanzetti. The United States government, ignoring the warnings from public opinion, executed them. Ba Jin was shocked and indignant. He wrote several articles to vent his feelings. In the summer of 1928 he revised these articles and turned them into his first novella *Death*.

The story is set in Shanghai under Beiyang warlord rule. There are descriptions of the ruined love of young people in feudal families and the execution of workers who spread pamphlets for revolutionaries. The story describes a violent world and the frustrations of young educated people who, spurred by the new ideas of the May Fourth Movement, seek social liberation. The book condemns those who cause suffering to others. The protagonist Du Daxin is determined to "perish for my beloved oppressed compatriots." But harsh reality, bitter personal experiences and a serious attack of tuberculosis filled him with pessimism. "He seeks death to end his endless struggles." His actions are rash and ill-considered. In order to avenge his comrades he attempts to kill the Shanghai garrison commander. The author lauds the young revolutionary's devotion, but makes it clear that individual acts of terrorism make little sense.

The character Du Daxin in *Death* shows the influence anarchism had on Ba Jin as well as his doubts about it.

In early 1929 *Death* appeared in the *Short Story Monthly* in installments. The struggle between revolutionary and reactionary forces makes it interesting reading. But more appealing to the young people of that time who were searching for a future were the questions posed by Du Daxin, Li Leng and Li Leng's sister Li Jingshu about life. Should one try to reform society or utterly destroy the old system? The sharply changing mood of the story —from uplifted determination to depression and perturbation —and Du Daxin's self-sacrificing action evoked a powerful response.

Readers followed the joys, agonies, disillusions and expectations described in the story. Thus, in spite of the crude writing style and ideological weaknesses, *Death* became a best seller when it was published in 1929. This unexpected success showed Ba Jin that literary works could give him a spiritual connection with the suffering youth. He said, "The publication of *Death* set me on the road of my literary career."

The New Life, a sequel to *Death*, is the story of Li Leng and his sister Li Jingshu who are inspired by Du Daxin's death to join the revolution. The novel, in diary form, tells about the insensitivity and backwardness of the people and the isolation of the revolutionaries. The revolutionaries survive and keep on fighting only because they have faith. The tone of the book is gloomy. Ba Jin was concerned with the fate of the Chinese people and the future that would be achieved through struggle and sacrifice. He hoped that the heroic deeds of pioneers would bring forth others to break down the old unjust order. Although this belief was not fully developed, it was inspiring.

Among the author's early works, the ones he likes most are the three medium-length stories in *Love Trilogy*. *Fog*, the first and the shortest, is about Zhou Ruoshui, a young man who has gone through the May Fourth Movement, but is still bound by feudal morals. Weak and indecisive in love, he loses his girlfriend. In *Rain*, the second part of the trilogy, Zhou loses his second lover and drowns himself. More characters are described in *Rain* than in the preceding story, and the plots are more complicated. The main story is woven around the love affair between the young man Wu Renmin and two girls, Zheng Yuwen and Xiong Zhijun, although it is not a love triangle. It brings up the serious question of how to handle the relationship between love and revolution. The two girls end up tragically, while Wu Renmin renounces personal sentiment and joins the revolution.

The characters appeared in the first two parts become more mature in the third part, *Lightning*. Love is no longer the main theme, instead, descriptions of the activities of trade unions, women's associations and students present a picture of the anti-warlord struggles. The main theme is about young people's friendship and dedication to their ideals. Ba Jin likes *Lightning* most for its presentation of society.

One point that deserves attention is the argument of whether individual terrorism should be used to fight reactionary forces. Ba Jin stresses time and again that "We hate the system, not individuals," and "It is an act of heroism to give up one's life, but we apparently need more ordinary people" who are "able to work silently without compliant." On this point *Lightning* is more clear-cut than *Death*. However, the novel gives too much space to terrorist acts and to praising self-sacrifice, so that the heroes outshine the ordinary people. This reflects the contradictions in Ba Jin's mind.

Ba Jin's early works—*Death*, *The New Life* and *Love Trilogy*—describe young and rebellious intellectuals in the old society. They were from the exploiting classes, but devoted themselves to the liberation of the exploited. They proclaimed themselves people's representatives, but could not see the strength of the people. They were unable to find the right direction in revolution. They were paradoxes of bravery and fragility, self-confidence and spiritual emptiness.

Ba Jin has said that the characters he wrote about were modelled on his friends. The stories are records of the lives of those young people, depicting their complicated and often abnormal psychology. There were many such frustrated young people in the 1920s and 1930s. Ba Jin's descriptions of such people in his literary works were a contribution to China's modern literature and his novels strongly influenced young readers.

Although Ba Jin is known for his works on educated youth, from the very beginning he also wrote about the struggles of workers in modern industry. He wrote about the revolutionary worker Zhang Aiqun in *Death* and about the Nanjing workers' strikes protesting the May 30th Massacre in the novella *The Sun Has Died* and many other works. In the early 1930s he wrote two novelle: *The Mould-Makers* about tin miners and *Snow* (originally named *Early Buds*) about coal miners. These two stories present a dismal picture of the life of miners who were paid next to nothing and suffered harsh working conditions. Lured to the mines for work only eventually to die either from harsh labour or in mining accidents, they had no freedom and no guarantee of personal safety. For them, the mines were literally a death house. The story also mentions the workers' progress from individual resistance to organized strikes. The author says, "I showed people a doomed system and told them: Here is the wound and here is the blood. Look at them!" Ba Jin was not particularly good at creating worker characters, but he showed the suffering and exploitation of the proletarian class.

From 1929 onward Ba Jin began to write short stories. By 1937 when the War of Resistance Against Japan broke out, he had published more than sixty. These were incorporated into eleven collections including *Vengeance*, *Light*, *The General* and *The Story of Fa*. Covering a broad range of subjects, many of them are about foreign countries and people—the French, Russians, Italians, Poles, Austrians, Jews, Japanese and Koreans. Many of the protagonists were either revolutionaries or rebellious young people. Except for those adapted from historical events and records, most of the stories originated in the author's association with foreigners and his understanding of them. They show that behind the colourful scenes in many foreign countries one also finds the brutal realities of class antagonism and struggles against unjust social systems.

The increasing social and cultural exchanges between China and other countries after the May Fourth Movement had a marked influence on both the content and form of Chinese literature. Many works used foreign themes as exemplified by Ba Jin's short stories.

Ba Jin's short stories on domestic themes touched upon many social contradictions. "Coal Mine," "Fifty or More," "Hometown Revisited," "Moonlit Night" and "A Trifling Matter," for example, describe the suffering and resistance of workers and peasants during natural calamities and under landlord and capitalist oppression. "The Intelligentsia" and "Sinking" criticize the decadence of upper class intellectuals; "After Father Has Bought New Leather Shoes," "Spring Rain," "Lightning" and "Stars" are about revolutionaries and the frustrated educated youth seeking new paths. The last group of short stories are more idealistic than the others.

Ba Jin liked to use the first person in his short stories, many of which were in letter or diary form. The narrator in the stories might be the protagonist or some lesser character. Later Ba Jin explained: the positive reason for such writing is that one can "pour out one's feelings"; the negative reason is that "I can circumvent what I don't known." His short stories contain more expressions of personal feelings than objective description. Ba Jin also said, "When I am writing, especially writing short stories, I feel a passion that must be released, a sorrow trying to get out. I don't have the time to think of what form to use. I write because I want to appeal and complain, and to commemorate." He did not pay much attention to structure, the arrangement of plots and the use of words. His short stories are like a torrential river, free and exciting.

Ba Jin's short stories are very colourful. Hidden in the singing of a destitute minstrel is a tragic love story ("Mr Luoboer"). "The Mute Balalaika" is the story of a Russian peasant exiled to Siberia who loves art and freedom. The story is criticism of autocratic rule. Three pieces set against the background of the French Revolution present a colourful picture of that stormy era and highlight several historical giants ("The Death of Marat" and two others). These works are imbued with romanticism. *Cleaning Rag* is a collection of short stories. In this collection "Sister Yang" tells the sad story of a maid servant; "The Second Mother" is about a woman who is forced by circumstances to be used in upper class society as a plaything. The kindness and love of life of these two women sets off the bleakness of the society they live in. The stories are permeated with the righteous anger of a humanitarian. *The General* is the story of a Russian aristocrat who flees the Russian Revolution to Shanghai and ends up living on the money his wife makes as a prostitute. The story contrasts the Russian general's former glory and his present sorry plight.

Another of Ba Jin's collections of short stories includes *Gods·Demons·Man*. The first two stories are about several Japanese who, weary of their sufferings, turn to religion for comfort and salvation. In the stories "Spectre" and "Dogs" the author uses symbolism. He also wrote "The Longevity Tower" and several other fairy tales. At that time with Kuomintang terrorism, Ba Jin used metaphors and fairy tales as a medium to protest class oppression. Although Ba Jin's short stories are less outstanding and influential than his novels, they have artistic merit and show his many-sided talent.

Early in 1927, when he was on his way to France, Ba Jin wrote several essays later incorporated in the collection *Random Notes on the Sea*. Written for his two brothers, these essays were not published in a book until much later, after Ba Jin had become a famous novelist. In "On My Essays" Ba Jin wrote: "My first collection of essays *Random Notes on the Sea* was written before I started writing novels." But for a long time the novel *Death* and not *Random Notes on the Sea*, was regarded as the beginning of his literary career.

Ba Jin wrote many essays in the form of travel notes, random notes, sketches, letters and reminiscences. About ten collections were published in the early days of his career. The most successful are about his personal life, thinking and writing (in the collections *Recollections*, *Succinct* and *Life's Remorse*). Ba Jin likes to "converse" with his readers, and he is always informal and frank. These essays are a pleasure to read, not only because they are lively, but also because they provide much material, about the author's life and writing career.

Some other essays portray different social classes. For instance "The Year of 193x, the Double Tenth Festival and Shanghai" portrays several scenes of the Chinese being bullied by the Japanese invaders; "In the Back of Evil Sheds" exposes the Kuomintang government encouraging prostitution so it could collect taxes; "Thirteen Hundred Dollars" is about prostitution; "Gambling" shows the shady world of gambling dens. "Carpenter Chen" and "A Cart Driver" praise the working people. "A Maidservant" is about a peasant's wife who kills a local despot in revenge and courageously accepts the consequences. "Peasant Gathering" depicts the rising political struggles waged by Guangdong peasants. "Bird Paradise" is a lively essay about landscapes in south China.

Using lively language, Ba Jin's feelings suffuse the narration. He pays little attention to the refining finishing touches. His deliberate, simple and conversational language conveys strong emotions and stimulates people to think.

II. *Trilogy of the Torrent—The Family, Spring, Autumn*

The publication of the novel *Death* drew public attention to Ba Jin and launched him into literary life. He began to write in earnest in 1931.

The original conception for the book was altered several times in the writing, and it took Ba Jin ten years (1931-40) off and on to finish this trilogy of three novels: *The Family*, *Spring*, and *Autumn*. The plots of these three novels are more coherent and unified than those of the twin novels *Death* and *New Life* and the three novels *Fog*, *Rain* and *Lightning* in *Love Trilogy*. The work is woven around the decline and disintegration of a big feudal family. It reveals the inner workings and collapse of the feudal patriarchal system and the rebellion of young people against the family.

The book is set in the city of Chengdu in Sichuan Province. The May Fourth Movement causes the eventual dissolution of the family. As the author puts it, he wants to "unroll a picture before the reader about the events of the last ten or so years." Inside the mansion of the rich Gao family which boasts a long heritage of scholars, family members are overtly or covertly fighting each other. Supporters of the old morality, as represented by the patriarch Master Gao and his second son Gao Keming, resort to every possible means to perpetuate the old values and family teachings. They suppress new ideas even at the cost of young lives. The antagonisms become keener between the old and the young, and between the oppressors and the oppressed. In *The Family*, Mei who cannot marry the man she loves, dies of melancholy; Ruijue dies when giving birth to a child; the rebellious Mingfeng drowns herself to protest being made a concubine, and Wan'er, a maid servant resembling Mingfeng, becomes her substitute. Through these tragic characters the author condemns the moribund feudal society.

The May Fourth Movement inspires the young generation to fight for new ideals. Their hatred for the old system and the life under its oppression deepens. Juehui in *The Family* stands out as the representative of the nascent democratic force that is struggling against the old order. He is single-minded, permitting himself "no hesitation, no fear, and no compromises" with the old order. But he is naive and still unable to explain the events around him. To his unsophisticated mind "this old family is an intricate knot he cannot unravel." But the May Fourth Movement has taught him to doubt and negate anything old; so he knows the family "is doomed." He has no hopes for the family, but likes to make new friends, discussing social problems with them and he edits magazines and runs a newspaper reading club. He "exaggeratedly assumes the duty of liberating mankind and reforming society." As madly in love with Mingfeng as he is, he "forgets" her when he is out in the world. Only when he comes home, where it is "as lonely as a desert," is he troubled by his longing for her. At last he breaks with the family and leaves.

Juehui's awakening is typical of the young people in the turbulent period of the May Fourth Movement. The novel describes the growth of the new forces in feudal families, and criticizes Juexin's "philosophy of appeasement" and the resigned attitude of other characters in the story.

In *Spring* and *Autumn* Juehui's influence on this family can be seen in the growth of Shuying, Shuhua and others. Juehui goes to Shanghai to join the New Culture Movement. The book does not tell how Juehui fares after he leaves the family. But the logical thing for him is to join the democratic revolution, as did so many young intellectuals who revolted against their feudal family background.

Trilogy of the Torrent shows the impact of the May Fourth Movement, the hardships resulting from constant fighting among warlords in Sichuan, the students' petitions to the governor and their strikes and rent collectors sent by landlords arriving in the villages. All this provides a background in which a rebellious generation seeks new roads. Among the young intellectuals seeking revolutionary solutions in Ba Jin's works, Juehui is one of the most successfully portrayed.

Two other major characters present throughout the trilogy are Juexin and Juemin, Juehui's brothers. Juexin, around whom all the plots in the book revolve, has paradoxical character and a troubled mind. Representative of a generation sandwiched between the old and the new, he was raised on old values but is stirred by new ideas. He knows he has been deprived of his happiness, his future, his sweetheart Mei and his wife Ruijue by the feudal ethical code, tradition and superstition. But the old values hold him to "correct" behaviour and obedience. As the eldest son of a deceased father who himself was an eldest son, Juexin carries a greater emotional burden than his brothers and more than others in the family, is bound by the feudal ethical code and bears more responsibilities. He is a victim and at the same time a defender of the feudal clan system and its values.

However, Juexin, at the risk of being reprimanded by his elders, protects and helps his rebellious brothers and sisters to escape the bondage of the family. The author arranges a fairly uneventful life for Juexin: he has a beautiful and understanding wife without experiencing the troubles of an arranged marriage; he changes and develops, but along a fairly smooth path. He thinks he has the ability to manage his own fate. In *Spring* and *Autumn*, he stands at the forefront of the struggle with his diehard elders and defends his two younger sisters. In a letter to Juehui he writes: "I have become one of the 'radicals.' You are the first 'radical' in our family and I am the second. I am going to do a lot of things they detest. I am going to create a third 'radical.'" The third "radical" is Shuying, his younger sister. The evolution of consciousness and escape of Shuying is the main thread of the plot of *Spring*. With mixed feelings, critical and sympathetic at the same time, Ba Jin creates in Juexin a full and well-developed literary character.

In *Spring* the female characters are more sophisticated. Shuying is disturbed by Juehui's departure from the family, and from the tragic end of Hui she realizes the danger in her own future. Encouraged by Juemin and Qin she takes the same road as Juehui —she leaves the family. She comes to understand the words: "Spring is ours." In *Spring* and *Autumn* the conflicts go deeper than those in *The Family*. With the hypocritical and decadent elders as a foil, the young people are described in *Spring* as innocent and provide the atmosphere in which Shuying's character develops. The development of the plot in *Spring* is slower than in *Family*, but the mood is consistent. Shuhua, the main female character in *Autumn*, is open-minded, and her bright character alleviates the gloomy atmosphere in some scenes, making the sad story a bit lighter. She gradually matures and starts to argue with her elders. Another girl, Shuzhen, goes in the opposite direction. Whereas Shuhua fights to win the chance to go to school, Shuzhen takes her own life by jumping into a well. Shuzhen, a girl who has lived amid ignorance and deceit and never tasted happiness, shows the hypocrisy of the older generation. She is a testimony to the spiritual and physical ruination of young people by feudal society.

Women are important in the *Trilogy of the Torrent*. The author treats them as individuals with their own minds. These unfortunate young women at the bottom of the social scale aroused the author's sympathy and he was influenced by the Chinese classics like *A Dream of the Red Mansions* and nineteenth century Russian literature.

The author does not caricature the hypocritical, the decadent and ignorant older generation, but he condemns them. He exposes the defenders of the old society through such characters as old Master Gao and Gao Keming (who dies in *Autumn*). They appear staid and dignified, but they are in fact cruel and deceitful. The author devotes much space to Gao Ke'an and Gao Keding, who steal and sell family property to keep prostitutes and use female servants as playthings. Juequn and Jueshi, of the younger generation, grow up following their elders' example. The author uses these examples to show the corruption and cruelty of the old order and its system of education.

Autumn relates to society on a larger scale. The negative features of "scholarly" families are further exposed through such characters as Zhou Botao, Zheng Guoguang, Feng Leshan and Chen Kejia. Zhou Botao is responsible for the death of his own son and daughter. His mother and wife reproach him for his obstinacy. But he prides himself on being a defender of feudal values, believing that what he has done is right. Through this character the rigid morality of feudalism is shown. This character supplements the expose of a degenerating generation of the Gao Family and shows that they are products of a system.

At the end of *Autumn* Juemin says, "There is not eternal autumn. The autumn will probably be gone soon." Ba Jin once said, "In the beginning I intended to give *Autumn* a 'grey' conclusion —to end it with Juexin's suicide and Juemin's arrest." But encouraged by friends, he "decided to wash away its gloomy colour." His original plan was very similar to those for the endings of *Love Trilogy*, *Death* and *New Life*. Urged however, by a desire to make the book optimistic and encouraging, he gave it a brighter tone. The anarchist sentiments in his early works are no longer seen in *The Trilogy of the Torrent*. This work exposes the destructiveness of feudalism and inspires hope for a better future.

Feudal society existed for thousands of years in China. Even in modern times, with revolution, its end was slow in coming. As feudalism approached its demise it destroyed people of all classes including some of the ruling class. *The Trilogy of the Torrent* showed the destructive nature of the feudal family and system towards the individual. It has stirred people of all generations. Many of the characters of this book were modelled after the author's own family members. Juexin is modelled after Ba Jin's eldest brother. Ba Jin tried to fuse his emotions with a description of society in this book, as opposed to his earlier novelle in which he was wont to lecture on politics or argue abstractly on the meaning of life. *The Trilogy of the Torrent*, as a consequence, was more realistic, a trait which was to be further developed in his later works.

III. *Fire Trilogy, Bitter Cold Nights* and Others

Ba Jin joined the national salvation effort immediately after the Japanese invaded China. He and Mao Dun were co-editors of *Beacon Fire*, a publication combining the periodicals *Literature, Midstream, Literary Season* and *Translations* that existed before the war. He was also an editorial board member of *Salvation Daily* sponsored by the Shanghai Anti-Japanese Association of Writers and Artists. Later he was elected executive secretary of the National Anti-Japanese Federation of Writers and Artists. Ba Jin had already established a good working relationship with Left-wing writers, joining the efforts to create a new literature. As the chief editor of several publications, he often published the works of Left-wing writers. He signed the "Declaration of Chinese Literary and Art Workers" and the "Declaration of Literary and Art Colleagues for Unity in Defending the Nation and for the Freedom of Speech," both launched by Left-wing writers.

During the war against Japan Ba Jin moved from place to place in southern China soliciting support for national liberation. At the beginning of the war Ba Jin mainly wrote about the atrocities committed by the Japanese and praised the struggle of the Chinese people. From 1937 to 1938 he wrote three articles in letter form: "To Mr Hitoshi Yamagawa," "To a Japanese Friend" and "To a Respectable Friend," rebuking the Japanese socialists who had betrayed their beliefs and were working with the Japanese imperialists. Ba Jin anticipated the awakening of the consciousness of the Japanese people, so that they would join the efforts of the Chinese people for the liberation of both nations and for world peace. In these articles the author's ideals for a better society can be perceived.

Ba Jin's major work of the early and middle period of the anti-Japanese war is *Fire Trilogy*, also known as the *War of Resist-*

ance Trilogy. The first part is about the anti-Japanese movement launched by Shanghai students. With the conviction that every Chinese should contribute to the movement, the main characters Feng Wenshu, Zhu Suzhen, Liu Bo and Zhou Xin enthusiastically nurse wounded soldiers and mobilize the masses. They are young and inexperienced, but honest and hardworking. As the Chinese troops withdraw from Shanghai before the Japanese take the city some of them leave for new battlefronts; others stay behind at the risk of their lives to continue fighting underground.

The second part focuses on two characters Feng Wenshu and Zhou Xin who work with a propaganda group in western Anhui Province. The members of the group come from all over China. With different family backgrounds, experiences, interests and personalities they have divergent views and come into conflict. Their tense and busy life in a collective endeavour tempers and matures them. As in the first part, the second part describes the young people's bravery and high spirits in the anti-Japanese war. The story touches broadly upon the social climate of that time, hinting at the more difficult struggles beyond that of propaganda work.

These first two parts of *Fire Trilogy* are about the atrocities committed by the Japanese and the resistance of the Chinese people. In the postscript to the first part Ba Jin wrote: "Let the reader see the future of China in the actions of these simple young people." The young people in *Fire Trilogy* have many similarities with the characters in Ba Jin's earlier works. Liu Bo, for example, reminds the reader of the revolutionaries in those stories. The difference is that Liu Bo, inspired by the anti-Japanese movement, breaks free of his isolation and despair to join in the struggle of the people. This gives the character an elevated and clear-cut personality not seen in Ba Jin's previous works.

Part three of *Fire Trilogy*, also called *Tian Huishi*, was written some time after the first two parts and its plot is not very closely linked to those in the first two parts. In the third part the young people who have been active in the anti-Japanese war go through great changes in their lives: Zhu Suzhen, who was an nurse in an army hospital, enters a university and Feng Wenshu leaves the army propaganda group. They are surrounded by young people indifferent towards the outcome of the war and cynical towards life. The main character in this part is an elderly intellectual named Tian Huishi, a devout Christian whose religion provides him with spiritual sustenance in his life and work. When his favourite son is killed in a bombing raid he poses a series of questions to God: "What sins have we committed to be punished so? Whose decree is this?" "Why do you call us sinners? We are innocent!" Shaken in his faith, he dies soon after.

Compared with the characters in the first two parts Tian Huishi lacks the spirits of the times, and the tone of this part is depressed. It was written when the war had reached a stalemate and the Kuomintang government was becoming increasingly corrupt.

Soon after *Fire Trilogy* Ba Jin wrote two novelle, *Garden of Leisure* and *Ward Four*. The first is the story of decline of two rich families. They have inherited great fortunes, but instead of bringing happiness, the wealth becomes the cause of corruption which leads to a tragic ending for the families. The Yang family falls apart when the incorrigible Yang Laosan is chased out and later dies in prison; the Yao family ends amid the misery of Wan Zhaohua after her son Xiaohu's death.

Through these two stories the author intends to convey the idea that feudal families which live on inherited property are faced with inevitable decline. He seeks a just way of life. The structure of the novels merges the two families in a story.

The author's original intention was to condemn the feudal patriarchal system as a whole, not individuals. To a certain extent Yang Laosan is also a victim of that system. But the system cannot be separated from the individuals who support it and Yang Laosan, as such an individual was responsible for his family's tragedy. Yang Laosan is modelled upon one of Ba Jin's uncles and is the equivalent of Gao Keding in *The Trilogy of the Torrent*. Towards Gao Keding the author was entirely negative, relentlessly accusing and deriding him. To Yang Laosan, however, he was both critical and sympathetic. This shows Ba Jin's quest for new ideas in plot conception and character portrayal.

Ward Four is taken from Ba Jin's experience at the Central Hospital in Guiyang in 1944. In the form of a patient's diary, the novel tells what happens in a ward during a period of more than ten days. Over twenty patients, crowded in one room, suffer from different ailments, but do not get proper treatment and some die. They get no sympathy either from the patients themselves or from the hospital staff. Even those who have been injured in the line of duty die in solitude. The author describes this small ward as "the epitome of Chinese society as a whole." Through description of the details of daily life, the novel spells out China's suffering and calamities under reactionary rule. But the story lacks artistic refinement—it is long, tedious and somewhat repetitious.

In *Ward Four*, Ba Jin has created a positive character. Doctor Yang Muhua does her best to alleviate the patients' sufferings and encourages them to go on living. This character is created from a doctor Ba Jin knew, but he idealizes her. "This is a wishful image," Ba Jin recalled later. "At least when I was lying in bed tortured I longed for some doctor who could give me a bit of comfort and encouragement." This character brings a bright spot to this otherwise gloomy story.

The novel *Bitter Cold Nights* was written at the end of the War of Resistance Against Japan and the beginning of the Liberation War. Ba Jin said he started to write this novel on a bitterly cold winter night. Beginning with a winter's night and ending with another the entire story is dark and cold and filled with humble characters in contrast with the gallant figures in his other works. Wang Wenxuan and Zeng Shusheng, the two main characters, are intellectuals who once had ambitions for successful careers. They challenge the old *mores* by living together without being married. But the long years of war and hard life eventually change them. Wang Wenxuan, a proofreader at a cultural organization, finds difficulty in supporting his family of four on his tiny salary. He dislikes his job, but is afraid of losing it. Life becomes harder after he contracts tuberculosis. As "Miss Vase" in a bank, Zeng Shusheng also brings home little money. She dislikes her "job," but poverty and the lure of material benefit draw her step by step into degeneracy. "If I can't save others, at least I must save myself" is her philosophy. Her mother-in-law is narrow-minded and quarrels incessantly with Zeng Shusheng. But both of them love Wang

Wenxuan, hoping that he will recover and become happier. Helpless to reconcile his quarreling wife and mother, Wang blames himself: "I have let everybody down. I should be punished."

Unable to stand the quarrels any longer, Zeng Shusheng leaves with her boss for Lanzhou. Wang Wenxuan goes from bad to worse and dies amid the celebrations marking the end of the anti-Japanese war. Meanwhile, Zeng Shusheng, who had not heard from the family for two months, comes back to Chongqing only to find all her family members either dead or gone. This sad story tells of the suffering people underwent in the bitter years of the war.

Ba Jin recalls in the article "About *Bitter Cold Night*," "As I wrote, I seemed to hear a voice saying constantly: 'I want to seek justice for these common folk!' It was my own voice, no doubt. I had friends and relatives who died as tragically as Wang Wenxuan. I think of them and I still cherish affection for them.... I also felt the pain of helplessly watching them suffer." Different from his previous works, this novel is not an outpouring of the author's emotions, but rather his feelings are subtly infused in objective description.

In Ba Jin's works there are several tuberculosis sufferers. His previous works only touch upon the psychological effects of this fearful disease. In *Bitter Cold Nights*, however, the author describes in detail the imminent death of a TB sufferer, a disease for which there was not yet any cure; the patient's coughing, laboured breathing and speech, fever, and coughing up blood.

Also impressive in the novel are characters such as the thin and expressionless 13-year-old son Xiaoxuan; Tang Boqing who tries to forget his worries by drinking wine in a tavern; and Zhong who dies unexpectedly of cholera. The author places the story in a broad social perspective. He describes events in China that had a close bearing on the fate of Wang Wenxuan and others: major events such as victories and defeats in the war, inflation and small changes such as changes in the attitudes of Wang Wenxuan's and Zeng Shusheng's superiors, all of which affected the family. The street noises and bustle of wartime Chongqing provide a colourful background for the tragic story. Stylistically *Bitter Cold Nights* is close to *The Trilogy of the Torrent* (especially *Spring* and *Autumn*). Of all Ba Jin's works, *Bitter Cold Nights* is the most realistic.

Ba Jin's short stories of this period, although few in number, go through the same changes as his novels from *Fire Trilogy* to *Bitter Cold Nights*. "Mona Lisa," written in the early days of the anti-Japanese war, is a story about the people's determination as expressed through the character of the French wife of a Chinese pilot Mona Lisa. "Resuscitating Grass" and "A Couple," written in the early 1940s, tell about the suffering brought on by the war. The collection *Common People* is about daily urban life. The quarrels and bickering among neighbours in "Pigs and Chickens" or among families in "Brothers" and "Husband and Wife" are described as common in a disintegrating society. The stories are tragic.

Ba Jin's essays of this period are collected in nearly ten anthologies including *Black Earth* and *Outside the Dilapidated Garden*. "Travel Correspondence" and "Random Travel Notes," continuations of two earlier essays of the same titles, are records of Ba Jin's impressions of different places. These two essays focus on his wandering life and the atrocities he saw committed by the Japanese, instead of the social sketches in his earlier writings. *Without a Title* is a collection of short pieces encouraging people to go on fighting amid adversity. *Dragon-Tiger-Dog* contains several prose poems which explain the author's philosophy in figurative language. *In Memory* consists of the author's reminiscences about his friends and relatives who died in the war, including Luo Shu, Bi Fanyu, Lu Yan, Liao Chongqun, Lu Li and his brother who was a translator of foreign literature. Ba Jin eulogizes them and affirms their contributions to literature and culture. These essays reflect the hard life of many intellectuals in those years. The essays of this period are more varied in style than before. The narration is interwoven with emotional expression which makes the articles exciting and thought-provoking.

Discussing his writing in the article "Recollections of My Life as a Writer" Ba Jin says, "From the time I took up the pen I have never stopped attacking my enemies. Who are they? They are all the old concepts, irrational systems that hinder social evolution and the development of human nature and all the attempts to destroy love. I have always defended my position and never compromised." In "Preface to *Subsidence*" he explains his attitude towards writing: "My attitude is consistent, my language is always simple, unreserved, humourless, unskilled, and intolerant. My work might be regarded by some scholars as shallow and vulgar. But in them beat the hearts of the youth of the times. I admit that in the negative sense I have not entirely expressed the ardent hopes of the youth of these times, nevertheless I would say in the positive sense that I at least have exerted myself: within the limits permitted by the scissors and the red pen (of the censors) I have painted the dark shadows they abhor."

Ba Jin's most prolific period was his youth, and many of his heroes and most of his readers are young. In a postscript to *Family* Ba Jin writes: "I always remember that youth is a beautiful thing. This has been a source of inspiration to me." And in fact, Ba Jin regards his works as a paean to youth; he praises the beauty and growth of youth and curses the life-destroying forces that oppose youth. This attitude of Ba Jin's is directly reflected in the style of his writing—simplicity, zeal, honesty, explicitness—qualities necessary for communication with young people. His fluent language draws the readers into the plots and elicits a strong response to the fate and the happiness and sorrow of the characters in the stories. His hatred for the restrictions of the old society and his call for change aroused anger and resentment in many young readers against the old order and guided them to the path of resistance and revolution. For a considerable period after the May Fourth Movement, young intellectuals and college students constituted the main readership of the new literature. But so far as impact on young readers is concerned Ba Jin's achievement is unique. As a writer he has always been deeply loved by young people.

Lu Xun once praised Ba Jin, saying, "Ba Jin is an enthusiastic writer with progressive ideas. He is one of the very few good writers."* A number of Ba Jin's works have been translated into English, Russian, Japanese, French and other languages. Ba Jin himself has translated works by Ivan Turgenev, Alexander Gertsen,

* "Lu Xun, "Reply to Xu Maoyong and Problems Concerning the Anti-Japanese United Front," *Essays of Qiejieting* (III).

Maxim Gorky and Oscar Wilde from Esperanto, English, French and Russian. He edited the publications *Literature Quarterly*, *Mercury*, *Literary Season* and *Literary Miscellany*. *Literary Collections*, of which he was chief editor, was the largest and most influential collection of literary works since the May Fourth literary revolution. Between 1935 and 1949 a total of ten collections of 160 titles were published, many of which number among the best works of modern Chinese literature, some of which are the first works of young writers. Ba Jin also supervised the selection and compilation of *Collection on Cultural Life*, *Junior Literary Collections* and *Collection of Contemporary Novels*. Ba Jin has made many outstanding contributions to modern Chinese literature.

Chapter 7
Literature of the Early Thirties (I)

I. Works by Jiang Guangchi, Rou Shi, Yin Fu and Other Writers

During the thirties, many new writers and a number of works depicting revolution emerged. The prominent writers were Jiang Guangchi, Rou Shi, Hu Yepin, Yin Fu and others.

Jiang Guangchi (1901-31), who sometimes used the name Jiang Guangci, began to participate in the student movement in Wuhu of Anhui Province in the period of the May Fourth Movement. He wrote poetry in a modern style during his studies in the Soviet Union from 1921 to 1924. In the preface to *The New Dream*, his first collection of poetry, he said, "I lived in the time when the tide of revolution was spreading all over the country and my heart burned at once like a boundless flame of fire. I will do my best to spread the revolution in eastern Asia!"

The New Dream was the first collection of poetry in modern Chinese literature which praised the October Revolution in Russia in 1917 and socialism. In "Before Lenin's Grave," he extolled the Russian leader "as the sun rising high up in the sky" and that, "Lenin, lying calmly under the Kremlin's wall, looks still at the tide of revolution surging far over the world and listens attentively to the rain and wind near in the red city." In "The Song of Moscow," he wrote with great enthusiasm for the October Revolution:

> *Oh, the October Revolution,*
> *You've come down like a fire from heaven,*
> *Burned all the remnants of the old times*
> *And illuminated the bright future to come!*

Oh, the October Revolution,
I dedicate my whole heart to you,
And mankind will be reborn for your coming.

Immediately after returning from abroad, Jiang Guangchi went to Shanghai. He wrote a new collection of poetry—*Lament for China* from 1924 to 1926. Although the poetry was somewhat melancholy, he had not been depressed. In poems like "Offering a Sacrifice with Blood" and "To Friends," he urged oppressed people to struggle against their oppressors.

After 1925, Jiang Guangchi spent most of his energy writing novels. In his novella *The Young Vagabond*, he depicted a young farmhand named Wang Zhong who had suffered a great deal when he began to wander after his father and mother were killed by a landlord. Wang Zhong was finally killed during a battle. Through Wang Zhong's experiences, the novel exposed the social struggles during the period from May Fourth Movement in 1919 to May 30th Movement in 1925.

In *On the Yalu River*, a collection of eight short stories written in 1926, Jiang Guangchi showed the suffering of the oppressed by depicting the lives of different characters.

In the beginning of April 1927, less than half a month after the third armed uprising of the Shanghai workers, he wrote a new novel—*Des Sans-culottes.* The novel depicted the process and failure of the Shanghai workers' second armed uprising and the scenes soon after the victory of their third armed uprising, showing truthfully this important historical event and the atmosphere of the society at that time. Jiang Guangchi created two characters who led the struggle, Yang Zhifu and Shi Zhaoyan. Out of his sense of responsibility to the revolution, Yang Zhifu persisted in his work though he fell seriously ill. The novel also included other characters, the workers Li Jingui, Xing Cuiying and others who bravely upheld their ideas.

However, there are some shortcomings in this work. It affirmed those who advocated assassination for personal vengeance. Also because the book was written in a hurry, the characters in this novel were not so distinct.

After the failure of the First Revolutionary Civil War (1924-27), the author passed through Shanghai and Wuhan several times, so that he had a chance to witness degeneration of the participants in the revolution. It made him both indignant and depressed and this mood was evident in his work. In *A Memorial Ceremony in the Wild Field*, some flinched in the wave of revolution, while others sacrificed themselves in the fight; in *Chrysanthemum*, the hero used assassination as a means to oppose reality after the defeat of the revolutionary struggle; in *The Last Smile*, the principal character felt he had no choice but to commit suicide to end his struggle. In short, though full of criticism for the enemy, these works were downcast and written with the formula "revolution plus love," which was in vogue in the early period of revolutionary literature.

It was in the novel *Liza's Sadness* that Jiang Guangchi's negative mood was most apparent. The novel was about a Russian aristocratic woman who went all the way to Shanghai soon after the October Revolution and finally became a prostitute. The novel was sympathetic to the Russian aristocracy so it was criticized by revolutionary literary circles for this reason.

In the summer of 1929, Jiang Guangchi went to Japan where he finished a new novel *The Moon Forces Its Way Through the Clouds*, in which he showed the splitting of the young intellectuals after the failure of the Great Revolution of 1927 and attempted to point out the path they should take. Following the revolutionary current, Wang Manying, a young college student, left home to join the revolution. Before long, suffering from despair caused by a reactionary coup, she became very rebellious, which only resulted in her own ruin. At last, with the help of a revolutionary named Li Shangzhi, she gave up her despair and took part in the workers' movement.

The diary *Foreign Land and Native Country* and the poetry *I Should Go Back*, which Jiang Guangchi wrote in Japan, showed that he had made a new commitment to the future of revolution and got rid of his previous doubts and worries. He missed China and his friends who were struggling, and longed eagerly to join them. At the same time, apart from having read many Marxist works on literature and art as well as much literature, he translated some

Russian literature and began to have close contact with Japanese proletarian writers. Consequently, he broadened his view of literature. On the basis of his new knowledge, he wrote *The Roaring Land* in 1930.

The Roaring Land succeeded in showing the class contradiction and class struggle in the countryside before and after the Great Revolution of 1927, and in showing the armed struggle waged by the peasants in the early period under the leadership of the Communist Party. *The Roaring Land* was the most mature work written by Jiang Guangchi. At the beginning of the novel, he depicts the atmosphere enveloping the countryside before the revolutionary storm. Class hatred began to arise gradually, and when the revolutionary worker Zhang Jinde and the intellectual Li Jie returned to their homes and spread the seeds of resistance, the oppressed peasants developed a consciousness of their situation and a rebellion broke out. They established the peasants' association, which undermined the power of the landlords and the despotic gentry. During this turmoil, a great change had taken place in the peasants' minds and many of them began to wake up to their oppression in the process of this struggle.

On May 21, 1927, Chiang Kai-shek launched a military coup in Wuhan and Communists and Left-wing Kuomintang members were arrested and killed. This was called the Ma Ri Incident. Shortly afterwards, no sooner than the news of the Ma Ri Incident spread out from the provincial capital, the landlords who had long fled their homes in the countryside came back with the armed restitution corps and attempted to disband the peasants' association and put the yoke once again around the peasants' necks. However, the peasants resisted them under the leadership of Zhang Jinde and others; breaking through the encirclement, they headed fifty kilometres for the Jingang Mountain where the worker-peasant troop was stationed. By the time progressive literary circles began to realize the importance of the struggle in the countryside, *The Roaring Land*, with its new theme and characters was soon widely acclaimed for its realistic description of the struggle. The first thirteen chapters of *The Roaring Land* were first published in the magazine *The Pioneers*. Due to reactionary persecution and censorship, the novel failed to appear in a single edition when the author was still alive. The novel was published finally only after it had changed its title to *The Wind on the Land* in 1932.

Writers like Yang Hansheng, Qian Xingcun, Dai Pingwan, Lou Jiannan, Feng Xianzhang and others emerged in the literary arena at about the same time as Jiang Guangchi and they had a similar style to his. Yang Hansheng (Hua Han) wrote the novella *A Woman Prisoner*, some collections of short stories such as *Auntie Shi's Distress* and a novel *The Fountain*. Though depicting a broad view of society, these works had the shortcoming of being too general. But later Yang Hansheng distinguished himself by writing plays.

Qian Xingcun (Ah Ying, 1900-77) published some collections of short stories and poetry, such as *The Burial Ground for the Destitutes*, *Revolutionary Stories*, *Marysha*, *Hungry Men and Hungry Eagles*, etc. However, his main achievements were in the field of literary criticism and the history of Chinese literature. During the period of the War of Resistance Against Japan he changed his literary direction and wrote historical dramas.

Dai Pingwan published some collections of short stories and poetry, such as *A Way-out*, *The Night of Municipality*, *Lu A'liu* and so on. Lou Jiannan (Shi Yi) wrote short stories collected in *Struggle for Existence*, *Illness and Dream* as well as others. Feng Xianzhang wrote some short stories and collections of poetry, such as *After Dream* and so on. At that time, with enthusiasm for the revolution, many young writers tried to describe society and the revolutionary theme from a class viewpoint. However, because they were inexperienced, their work turned out to be formula writing and was all quite similar. This was the common defect of revolutionary literature in the early period. In the summer of 1932, taking the opportunity when the novel *The Fountain* was reprinted, some writers of the new literature wrote articles, to teach young writers about writing and Lu Xun also published a couple of essays to instruct young writers to overcome this defect.

The development of revolutionary literature in the first years of the thirties aroused fear and anger among the reactionary ruling class. They suppressed the revolutionary literary movement by a fascist cultural dictatorship. They went so far as to assassinate revolutionary writers.

On February 7, 1931, Rou Shi, Hu Yeping, Yin Fu, members of the Chinese League of Left-Wing Writers, and Li Weisen, who was associated with the League but not a formal member, Feng Keng and eighteen other members of the Chinese Communist Party were secretly murdered in Longhua, Shanghai. A few years later, the young writers Ying Xiuren, Hong Lingfei, Pan Mohua and others were also murdered. Soon after the death of Rou Shi and four other writers, the Chinese League of Left-Wing Writers lodged a strong protest against the atrocities of the Kuomintang government and published a declaration which won extensive support from progressives both at home and abroad. The League of International Revolutionary Writers issued a manifesto at that time, calling upon "all the revolutionary writers and artists of the world to unite and oppose the Kuomintang's oppression of our comrades."* Having been involved all along with these young writers, Lu Xun had pinned great hopes on them. When he learned of the murders, he wrote an article at once to mourn the dead writers saying that they had written down with their own blood "the first essay" for the revolutionary literature of the Chinese proletariat.** Later he wrote "Written for the Sake of Forgetting" (1933), "Preface to Bai Mang's *The Children's Pagoda*" and other essays, praising their integrity and their literary achievements.

Rou Shi (Zhao Pingfu, 1902-31) devoted himself to teaching at the outset of his career, and later he joined the new literature movement. Taking up creative writing in 1923, he wrote *Madman*, a collection of short stories, which demanded freedom for the individual. His novel *The Death of the Old Time* and novella *Three Sisters* criticized young intellectuals for their hesitant psychology. He had more contact with Lu Xun when he went to Shanghai in the summer of 1928. With Lu Xun's help, he began to translate foreign literature, especially the progressive literature of eastern and northern Europe and he also edited periodicals, such as the magazine *Tattler*, the fortnightly *Dawn Blossom*, the *Germination*

---

* *Literary Guide*, Vol. I, No. 3, August 20, 1931.

** "The Revolutionary Literature of the Chinese Proletariat and the Blood of the Pioneers," *Two Hearts*.

Monthly and others. All these activities subsequently influenced his work. In *The Hope*, a collection of short stories finished during this period, he depicted a wider view of society than in his previous works. He developed a unique artistic style: succinct and simple in writing with deep feelings.

The novel *Threshold of Spring* (1929) was relatively important among his literary works. When this novel was sent to press, Lu Xun wrote a brief introduction for it. About the hero of the novel Xiao Jianqiu he said, "Though ambitious and full of enthusiasm, he was hesitating and too restrained."* Having wandered a zigzag path for six years since his graduation from school, Xiao Jianqiu came to Furong Town with the intention of leading a calm and leisurely life. However, what he experienced there was still sadness, bitterness and vulgarity. He made up his mind to change his present existence with his own individual effort. He began to help a girl and her widowed mother, thinking that they would thus be delivered from their miserable situation. As a result, however, he was slandered and reproached and he grew perplexed. Though love brought him a bit of warmth, it failed to satisfy him emotionally. At last he left Furong Town. This story showed the author's dissatisfaction with reality and his reflection of what kind of a life an intellectual should lead. With its moving narration and distinct characterization, the novel made a deep impression on readers.

"A Slave Mother," written in 1930, was Rou Shi's best short story. Depicting the life of the poor, this story adopted an even more simple style, from which it was evident that the author was trying to "transform the content and form of his work."** In this work the melancholy of *Threshold of Spring* had disappeared, and in its place emerged a concern for the bitterness of the poor. The story depicted a poor woman who for the sake of supporting her family, was mortgaged by her husband to a scholar-landlord in the neighbouring village. For three years, she left her home and child, becoming a servant in the landlord's family. In the end, she was driven back to her original home soon after giving birth to a baby boy. Endless misery awaited her. The story depicted ordinary

* Lu Xun, "Preface to *Threshold of Spring*."

** Lu Xun, "Written for the Sake of Forgetting."

people and their everyday life, and with simple narration the author revealed that the exploitive system was the root of the misery and misfortune of the working people. Although it did not reflect the class struggle in the countryside directly, the story depicted a corner of the miserable life existing in the vast rural area and was a strong protest against the old society.

After the establishment of the League of the Left-Wing Writers, Rou Shi worked successively as a member of its executive and standing committees, was the director of the editorial board and held other positions in the League. Rou Shi kept up his creative writing no matter how busy his administrative work was. In June 1930, he wrote an article "A Great Impression," on the National Congress of the Soviet Areas in China held in Shanghai in May that year which he attended. In October of the same year he wrote a long poem, "The Boiling of Blood" in memory of a 16-year-old group leader of the Young Pioneers who was murdered by the reactionary clique.

Hu Yepin (1903-31) began writing in 1924. In collaboration with others he edited *The Popular Literature*, one of the supplements of the newspaper *Jing Bao* in Beijing; he also wrote for this periodical under the penname of Hu Chongxuan. Within a few years he had produced more than ten collections of short stories and plays such as *Holy Disciple* (short stories), *The Selected Poems by Yepin*, *Three Different Characters* (short stories), *Other People's Happiness* (plays) and *A True Record of the Tragedy* (a novella). In his early works there was a wide range of subject matter which he drew from his own observations and experiences. But later on he concentrated on portraying the life of intellectuals. Though written in clear and fluent language and at times with humour and satire, these works did not reflect reality very deeply and were not politically defined. However, in his novels *Go to Moscow* (written in 1929) and *Brightness Is Ahead of Us* (written in 1930), there was important development in these respects.

In *Go to Moscow*, Hu Yepin portrayed a modern thinking woman named Su Shang, who though disgusted with the bourgeois way of life and seeking a new meaningful life, was still perplexed by the various ideological tendencies emerging at that time. The appearance of the Communist Shi Xunbai enabled her to find a lifestyle and strengthened her confidence in revolution. They decided to go to Moscow together. Then her husband Xu Daqi, a bureaucrat, suddenly arrested and killed Shi Xunbai. This deepened Su Shang's hatred for the old life, so she resolutely made up her mind to set out alone. Su Shang's transformation was presented mainly through dialogue. The characterization of the Communist Shi Xunbai was weak, disclosing the author's lack of life experience.

Through a description of a pair of young lovers, *Brightness Is Ahead of Us* raised the political question of what kind of path one should take. Liu Xijian firmly believed in communism, whereas his girlfriend Bai Hua was attracted by anarchism. Though they discussed and argued, it did not shorten the ideological distance between them. When the May 30th Massacre took place, these ideologies had to undergo a test in the presence of the facts: the Communists had support from the broad masses, whereas the anarchists acted frantically and proved of little use for the struggle of the masses. Eventually, Bai Hua turned to the revolutionary path. The novel depicted how the massacre aroused a strong reaction in Beijing and how the young people enthusiastically went to factories and the countryside. In *Cohabitation*, his last work, Hu Yepin tried to show the life of the people in the revolutionary areas, but it was written rather simply because he had no practical experience.

Yin Fu (Xu Bai, 1909-31) began to write poetry in 1924. Many of his early poems were about love, home and his yearning for a bright future. His later poetry, however, mainly expressed his opposition to the oppression of society as well as his own worries. He wrote, "I desire to glimmer in the grey distance like a tiny star" ("The Footprint of Times"). He also felt that he was "lying on a volcano that is going to erupt and will make the whole world red with flames and fire" ("The Heart of Land").

Yin Fu began to have contact with revolution quite early. In April 1927 he was arrested in Shanghai by the Kuomintang reactionaries. His writing reached a climax at the time when he joined the young workers' movement after his departure from school in

1929. Under the names of Yin Fu, Bai Mang, Sha Fei and others he published many poems, prose and essays. In addition, he also wrote a lot of political poetry. Instead of being worried by loneliness, he was confident he could determine his life as well as remould the times. In 1929 on the commemoration day of the second anniversary of the April 12 Incident, he wrote the poem "Farewell, Elder Brother!" Keeping to the side of the proletariat, he resolutely broke with the reactionary class represented by his elder brother. At the end of this poem, he wrote:

Farewell, my elder brother, farewell,
We take from now on a different path,
And the time we'll meet again is
Only when we open fire with your class.

In "Resolution," he described how the workers held an assembly at midnight; though very tired, all those participating were still in high spirits. In "On May First, 1929," he depicted the march of the workers, the crowds shouting slogans, waving papers:

I walk amidst the crowds of people,
With both hands in my pockets,
While thick reams of paper-sheets
Dearly kissed the tips of all my fingers.

The poet was involved with the struggle he wrote about, giving it more immediacy.

Lu Xun spoke highly of Yin Fu's poetic works in his "Preface to *The Children's Pagoda*." He wrote: "This is a ray of light in the east, a sounding arrow in a dense forest, and a bud at the end of winter, and the first step in a march. It is a banner of love for the forerunners and an epitaph of hatred for the vandals. None of the works marked by 'mature thought and skillful writing,' or showing 'calm grace and awe-inspiring profundity,' need be compared with these poems, for they belong to a totally different world."*

Li Weisen (Li Qiushi, 1903-31) was mainly involved in practical revolutionary work. He wrote many essays and miscellaneous

* Lu Xun, "Preface to *The Children's Pagoda* by Bai Mang," *Essays of Qiejieting* (III).

articles, compiled *A Collection of Revolutionary Songs* and translated the biography of *Dotoyevsky*. He also produced some short commentaries on literature and art and translated a few foreign literary works. Feng Keng (1907-31) mainly wrote lyrics in her early period. Soon after taking part in the revolutionary struggle, she concentrated on writing stories and from then on her writing style also changed greatly. Her short story *A Woman Baby-monger* movingly depicted the miserable life of a poor working woman; *The Vanishing of a Paradise* and *A Sudden Transformation* were about the collective struggle; *Little A'qiang* and *The Red Diary* described the struggle of the people and the Red Army.

Ying Xiuren (1900-33) was originally one of the Lakeside poets. With the same theme, his two children's stories *The Story of a Flag* and *The Golden and the Silver Pagodas* written in this period vividly describe how the Red Army soldiers fought bravely, and how working people had firm belief in the revolution. Hong Lingfei (1901-33) wrote the novels *Going into Exile*, *The Frontline* and *Transformation*, a collection of short stories *Return Home* and others, describing the young revolutionaries' struggles, suffering and their love stories, mostly from his own experiences. The novel *The Great Sea* published in the monthly *The Pioneers* shows progress in his work. The first part of the novel depicted the spontaneous revolt of three peasants against feudal rule, while the second part related how they waged an organized struggle under the leadership of the Soviet regime.

Most of the young revolutionary writers like Rou Shi, Yin Fu and others were murdered while they were just starting to embark on a new literary path. It was no doubt, a loss for China's proletarian revolutionary literature. However, as Lu Xun had pointed out, "So long as the broad masses exist and gain strength, the proletarian revolutionary literature will still grow."* The martyrs had written their work not only with ink, but also with their own blood, so that the revolutionary literature had close ties with the people's cause.

---

* Lu Xun, "The Revolutionary Literature of the Chinese Proletariat and the Blood of Pioneers," *Two Hearts*.

II. Ding Ling and Zhang Tianyi

The Chinese League of Left-Wing Writers cultivated many new writers and helped the creation of new literature. It was under the guidance of the League that a good number of well-known authors such as Ding Ling, Zhang Tianyi and others developed their work in the early thirties.

Ding Ling, the penname of Jiang Bingzhi, was born in 1904 in Linli, Hunan Province. She studied in Changde, Changsha, Beijing, Shanghai and other places. While in Shanghai, she studied in girls' school and then at the Chinese Literature Department of Shanghai University. During her schooling, Ding Ling was influenced by the new ideas ushered in by the May Fourth Movement. She started writing stories in 1927 and published them in the *Short Story Monthly*, stories such as *Dream*, *The Diary of Miss Sophia*, *In Summer Vacation*, *The Girl Named A'mao* and others, all of which she later compiled into a collection entitled *In the Darkness* published in 1928. Soon afterwards, she published *The Diary of Committing Suicide*, *A Woman*, *Wei Hu*, etc. After joining the League of Left-Wing Writers in 1931, she edited its magazine *The Dipper* and wrote *The Birth of a Man*, *Water*, *Night Meeting*, *Mother* and others. These works were well received by the public, and she became the most prominent woman writer of the new literature. Ding Ling was arrested by the Kuomintang government in 1933. Immediately after being released from prison in 1936, she went to the central revolutionary base in northern Shaanxi Province, and did revolutionary work. She went to the front many times with the troops. During this period, she wrote a good deal of prose and reportage and published two collections of short stories entitled *An Unfired Bullet* and *When I Was in Xia Village*. Later, she went back to Yan'an and edited the art and literary supplement of *Jiefang Ribao* (*Liberation Daily*). After the Yan'an forum on literature and art, her writing progressed and she wrote an excellent novel in 1948, *The Sun Shines over the Sanggan River*.

Most of Ding Ling's works in the early period portrayed young heroines who were usually rebellious and at the same time hesitant. Her main theme was woman's emancipation, but she did not have a clear vision of the future. Just as the author herself said, "I wrote stories, because I felt lonely. Being discontented with society and my life, I had much to say, yet I could not find anyone who would listen to me. I longed to do something, but there was no opportunity. Therefore, I tried to analyse society for at that time I was the one who happened to be good at venting grievances."*

The Diary of Miss Sophia is one of the most important of Ding Ling's early works. Written in the form of a diary, this story portrayed a young woman Sophia ,who was unbending and arrogant and at the same time, depressed and dejected. Being rebellious, she fled from her family under the influence of the May Fourth Movement. She was cynical about everything around her, not knowing what to rebel against or how to rebel. Her relationships were full of contradictions. She was in love with a college student named Ling Jishi, who was "tall and slender in stature, with a white and soft-skinned face, small and thin lips and soft hair." However, she discovered afterwards that his character was not so good, so she deserted him. Sophia rebelled against feudal ethics and was an individualist. She reflected those young intellectuals who, divorced from the collective struggle, sought freedom for the individual. Mao Dun once pointed out, "Miss Sophia is a young woman rebel who had a mental scar caused by the worries of the time in which she lived.... This is a bold description, at least it is so for the Chinese women writers at that time. So, Miss Sophia is the representative of those women who had suffered mental contradictions after being emancipated since the May Fourth Movement."** This work and the other three stories compiled afterwards in the collection *In the Darkness* were all produced before Ding Ling joined the revolution. Although sentimental, her work demonstrated that Ding Ling had remarkable writing skill especially when it came to depicting the inner world of her characters.

In the last years of the twenties and the first years of the

---

* Ding Ling, "My Writing Career," *Experiences on Writing*, Tianma Book Company.

** Mao Dun, "On Woman Writer Ding Ling," *Literature Monthly*, Vol. 1, No. 2, July 15, 1933.

thirties, new writers had used the formula of "love plus revolution." So did Ding Ling before she participated in the revolution. Her novel *Wei Hu* written in 1930 and short story "In the Spring of 1930 in Shanghai" (the first part) also had the theme of revolution and love, however she was able to reveal her characters' psychological state and personalities without using the formula in vogue at the time which often led to generalization. In *Wei Hu*, the hero Wei Hu took part in the revolution, determined to give up love for the cause. In the short story "In the Spring of 1930 in Shanghai" the hero Zi Bin was a young writer with some reputation. Ignoring politics, he worked hard at his writing. His girlfriend Meilin was both lively and naive. Rou Quan, Zi Bin's best friend, was a revolutionary who urged Zi Bin to become political, but Zi Bin turned a deaf ear to his friend's advice. However, Meilin was influenced and became enthusiastic in the progressive activities. As the distance of ideology between Meilin and Zi Bin grew wider, she left him. Compared with those stories compiled into the collection *In the Darkness*, these two works showed an improvement in Ding Ling's writings.

The short stories "Water" and "Tianjiachong" written in 1931 marked that Ding Ling had progressed in her writing and it was also a new achievement for realist literature at the time. "Water" was serialized in the monthly *The Dipper* published from September to November 1931, and was printed in a separate edition in 1932. With the flood which affected sixteen provinces in the summer of 1931 as background, the story depicted the miserable scenes in China's countryside and showed how the peasants were determined to emancipate themselves. Instead of portraying merely a few heroes, Ding Ling also described the collective action of the peasants. She described stirring scenes of the life-and-death struggle, demonstrating the strong will and stamina of the Chinese peasant. When they came to realize that their suffering was not only caused by natural calamity, but also by the man-made problems, the peasants resolved to take their destiny in their own hands: "Before the dawn, a huge procession of peasants, the ranks of hungry slaves, with men in the front and women running behind, rushed towards the town with loud cries and shouts all along the way, and with strength even more fierce than that of a rapid current of water." It was the irresistible torrent of water that eventually drowned the old ways. With a new form, this work had great influence at the time. Just as Mao Dun had once pointed out, the emergence of the short story "Water" showed that "the formula of 'revolution plus love,' in vogue for a long while, has already been cleared away,"* and a new important beginning had appeared.

Different from "Water" in form, "Tianjiachong" was the story of how a tenant-peasant's family boarded a Communist who was born in a landlord family. Through the eyes of the young girl named Yaomei, the author portrayed the activities of the Communist Party in the countryside. The portrayal of the 16-year-old peasant girl Yaomei and the young woman revolutionary was very realistic.

Some short stories, such as "On a Certain Night," "The News," "Fleeing" and the others which she wrote later on and compiled into the collection *Night Meeting*, were all permeated with optimism even amidst a depressed atmosphere. "Fleeing" portrayed six peasants who fled to Shanghai from the bankrupt countryside. Unemployment and hunger awaited them there and they went back to the countryside again, realizing in the end that the only way out for them was to struggle against their landlords. These works showed that the novelist began to turn to the path of revolutionary realism in her writings.

From 1931 to 1933, Ding Ling worked hard at writing the novel *Mother*. She planned the plot's time frame from the end of the Qing Dynasty, through the Revolution of 1911 and the Great Revolution of 1927, until the land reform in the rural areas in the first years of the thirties. With a small city and several towns and villages in Hunan Province as the setting and local gentry and landlords' families at the centre, the novel showed how women lived through the endless tribulations caused by the feudalism. In the first volume of this trilogy, the story ended at the period after the Revolution of 1911. Ding Ling did not finish the remaining two

* Mao Dun, "On Woman Writer Ding Ling."

volumes because she was suddenly arrested. Using her own mother as the prototype Manzhen, the heroines of this novel epitomized the women previous to Ding Ling's generation. Mao Dun wrote, "The unique virtue is no other than how Manzhen, the representative of the women of the previous generation, struggled to break through the heavy bonds of feudalism and how she longed for a bright future."*

After having arrived at Yan'an and taking part in revolutionary work, Ding Ling underwent a new change in her ideology and work. The stories compiled into the two collections, *An Unfired Bullet* and *When I Was in Xia Village*, portrayed worker and peasant characters, as well as revolutionary soldiers. "An Unfired Bullet" depicted a young soldier of the Red Army who showed courage in the face of the enemy troops, which aroused a sense of justice in a Kuomintang company commander. The commander could not bear to kill the brave boy, so he did not fire. Another story, "Enlist in the Army," described a journalist named Xu Qing and a soldier, Yang Mingcai, who was assigned to accompany the journalist to the front. They lost contact with the troops and suffered various difficulties for several days and nights. Although the intellectual was frightened because of having never gone through a battle, he was very complacent afterwards. The soldier was unruffled, and longed to go to the battlefield.

In the work *When I Was in Xia Village*, Ding Ling portrayed a young woman named Zhenzhen who lived in a village near the front. In spite of being tortured after being imprisoned by the Japanese invaders, Zhenzhen insisted on sending information to the anti-Japanese troops, showing her courage.

Apart from the already mentioned works, Ding Ling also published a short story entitled "In the Hospital" in the first issue of the *Spring Rain* and was later reprinted in the magazine *Literary and Art Front*. Through the observations of a young doctor Lu Ping in a newly-built hospital, the story criticized the administrative work in some units. This work caused controversy in literary circles for exposing the shortcomings in the work of the revolu-

---

* Mao Dun, "On Ding Ling's *Mother*," published under the penname of Fang Weiming in the magazine *Literature*, Vol. 1, No. 3, September 1933.

tionary organizations.

During her stay in the northern Shaanxi base and later on in North China, Ding Ling wrote a lot of prose and reportage which were compiled later into collections, such as *The Life in the Western Front* and *The Scenes in Northern Shaanxi*. "The Sketch on Peng Dehuai," "The Records on Comrade Zuo Quan's Talk About the Shanchengbao Campaign," "Division 129 and the Shanxi-Hebei-Shandong-Henan Border Region" and others were well received for their positive influence. However, Ding Ling's main achievement was her novels. Her representative work *The Sun Shines over the Sanggan River* will be discussed later.

Zhang Tianyi began to publish fiction two years later than Ding Ling, but he was also one of the new figures who had been active in the literary arena of the Left-wing writers in the first years of the thirties. However, the style of their writings had nothing in common with each other. Quite different from Ding Ling whose language was fresh, lucid and elegant, compact and lively, Zhang Tianyi wrote in a succinct and brisk way, which was somewhat "too jocular"* especially in his early work. But, later on, he "did become practical."**

Zhang Tianyi, originally called Zhang Yuanding and Zhang Yizhi, was born in 1906. Zhang Tianyi lived in many places during his childhood with his father who was a school teacher. After graduating from a middle school at Hangzhou in 1924, Zhang enrolled in the preparatory school of Beijing University, and studied for only one year, and then went to work. Working as a clerk, teacher and journalist, he gained an understanding of different social classes. His observations and work experiences laid the foundation for his writing career. In his early years he wrote detective stories for some old magazines. His first new story "A Three-and-a-Half-Day Dream" was published in 1929 in the periodical *Torrent*, edited by Lu Xun. In the early thirties, he published the short stories: "From Hollowness to Substantiality," "Little Peter," "Bees," "Counterattack," "Moving," "Reunion,"

---

* Lu Xun, "To Watari Masuda," *The Collection of Letters by Lu Xun*, Vol. II, p. 1111.

** Lu Xun, "To Zhang Tianyi," *The Collection of Letters by Lu Xun*, Vol. I, p. 349.

"A Steep Gully," "Spring Breeze," "Pursuing" and others; the novella *Qingming Festival*; the novels *Diary of Ghost Land*, *One Year*, *In the City*, as well as others. When readers grew tired of the sentimental and stereotyped "revolution plus love" novels of the time, Zhang Tianyi's and Ding Ling's works brought fresh air to literary circles. In 1932, Lu Xun recommended Zhang Tianyi's "Little Peter" to the Japanese scholar Watari Masuda for translation and publication in his *Collection of World Humour*.

Zhang Tianyi's works cover a wide range of themes, but he mainly wrote about urban life, and the philistinism and hypocrisy of some intellectuals, who idled away their time by leading a hollow and meaningless life, indulging in drinking and philandering. At times, they felt depressed and dissatisfied, but they were unable to extricate themselves from their lifestyle. Jing Ye in "From Hollowness to Substantiality" and Sang Hua in "Moving" are representative of such people. Zhang Tianyi portrayed them with sarcasm and humour. He caricatured as a form of social criticism. Among his many short stories aimed at depicting the mentality of the petty bourgeois, "Father Bao and His Son" has generally been acknowledged as the best one in which the author explored their mentality more deeply than in his other works.

Old Bao, the hero of this story, was a servant of a rich family who wanted his son to advance through education. He therefore did his utmost to borrow money to pay his son's school fees, however, Bao Guowei, his son, became decadent, influenced by the son of a rich family. When the old man learned that his son was dismissed from school because of having beaten a schoolmate and in addition he had to pay the medical fee to the wounded fellow, Old Bao was unable to endure this unexpected disappointment and the heavy debt he had incurred. The story describes how the old servant had pinned a great hope on his son and how proud and foolish his son was. The writer revealed how decadent ideas had harmed the younger generation.

In another short story entitled "A Welcome Party" which satirized the sordid merchant mentality of going to all lengths to climb the social ladder, Zhang Tianyi ridiculed Zhao Guoguang, who tried to gain favour, with the reactionary authorities. At the same time, the author criticized the Kuomintang reactionaries, who betrayed China. These works demonstrated Zhang Tianyi's mastery of satire.

Following the broadening of Zhang's political vision, themes reflecting class oppression and class struggle became more frequent in his fiction. In "Third Grand Master and Guisheng," the author exposed a despotic landlord's crime of burying a revolutionary peasant alive, while in "Laughters," he denounced the local tyrant and the gentry's oppression of their fellow villagers. His novella *Qingming Festival* is the story of two landlords. At first, they fought each other for a small graveyard and finally became reconciled by victimizing three soldiers. The novella depicted the landlord named Xie who, in an attempt to keep his family graveyard, held a feast for three soldiers stationed in the village. He first instigated the soldiers to beat up another landlord who had occupied the graveyard, and then he betrayed them. The other landlord Luo was described as imperious, sinister and greedy. The three soldiers were depicted as honest and straight forward, as foils for the landlords.

Zhang Tianyi also used his writing to portray the labouring class who had begun to awake gradually from the oppression and duplicity of the ruling class. The character of the peasant Guisheng in "Third Grand Master and Guisheng" was still indistinct, but the new generation in "Children" were described in more detail. "Twenty-one Soldiers" relates the story of a group of soldiers who, having escaped death in the war among the warlords, ultimately rebelled, unable to endure the reactionary officers' maltreatment any longer. Aware that soldiers of both sides were forced to enlist in the warlords' armies to survive, the soldiers saved a wounded soldier of the opposite side and together they started a rebellion. This novella and a later book "Hatred" with a similar theme are regarded as among Zhang Tianyi's better works.

During the War of Resistance Against Japan, Zhang Tianyi's most famous short story, "Mr Hua Wei" published in April 1938 in the first issue of *Literary and Art Front* was compiled later into the collection of his short stories entitled *Three Sketches*. In this story Zhang Tianyi depicted the character of Hua Wei, a Kuomintang official on the anti-Japanese side. As a member of the upper class on the anti-Japanese side, Hua Wei tried to control the anti-Japanese activities. In order to reveal the character of Hua Wei who was egotistical and greedy, the writer showed those fragments of his life which best reflected his personality. Hua Wei wanted to be the centre and to maintain his position he tried to suppress the people's demand to resist Japanese aggression, trying to monopolize and manipulate the people's organizations. However, the masses could not be shackled. People despised Hua Wei and refused to listen to his speeches. Though he had sent someone to drag listeners to his speeches in the end, even the person dispatched to do this did not attend the meeting. Through irony the novella showed the contradiction between high-sounding outer appearance and the weak inner world of Hua Wei. Through the character of Hua Wei, Zhang Tianyi criticized the Kuomintang rulers who opposed the people in the name of carrying out the resistance against Japan.

The two other short stories compiled later on into his collection entitled *Three Sketches* were "Mr Tan the Ninth's Work" and "New Life." Mr Tan the Ninth, the hero of the first story, is a university-educated landlord. Taking advantage of the resistance against Japanese aggression, he sought profit and power through hoarding and speculation, strengthening his personal power. This work exposed how local feudal power weakened the War of Resistance Against Japan. But, from an artistic perspective the story is a bit slow and the characters are indistinct.

"New Life" shows the problems of the anti-Japanese side. Apart from praising the middle-school teachers who worked for the resistance against Japan, this story showed the process of gradual degeneration of an artist who separated himself from politics and led a comfortable life.

As well as producing a great deal of fiction with realistic themes, Zhang Tianyi also published children's literature, such as the short stories "Big Lin and Small Lin," "The Bald King" and the fairy-tale novel *The Empire of the Golden Duck* and others. Rich in imagination there were moral lessons in these stories. Zhang Tianyi suffered from both poverty and sickness during the first years of the forties, which greatly influenced his writing capacity, so he later mainly wrote children's literature.

III. Fiction by Ai Wu and Other Writers

During the first year of the thirties, as well as Ding Ling and Zhang Tianyi, many other good writers emerged. Among these authors some wrote in the twenties and were influenced by the Left-Wing Literary Movement; others were newcomers who began to write with the help of Lu Xun and the Left-Wing League in the beginning of the thirties.

Both Wei Jinzhi and Peng Jiahuang started to write short stories in the late twenties and in the thirties. Wei Jinzhi (1900-72) was known for his works, "West Nurse," "The Bearer of the White Banner," etc. Portraying the struggle of a woman revolutionary who died a heroic death, "West Nurse" reflects the ruthless class struggle after 1927, and criticizes the petty bourgeois who led an undisciplined and decadent life. "The Bearer of the White Banner" tells the story of a group of newly-recruited soldiers who, dissatisfied with living "worse than beasts of burden," embark on the path of revolution.

Peng Jiahuang (1898-1933) had a writing style similar to that of Wei Jinzhi's. In his short story collections such as *Instigation*, *The Storm Risen in a Teacup*, *Happy News* and others, Peng Jiahuang protested against social injustice. "A Thief" depicts some selfish and ruthless intellectuals. "Hastening Home for the Funeral" describes the bankruptcy in the countryside. "Happy News" tells the story of an old man named Ba, who longing impatiently for the return of his son, becomes depressed upon hearing that his son was sentenced to ten years' imprisonment as a political suspect. The story shows the widespread terror at the time.

Jiang Muliang (1901-73), born in Hunan, had a writing style similar to that of Zhang Tianyi's. Jiang Muliang published two collections of short stories, *The Placer* and *A Night Worker* and a novella, *Drought*. Most of his work was drawn from the peasants' miserable life and their resistance against their oppression. His characters ranged from peasants, miners and soldiers to government bureaucrats. His work revealed the sharp social contradictions existing in China by presenting brief fragments of life. "Relief Rice" relates the story of an officer in charge of a relief mission who lends the relief rice to merchants as a pledge which arouses a revolt by local peasants. "A Night Worker" describes an unsuccessful old scholar who made his living by relying on his daughter. The daughter was later forced to become a prostitute to support her family. In order to cover this up, she said she was working as a night worker. When the truth was finally discovered, the old man felt very bad. "The Fourth Master Jicheng," which the author did not include in his collection of short stories, depicts an overbearing and cruel landlord who became frightened upon learning of the peasants' revolt. Under Jiang Muliang's gifted pen, the landlord was vividly described as strong in appearance, but weak in reality.

Both Ai Wu and Sha Ting are well-known writers who began to write in the beginning of the thirties. Shortly after they started their literary careers they wrote a joint letter to Lu Xun, consulting him about story-writing. Lu Xun's famous essay, "Communications on the Subject Matter of Fiction" is a reply to them.

Ai Wu, originally named Tang Daogeng, was born in 1904 into a rural primary-school teacher's family in Xinfan, Sichuan Province. During the period of the May Fourth Movement, he took a keen interest in reading progressive periodicals, such as *New Youth*, *New Tides*, *Young China* and others, so he was greatly influenced by the new anti-feudal ideas. By the time he studied at the First Provincial Normal School in Chengdu, Ai Wu left home because he was dissatisfied with the education given in school and he wanted to escape an arranged marriage. From then on, he wandered first in the southwest border region of China, and then in Burma, Malaysia, Singapore and other countries. At that time, though very poor, he earned his own living. He did odd jobs in Kunming; he collected manure in the frontier area around Burma and Yunnan Province, he was a temple cook in Rangoon, and later on, a contributor to the newspaper run by the overseas Chinese. It is from his experiences that Ai Wu "drew the material for his works in the initial period of his creative writing."* In 1931, due to his participation in the anti-imperialist movement in Burma, he was expelled by the colonial authorities. On his return to Shanghai, he at once began to write with the intention "to portray what he had experienced and seen; the struggle of the poor who rose up against their oppressors."** In 1932, Ai Wu joined the Chinese League of Left-Wing Writers, and threw himself into writing revolutionary literature. In 1933, he was arrested by the Kuomintang government, but as a result of a rescue effort made by the Left-wing literary circles, Ai Wu was released after half a year's imprisonment. Immediately after getting out of jail, he began writing stories and finally became a writer noted both for his unique writing style and his prolificness.

Ai Wu's first collected works entitled *Travels in the South* consist of eight short stories, all of which tell of his wanderings. It begins with "A Lesson in the Philosophy of Life," which is a first-person narration of an educated young man outcast in Kunming, utterly at the end of his tether. Penniless, without any employment prospects, the young man finds himself in danger of being driven out of the tavern and will have to live without shelter. It is an autobiographical account to some degree. The contempt he felt for these circumstances and the toughness with which he challenged life is a vein that runs through many of Ai Wu's works. "In the Midst of a Gorge" was about the misfortunes of those oppressed by social injustice. The protagonists were a rough bunch reduced to pilfering in their wandering life, who realized that "cowardice will only lead them to be trampled upon," but they failed in finding the right path in their struggle for survival. Little Black Bull, the hero of the story, is portrayed as an honest peasant who left his native area to get away from Lord Zhang's tyranny, only to be swallowed up by the evils of the society. In describing the miserable life of Little Black Bull, the author criticized the old society which brought about the hero's ruin. Much detail is devoted to the description of a young girl called Wild Cat, whose enthusiasm, shrewishness, naivety and kindness not only lighten up the

* "Preface to *The Collection of Short Stories by Ai Wu.*"
** "Preface to *Travels in the South.*"

oppressive atmosphere of the story, but represent the wanderers' simple and fine qualities hidden behind their outward personas.

"Foreign Officials and Hens" and "A Cursed Smile" are about the imperialists' blackmail of people in the border areas. "Foreign Officials and Hens" is contemptuously ironical in its condemnation of the imperialists, while "A Cursed Smile" is indignant. "A Night in South China" and "Winds from Europe" which have been included in his collected works entitled *A Night in South China* are not narrated in the first-person. Ai Wu attempted to interweave characters into various plots in order to mirror life in Burma and the Sino-Burmese border areas and to depict the hardships and miseries of the colonial people as well as their struggle. "Xujia Village in an Uproar" is about the bloody struggle waged by the people of Northeast China against the Japanese aggressors. The story which came out in 1933 when the anti-Japanese movement was on the rise inspired the people's struggle. Apart from *Travels in the South* and *A Night in South China*, the works that Ai Wu produced early in the 1930s include a novella entitled *The Banana Valley* and two collected works, *Night Scene* and *On an Island*. An earlier story, "Aboard a Ship Bound for Taiyuan," is not included in any of his collected works. It is about a Kuomintang soldier who once fought the Red Army and was captured. It met with Lu Xun's approval for "its plain writing."*

Ai Wu's works produced during that period broke fresh ground in describing the life of the poor in southeast China border area and Burma and their struggles. Adept in weaving scenic description, narration and characterization he created a series of pictures imbued with local colour in an exotic atmosphere. In his strongly lyrical style he wrote about human tragedies set in the beautiful southern scenery. For all their crookedness, Ai Wu's characters, including those who pilfered for their survival, were still kind, honest and sincere in their inner-mind. In contrast with the prevailing squalor and depravity as well as the social injustice and cruelty inflicted upon them, these qualities shone all the more and gave them confidence in their struggle for survival. His works

* Quoted from "Preface to the New Edition of *Collection of Short Stories by Ai Wu*."

are lucid and optimistic, achieved not by high-sounding slogans or unrealistic bright endings, but through the qualities of the characters in the face of adversity.

Even during the War of Resistance Against Japan and throughout the late 1940s when life was very hard for him, Ai Wu continued to write prolifically. Compared with his early works, those of that period were more serious, broader in perspective and less romantic. Like many of the literary works of the period, *On a Voyage Along the River*, a novella written in the early period of the war against Japan, and some of the stories under the title of *The Wasteland* lacked depth. This was a defect set right in his later works. *A Woman's Tragedy* and *Nostalgia*, both of which are novelle and the short story "Sister Shiqing" was a deeper work. *A Woman's Tragedy* is the story of a peasant woman named Fourth Sister Zhou who is hounded by the local reactionaries and finally commits suicide by jumping from a precipice. *Nostalgia* describes how a poor peasant named Chen Yousheng revolts against oppression. "Sister Shiqing" gives an account of a peasant woman's hard work and how she endured bitter experiences. These works expose the reactionary rule in the countryside, showing how Chinese people suffered on the eve of liberation. It was Ai Wu's belief that social injustice would soon be over and a new social order was dawning upon China. "On a Gloomy Night," a story about two young men of different characters picking their way to the guerrilla areas on a gloomy night, reveals the author's aspiration for better future.

In the 1940s Ai Wu turned out three novels, *The Fertile Plain*, *Hometown* and *A Mountain Region*. *The Fertile Plain*, which abounds in local details, was not published until 1946. The novel has two volumes: the first volume, *Spring*, was written before the anti-Japanese war broke out and the second volume, *When the Flowers Fall*, when the war was going on. The story unfolds the life of the people in the Mintuo River Valley in Sichuan Province. Attractive as the scenery is, the fertile plain is by no means a paradise for the labouring people. Three farmhands of different characters are depicted. Their reactions against oppression vary: one takes it lying down, another rises in uncompromising revolt, the third takes a middle course. In spite of this potentially moving theme, the novel lacks a complete, touching plot and the characters are inadequately portrayed. *Hometown*, a six-volume novel, appeared in serial in 1942 *Literary and Art Magazine* of Guilin. The novel came out in book form in 1947 and turned out to be the lengthiest of all Ai Wu's novels. Set in a remote county town located in the hilly regions south of the Yangtse River, it portrays a college graduate named Yu Junting, who is visiting his hometown. Ai Wu writes about all aspects of the county's society and depicts many different characters. In so doing, he has succeeded in providing a social panorama of a Kuomintang-controlled county town during the anti-Japanese war. Ai Wu also describes the crimes that the local tyrants and gentry have committed, how the bureaucratic politicians have tried to put the clock back, how the oppressed peasants have endured hardship and how patriotic intellectuals have made appeals on behalf of the people. Some of the scenes, for example, the scene of the enraged peasants attacking the bank and the county government office, have a dramatic effect. Yet interspersed with these more interesting passages are excessive trivial description and scanty details of characterization, so the book strikes the reader as lengthy and tedious.

A Mountain Region, written in 1947, signified that Ai Wu had come into his own as a novelist. "My limited perspective has made it impossible," said the author, "for me to write an epic of the whole anti-Japanese war. I can only note down to the best of my capability what had happened in a small mountain village on an eventful day."* The novel mirrors the relationships among the rural people of different class backgrounds, and their varying ideological outlooks. He creates dozens of characters and the principal characters are more distinct and lively than those of *The Fertile Plain* and *Hometown*. The poor peasants in the novel are described in detail, as are the members of the upper classes. Rarely had any other literary work produced in Kuomintang-controlled areas reflected rural class relationships so accurately and so distinctively.

---

* "Postscript to *A Mountain Region*."

The novel was highly praised by the progressive literary circles of the time.

IV. Plays of Ouyang Yuqian, Hong Shen and Others

In the early years of the thirties, the drama movement developed under the leadership of the Chinese Communist Party. In August 1929, the Shanghai Art Drama Society was formed by Shen Duanxian, Zheng Boqi, Feng Naichao, Qian Xingcun, Ye Chen, Ling He, Chen Bo'er, Liu Baoluo and others. Apart from staging performances, the society had the goals to develop new drama and to create a proletarian drama. The society also emphasized that drama should serve the revolution. Under the influence of this society, the political tendency of many other drama societies, such as the South China Society, the Modern Drama Society, the Xinyou Drama Society, the Fudan Drama Society, etc., had also become more radical. In April 1930, the Shanghai Art Drama Society was suddenly closed by the Kuomintang. On August 1 of the same year, theatre workers established the Federation of the Chinese Left-Wing Drama Troupes; before long, it was reorganized into the Federation of Left-Wing Dramatists (briefly called the Drama Federation) with branch organizations in Nantong, Beijing, Wuhan, Guangzhou and Nanjing and small groups in Qingdao, Hangzhou and other places. They coordinated their activities closely with those of the League of Left-Wing Writers.

Soon after the events of September 18 and January 28, with rapid development of the anti-Japanese patriotic movement throughout China, theatre flourished. The Dadao Drama Troupe sponsored by Tian Han, the Morning Star Drama Troupe sponsored by Shi Yi and many other drama societies and troupes staged modern dramas with the struggle against Japan as the principal theme. They also gave performances in factories and suburbs, as well as in the cities, which helped popularize modern drama. In 1933, owing to the sabotage of the reactionary clique, it was difficult to stage progressive productions in the cities. The Federation of Left-Wing Dramatists issued a slogan—"Drama should go to the countryside"; and so many drama troupes left Shanghai and toured China's countryside. It was impossible for modern drama to really develop in the countryside, yet the movement had finally begun to break the limitation that modern dramas were only staged in big cities and it was the first step to popularize drama among the masses. In the beginning of 1936, the Drama Federation dissolved of its own accord, and in its place the Association of Chinese Dramatists was established; it united playwrights and stage workers, and mobilized them for the anti-Japanese movement.

During the first years of the thirties, together with the flourishing of modern drama, an unprecedented period of playwriting also emerged. Many dramatists who had made their names in the twenties, such as Tian Han, Hong Shen, Ouyang Yuqian and others, continued to produce new works, while new playwrights such as Xia Yan, Yang Hansheng, Chen Baichen, Song Zhidi and Yu Ling appeared. The appearance of *Thunderstorm* and *Sunrise* written by Cao Yu marked a higher level of playwriting by modern Chinese dramatists.

Ouyang Yuqian (1899-1962) was a famous contemporary Chinese dramatist, who began to write modern drama very early. Born in Liuyang County, Hunan Province, Ouyang Yuqian studied in Japan in his early years. Before the Revolution of 1911, he had been one of the key members of the Spring Willow Society, and took part in the play adapted from Mrs Stowe's *Uncle Tom's Cabin*. While organizing the Wen Club soon after his return to Hunan in 1913, he wrote and performed in the five-act play entitled *The Strength of Movement*, in which he satirized the degeneration of some members of the Revolutionary Party after the Revolution of 1911. The May Fourth Movement further stimulated his work. He wrote *The Shrew* in 1922 and *After Returning Home* in 1924. The conflicts in these two plays were both brought about by unfaithful love. *The Shrew* criticized decadent feudal morality. Though lacking in depth, it praised Yu Suxin who was regarded as a "shrew" by adherents to feudalism. She left home at last because of too much frustration. *After Returning Home* criticized the irresponsible act of Lu Zhiping who abandoned his wife. This might have been used to develop the play into a tragedy, however, instead of writing a tragedy, Ouyang Yuqian handled it so that the significance of the struggle was somewhat reduced. *Pan Jinlian*, another five-act play, was written in 1928 "under the influence of the ideology of opposing feudalism, demanding the emancipation of individuality and doing away with superstition, the ideology that was spread during the May Fourth Movement."* Pan Jinlian, a character from *Outlaws of the Marsh*, was a woman seeking the emancipation of individuality and choice in marriage. The playwright attacked feudal power and the system of arranged marriages.

During the early years of the thirties, Ouyang Yuqian threw himself into the progressive drama movement. The range of themes in his work expanded. In *Behind the Screen*, through depicting the unfortunate encounters of the actress Yiqing and her mother as well as the degenerate life of the director of "the Society for Maintaining Morality" and his son, the author exposed the evil doings of the defenders of feudalism. *The Family of a Rickshaw Puller* described the miserable life of the poor townsfolk and denounced the criminal acts of both the imperialists and the comprador class; *A Piece of Business* disclosed the sordid conduct of a comprador who was willing to make a deal by selling his own relative; *Three Families Living Together* showed the hellish life of workers in the city, who were sometimes slaughtered by warlords and suffered during frequent civil wars as well as from economic deprivation when the money was devalued. These themes were drawn from Ouyang Yuqian's own observations so he was able to described them very realistically. Due to his stage experience and his writing skill, he succeeded in creating vivid characters and his work was significant in its criticism of society.

In the early winter soon after the outbreak of the War of Resistance Against Japan in 1937, Ouyang Yuqian, adapted *The Peach Blossom Fan*, a work of the famous Qing Dynasty dramatist Kong Shangren, into a Beijing opera, and in 1939 he adapted it into a Guangxi opera, which created a furore when it was staged. Then, in 1946, he once again adapted it into a modern drama, with the

* "Preface to the *Selected Works of Ouyang Yuqian*."

love story of Li Xiangjun and Hou Chaozong as a thread. In this play, the author praised the patriotic spirit of his heroine and gave "a good beating to those fellows who sought power and wealth by betraying their country."* After 1939 Ouyang Yuqian also wrote several one-act plays, such as *The More He's Beaten, the Fatter He Gets* and others, most of which satirized the corrupt members of the Kuomintang."** In 1942, he wrote the five-act historical play *The Royal Prince Li Xiucheng*.

In *The Royal Prince Li Xiucheng*, Ouyang Yuqian portrayed Li as a revolutionary hero who was "always loyal and firm, without a moment of vacillation." As the author himself had once said, "Revolutionaries should have the spirit of daring to sacrifice their lives for their belief, and what supports the nation is none other than its strong citizens. Those double-dealers who vacillate and seize every chance to gain advantage by trickery are doomed to be cast aside. It is with this purpose I've written the play."*** At the beginning of this play, the Taiping Heavenly Kingdom was in a critical situation, its capital besieged by Zeng Guoquan's troops. The Heavenly King was still suspicious and jealous of Li Xiucheng, and many relatives of the imperial family scrambled for power and profit and tried to break up the revolutionary force. Thus it was impossible for Li Xiucheng to carry out his plans to save the Heavenly Kingdom from being totally destroyed. Though repeatedly defeated, Li Xiucheng persisted all the more in his struggle until the Heavenly King committed suicide and the capital fell into the hands of the enemy and Li Xiucheng himself was taken prisoner. Through this tragic story, the playwright explained that the failure of the Taiping Heavenly Kingdom was caused mainly not by the suppression of the Qing government and the imperialists, but by the split inside the revolutionary camp. It was caused by the treacherous court officials who were in power and traitors who betrayed the peasant uprising. Although the play had many characters and was long it was tightly knit, vivid and touching.

Hong Shen (1894-1955) was also a well-known Chinese mod-

---

* Ouyang Yuqian, "Preface to *The Peach Blossom Fan*."
** "Preface to *Selected Works of Ouyang Yuqian*."
*** Ouyang Yuqian, "Preface to *The Royal Prince Li Xiucheng*."

ern dramatist. Born in Wujin County, Jiangsu Province, he studied drama abroad at Harvard University soon after his graduation from Tsinghua University in 1916. On his return to China in 1922, he taught at several universities successively, and spent most of his energy on drama. In 1916, he wrote a play entitled *The Tragedy of the Poor*, in which he showed his sympathy for the poverty-stricken masses. Hong Shen completed *The Yama Zhao* in 1922 which he said was "not a work following the fashion." Zhao Da, the hero of this play, was originally a peasant. When foreign capitalism made its incursion into the Chinese countryside, his whole family was ruined. Zhao Da was forced to become a soldier in a warlord's troop. He was full of contradictions and fought within his mind even when committing crimes, such as stealing his fellow soldier's meagre pay pocketed by their battalion commander. Of course, compared with the battalion commander, he was a little better than his superiors. Being obedient to his battalion commander, Zhao Da submitted meekly even to being coursed or beaten. After Zhao Da was beaten to death, his fellow soldier Lao Li ran away with Zhao's money. At that time, in the warlords' troop, people like Zhao Da, Lao Li and the battalion commander were not rare. Hong Shen exposed the crimes of the warlords' rule by presenting these evil characters. The play had its limitations, just as Hong Shen put it later on in his preface, "I merely want to say that this kind of crime is caused by society, but I failed to draw the due conclusion...."* With its concise and convincing dialogues and the vivid description of the characters, the first part of the play is more successful. But, in the second half of the play, in recounting the crimes Zhao Da had committed, Hong Shen adopted the artistic method used by O'Neill in *The Emperor Jones* and devoted long paragraphs to the description of abnormal psychology, a method to which the audience and readers were not accustomed.

In 1930 Hong Shen joined the League of Left-Wing Writers and the Drama Federation, devoting himself to the work of progressive drama and film plays with even greater enthusiasm. Soon after producing *The Yama Zhao*, he completed three other plays in the

* "Preface to the *Selected Works of Hong Shen*."

early years of the thirties *Wukui Bridge* (one act), *Fragrant Rice* (three acts) and *The Black Dragon Pond* (four acts). These three works were called collectively *The Trilogy of the Countryside*.

In this trilogy, *Wukui Bridge* is the one that received the most praise. The Wukui Bridge was located on a river which, though small, was the important waterway for the nearby villages. Due to the narrow bridge opening, the peasants found it difficult for their pumping boats to pass through when there was a drought. Therefore, the question of whether the bridge ought to be kept or torn down had much to do with the harvest of more than twenty-six hectares of rice fields on the eastern side of the bridge. At the same time, according to geomancy the bridge was closely connected with the landlord Zhou's ancestral tomb and was the symbol of the feudal landlord's prestige. The question of tearing down the bridge thus became a conflict between the peasants and the gentry landlord class.

It was precisely around this question that the playwright unfolded his description of the class struggle in the countryside. He successfully created two characters in this play: the young peasant Li Quansheng and the local despotic landlord Zhou. Daring to wage a struggle against feudal power, Li Quansheng won the victory to finally remove the Wukui Bridge by exposing Zhou's deceitful trick to crush the peasants' determination. No matter how Zhou tried to threaten the peasants with the soldiers, policemen and the law, and no matter how much he tried to disunite the peasants, both his schemes and armed suppression met with failure in the end. This play held the audience's attention with the tension running higher and higher with the development of the story. In the history of modern Chinese literature, *Wukui Bridge* is an excellent play reflecting the peasants' struggle against feudal landlords and was well received by audiences.

During the anti-Japanese movement which spread all over China after the September 18 and January 28 incidents, Hong Shen wrote plays advocating anti-imperialism and resistance against Japanese aggression. The play *Smuggling* (which was first discussed by a group and then written by Hong Shen) was very popular. In the early years of the War of Resistance Against Japan, Hong Shen took an active part in organizing and leading the activities of the national salvation drama troupes, and he wrote a series of plays at that time, such as *Rice*, *Bao Dexing*, *Money and Painting*, *Oh, Woman, Woman* and others. Exposing the corrupt Kuomintang recruiting system, the four-act play *Bao Dexing* was written in Sichuan dialect. After the victory of the anti-Japanese war, Hong Shen finished *Look at the Sky When the Cock Crows*. Set in an inn near the highway in the northern part of Sichuan Province, this play revealed the gloomy society even after the victory of the war against Japan through the description of the ideological conflicts of the inn-owner's family as well as his customers. In this play the author called for democracy and freedom through his characters. Though the play won a popular audience it did not reflect reality deep enough.

Immediately after the founding of New China, both Ouyang Yuqian and Hong Shen threw themselves into the work of popular drama with all their energy.

V. Tian Han

Tian Han, one of the most outstanding Chinese modern dramatists, was generally acknowledged as one of the pioneers of the early drama movement after the May Fourth Movement in 1919 and the revolutionary drama movement after the Great Revolution of 1927.

Tian Han (1898-1968), who was also known as Shouchang, was born in Changsha, Hunan Province. With financial help from his relatives and friends, he studied in Japan in his youth. Joining the Young China Society immediately after the May Fourth Movement, together with Guo Moruo, Yu Dafu, Cheng Fangwu, Zhang Ziping and others, he sponsored the establishment of the Creation Society. Starting his career of play-writing as early as 1919, Tian Han produced many plays, such as *Violin and Rose* and *A Night in a Cafe*. He also translated Shakespeare's *Hamlet* and *Romeo and Juliet*. On his return to China in 1921, he edited and published the magazine *The Southern China* while continuing to write plays. The Southern

China Society, formed on his initiative and under his leadership, promoted modern drama in China. As well as expressing anti-imperialism and anti-feudalism through its activities in the early period, this society had the tendencies of both romanticism and aestheticism.

A Night in a Cafe, a one-act play written in 1920, influenced the drama movement during the early period. It is story of how Bai Qiuying, the daughter of a poor scholar, was forsaken by Li Qianqing, the son of a salt merchants. The play denounced the bourgeois notion that relationship was connected to money and social status. In the play, Bai Qiuying said to Li Qianqing, "You, both you and your father, are really good at making deals! Your father used to engage in the illegal salt business, and now, you yourself have taken up the trade in love letters." Finally, she burned all the money and love letters Li had given her. Through this play Tian Han criticized philistinism. The defect of this play is that it was tinged with too much sentimentalism, and the heroine Bai Qiuying was too weak in some respects. When the play was revised in 1932, the sentimentality of the play was toned down and Bai Qiuying's character became more balanced.

Not long after *A Night in a Cafe*, Tian Han produced a series of one-act plays. Among them, *Before Lunch* (renamed later as *Sisters*), published in the quarterly *Creation*, was the earliest work in which the playwright reflected the life of workers, and was therefore generally regarded as the earliest play in modern Chinese drama depicting the struggle between workers and capitalists. The woman workers were not impressive and the major struggle was behind the scenes, yet the play is commendable for its description of the workers' exploitation by capitalists.

In *The Night When the Tiger Was Captured* the author wrote about class antagonism. Published in installments in the magazine *Southern China* in the beginning of 1924, this play was one of Tian Han's finer works of his early period. It mainly concentrated on the love story between Liangu, the daughter of a rich peasant, and Huang Dasha, a tramp. Owing to the wide class gap of the young couple, their love ended in tragedy. When Huang Dasha became crippled, Liangu's father tried to part the young lovers, but Liangu protested. Liangu was honest, tender and bold, but Huang Dasha's character, compared with Liangu, turned out to be quite weak. His melancholic character was common to the young intellectuals at the time. The local colour of the mountain district in Hunan Province added a pastoral tone to this play.

When he sponsored the Southern China Society, Tian Han wrote a series of plays, such as *A Minor Scene in a Riverside Village*, *The Night Talk of Suzhou*, *The Tragedy on a Lake*, *Return to the South*, *The Death of a Noted Actor* and others. *A Minor Scene in a Riverside Village* and *The Night Talk of Suzhou* all had as their theme the civil wars waged by the warlords. Tian Han showed that the tragic death of two brothers in *A Minor Scene in a Riverside Village* and the separation of the old painter Liu Shukang from his wife and daughter in *The Night Talk of Suzhou* were all caused by the wars between warlords. *The Night Talk of Suzhou* depicted how Painter Liu's philosophy of art above everything was shattered by reality. *The Tragedy on a Lake* and *Return to the South* deal with tragic love. Though still retaining "the remnant dream of aestheticism" and "the sorrow of youth"* of his early works, these two plays revealed the author's dissatisfaction with reality and his search for a bright ideal.

Depicting the tragic lot of its characters, *The Death of a Noted Actor*, written in 1929, showed that the old society was antagonistic towards the development of art. Valuing art all his life, Liu Zhensheng, the hero of the play, hated these opponents of art. Lured by Master Yang, his student Liu Fengxian embarked on a path of degeneration. Filled with indignation and bitterness, Liu Zhensheng struggled against Master Yang, exposing his bad conduct. Master Yang humiliated the old actor and finally caused his death. The author modelled the play's hero Liu Zhensheng after the celebrated Qing Dynasty Beijing opera actor Liu Hongsheng. As Master Yang's behaviour became more and more reckless, and Liu Fengxian's degeneration grew more obvious, Liu's rebelliousness increased and finally, through the death of the principal character, the play raised a strong protest against the old society. *The Death*

---

* Tian Han, "Preface to the *Collection of Dramas by Tian Han*."

of a Noted Actor was a realistic record of the hellish life of artists in old China. The success of this play marked Tian Han's maturity in his mastery of drama techniques.

From 1928 to the end of 1929, when the Southern China Society made a performing tour under his leadership in Shanghai, Hangzhou, Nanjing, Guangzhou, Wuxi and other cities, Tian Han wrote a number of plays, including the one-act play *Of One Mind* and the three-act play *The Dance of Fire*. In these plays Tian Han praised the popular revolutionary movement. The performance of these plays pushed modern Chinese drama into a new stage of the revolutionary drama movement.

From 1930 onward, Tian Han's ideology and work developed further. Under the encouragement and influence of the revolutionary movement at that time, as well as the Chinese Communist Party, he began to write about the proletariat. In April 1930, he published an article entitled "My Self-Criticism," in which he criticized the petty bourgeois romantic and sentimental tendencies appearing in both his own works and the works written by the other members of the Southern China Society. Then, he adapted Mérimée's *Carmen* into a six-act play and staged it, venting his antagonism towards the feudal society by borrowing this foreign story. In the same year, he joined the League for Freedom in China, the League of Left-Wing Writers and the Drama Federation. Two years later, Tian Han took charge of the Drama Federation and wrote many plays for the troupe attached to the Federation such as *The Plum Rain, Moonlight Serenade of 1932, Floodwater, The Alarm Bell, Comrades-in-Arms, Song of the Return of Spring, Seven Women in the Storm* and an opera *The Storm on the Yangtse River*. The themes of most of these works were drawn from social and political struggles. *The Plum Rain* and *Moonlight Serenade of 1932* reflected the life and struggle of the jobless workers while *Floodwater** depicted the peasants' sufferings and struggles. *The Alarm Bell*,

* Tian Han wrote two plays with the same title "Floodwater," one of them was set in a village in the middle area around the Yangtse River, which was later compiled into the collection *Song of the Return of Spring* and the other play took place in the area of a dyke surrounded by the floodwater from the Yellow River, which was compiled afterward into the collection named *Before the Dawn*. The play mentioned here is the former one.

Comrades-in-Arms and *Song of the Return of Spring* described the ever-growing anti-Japanese feeling of the common Chinese people and denounced the traitorous crimes of the Kuomintang reactionary government. Due to the fact that the author did not have enough practical experience with the struggle and life of workers and peasants at the time, some of his characters were not so realistic or moving. For instance, the workers in *Moonlight Serenade of 1932* and the peasants in *Floodwater* were not very convincing. However, since these plays reflected important events timely they did influence the reading public.

Song of the Return of Spring, a three-act play written in 1935, was the story of the heroic deeds of some overseas Chinese. Filled with patriotism, Gao Weihan, a young intellectual living in southeast Asia, returned to China together with one of his friends to fight against Japanese aggression immediately after the September 18th Incident in 1931 when the Japanese seized Shenyang. Seriously wounded in battle on January 28, Gao Weihan had completely lost his memory because of a shock to his cranial nerve. Yet, he continued his struggle against the enemy showing his determination to fight to the bitter end. Apart from the main theme of resistance against Japan, the faithful love between Gao Weihan and Mei Niang was also important in this play. When Gao Weihan was confined to bed, Mei Niang rushed to him from southeast Asia. She looked after him and firmly refused the seductions of other men. With her care during his convalescence, Gao Weihan regained his health at last. Though there were only a few scenes in which Mei Niang appeared on the stage, her character was convincing. The dialogue was natural and fluent and some songs added a poetic element to this play. Reflecting the masses who resisted the Japanese invaders, *Song of the Return of Spring* was influential at that time.

During the early thirties, apart from leading the progressive drama movement as well as producing many plays, Tian Han had also written many film scripts and songs. For example he wrote *March of the Volunteers*, which was later set to music by Nie Er. It became very popular and was chosen as the national anthem soon after the founding of the People's Republic of China in 1949. In the spring of 1935, Tian Han was arrested by the Kuomintang government; he was released in the autumn of that year when someone paid bail for him. After getting out of jail, he wrote many new works, including *Mother of Abyssinia* and *Floodwater*.

With the outbreak of the War of Resistance Against Japan in 1937, Tian Han wrote the play *Lugouqiao Bridge* (*Marco Polo Bridge*), about the effort of both the army and people in the Lugouqiao district against the Japanese aggressors. From then on, he devoted himself to the anti-Japanese drama movement, writing new plays, such as the opera *New Yanmen Pass*, *Fisherman's Song*, *Yue Fei* and the modern drama *Ode to Autumn Insects*. The main theme of these works was the resistance against Japanese aggressors. After the victory of the war against Japan he finished a new film script entitled *The Remembrance of South China* and a modern drama *Song of Beautiful Women*, resolving to expose the Kuomintang's oppressive rule. With their influence on literary and art circles, these two works helped to push the democratic movement forward.

Finished in the spring of 1947, *Song of Beautiful Women* depicted the revolutionary struggle. Set in Shanghai, under the Japanese imperialist occupation on the eve of the victory of the war of resistance, the play depicted the zigzag life paths of three young women from different social classes. Liu Jinmei, a simple and kindhearted textile worker, was very poor. Apart from being humiliated by the Japanese occupants, she suffered another misfortune—her husband was poisoned by hooligans which resulted in blindness. The heavy burden of supporting the whole family thus fell on her shoulders. She was finally forced to become a prostitute to support the family. Even so, Liu Jinmei still could not change this miserable situation. In despair, she went to the bank of the Huangpu River to drown herself. She obtained a fresh outlook on life soon after being rescued by a revolutionary.

Liang Ruoying, a young woman intellectual who, though cherishing the ideals of justice and patriotism, was weak by nature and easily wavered. She married Zhang Yuliang, a young revolutionary, before the outbreak of the war, and they had a child. Liang Ruoying suffered bad experiences in the chaotic years of the war after she had parted with her husband.

Li Xinqun, a woman underground worker, was assigned to remain in the enemy's rear area. Together with her husband, she worked hard for the revolution, confident of victory. *Song of Beautiful Women* portrayed these three young women as well as the revolutionaries Zhang Yuliang, Meng Nan and the leader of the Party organization, Brother Liu. Breaking up the conventional formula that every play ought to be separated into acts, Tian Han used a technique from Chinese opera and divided his play into twenty-one scenes of different lengths in accordance with the plot. In this way, he described the lives of the three young women, linking them with the anti-Japanese struggle under the leadership of the Chinese Communist Party, which was the main theme of this play. It was staged when students throughout China were launching protests soon after the rape of a Chinese student in Beijing by U.S. soldiers. *Song of Beautiful Women* criticized Japanese imperialists and their puppet regime and also criticized Chiang Kai-shek's reactionary clique supported by the United States.

Chapter 8
Literature of the Early Thirties (II)

I. Qu Qiubai's Works and Other Essays, Prose and Reportage

Essays, prose and reportage flourished in the early thirties. Apart from Lu Xun, Mao Dun, Ba Jin, Yu Dafu and other writers who wrote prose or reportage as well as fiction, Qu Qiubai's essays were also considerably influential.

Qu Qiubai was born into an impoverished literary family in 1899 in Changzhou, Jiangsu Province. After graduating from middle school he was admitted to the special institute for Russian in Beijing and was active in the May Fourth Movement and the new literary movement. In 1920 he went as a reporter for the Beijing *Morning News* to the Soviet Union where he wrote two collections of prose and reportage entitled *Journey to the Land of Hunger* (also known as *Travel Notes in New Russia*) and *Thoughts in the Red Capital.* Parts of the articles were published in the *Morning News.* These are the earliest reportage articles after the May Fourth Movement. He wrote about the struggle between old and new orders and between revolutionary and counterrevolutionary forces after the October Revolution in Russia. In his articles "Lenin" and "The Red October" he wrote about Lenin, showing the Russian people's affection for their leader. The two books also record the author's ideological development from a progressive, educated youth who held the ideal of the October Revolution to a dedicated Communist as expressed in his "Letters to My Family," "I" and "Existence." These works contain travel observations, short essays, miscellaneous thoughts and prose.

After his return to China in 1923, Qu Qiubai supervised the publication of the magazines *New Youth*, *Guide* and *Vanguard* and later taught at Shanghai University. In 1925 he shifted to revolutionary work and then returned to literary work in 1931, promoting revolutionary literature with Lu Xun. He translated many famous works by Gorky, Pushkin, Gogol and Tolstoy, wrote articles to introduce Russian literature to the Chinese people, and compiled and translated works on art and literature by Marx, Engels, Lenin, Lafargue and Plekhanov. His versions are smooth and true to the original, as Lu Xun put it, "faithful and convey the ideas well."*

Apart from his translation of Marxist theoretical writings on art and literature, Qu Qiubai related them to the Chinese literary movement. His "Preface to the *Selected Essays of Lu Xun*" is an article on literature using Marxist analysis. Through analysis of Lu Xun's essays Qu explained Lu Xun's thinking and its development. As well as an appraisal of Lu Xun, this article was instructive in the further development of the new literary movement.

In other articles on art and literature Qu Qiubai applied the Marxist view to the new literary movement since the May Fourth Movement, trying to find a way to serve the revolutionary struggle and to popularize literature.

In the thirties he published dozens of articles in Shanghai in *The Dipper* and *Literary Guide* under the pennames Shi Tie'er and Chen Xiaofeng and later in "Random Talk," a supplement of *Shen Bao* and *Shen Bao Monthly* under the pseudonym Lu Xun. His articles were similar in content to those of Lu Xun's. To fight against the Kuomintang government's policy of yielding to pressure from outside and suppressing the people, he wrote "A Gloomy Answer," "Liberation by a Devious Path," "Head-on Sutra" and "Interior and Exterior." To oppose scholars such as Hu Shi, who covered up for the reactionaries and advised the invaders, he wrote "Poems of the Kingly Way," "The Trick of Selling Yourself" and "Talents in the Grand Garden."

Criticizing the old society, Qu envisioned a new society. "A Kind of Cloud," "Before the Storm" and "*Iron Stream* in Paris" are

* Lu Xun, "Introducing *Notes on the Sea*, Part I," *The Complete Works of Lu Xun*, Vol. 7, Chinese ed. p. 778.

articles which call for a new society. These articles have novel themes compared with those of his contemporaries. Qu was good at presenting social conflicts through the words and deeds of upper-class characters with metaphors and a simple, straightforward style. Sometimes he used symbolism, such as in "A Kind of Cloud"; sometimes he made a point by describing social customs, such as in "The National Spirit." He adopted various writing forms including political essays, short commentaries, book reviews, lyric prose, *zaju* (poetic drama set to music), short verse and fables, explaining profound themes in simple terms.

In January 1934 Qu Qiubai went to the Central Revolutionary Base in Jiangxi Province. When the Red Army began its Long March, he could not go north with the army because he was ill. He was arrested by the Kuomintang reactionaries in February 1935 and killed in June of the same year. After his death Lu Xun, while ill in bed, compiled and published his translated works under the title *Notes on the Sea.*

Under the guidance and instruction of Lu Xun, many young writers wrote essays writing to criticize politics, to expose social contradictions, and to offer advice or to discuss art and literature. Wide in content and varied in style these articles are terse and incisive and full of vitality. Xu Maoyong (1910-77) wrote the collections of *Non-astonishment* and *Miscellaneous Notes* to criticize current events. Lu Xun wrote a preface for *Miscellaneous Notes* which had a considerable influence in literary circles. Tang Tao's collections *The Back Side of the Story* and *The Sea and the Sky* exposed evil social practice. Influenced by Lu Xun's artistic style, his essays were sometimes written in lyrical prose. During the anti-Japanese war and the Liberation War, Tang wrote collections of essays including *Projections*, *Short and Long Notes*, *Hard-Earned Money* and *Distinguishing Nonentities*. With the assistance of Lu Xun, another writer Xu Shiquan published short commentaries under different pennames in "Random Talk," a supplement of *Shen Bao*, criticizing politics of his time. Other essayists were Nie Gannu, Zhou Muzhai and Ke Ling. *Beneath Common Sense* is a collection of essays written with keen insight by Ba Ren (Wang Renshu). Ba's other collections include *Life, Reflection and Study*, *Narrow Door* and

Side Wind.

Lyric prose developed further in the early thirties. Not only veteran writers of the twenties continued to contribute to this field, but also new writers arose during this period and wrote a great deal of lyric prose. They uncovered the vicious reality and extolled the struggle of the people.

Li Guangtian (1906-68) and He Qifang (1912-77) wrote lyric prose. Li's collections *Gallery* and *The Silver Fox* are mainly "about people who suffered in the old society and could find no way out."* In one work the character Wen Qu is bullied and cheated and finally killed because he has talked about revolution ("About Mr Wen Qu"); in another work an old ferryman has to endure humiliation throughout his life ("An Old Ferryboat"). Another story tells of a mute who takes up flower-collecting like his father and elder brother and then falls to his death when climbing up a gully to pick lilies, risking his life to support his family ("Son of the Mountain"). "I am from the countryside," Li Guangtian said in his "Preface to *Gallery*." "So I love the countryside and the people who live there." He described the scenery of his birthplace, Shandong Province, and his early life there. Excelling in characterization, Li wrote in a natural and vigorous style. Even ordinary people come to life under his pen. In the early days of the anti-Japanese war he published the collections *The Straw Cape* and *Another World* and in the forties *Echoes*, *The Gold Jar* and *Jottings by the Sun.* *Another World* depicts his life in exile and his withdrawal to the rear with his school in the early days of the anti-Japanese war. *Echoes* and *The Straw Cape* are collections of essays. Most of the essays in *Echoes* (written around 1941) portray a lonely and depressed intellectual who had a hard time in the rear area, showing his relation with the poor and his tireless pursuit of a brighter future.

Records of Painted Dreams by He Qifang is a popular collection. In 1937, together with Cao Yu's *Sunrise* and Lu Fen's *Paddy*, it won the art and literature award issued by *Da Gong Bao.* Different from Li Guangtian's style, this collection and the collections *Painstaking*

* "Preface to *Thirty Essays.*"

and *Notes on the Visit to My Hometown* published later reflect the loneliness and sadness of the intellectuals who were dissatisfied with reality and their search after truth. He Qifang wrote lyric prose with delicate, refined language. "I never search for its form from the glimmering of a concept," he once said. "What has been floating in my mind are some ready-formed colours and patterns" ("The Path in My Dream" in *Painstaking*). His approach was influenced by impressionism prevalent in Europe at that time. *Notes on the Visit to My Hometown* reflects a change in the author's thinking and writing, showing how he had experienced life and began to turn from illusion to reality.

Other noted contemporary essayists were Lu Li (1908-42) and Li Ni (1909-68). Before the outbreak of the anti-Japanese war Lu Li wrote the essay collections *Sea Star* and *Bamboo Knife* bluntly denouncing the old unjust society. "Water Rice-Pounder" in *Sea Star* tells the story of a child bride who is killed by the water rice-pounder. "The Mute" in the same collection depicts the suffering of a poor labourer who is exploited, but who cannot take action to better his situation. It expresses the author's sense of justice for the working people. Lu's *Notes in Beseigement* was published in 1940. Remaining in Shanghai, the author expressed his loneliness. He was killed by the Japanese in 1942. Li Ni's collections *Contributions at Dusk*, *Song of the Eagle* and *White Night* mirror the author's depression brought on by the difficulties of the times. In other essays such as "Song of the Eagle" the dissatisfaction with reality, and longing for a brighter future are expressed in a despondent tone. The writing is fresh and elegant, but sometimes lacking concrete description.

Feng Zikai (1898-1975) was another essayist who used techniques of Chinese traditional prose. In 1931 he published *Jottings at Yuanyuan Study* and later *More Jottings at Yuanyuan Study* and *Carriage Society*. His early writing praises children's naivety and integrity of personality. In his writings he also deplored the boundlessness of the universe and the boundaries of time, comparing the birth and death of human beings in the universe with the rise and fall of the waves in the sea ("Ananda," *Jottings at Yuanyuan Study*). His later essays are more related to society, describing characters and events. For instance, in "Third Aunt" (*Carriage Society*) he shows sympathy for the hard life of the urban poor. Feng Zikai depicted events in a plain style that compels the reader to reflect upon his essays.

The "Analects" school rising in Shanghai in the early thirties mainly deals with short essays in prose style with Lin Yutang (1895-1976) as one of principal writers of such essays. He was one of the chief contributors to *The Tattler* in the late twenties. His essays showed his dissatisfaction with the feudal warlords' rule and his support for the progressive movement of the students. *Cutting and Whisking* contains his essays of this period. In the thirties Lin and other writers started the fortnightly magazines *Analects*, *Human World* and *Wind of the Universe* to advocate "humourous literature" and to "make a point of telling the truth, express seriousness through humour, breaking the boundaries of the two" ("Reply to Ping Fan," *My Remarks*). They advocated the study of the "natural and lively outlook of life" from the West ("the Study of Pedantry," *My Remarks*). Later his articles were collected in *Essays About Nothing*, *My Remarks*, *Notes of Yutang*, *Selected Humorous Essays of Yutang*, *Essays of Youbuwei Study* and others. Some of them have retained the anti-feudalism stand of his *Tattler* period. For example, "On the Freedom of Speech," "Appropriate Articles," "The Revised and Enlarged Edition of Aesop's Fables" and "Study Confucian Classics for the Resistance Against Japanese Aggression," ridicule the reactionary rule with humour. Lin eventually advocated *feuilleton*, spreading the idea of "taking 'I' as the centre of all and leisure as our style," and took a critical stance towards the Left-wing literary movement. This tendency came under criticism from Lu Xun. After his migration to the United States in 1936, Lin Yutang continued to write humorous articles in English and then translated them into Chinese. Collections of these articles include *My Country and My People*, *With Love and Irony*, *The Life and Times of Su Tungpo*, *The Importance of Life* and *Between Fears and Laughter*. These articles advocated "living in ease and comfort," "saving the nation by production," and encouraged people to read the classic *The Book of Changes*. All this deviated further and further from the reality of the Chinese people's struggle against imperialism and feudalism and even distorted the facts. Apart from essays, Lin also wrote a novel in English entitled *Moment in Peking* describing the large family of a feudal official living in luxury in Beijing before the 1911 Revolution. The book was later translated into Chinese and published.

After the publication of Qu Qiubai's *Journey to the Land of Hunger* and *Thoughts in the Red Capital*, reportage went a step forward in the early thirties thanks to the work of the Chinese League of the Left-Wing Writers. *The New Situation of the Proletarian Literary Movement and Our Tasks*, published in August 1930, and *The New Tasks of China's Proletarian Revolutionary Literature*, printed in November 1931 by the Executive Committee of the League pointed out that writers must study and adopt the form of "reportage literature in Western Europe" and "create our own reportage." After the September 18th Incident, some short reportage on the anti-Japanese struggle began to appear in newspapers and magazines. *News on Literature and Art* published articles such as "To Our Brothers in Factories—The Task and Content Concerning the Communication of Factories" and "Our Reportage" to recommend reportage writing. *The Dipper* also published translations concerning the theory of reportage. During the January 28th Incident when Shanghai resisted Japanese attack, many progressive writers went to the front and reported on the battle. Their articles were published in *Beacon Fire*, the wartime special issue of *News on Literature and Art* and *The Dipper*. The contributors included Zheng Boqi, Shi Yi and some other young writers. With the development of the anti-imperialist movement and the combination of reportage with "the movement of literary reporters," and with the participation of workers, peasants, soldiers and students, the scope of writers and the themes expanded. Their main themes were the suffering and the resistance of the Chinese people under the Japanese imperialists. *Living Records* published in 1936 was a selection of good reportage literature collected from all parts of China. Some pieces were compiled in *A Day in China*, published in the same year with Mao Dun as the chief editor, and *A Day in Shanghai*, published later with Mei Yu as the chief editor, reported the facts, but they lacked a cohesive style. Xia Yan's "Bond Labourers" written in 1936 and Song Zhidi's "Spring in Taiyuan in 1936" marked an improvement in reportage. "Bond Labourers" shows the hard life of a group of women workers who had no personal freedom working in a Japanese textile factory in Shanghai. Written after an investigation it aroused a strong sense of rage against the Japanese imperialists and feudalism. In a tone of biting sarcasm "Spring in Taiyuan in 1936" presents a lifelike picture of the Shanxi reactionary rulers. During the anti-Japanese war reportage made further progress.

II. Ye Zi, Wu Zuxiang and Other New Writers and New Works in the Later Period of the League of Left-Wing Writers

Many new writers emerged at the early stage of the revolutionary literary movement and the formation of the Chinese League of Left-Wing Writers and even more at the later stage of the League. Among them were Ye Zi, Zhou Wen, Wu Zuxiang and Luo Shu who mainly wrote fiction, as well as Xiao Jun and Xiao Hong, representatives of the "Northeast Writer Group."

Ye Zi (1912-39), originally named Yu Helin, was a native of Yiyang, Hunan Province. During the upsurge of the peasant movement in Hunan between 1926 and 1927 his uncle was one of the principal leaders of the Yiyang Peasants' Association. His father and sister also took part in the struggle led by the association. Educated by the mass movement, Ye Zi, then a middle school student, entered the Wuhan Military School. When Chiang Kai-shek betrayed the revolution in 1927 Ye Zi's uncle, father and sister were killed. He fled his hometown and lived in exile for a period of time elsewhere, where he acquired a deeper understanding of the life of the poor, especially that of the peasantry. The struggle in his hometown became the main theme of his works when he took part in proletarian revolutionary literary movement and began to write in 1933. He wrote against the exploitation of the poor by the rich.

His works include *Harvest* and *One Night in a Mountain Village*, collections of short stories, *Star*, a novella and some essays. All the stories in *Harvest* are about the life and struggle in the Hunan countryside except for "Grandad Yang Celebrates the New Year" which was about the hard life of the peasant refugees in Shanghai. "Harvest" was Ye's first story, telling how the peasants organized themselves and resisted the grain tax under the cruel exploitation of the landlord class after the failure of the revolution in 1927. Uncle Yunpu, the hero of the story, worked the year round, harbouring illusions about his landlord, but in end the "rice he has painstakingly grown was taken away load after load." Worried and furious, he finally fell ill. The story advocates that the only way out for the peasants is to organize themselves and defend their work. This is the path Uncle Yunpu's son, Liqiu took. After the story's publication in *Unnamed Literature*, Ye Zi won praise from literary circles as a new emerging writer. "Fire" is sequel of "Harvest." It described the further development of the peasants' struggle. The older generation like Uncle Yunpu also rose in rebellion; the struggle converged with the revolution of the Workers and Peasants Red Army in the Snow Peak Mountain.

Like Uncle Yunpu in "Harvest," Uncle Wang in "Outside the Electric Wire-Netting" was also an honest and hardworking peasant of the older generation. When the Red Army approached his hometown and the reactionary troops set up electric were-netting in an attempt to check the Red Army, he could not bear to part with his house and refused to go with his son to the Red Army. In the end his house was burned down and his daughter-in-law and grandson were killed. But Uncle Wang was unflinching and courageous in the face of the reactionaries' slaughter.

Lu Xun wrote in his preface to *Harvest*: "In the face of the destruction, his works gained in maturity. They not only won the warm approval of many young people in China, but also of readers of other countries as with "Outside the Electric Wire-Netting" when published in the magazine *New Land of Literature* under the title of "Uncle Wang." The author fulfilled his immediate task in giving his answer to the oppressors: 'Literature is militant!' "*

"One Night in a Mountain Village" in the collection of the same title is another important work by Ye Zi. The story was told by a lonely old man Gui living in a remote mountain area. Deceived by the landlord class, the timid and overcautious old man gave up his son who was involved in the revolution, believing that by doing so he could receive clemency from the landlords. But he had, in fact, sent his son to death. The young man was immediately killed by the enemy. Through Gui's narration the author expressed his strong indignation against the old social order. The story depicts the old man's cowardice and ignorance and his son's courage.

Compared with other writings reflecting rural life, Ye Zi's works are more distinctive and profound. He not only portrayed the poverty-stricken countryside of old China, but also the victory of the peasants in their struggle for a better life. He did not limit his portrayal to isolated and accidental events, but presented a picture of the whole revolutionary movement. He showed the ideology of the younger generation who were involved in the revolution, as well as the older generation of peasants. He portrayed the suffering and conservative thinking of the older generation as well as their rise in consciousness. Ye Zi said he wrote "to depict the injustice in the world ... until it was eliminated forever!"**

After the outbreak of the anti-Japanese war, Ye Zi returned to Hunan from Shanghai. He had finished forty thousand characters of the novel *The Sun Rises from the West*, which he had been planning for many years, when he died of illness in poverty at the age of twenty-seven.

Zhou Wen (1907-52), also known as He Gutian, was once in the ranks of the warlords in the Sichuan-Xikang border area. He drew material from the warlords' troops and local authorities, showing how the upper classes conflicted with one another as well as the suffering of the poor. In his short stories he wrote about people from all walks of life. From 1933 to 1937 he published four

* Lu Xun, *Essays of Qiejieting* (II).

** Ye Zi, "How I Built My Relation with Literature," *Literature and I*, p. 41, Life Bookstore in 1934.

collections of short stories including *Division* and *Love*, a novella *In Baisen Town* and a novel *The Tobacco Seedling Season*. His stories emphasized characterization as in "Several Meals a Day" and "Executive Chen," and setting as in "A Stuffy Day" and "Between Father and Son" without complicated plots. Many of his short stories are character sketches and Zhou was especially good at showing the thoughts of the characters, thus creating distinct personalities. However, in some of his works the social range is narrow and the ideological content lacks depth. When the war of resistance broke out he spent most of his time doing revolutionary work while writing the novella *Refugees*.

Wu Zuxiang's collections of stories and essays include *Xiliu* (*West Willow*) and *After Meal*. His early stories tell how the obstinate, conservative social forces destroy new possibilities and how vicissitudes wear people down. Later he wrote about the poor in the countryside in southern Anhui Province. "Eighteen Hundred Piculs" and "Fanjia Village," which were influential around 1934, are excellent stories in the above-mentioned collections. The subtitle of the "Eighteen Hundred Piculs" is "A Sketch of the Song Ancestral Hall on July 15," in which several hundred landlords and despotic gentry from the Song clan fought for the eighteen hundred piculs (a Chinese unit of weight equal to fifty kilogrammes) of rice stored in the ancestral hall. The story ends when the peasants seized the rice, showing the revolt in the countryside and the doom of the landlord class. The young couple in "Fanjia Village" were simple hardworking peasants. But under the exploitation of the landlords and blackmailed by the local officials, the husband was forced to steal, while the wife, in order to get money to rescue her imprisoned husband, killed her own mother. Through this tragedy the author repudiated the old society. Although the theme is gloomy, the author concentrated on revealing the poverty of the Fanjia Village, as well as the panic of the landlords as their lifestyle was threatened. By Showing the class conflicts of a particular village the author gave an immediacy to the conflicts of the broader social climate of the time. "Peace Across the Land" and "At a Certain Date" are also popular. During the anti-Japanese war Wu wrote a novel entitled *Yazuilao* (later also published under the title of *Mountain Torrents*) and a short story "Iron Dummy." Set in the Anhui countryside in the early period of the anti-Japanese war, *Mountain Torrents* shows how the peasants became politically conscious when their town was ruined in the war. The hero Zhang Sanguan is successfully depicted. Meticulous description shows how this young peasant, educated by the New Fourth Army, overcame his backward ideology and plunged himself into the war for national liberation. Because of the author's understanding of the psychology, customs and habits of various classes in southern Anhui Province and his use of the local dialect, the story paints a rich picture of rural life. "Iron Dummy" is the story of a deserter from the Kuomintang troops. Wu excelled in portraying various crowd scenes and at character dialogue. His works clarify the complicated situation in the countryside.

Luo Shu (1903-38), originally called Luo Shimi, was born in Jianyang County, Sichuan Province. She went to France to study in 1929. After she returned in 1933, she settled down in Shanghai, writing and translating. She had published three collections of short stories and prose in the early thirties *Twice-Married Woman*, *A Corner of the Land* and *The Fish Col.* The story "Twice-Married Woman" is about a peasant living in a mountain area at the upper reach of the Tuojiang River in Sichuan Province, who was so poverty-stricken that he had to eventually sell his wife. Luo Shu presented the tragic life and the simple but sincere feelings of the peasant couple with sensitivity. The theme is similar to Rou Shi's "A Slave Mother," but the class struggle in the countryside in her story was developed further. Rou Shi concentrated on expressing the suffering and humiliation of the mother, while Luo Shu highlighted the stubbornness of the wife and her resistance. After its publication "Twice-Married Woman" attracted attention because of its moving theme and was well-received by literary circles.

After the September 18th Incident in 1931 a group of young writers fled Northeast China then occupied by the Japanese invaders to south of the Great Wall. Some had already been writing for some time, and some, inspired by the revolutionary literary movement, also began to write. They wrote many works about the struggle of the people in the Northeast. Notable among these writers were Xiao Jun, Xiao Hong, Duanmu Hongliang, Shu Qun, Bai Lang, Luo Feng and Hei Ding, known as the "Northeast Writer Group." Their most influential works were *The Village in August* and *The Field of Life and Death.*

Written by Xiao Jun (also known as Tian Jun) and published in 1935 the novel *The Village in August* is about the anti-Japanese guerrilla forces led by the Chinese Communist Party, showing the struggle of the guerrilla fighters with the enemy, as well as the landlord traitors. The novel also shows the conflicts between members of different family backgrounds and different social classes. The characters, Commander Chen Zhu and Aunt Li who had become more politically and socially conscious under the humiliation of the enemy, embody the Northeastern people's demand for unity and their resistance against the Japanese aggressors. The novel shows the guerrilla battles. Appraising the novel Lu Xun wrote, "Brightly unfurled before readers' eyes are the author's painstaking labour, the lost sky, the land, the suffering people as well as the lost grass, sorghum, grasshoppers and mosquitoes twisted in a skein, revealing a part and the whole of China, present and future, the road to ruin and the way to survive."* At the time when the national crisis became increasingly serious and the anti-Japanese movement developed vigorously, the novel was widely read. As well as the collections of short stories *Sheep* and *On the River*, Xiao Jun wrote another novel *The Third Generation* (later also published under the title *The Bygone Years*) which describes the struggle of the people in the Northeast after the 1911 Revolution. This novel is more mature artistically.

The Field of Life and Death, written by Xiao Hong (1911-42) and published in 1935, is a novella which vividly reflects the life of the people in the Northeast after their land was occupied by the enemy. Lu Xun wrote about the book "... The description of the northern China's people's firm resolution in life and their struggle against death ... show the author's keen observation and unusual skill in handling the theme." The first ten chapters of the book deal with the villages near Harbin before the fall of Northeast China

* Lu Xun, "Preface to Tian Jun's *The Village in August*," *Essays of Qiejieting* (II).

when "human beings and animals were busy giving birth and dying." The peasants sent their old cattle to the butcher for money, but the money was seized by the landlords. They tried to rebel against the vampiric landlords, only to be imprisoned. A still graver disaster befell them. The miserable death of their elders was embedded in the memories of the younger generation. They wanted to take revenge on the despotic landlords. But pestilence and starvation had killed many and threatened every one. The book shows the suffering and struggle of the masses after Japanese imperialists occupied the Northeast. They resolved "to remain Chinese, life or death"—to die rather than surrender. When they were defeated they came to realize that the only solution was to organize themselves and join the revolutionary army. So they left their native land and took an even harder road. Xiao Hong showed the disaster of the Northeast under the dual oppression of imperialism and feudalism. After *The Field of Life and Death* Xiao Hong wrote the short stories: "A Cry in the Wilderness," "Hands," "Spring in a Small Town," the novella *Mr Ma Bole* and *Tales of Hulan River*. She also published collections of prose essays *The Market Street* and *The Bridge* under the penname Qiao Yin.

Before the War of Resistance Against Japan Duanmu Hongliang's collection of short stories *Hatred* and Shu Qun's *Children Without a Country* had the same theme of resistance against aggression.

To sum up, compared with the early proletarian revolutionary literature, literary works from Ye Zi to the "Northeast Writer Group" developed in the range of themes, ideological content and writing technique. Especially in the description of class and national struggle these writers reflected the growth of consciousness of the masses and their strength.

In Taiwan, which was invaded by the Japanese over a long period of time, a literary movement was carried on under conditions as difficult as those in the Northeast under the rule of the Japanese. In October 1921, impelled by the May Fourth new literary movement and the Japanese proletarian literary movement, the Taiwan Federation of Culture was established, uniting writers of the new literature. Influenced by the Left-wing literary movement, the Taiwan new literary movement developed in the thirties. In defiance of long imprisonment, the well-known writers Lai He (1894-1943) and Yang Kui persevered in their struggle and their writings. In *A Steelyard* Lai exposed how the Japanese oppressed and exploited the Taiwan people in a sugar refinery. In *The Story of a Pettifogger* he told the story of the struggle in Taiwan during the Qing Dynasty in the form of a folk tale. Yang Kui's short story "A Newsman," written in Japanese and translated into Chinese by Hu Feng, shows the cruel exploitation and oppression of the Taiwan people, as well as the exploitation of the Japanese people by colonialists and capitalists, through the suffering of a Taiwan youth who wandered destitute in Tokyo as a newsman. It shows how Japanese and Taiwanese working people shared a common fate. These stories helped the development of Taiwan's progressive literature later on.

III. The China Poetry Society and Works of Zang Kejia

Like fiction, drama, essay and prose, poetry also developed in the field of new literature in the early thirties. The China Poetry Society was an organization under the leadership of the Chinese League of Left-Wing Writers, founded in September 1932 by Mu Mutian, Yang Sao, Ren Jun (Sen Bao), Pu Feng and others. In "About the China Poetry Society" they wrote, "In China, a semi-colonial country, everything is bathed in a rainstorm. A great deal of material for poetry is waiting to be gathered and expressed. But China's poetry circles are sunk in silence. Some of the poets clamour for Westernization, while some are intoxicated by the beauty of poetry on natural themes." In February 1933 the society started a publication, *New Poetry*, published every ten days. Later it changed into a monthly. To express the common aim of the poets of the society, the introductory poem declared:

We will not visit historical ruins
Because they belong to the past.

We want to seize the present reality
And sing the praises of the new century.
......
In the face of the oppression, exploitation and slaughter by the imperialists,
High is the people's morale in the resistance against Japanese aggression.
We want to sing this contradiction and its significance,
Through this contradiction we create a great century.
In colloquial language
We will write this contradiction into folk songs and drum ballads,
Turning our poems into popular rhymes,
And make ourselves one of the masses.

The society promoted both poetry and research. It tried to popularize poetry and published "Special Number of Ballads" and "Special Number of Creations," trying "to make use of pop songs, ballads and popular rhymes of the day, in our future poetry."* Apart from its main office in Shanghai, the society also had branches in Beijing, Guangzhou, Qingdao and Tokyo, most of which set up their own magazines or supplements to newspapers.

Pu Feng (1911-42) was the most enthusiastic and active poet in the society. His works include collections of *The Dark Night*, *Life*, *The Song of Steel*, *Lullaby*, *The Trilogy of the War of Resistance*, *In the Dark*, *Shabby Corner* as well as long poems "Meteors in June" and "Pitiful Creatures." He wrote about two themes: the revolutionary change of the people in the countryside from suffering to a new consciousness and their resistance against Japanese aggression. Pu Feng's poems are emotional, although not so developed artistically. The style is plain and the language, simple. His poems criticized the old order.

Pu Feng's first collection *The Dark Night* concentrates on the struggle of the peasants, describing their oppression and exploitation and their resistance. Some poems such as "Roaring" depict the vitality of the villages after the revolution with "red flag bathing in

* "Our Remarks," *New Poetry*, Vol. II, No. 1.

the sunlight." "The Dark Night" expresses in a dialogue between mother and son the awakening of the younger generation in the countryside. On a stormy dark night an old mother missed her son, wondering why he should go far away leaving her and his wife behind. She wished he would come back soon. But in the howling wind she faintly hear his reply in the wind:

For the sake of us all I have to leave my home,
For our cause I have to go far away from you and her!
Oh, Mother, don't worry about me!

Her son Qing was a revolutionary who left home to join "the army of the poor" and fight for the liberation of the people. Many poems in this collection imply that when hundreds of thousands of people became conscious there would be strength that could transform heaven and earth. "Light shall be born from darkness."

The long narrative poem "Meteors in June" shows through the struggle of the peasants against the construction of a highway, the counter-revolutionary "encirclement and annihilation campaign" of the Kuomintang reactionaries and the development of revolution in the countryside led by the Communist Party. In order to attack the revolutionary base the Kuomintang reactionaries seized the peasants' land to build a highway. The Wangjia Village protested angrily: "Protect our land"; "We can't starve to death for nothing."

Like the water of the Yellow River breaking through the dam.
Who will be strong enough to block it?
Like the waves surging in the sea
Are our troops marching forward.

Although bandit troops came to the village later and massacred some people, the peasants supported by the Workers and Peasants Red Army finally drove the enemy away. The poem deals with the events in one village, but it showed how a single spark can spread.

At the early period of the anti-Japanese war Pu Feng continued to compose militant poems. He died of an illness at the anti-Japanese front in southern Anhui in 1942.

Other members belonging to the society in Shanghai include

Mu Mutian, Yang Sao, Ren Jun and Liu Qian. In Yang Sao's collections *The City of Recollection*, *The Sufferers' Canzonet* and *Sorrowful Spring*, most of the poems use the theme of love to express his resentment of suffering and his pursuit of a bright future. His long poem "Village Tune" describes the wretched life of the peasants caused by oppression and natural calamities: the oppression of the landlords, the harassment of bandit troops, taxes and levies and famine due to crop failure. Although traces of classical forms can be found in his work, Yang Sao wrote in a fresh and novel style, imbued with romanticism. Ren Jun's poetry collections include *Battle Song* and *Cold and Heat*. His poems have a militant quality. Mu Mutian, who had witnessed the ruin of the countryside in the Northeast and experienced the September 18th Incident when the enemy occupied his native area, published collections of poems such as *Song of Wanderers*, "elegies to mourn for the fall of their native land."* Liu Qian's "The Shocking January" depicts the people's strength in the struggle against Japanese aggression during the January 28th Incident in 1932. "The Shallow Track of Life" tells about his personal misfortune. Shi Ling's short poems, "The New Cowherd's Song" and "Song of the Longshoremen" were set to music by Nie Er and became popular.

Wang Yaping, chief leader of the Hebei branch of the society, was the chief editor of the magazine *New Poetry* in Beijing. He wrote the collections of short poems *Winter of the City*, *Song of Petrels* and a long narrative poem "The Wind of December," set in the December 9th student movement in 1935. In the "Lighthouse Keeper" he wrote, "On the eve of daybreak, I dedicate my life to light." He wandered from the ruined, poverty-stricken village to the city, experiencing "a life that was like an iron whip that lashed him mercilessly on the back, with devilish hands stretching out all around."** He described the ruin of the countryside, the poverty in the city and the tragic lot of the working people from his observations, expressing the Chinese people's patriotism in the resistance against Japanese aggression. His representative works include "The Lighthouse Keeper," "The Huangpu River," "The Child's Won-

* "Preface to *Song of Wanderers*."
** "Postscript to *Song of Petrels*."

der," "The Dagu Estuary" and "A Village in Summer." "A Village in Summer" depicts the misery resulting from serious drought and how government officials pressed for grain taxes. Villagers were compelled to leave their homes:

Summer does not look like the season of summer,
Not a soul in the field to do ploughing or rice-planting.
The road's swarmed with starving crowds
Leaving their homes to search for living.

Wang used colloquial language because he studied the techniques of folk songs and ballads. During the anti-Japanese war he published the collections *Red Roses* and *Song of Life*, most of which are about the battles of the war.

Wen Liu (1912-37), principal leader of the Guangzhou branch of the society, was the chief editor of the magazines *Poetry* and *Poetical Life*, which played a strong role in promoting poetry in South China. His two collections of poems are *Our Fortress* and *The Last Road*. Most of his poems reflect the life of the working people in towns and the countryside, and use the techniques of folk songs to depict a concept. While praising the working people he expressed his ties with them and reflected the times, exemplified by the poems "Song of Brick-Makers," "Song of Stele Chisellers," "New Year's Eve" and "Young Vegetable Sellers." The second passage of the last poem is a desolate scene:

"Vegetables, fresh vegetables!
Two coppers for a bundle!"
I look around to find
Basket after basket of vegetables
And boys of the same age with the same look,
Doing the same slack business.

Many of Wen's poems praise revolutionaries and patriots, expressing his firm faith in a bright future and in the Chinese people's increasingly urgent demand of national freedom and liberation. In his poem "Charge," the poet voiced the resistance against Japanese aggression. He described the people resisting Japanese aggression as "like the storm in the sea, like the spurting volcano," their shouting would "arouse their comrades" and "make traitors tremble" ("Fifty Men"). In his short life of twenty-five years, Wen Liu wrote many patriotic poems.

Zang Kejia was an influential poet in this period. His collection *The Brand* appeared in 1933 and, *The Black Hand of Crime* in 1934. Born in the countryside of Zhucheng County, Shandong Province, Zang was familiar with rural life and had loved the peasants since childhood. That is why the majority of his poems are about the countryside. These poems which reflected rural life brought freshness to poetry circles and attracted the attention of the literary world.

Zang has a distinctive style of his own. With carefully polished verses he showed the misery and misfortune of the hardworking peasants. His poems "Refugees" and "Old Brother" are about the suffering of the peasants. In "Night in a Village" and "Reply to a Guest" he described the upheaval in the northern Chinese countryside in the early thirties. Sometimes he used metaphors to make his point. For instance, in "The Old Horse" from *The Brand* he wrote:

> *The cart is always fully loaded,*
> *He just pulls on without a word.*
> *The heavy yoke cuts deeply at his back,*
> *He droops his head low!*
>
> *Not knowing what would befall on him the next moment,*
> *He can only swallow the tears he sheds.*
> *Before his eyes the whip flashes,*
> *Raising his head by instinct he looks ahead.*

The old horse under the yoke symbolizes the heavy load of the peasants. Simple and compact every other line rhymes. Zang's "Workers at Lunchtime" and "Rickshaw Pullers" were also widely read when they were first published.

Zang Kejia took part in the 1926-27 revolution. After the revolution failed he lived in exile, which enabled him to see the wave of struggle from the apparently quiet land. He predicted the coming of the revolution in "The Heavenly Fire," "The Day Will

Soon Come" and "The Black Hand of Crime." In "The Black Hand of Crime" he says: Tempest will rise in the sea and waves surge in an ancient well. The days when workers bow their heads are numbered. Some day they will

> *Tear to shreds with their rude hands the accumulated scrolls of ten thousand years,*
> *Rising in violent rebellion!*

The composition of "The Black Hand of Crime" is compact and symmetrical and the images are distinct and vivid. The poet said, "In content, I strive to abandon personal blind adherence and make myself face reality"; "in form I try to do away with overcaution and turn to an unrestrained style."* His long poem "My Own Portrait" reflects the advancing era through his own experience of life. The poem is one of his masterpieces in this period. In the forties he continued to publish quite a number of poems.

Ai Qing and Tian Jian also began to write poetry in the early thirties. Ai Qing's poem "Dayanhe—My Wet-Nurse" was one of the most important poems of this period.

Dai Wangshu (1905-50) had a style different from his contemporaries. He was a typical poet of the Modern School. His poems were collected in *Recollections*, *Wangshu Grass* and *Years of Catastrophe*. His early works contained poignant melancholic recollections. Greatly influenced by Chinese classical poetry and French symbolism, he sought conceptional novelty as well as new terms. "The Alley in the Rain" is a typical example of this. Concisely written with rich metaphors, his poems are appealing and compelling. "A Finger Cut Off" in *Recollections* was written in memory of a friend who had died for the revolution. "Country Girl" in *Wangshu Grass* is about a hardworking country girl. "Song of the Wanderer" in the same collection is optimistic and shows how Dai was awakened from his melancholy by the national liberation movement. In *Years of Catastrophe* he wrote in a different style in praise of the War of Resistance Against Japan. When he was arrested by the Japanese invaders he wrote in a jail in Hong Kong "Inscriptions on the Prison Wall" to show his hatred for the enemy

* "Preface to *The Black Hand of Crime*."

and his willingness to sacrifice his life:

When you come back, from underground
Dig out his injured body
And hoist his soul high
With your cheers for the victory.

Here he expressed his love for China and freedom. Other similar poems include "I Use My Mangled Palm." From expressing personal melancholy to fighting for the freedom of China, Dai Wangshu's life and poetry were typical of petty-bourgeois writers at that time.

IV. Works of Lu Yan, Shen Congwen and Other Writers

In the twenties and thirties Lu Yan, Zheng Zhenduo, Jian Xian'ai, Li Jieren, Li Jianwu, Shen Congwen and other writers contributed to the development and enrichment of modern Chinese literature.

Lu Yan (1901-44), also known as Wang Heng, was a native of Zhenhai County, Zhejiang Province. Starting his literary career a little later than Wang Tongzhao he was also one of the writers in the early period of the Literary Research Society. *Pomelo* is a collection of his early works. In his article "About My Creative Writing" he wrote, "I was young when I wrote those articles and I did them with special passions, often expressing my feelings through slogans, curses and satire." In a bantering tone the article "Pomelo" denounces the Hunan feudal warlords' bloody rule through comparing a human head to a pomelo, "revealing indignation under the cloak of cynicism."* His short story "Perhaps He Can't Go So Far" humorously exposes the wicked mentality of the money bags Wang Ayu and his craftiness. Lu's unique style began to show in this work. His later work became more realistic. For example, the story "Gold" from his collection of short stories of the same name shows the decline of a comfortable family, how petty

* Lu Xun, "Preface to *The Short Stories*, Vol. II, *Major Works of New Chinese Literature*."

proprietors went bankrupt under the pressure of an imperialist economy and feudalism in the countryside. It criticizes the negative power of wealth, snobbery and old habits and customs. The influence of Lu Xun and some Russian and Eastern European realistic writers on Lu Yan's writing technique is apparent in these works.

Lu Yan's five collections of the early thirties are: *The Tragedy of Childhood*, *The Young Heart*, *Under the Roof*, *Sparrow and Mouse* and *Riverside*. He also wrote a novel *Prairie Fire* (later also published under the title *The Enraged Village*). In his article "About My Creative Writing" he said that after the publication of *The Tragedy of Childhood* he was "inclined to observe the evil and wicked side of things." In *Under the Roof* Granny Bende eked out a living with twenty years of hard labour. The shadow of her miserable experience hung over her, so she was always anxious in spite of her comparatively well-off life. The story "Crossroads" tells how peasants in two villages attempted to wipe out the plague through a prayer procession which aroused a fight between the two villages. It uncovers how the old social system seriously poisoned the people's thinking. "On the Bridge" is another story about competition among industrialists and businessmen who always tried to outdo each other. In these stories the author depicted the characters' psychology and deeds, criticizing the old society, and the narrow-mindedness, selfishness and ignorance of the petty proprietors. But his tone is too rigid and there is not a gleam of hope in the dismal picture. The story "Amah Li" describes a maidservant from the countryside. Apin in "The Young Heart" was an orphan who had been deceived and sold as a slave. The whole story is shrouded by despondency. "The Tragedy of Childhood" portrays the misfortune of the cheerful hired farmhand Acheng. The author praised this friend from his childhood and mourned his lost childhood. Unlike in *Under the Roof*, in these stories the author expressed his mind frankly and with strong emotion in his narration and descriptions.

Lu's novel *Prairie Fire* shows the suffering of the peasants and their struggle against the landlords, who collaborated with the township head and the local despotic gentry to persecute the peasants. Although the author sympathized with Brother Gesheng who had suffered too much and become a coward, he criticized his servility. The novel lacks authenticity in the depiction of Hua Sheng, a young rebellious peasant, revealing the sentimentality of the petty bourgeoisie, somewhat out of tune with the characters. Lu Yan's works vividly exhibit the acute class antagonism in the countryside and the trend from individual peasant resistance to an organized class struggle.

Zheng Zhenduo (1898-1958) was one of the sponsors and key members of the Literary Research Society. In his early years he was involved in the administration of literary activities. Later he edited literary magazines, wrote commentaries, translated foreign literature and also did some writing. Apart from the poems collected in *Snowy Morning* and the collection of prose *Miscellaneous Notes in the Mountains*, he wrote a collection of short stories, *The Story of Family*, which is as he said in his preface to the collection, "a fragment of the vanishing old families in China." In the early thirties, under the penname Guo Yuanxin, he published "The Arrest of the Fire Fetcher," "The Lure of Aqueloo," "The Destruction of God" and other stories which reflected the events of the time using Greek mythology.

Some time later he wrote "Guigong Pond," "The End of Huang Gongjun" and "Destruction" displaying the moral integrity of Chinese historical characters who would rather die for the realization of their ideals than yield to the forces of darkness. Drawing material from *Guiding Notes* written by the Song Dynasty hero Wen Tianxiang, 'Guigong Pond" is solemn and stirring.

Jian Xian'ai joined the Literary Research Society in 1926 when he was a young writer and was influenced by Lu Xun, Ye Shaojun as well as Maupassant and Chekov. He mainly drew his material from his birthplace in the Guizhou countryside, describing ordinary people and their daily life. Lu Xun called Jian Xian'ai, Xu Qinwen and Wang Luyan "writers of country literature."* *Morning Mist* is Jian's early collection of short stories.

In the thirties Jian published collections of short stories *Return*

* Lu Xun, "Preface to *The Short Stories*, Vol. II, *Major Works of New Chinese Literature*."

Home, *Tavern*, *Hesitation*, *The Story of Salt*, *Tragedy in the Countryside*, and a collection of prose *Under the City*. The stories "Tragedy in the Countryside," "The Packer," "Hesitation," "Mystery," "The Story of Salt," "Salt Sellers" and "En Route to Guizhou" depict in a simple and compact style the misery and oppression of the labourers in the Guizhou mountain area.

Li Jieren (1890-1962), translator of many famous French literary works and author of the novel *Sympathy*, wrote since 1935 three novels *Ripples Across Stagnant Water*, *On the Eve of the Storm* and the first volume of *The Great Wave*. The three books mirror society before the 1911 Revolution in Sichuan, the author's birthplace. *Ripples Across Stagnant Water* deals with the licentious life of Skewmouth Luo, a senior member of the Elder Brothers' Society in a small town during the period from the Sino-Japanese War of 1894-95 to the signing of the 1901 *Xinchou* Treaty. Apparently generous in aiding needy people, Luo had a dark side too and opened gambling houses, visited prostitutes and forcibly seized others' wives. The novel realistically describes the local conditions and customs of the time, the mentality and way of life of the townspeople, also showing the seamy side of life. With the incursion of European and American civilization, the growth and decline of Christian converts and members of the Elder Brothers' Society, the conflicts of these interests stirred up the stagnant society. The novel also shows the imperialist aggression against China and the Qing Dynasty government's humiliating surrender to foreign forces. *On the Eve of the Storm* mainly reflects the awakening of the people after the signing of the 1901 *Xinchou* Treaty. The author began to shift his view from small towns to the city Chengdu, dealing with the Red Lantern Society's secret society against the rulers in the late Qing Dynasty which assaulted on the city, the activities of the bourgeois reformists and the revolutionaries and the meagre social reform of the constitutionalists. This turbulence swept the big cities before the storm of the 1911 Revolution. Compared with *Ripples Across Stagnant Water*, this novel has a wider range of subjects and a more intricate plot, but it is less detailed and vivid than the former. The first volume of *The*

Great Wave mirrors the Sichuan railway incident* in 1911, the cause of the Wuchang Uprising in October of the same year. The author's life experience and writing technique fail to meet the need of the wider range of subjects, and therefore the description of the popular movement is weak. Nevertheless his extensive knowledge of the society and his ability to depict local conditions and customs provide these novels with strong local colour. Drawing on the techniques of Zola and Maupassant, Li Jieren wrote about the local people with flare.

In this period Li Jianwu, who was commended for his novel *Legend of Zhongtiao Mountain*, mainly wrote plays while continuing to write fiction. His one-act play *Mother's Dream* reflects the disaster brought by the civil war, vividly representing the people's denunciation of the war among the warlords. Another play *Liang Yunda* tells how a warlord's garrison collaborated with local tyrants to traffic opium. The three-act play *It Is Spring Only* is his representative work. It is set in Beijing disrupted by warlords during the 1911 Revolution, describing how the wife of the police chief tried to rescue an arrested revolutionary. The crafty character of the police chief, his secretary and secret agents, and the loneliness of his wife are vividly described.

At the outbreak of the anti-Japanese war Li Jianwu worked in the Shanghai Art Drama Society and later wrote many plays. Although they lack depth, the plots are compact and the tone humorous. Li developed a style of his own in comedy writing.

Shen Congwen, born in Fenghuang County, western Hunan in 1902, was a renowned writer in literary circles in the thirties. His father was a staff officer in a garrison force in the last years of the Qing Dynasty. Shen Congwen left home to work as a secretary in a local army unit at the age of fifteen and then followed the army to the area bordering Hunan, Sichuan and Guizhou. He was drawn to Beijing in 1922 and under the influence of the May Fourth new literary movement he began to publish stories in 1924. In seven or eight years from the end of the twenties to the beginning of the

* When the Qing Dynasty government decided to nationalize the railways in Sichuan Province built by the local people, the Sichuan Railway Protection Society was formed to fight against the government's decision.

War of Resistance Against Japan he published more than twenty collections of short stories including *Busybody*, *Stone Boat*, *Inn and Other Stories*, *The Honest Man*, *A Scene in the Moonlight* and *Eight Steeds* and became one of the most prolific writers in literary circles.

Some of Shen's works are about military life such as *After Recruit*, *Huiming* and *The Messenger*, while others depict urban life such as *The Wife of a Gentleman*, *Eight Steeds* and *A Couple*. The best works portraying the conditions and social customs of the minority nationality region in the border of Hunan and Guizhou include *Inn*, *Night*, *Return to My Native Place* and *The Border Town*. In his "Preface to *Selected Stories of Shen Congwen*" he says, "My writing relates to a rather vast range of the society, but to me perhaps the most amiable and familiar places and things are my hometown and the villages scattered on the banks of Yuanjiang River which meanders a thousand *li* (1 *li* = 0.5 km.). The loves and hates, sorrows and happiness of the people in this area have distinctive features of their own." The novella *The Border Town*, written in 1934, is such a work. Set in Chadong, a small mountain town on the Sichuan-Hunan border, and the villages in its vicinity, the novel tells the life of an old ferryman and his granddaughter and the romance of the girl and the two sons of the wharfinger. The ferryman was seventy years old, candid and honest and he had worked on the ferry for fifty years, never delaying a single crossing or taking extra cash. Always keeping him company was his 16-year-old granddaughter Emerald. Pretty and warmhearted, she liked two young brothers, but at heart was in love with the younger brother. The two brothers serenaded her at night according to the local custom. Realizing that he could not win her heart the older brother rowed a boat into the torrent and drowned himself. Known that his brother's death had something to do with Emerald, the younger brother dared not publicly propose to her, though he still loved her. Centering on the story of the old ferryman and his granddaughter, the author vividly described the landscape of the remote border town and the customs of the local people. Full of local flavour, the novella sketches daily events in vivid detail as well as festive activities, like the exciting dragon-boat race. Other works such as *Return to My Native Place* and *Aboard and Ashore* also depict the scenery and customs of border towns in western Hunan, showing the tranquility and simplicity of life there.

Characters of various types figure in his work: bureaucrats, warlords, capitalists, politicians, local tyrants, as well as soldiers, boatmen, fishermen, pedlars, prostitutes, workers and students, forming a panorama of the society at that time. The characters such as Huiming, the sincere and honest cook, devoted to his work for thirty years in *Huiming*, the old diligent section leader of general affairs who was loyal to his master in *Lamp*, the company commander who loved the widow in a border hotel in *The Company Commander*, the child bride Xiaoxiao in *Xiaoxiao*, all leave a distinct impression on readers. However, as the author often depicted his characters in isolation, instead of showing them in a social context, the reader cannot see their social significance.

The author himself was critical of his portrayal of the society at the time, he said, "It was exceedingly radical in social changes, but my way of life and work was extremely narrow and had little change. Besides, my thinking was conservative and stagnant. It is only natural that my work lagged behind the realities."* However, he tried to remedy this. "The Mountain Climber" written in the latter part of 1934, "The Military Adviser," "Big Ruan and Little Ruan" and "Unemployment" written in 1935 as well as "Survival" written in 1936 illustrate a more comprehensive social view. "The Mountain Climber" is about a messenger of the Red Army who trekked across mountains on his missions and shows the struggle between the Red Army and the Kuomintang troops. "Big Ruan and Little Ruan" describes the different life paths of two young men, Big Ruan and Little Ruan who were "uncle and nephew in the clan, but like brothers in age, like friends in life and like enemies in thinking." Little Ruan was enthusiastic and always forging ahead, but Big Ruan was obstinate, selfish, opportunistic and always tried to secure personal gain, forming a foil for Little Ruan. "The Military Adviser" and "Unemployment" show the corruption of the old

---

* "Preface to *Selected Stories of Shen Congwen*."

army. "Survival" is the story of a poor, suffering unemployed youth. All these stories are true to life. Shen Congwen also wrote fairy tales and myths based on Buddhist scriptures and legends. Among them *Aris' Travel Notes in China* satirizes the evil rule of the imperialists and feudal warlords in China.

Shen's early works were stories of the genre of "country literature," the recollections of a person's hometown. His work was influenced by the lyric tone and techniques of Yu Dafu and Fei Ming. A prolific writer, he gradually formed a unique style of his own. Influences of this style can be found to varying degrees in the works of Xiao Qian, Luo Ailan, Wang Zengqi and other writers. In the mid-thirties and the later forties Shen was the chief editor of the literary supplements of *Da Gong Bao* and *Yi Shi Bao* published in Beijing and Tianjin.

Shen Congwen explored new forms of expression and composition in fiction and won a reputation as a stylist writer. His language is fresh and lively, his sentence structure terse and concise. He blended melancholy with humour and effectively described local customs and created interesting characters all of which is very entertaining to read.

Chapter 9

Cao Yu

I. *Thunderstorm, Sunrise* and *The Wilderness*

Cao Yu, the penname of Wan Jiabao, was born in 1910 in Tianjin in a declining bureaucrat family. His father was an unsuccessful military man, who had retired very early and stayed at home, often gathering poor scholars and office assistants in his home for poetry recitals. Cao Yu always spoke in a disdainful tone about the suffocating atmosphere of his home, "I have seen many high-class ruffians, high-class hooligans; I have seen too many characters such as those that appeared in *Thunderstorm*, *Sunrise* and *Peking Man*."* These experiences supplied him with rich material for his description of the landlord-capitalist class later on. At the same time, his home was also full of literary influences as his father was an avid reader and his mother was very fond of plays and operas and frequently took Cao Yu to the theatre. All kinds of theatre; Beijing opera, *kunqu* opera, Hebei *bangzi*, Shanxi *bangzi*, Tangshan *laozi* and various folk songs and plays, enchanted Cao Yu. "After having seen the performances, I used to re-enact the stories together with my schoolmates, and at other times we created plays of our own."** So much exposure to theatre naturally influenced his later career of playwriting.

In 1933, when Cao Yu was still studying at Qinghua University, he completed his first work *Thunderstorm*. The play was written in six months in five successive drafts, after five years' planning and deliberation. It was published in the *Literature Quarterly* of 1934.

---

* "Cao Yu on *Thunderstorm*," *People's Drama*, No. 3, 1979.

** "Parts of Cao Yu's Life as a Playwright," *Plays*, July 1957.

The four-act play *Thunderstorm* depicts thirty years' relationship between two families in one day's time (set in the guest hall of the Zhou family and the living room of the Lu family). It was about the crimes and tragedies of the two families. The author wrote about the capitalist Zhou family, and about the Lu family which was robbed and humiliated. Of the principal characters in *Thunderstorm*, some died, some ran away, and still others became mad. The tragic play shows the exploitation of the workers and the social causes of the tragedy. This is the ideological significance of the play *Thunderstorm*. There are not many characters in the play, but all the principal characters elicit sympathy from the reader regarding their individual encounters and fate.

The Chinese upper class was usually influenced by feudalism; Zhou Puyuan was just such a person. He was a capitalist with a deep respect for the old morality and also an intellectual who had studied abroad. Through this character the author has exposed and criticized the hypocrisy of the upper class hidden under the cloak of benevolence and good upbringing. Lu Gui, another character, was a flunkey who curried favour with the wealthy and powerful. He knew no shame, always thought that he was right. The author did not caricature him, but exposed his meanness. Another complicated and contradictory character is Fanyi. Fanyi was an upper class woman who was clever and pretty, and sought freedom and love; but she was headstrong and fragile, enthusiastic and lonely. She had suffered spiritual torment, and was eager to get free from her position, but could do nothing but surrender to it. Thus the author said about Fanyi, "Among the eight characters in *Thunderstorm* the one whom I have thought out the earliest, and who is also comparatively more real to me, is Zhou Fanyi."* Cao Yu effectively depicted her thoughts. She felt that the vulgar and monotonous life of the Zhou family was unbearable. She was stifled by the gloomy, heavy atmosphere and wished to get free from it all. But the environment made her become cynical and she lost her emotional balance. Cao Yu said, "Many of these women have beautiful souls, but owing to abnormal development and the

---

* "Preface to *Thunderstorm*."

suffocation of their surroundings, they become perverse and incomprehensible. People project anger and hatred at them and they are oppressed by society, and thus they sadly end their lives without being able to breathe any freedom. Do we know how many such women there are in our present-day society?"* The author also showed sympathy in the treatment of the character Zhou Ping, who was a product of his family upbringing. Zhou Chong was still young, lived in longings and dreams, and lacked a deep understanding of reality. The tragic death of this young man exposes the destructiveness of this feudal capitalist family.

Apart from Lu Gui who was attached to the family both spiritually and materially, the three other members from the Lu family all belonged to the lower class. The similar experience of Lu Ma and her daughter Sifeng of getting pregnant from their rich masters and then being driven from the household shows the fate of these ordinary good people in the society at that time. Although Lu Ma hated wealthy people, she was unable to prevent her daughter from associating with them and having a similar experience as she had in her youth. Sifeng was ignorant of social realities. Lu Ma and Sifeng were simple and easily deceived. Their fate was different from that of Fanyi and Zhou Ping, and won the reader's sympathy. Although the figure of Lu Dahai was insufficiently drawn, he was a figure that expressed the author's ideals. He was rough and forceful; when finally all the other characters in *Thunderstorm* met with destruction, he alone proceeded on the road he should take. The appearance of Lu Dahai gave some ray of light and hope to the dark and heavy atmosphere of the play.

As the author at that time still lacked an understanding of the social problems that produced these tragedies, he explained the cause of the tragedy "as the laws of nature," and wrote, "you could never escape from this dark pit no matter how loudly you cried, once you had fallen into it."** This idea weakened the play somewhat.

The play *Sunrise* was written in 1935 and was published serially the next year in the *Literature Monthly*. *Sunrise* depicted

---

* "Preface to *Thunderstorm*."

** *Ibid.*

a cross section of society including the upper and the lower classes in the limited space of the stage. From predestination hinted at in the *Thunderstorm* to the actual causes of social problems as described in *Sunrise*, we can see progress in the author's understanding of reality. The play *Sunrise* describes a big Chinese city in the early thirties under the influence of the economic crisis of world capitalism. The author hoped to raise social consciousness through his play: "After reading *Sunrise* people will ask angrily: Why is it that so many people lead such a hard life? Should this world go on like this? What is the cause that has brought about this world of injustice? Whether or not this situation should be improved or totally changed? If there are really some people who will ask this, it will be beyond the hope of the author."* This shows that Cao Yu was criticizing the system and trying to shake it at its roots.

The atmosphere in *Sunrise* was tense and noisy; it was the atmosphere of life in the big cities at that time. With the unfolding of the play, the audience grasped the social inequalities. The play depicts various aspects of urban life: women living in hotels, bank managers, doctors, hooligans, prostitutes, waiters, rich widows, etc., who all had different social status, temperaments and cultural backgrounds. There are more characters in this play than in *Thunderstorm*; the scope of life is also wider and more complex. The events in the play unfolded in the rooms of Chen Bailu and Cuixi. These two women were connected with different social classes, but they were both downtrodden, products of urban problems. The plot developed around the principal character Chen Bailu who was a prostitute. She was on the one hand connected with Pan Yueting, thus exposing the decadence of the upper class; on the other hand her relationship with Fang Dasheng showed the misery of the lower class. Chen Bailu was young and beautiful; she was proud, willful and cynical, but at the same time she sought a comfortable and stimulating life. She was conscious, but also confused, enthusiastic and cold. She always had a sarcastic smile, and cynically lived a pessimistic and contradictory life. She was a

* See the last note to the "Postscript to *Sunrise*." This note was deleted in the first edition of *Sunrise* published by the China Drama Press, September 1957, Beijing.

tragic character. However, she had not entirely lost her integrity. She defended a young girl against Black San. The girl, named "Little Thing," was kidnapped by Black San and forced to become a prostitute. But her cynical attitude towards life could not sustain her and she committed suicide before sunrise.

In the activities of Pan Yueting, the economic panic in the big cities at that time began to appear: factories stopped work, banks closed, land depreciated, and speculation on government bonds was rampant. Pan Yueting's intense struggle with Li Shiqing exhibits the evil of these characters and their impending downfall. The dialogue between Huang Shengsan and Li Shiqing expresses the cruel class oppression of that society and the pitiless class relations. Through the action of the play, the special temperament of each character is shown. Fang Dasheng is a foil for the people in the hotel. His reserved nature and kind temperament convince the audience of his affection towards Chen Bailu. He was a socially inexperienced intellectual with good intentions. He hoped to reform Chen Bailu by setting an example for her, and also to save Little Thing.

The author took the work song of the pile-driving workmen as a symbol of light after sunrise. He said: "What really makes me hope is the powerful work song of the pile-drivers; it symbolizes the vigorous life of the great future."* This shows that Cao Yu placed the hope of reforming the society on the workers. Although no working class characters appeared in the play, the work song was used principally to offset the atmosphere. The scene with Fang Dasheng walking towards the rising sun in the direction from which the singing of the workers came is very suggestive. Although this character still has defects, the author has depicted him as a positive character. His appearance in the play gives us hope and encouragement.

Apart from the above-mentioned principal characters, the play includes Eighth Mistress Gu, who was vulgar and foolish and Li Shiqing, who was cunning, sinister and worldly-wise. The power of Jin Ba was shown through the brutality and ruthlessness of

* "Postscript to *Sunrise*."

Black San, and through the miserable experiences of Cuixi the goodness of the lower class was shown. Through these characters, the author has shown the class inequalities existing at the time. Jin Ba, the agent of the feudal, bureaucratic and comprador classes, who wielded the power, did not appear on the stage, neither did the pile-drivers who represented future appear on the stage. When the play is drawing to an end, the audience is shown that a brighter day for the working class is not far away and the wealthy class is nearing its downfall.

The publication and performance of *Thunderstorm* and *Sunrise* met with wide attention and enthusiastic praise from literary circles. Ba Jin, recalling his first reading of the manuscript of *Thunderstorm*, said, "I read it through at one sitting and was deeply touched, and I cried.... At the same time, I felt an earnest hope, a force emerged in me. I wished to do something to help people, I wished to find an opportunity to unselfishly offer my small ability."* At that time, authors, critics and playwrights of different literary schools, like Guo Moruo, Mao Dun, Ye Shengtao, Zhang Geng, Shen Congwen, Meng Shi (Zhu Guangqian), Liu Xiwei (Li Jianwu) and Jin Yi, all wrote to introduce and praise this new dramatist. They pointed out the weak points existing in his work but all of them evaluated his achievements highly. They considered Cao Yu as "outstanding among Chinese writers."** Zhou Yang further affirmed the profound social significance and great artistic force of *Thunderstorm* and *Sunrise* in contrast to the simplifying tendency of Left-wing critical circles.*** The supplement of the *Da Gong Bao* published a special issue for *Sunrise* as it had done with *Thunderstorm* and then awarded a literary prize to Cao Yu.

In *The Wilderness* written on the eve of the War of Resistance Against Japan, Cao Yu's setting shifted from the city to the countryside. The local tyrant Jiao Yanwang buried the father of Qiu Hu alive, sold his younger sister into prostitution and forcibly took possession of his family's land. He also wrongly accused Qiu Hu of

* Bai Jin, "Postscript to *Transformation*."

** Guo Moruo, "On Cao Yu's *Thunderstorm*," *Eastern Current*, Vol. 2, No. 4.

*** "On *Thunderstorm* and *Sunrise*, and a Criticism of Huang Zhigang's Criticism," *Light*, Vol. 2, No. 8.

being a thief for which Qiu Hu spent eight years in prison. The play begins with Qiu Hu's escape and return to his home village to take revenge. Jiao Yanwang had already died. Jiao Yanwang's son, Jiao Daxing had married Jinzi whom Qiu Hu had once loved. The couple were not leading a very harmonious life. The mother-in-law and the daughter-in-law did not get along. The arrival of Qiu Hu brought a new crisis to the family which was already full of conflicts. The play has only four principal characters. Mother Jiao although blind was not only openly tyrannical, but secretly ruthless. She was clear about the significance of Qiu Hu's sudden intrusion into her family. She promised to allow him to take away Jinzi; at the same time she secretly reported Qiu Hu to the detective squad and even attempted to kill him herself. She did not expect that it was her beloved grandson that she had killed. Her actions exhibited the ruthless nature of the exploiting class. Jinzi's pursuit of personal happiness, her enthusiastic yearning for a free life, and her fearless resistance when these wishes met with suppression, showed her strong character. She did not like Jiao Daxing, but she did her best to pursuade Qiu Hu not to kill him, which showed that she was also level headed. Long suffering had made Qiu Hu give up any illusions towards life. He chose individual revenge to oppose the unjust world. The experience of Qiu Hu had a general significance in rural villages in old China. It is regrettable that the author's characterization of him included too much primitive energy which dims his class consciousness.

Qiu Hu's desire for revenge comes entirely from a feudal, patriarchal view of ethics. He firmly believed that it was his duty to avenge the wrong done to two generations of his family. Even if the enemy was already dead, the debt must be repaid by the son. The play emphasized the honesty and tolerance of Jiao Daxing; he was once a good friend of Qiu Hu and had nothing to do with the enmity between the two families. Moreover, he also did not know about the former relation between Qiu Hu and Jinzi. Even when Qiu Hu had intruded into his home, and Jinzi admitted that she had a lover, he still put himself in Qiu Hu's place and did not doubt him. This made Qiu Hu hesitate before he took action and created conflict within him. After killing Daxing, Qiu Hu felt regret and became spiritually despondent. This however, was not a split in his personality, but the logical development of his irrational views about revenge. The portrayal of Qiu Hu as a tragic character shows that revenge cannot alter the humiliated position of the victim, that it only destroys the person taking revenge himself. When the play ends, Qiu Hu, surrounded by the detective squad, prepared to commit suicide. He told Jinzi to tell his brothers: "You must fight against them together, then you can come out alive; if you fight with them alone, you will die." He predicted: "Some day our sons and grandsons will rise up." This shows that in the course of seeking the liberation of the working people, Cao Yu criticized revenge. This is the significance of the play *The Wilderness.*

When he was young, Cao Yu had frequently heard from his nurse and relatives about the peasants and class struggles in rural villages, but as he has no personal experience of such incidents, his description of rural life in *The Wilderness* was not as good as his description of urban life in *Thunderstorm* and *Sunrise*. In the third act, he broke through the limits of time and space on the stage, and recapitulated the crimes of Jiao Yanwang in the earlier years, but played up the terrifying atmosphere too much, thus weakening the play's realism which met with criticism from readers. Of all Cao Yu's works, *The Wilderness* is probably the one of which opinions are most divergent.

II. *Beijing Man* and Other Drama Works

Right after the outbreak of the War of Resistance Against Japan, Cao Yu went inland together with the teaching staff and students of the Nanjing Drama School where he was teaching. The national crisis and the growing cooperation between the Kuomintang and the Chinese Communist Party at its initial stage widened his political vision and stimulated his political enthusiasm anew. He tried to link his literary work with the political struggle. In 1939, in collaboration with other authors, he wrote a play entitled *Twenty-Eight in Black Characters*, praising the anti-Japanese war fighters and patriots, condemning traitors and calling for nationwide mobilization for the War of Resistance. The play was political propaganda, but lacked artistic refinement. Therefore it was rarely mentioned by literary critics later on. The four-act play *Transformation* written at a later date reflected his political enthusiasm during this period.

Transformation reflected the vicissitudes of a provincial field hospital in wartime. The first two acts described the hospital's corruption and confusion. The superintendent was a typical bureaucrat who was unconcerned about the wounded soldiers. He was concerned only about his own interests and he finally became a traitor. His close follower, Ma Dengke was also opportunistic and made a fortune through the national crisis. The functioning of the hospital was impeded by disorder and slowness. The playwright showed the inefficiency of the hospital which obstructed the progress of the War of Resistance. In striking contrast with the selfish and vicious superintendent, was Doctor Ding. For the sake of winning the war, she was willing to sacrifice all, even sending her only son to the frontline. As a devoted doctor and a loving mother, this character was very appealing. It was because of his political enthusiasm that Cao Yu has written this play and created this principal character. The positive and progressive ideals embodied in this work remained powerful, instead of being destroyed or spoiled by the war which was not the case in any of his previous works.

With the eager hope of China's reformation in the course of the war, the playwright portrayed a new hospital administrator who was not corrupt like many who had previously abused their power. Commissioner Liang, who had none of the bureaucratic airs or selfishness, acted in the interests of the people and integrated with them. Under Liang's wise leadership, the hospital changed in a short time. Cao Yu once explained that this character was created after a veteran Communist.* However the majority of administrators who constituted the upper levels of state administration could not bring about reforms in the ruling organs of the Kuomintang, regardless of good intentions or qualities. In this play, Liang was

* "Comrade Cao Yu on Playwriting," *Literary Gazette*, No. 2, 1957.

sent to reshuffle the hospital by the order of the central government. The reform had quick results and went well. But the easy success of the reform weakened the message that old China ought to be transformed, a theme put forward by the playwright. As Cao Yu's understanding of the national reform process was too simple, the play *Transformation* had its limitations.

The stern realities of the day set Cao Yu thinking about life in a new way. Completed in 1941, *Beijing Man* returned to his familiar theme of anti-feudalism. The play presented a once very rich and powerful family, rapidly collapsing with each family member going their own way. Having enjoyed a happy life of prosperity for several decades, but now meeting with frustration in his later years, the old master of the house, Zeng Hao, was determined to protect the coffin which had been painted almost a hundred times for his eventual death and to make his wife's niece, Sufang wait on him as his slave. Brought up under Beijing gentry's culture, Zeng Wenqing, his son, was good at chess, writing verses, drawing and tea tasting, yet, he was unable to earn a decent living by himself. He often picked quarrels with his wife Siyi, while he secretly loved his cousin Sufang. Both of them kept their feelings secret. In order to improve his life and his family's situation, he left home to find a new life. Having no courage to endure hardships, he quietly returned home before long and committed suicide by taking poison. Jiang Tai, his younger sister's husband, was a student majored in physics and technology. Although he had great ambition, he repeatedly failed in business, and eventually became parasitic on the family of his father-in-law. He often exaggerated things and complained a lot, looking down upon other people and making unrealistic plans, but he was unable to escape from the doomed failure. Zeng Wenqing said about his brother-in-law, "I've kept quiet about all things, and achieved nothing. He has raised hell about nothing, yet so far he hasn't accomplished anything either." Their temperaments were very different, but they were both good-for-nothing. Siyi alone was a women of action, who managed the household affairs with diligence and frugality. She was thinking of how to rescue herself from the sinking ship. She had a kind face, but a wicked heart, greeting the people all around with smiles while harbouring deep-seated contempt or bitter hatred for them. Being clever and skillful, hypocritical and cruel, she made jokes at other people's expense. Like her elders, she failed to save the family's situation and herself despite her talent and schemes.

The play showed the weakness of the feudal class, the feudal family system and ideology, such as Zeng Hao's selfishness and Siyi's insidious schemes causing the family to go to ruin.

There were people who left the corrupt family, for instance, the runaways Ruizhen and Sufang. From the youngest generation of the family, Ruizhen was oppressed by an arranged marriage and a cruel mother-in-law. The suffering she endured during her early teens showed her that it was impossible for her to continue living in such a feudal family. Some progressive friends and revolutionary books showed her a new course to follow. However, it was more difficult for Sufang to make the break and become independent because she had long been closely intertwined with the Zeng family. In spite of being slighted and maltreated, she was good-natured and innocent, and her life creed was: "One should rejoice in other's happiness." She secretly fell in love with Zeng Wenqing, and was willing even to sacrifice her life for him. She knew that there would be a time when she might find it impossible to endure her situation any longer. With her hope in Zeng Wenqing frustrated, and her integrity threatened, she took Ruizhen's advice to break off relations with the Zeng family and run away with her. Their move of independence and particularly the development of Sufang's character was contrasted with those who were faltering in the feudal order.

The play devoted a comparatively large space to describe a "Beijing man," a truck mechanic, an image symbolizing the primitive people who denied any restraint of rules. Through him the playwright expressed his ideal: "This is the ancestor of our human race, and the hope of human beings too!" The play was a scathing satire on the decaying feudalistic civilization. Since the Chinese people had already found the correct course to liberation, the playwright's ideology could hardly be expected to produce any significant effect. The activities of Ruizhen's revolutionary friends merited attention, but these episodes were unfortunately neglected, dulling and lessening the force of the climax of the whole play —the flight of the two girls.

Beijing Man had no intricate and large-scale plot. It depicted daily family life and household gossip, and the tense atmosphere and sharp collision of opinions resulting from conflicts within the family. The play *Beijing Man* was both tragic and comic.

In 1942 Cao Yu adapted Ba Jin's novel *The Family* as a play. Juexin's marriage, the mutiny, Grandfather Gao's birthday celebration and his burial service, and Ruijue's death—these four parts were chosen from the novel, and adapted to the limitations of the stage. Cao Yu included the main contents of the original work, cutting out a few characters and episodes while developing some personages and details. Other writers had also tried to do the same thing before, yet only Cao Yu's adaptation lasted together with Ba Jin's original work. It was Cao Yu who furnished us with a successful example as to how to adapt a play from a novel.

Ba Jin's novel emphasized the young people's rebellion and struggle against the feudal family and the old order. Cao Yu's drama exposed the damage wrought by the corrupt family and the old marriage system. In the feudal family, genuine feelings not only failed to gain the esteem of the elders, but also met with ruthless oppression and destruction. Feudal ethics mixed with ignorance and superstition resulted in emotionally damaging situations. Ruijue was married to Juexin by order of their parents, and despite their obedience, their harmonious married life did not last long.

Owing to its omission of many descriptions of the characters and political activities, the scope of the old society reflected by the play was narrower than the novel, and the young people's desire to seek a new life which was originally a strong thread in the novel was weakened in the drama.* The young people struggled hard to accomplish their goals, and managed to escape from some of the shackles of the old traditions. At the end of the play, when Juexin sorrowfully exclaimed, "Now it's hard winter time!" The dying Ruijue added, "But the bitter winter is going to have its end too!"

---

* He Qifang, "A Few Remarks About *The Family*," which was later compiled into his collection entitled *On Realism*.

This presented the force and hope coming from the life impulse.

After his adaptation of *The Family*, Cao Yu did not write anything for a long time until his new drama *Bridge* appeared in a magazine in 1946. This play was about the bureaucratic capitalist's cruel seizure of national bourgeois enterprises. Because he went to the United States for a lecture tour, Cao Yu left the play unfinished. In 1948 he wrote the filmscript *Bright Day*, which showed the hardships in the Kuomintang-ruled region since V-J Day and the people's hopes for a better life.

Cao Yu could handle the themes of the intellectuals, bourgeoisie and feudalism with ease. *Thunderstorm*, *Sunrise*, *Beijing Man*, etc., show his hope and belief in the Chinese people's future and capacity to create a new social order with equality. However as Cao Yu had not yet built up a scientific world outlook then, his works were affected to a certain degree by this limitation. His works sometimes tend to be too idealistic. The fatalistic point of view expressed in *Thunderstorm*, the hallucinations and mysteriousness of *The Wilderness*, the unrealistic portrayal of Commissioner Liang in *Transformation*, the symbolic figure in *Beijing Man*—were shortcomings resulting from this limitation.

All in all, Cao Yu's works reflected a certain section of Chinese society. Prior to his plan to write *Thunderstorm*, he read many European classical plays and the old Greek tragedies. He had read Shakespeare, Ibsen, Chekov, Gorky, Bernard Shaw and O'Neill's plays, and translated Shakespeare's *Romeo and Juliet* into Chinese. His knowledge of world literature doubtlessly aided his literary development. During his youth he read the Chinese classics, and knew quite a lot of the northern folk literature, and its inference can be found in his one-act play, *Just Thinking*, written in 1940. Cao Yu had also seen a great deal of Chinese traditional operas, which left an indelible impression on him.

He thought his play should be accepted by ordinary people "Only the masses are 'the lifeblood of the theatre.'" This was a clear indication that Cao Yu esteemed his audiences and he was entirely different from those who thought that an expert's appreciation was much better than the praises of popular theatre-goers.* Because Cao Yu's plays were very popular, he influenced the whole society.

The May Fourth literary revolution gave rise to deep changes in literature. The modern play was very different from Chinese traditional opera, and was influenced by foreign literature more than any other kind of literature. For this reason, the development of the modern play was rather slow, and its maturity was a long time in coming. The appearance of Cao Yu's work was the milestone of modern Chinese plays since the May Fourth Movement. His works not only attracted extensive attention and heightened the writing level of plays, but were also universally well-received during their run in the theatres. *Thunderstorm*, *Sunrise*, *Beijing Man* and Cao Yu's other works opened a new field for modern drama, and he had made a valuable contribution to the history of modern Chinese drama.

---

* "Postscript to *Sunrise*."

Chapter 10
Ai Qing and His Contemporary Poets

I. Ai Qing

Ai Qing is an important poet who began writing poetry in the late thirties. His poems influenced the development of modern Chinese poetry.

Born in 1910 in Jinhua County, Zhejiang Province, Ai Qing spent his childhood among the peasants in a mountain area and this experience developed a profound feeling for the countryside in him and later provided important material for his poetry. During the First Revolutionary Civil War (1924-27) when he was still a middle school student, he read some books on the materialist conception of history and he began to embrace socialism. He loved painting since childhood and after he graduated from junior middle school, he entered the West Lake Academy of Fine Arts in Hangzhou and later went to study in France in 1929. Three years later he came back to crisis-ridden China in early 1932 and in May that year he joined the Chinese League of Left-Wing Artists and became a member of the art organization, the Spring Field Painting Society. In July he was arrested together with a dozen other young artists under fabricated charges of subverting the government and was imprisoned for more than three years.

While still in France, Ai Qing began to write poems, but most of his important early poems were composed during his imprisonment in Shanghai. In 1936 his first poetry collection, *Dayanhe*, consisting of nine poems was published. It was well-received for its expression of profound feelings and novel style. "Dayanhe—My Wet-Nurse" was the best among the nine poems. In the poem Ai Qing praised his nurse, Dayanhe, and expressed his indignation for her tragic lot in the world. The poem not only expressed sympathy for a poor peasant woman, but also showed deep concern for the miserable life in the countryside. In this collection there were also a few poems that recorded the poet's experience abroad. For example, "Marseilles" and "Paris" expressed some affection for these two cities, but were mainly filled with condemnation for the inequalities of capitalism.

Ai Qing's deep love for the peasants and his rupture with the exploiting classes and criticism of capitalist society are reflected in *Dayanhe*, which serves as a summary of his feelings, as well as a starting point of a new path in ideas and artistic creation.

Ai Qing's poems written during the period from his release in October 1935 to the eve of the War of Resistance Against Japan were collected in *Wilderness*. Some of them further reflected the increasingly bitter life in the countryside, but most of the poems were imbued with hope, expressing the longing for a bright future. He believed the bloodshed of the martyrs would bring about change and expressed his confidence: "I firmly believe in the regeneration of mankind."

When the War of Resistance Against Japan broke out in 1937, Ai Qing travelled all over China which enabled him to widen his horizons and to understand the spirit of the times. During the first years of the war he wrote prolifically. His works were assembled in collections such as *The North*, *Facing the Sun*, *He Died at the Second Time*, *Wilderness*, *The Announcement of the Dawn*, *Torch*, *Defeat and Destruction*, *Poems Dedicated to the Countryside* and *Against Fascism*.

The North included Ai Qing's important poems written in the early period of the war against Japan, which recorded the suffering and adversity brought to the Chinese people by the war, for instance, "Snow Falls on China's Land," "The North," "Beggar" and "Wheelbarrow." These poems depict the enthusiasm and confidence of the people against the enemy. "He Has Risen" symbolized the awakening of the nation.

Facing the Sun, written in the spring of 1938, was Ai Qing's first long poem. It is in keeping with the fervent enthusiasm in the early period of the War of Resistance Against Japan, imbued with zeal, optimism and hope. The poem is divided into nine stanzas. The first three stanzas depict how the poet greeted and blessed everything in the cheerful dawn. The fourth and fifth stanzas say that sunrise was "more beautiful than everything," and it enlightened creation and inspired people. The sixth and seventh stanzas say that the cities, villages, fields, rivers and mountains had awakened from despair, pain and melancholy and were moved to action. The last two stanzas express the poet's inner feelings. The sun had dispersed his solitude, hesitation and sorrows and brought him back to the joy of childhood.

Among the poems in the collection *He Dies at the Second Time*, "The Bugler" and "He Dies at the Second Time," two long poems written in the spring of 1939, are the most important. The latter depicts a wounded soldier who longed to return to the battlefield and how he went back to the front where he was killed. Ai Qing praised the soldier's heroism. The soldier's enthusiasm was based on the hope of new life for China which inspired him to fight and sacrifice his life. "The Bugler," another poem with a similar theme, is more lyrical and touching. The poem is mournful and solemn. This long poem vividly depicts the bugler's longing for dawn:

Now, he begins,
Standing underneath the blue and lucent dome of heaven,
He begins, and, with the fresh fragrant air of the open country,
Blows his breath through the bugle,
—And, along with it, perhaps a trace of blood?
From the bugle, out of deep feeling,
A fresh, full sound is given back to the countryside,
—With devotion to the beautiful dawn,
He blows the sounds of reveille:
How that sound resounds for miles and miles! ... *

When the bugler laid down his life, the poet wrote: "But the sun, the sun / Made that bugle glint and flash in its light.... / Listen: / That bugle seems to be sounding still...."** This poem inspired the morale of the people fighting against the Japanese aggressors.

---

* Ai Qing: *Selected Poems*, p. 74, Foreign Languages Press, Beijing, 1982.
** *Ibid.* p. 76.

Ai Qing's accomplishments of this period are also reflected in the short poems included in *Wilderness, The Announcement of the Dawn, A Poem Dedicated to a Village* and other collections. These poems not only reflect the struggle and the hope for China, but also clearly mark Ai Qing's artistic and ideological development. The early poems in these collections are bright in tone, but some of the poems written right after the autumn of 1939 have a heavier atmosphere. At that time the enthusiasm at the initial stage of the war had gradually died down and people felt the increasing difficulties of the struggle. The poet was then in the rear area under the Kuomintang rule and far away from the battlefront, and was affected by the desolate, lonely atmosphere. So the tone of his poetry became downhearted. For instance, if comparing the two poems written in 1938 and 1939 under the same title, "Autumn Morning," the latter poem is more gloomy. While depicting in "The Colt" how happy and fresh the little horse felt, the poet also said that "it had never tasted any hardship." The heavy-heartedness that occasionally appeared in Ai Qing's poems showed that the poet was in reflection.

Before long he composed another long narrative poem, "Torch," which depicts how a petty bourgeois intellectual was educated in the mass movement and strengthened his resolve in revolution. It reflects the protagonist's longing for revolution, his hesitation and changes in his thinking.

"Torch" not only encouraged people to find the right path, but also lit the revolutionary road for the poet himself. In the spring of 1940, Ai Qing went to Chongqing with the manuscript of "Torch," where he met Zhou Enlai. Since then he had got rid of his depression and wrote many joyful and fresh poems. For instance, "Sorghum" which praises the harvest and life, "Old Man" and "Bonfire" express his love and respect for the peasants. "Highway" and some other poems praise the achievements of the working masses, from which the poet drew inspiration:

> "Walking on this newly opened highway / My heart following its bent / And sensing a limitless joy: / The road stretched out before me / Is so broad, so smooth, / So independent and without obstruction,

/ Leading off into the distance—"*

The following year the South Anhui Incident occurred. Helped by Zhou Enlai, Ai Qing went to Yan'an, where he felt that he had entered a new era as well as a new area. Educated by Mao Zedong and his theory on literature and art, he began a completely new period in his career. "Poetry must serve the ideological education of the masses and become a weapon for propaganda for the revolutionary cause."** He wrote this after he had attended the Yan'an Forum on Literature and Art and it showed that Ai Qing had become increasingly conscious about the political orientation of poetry. To reflect the new life, to serve the workers, peasants and soldiers and to serve proletarian politics were the important features of his poems written during that period, which were later included in the collections of *The Announcement of the Dawn*, *A Poem Dedicated to A Village*, *Against Fascism* and *Amidst Snow*. So the poet recalled later, "My style changed greatly during this period."***

This change was reflected in the subject of the countryside. Though these poems are few during this period, because he was educated by the revolutionary thinking and inspired by the life in the liberated areas, Ai Qing gained new understanding of the countryside. "A Poem Dedicated to A Village" recalled the bright and beautiful scenes in the native area of the poet, which was in sharp contrast with the miserable life of the peasants there.

In November 1941 while attending the assembly of representatives of the border region, he wrote the poem "Mao Zedong" to praise the leader of the Chinese people; in 1942 he wrote "Announce to the World" to refute the slander of the reactionaries and extoll the happy life and struggle in the liberated areas. To denounce the Kuomintang's assault on the Shaanxi-Gansu-Ningxia Border Region, he composed "Rise Up in Defence of the Border Region!" which called upon the people to unite under the leadership of Mao Zedong and Zhu De. "Amidst Snow' was the poet's first

* "Highway" in *The Announcement of Dawn, Ai Qing: Selected Poems*, p. 108, Foreign Languages Press, Beijing, 1982.

** "Poetry Comes into the Street" in *On Poetry*.

*** "Preface to *Ai Qing: Selected Poems*."

long narrative poem which portrayed the revolutionary army led by the Chinese Communist Party.

During this period Ai Qing praised the life in Yan'an and, from this revolutionary base in northwest China, he also addressed "The Announcement of the Dawn" to the whole country, to "the distant towns and villages steeped in misery":

While the night is nearly over, please tell them
What they've been waiting for is coming.

In this poem, Ai Qing expressed his desire for the light, warmth and comfort which he himself had been waiting for many years. The other two poems written in Yan'an, "To the Sun" and "Words from the Sun," showed similar feelings. But, instead of the anxiety in pursuing and longing for the sun and brightness, they expressed the happiness when he was bathed in the light and warmth of the sun:

After the lonesome, long winter,
Today I want to climb up the summit,
Unbuttoning my clothes and bathing my soul in your brilliance....

During this period the poet also wrote a number of poems to protest against fascist crimes and praise socialist construction in the Soviet Union and their struggle against aggression, such as "Revolt of Toulon," "Hitler," "Congratulations in October," and "Salute." "Against Aggression," "Time Is Up," "Lament for Paris," "Gambling" and other poems written in the early period oppose the German and Japanese fascism and view major international events through the method of class analysis. They also reflect the belief of victory over the anti-imperialist struggle from the viewpoint of historical materialism.

After the victory of the War of Resistance, Ai Qing left Yan'an for north China where he stayed until Liberation in 1949. During this period he mainly did other work and took part in land reform and wrote only a few poems which were later included in *Cheers* and other collections. "People's Carnival," "The City of the People" and "Cheers" showed the joy after the victory of the war. *Cheers* praised the peasants in the countryside. "Cuckoo," "Seeing People Off to Join the Army" and some other poems reflected Ai Qing's joy in participating land reform movement, which seemed to be a good answer to his concern for the fate of the peasants.

Ai Qing has a unique style. Out of his concern for the peasants in the countryside, he composed many poems for them. During the time from the collection *Dayanhe* to the poem "Cuckoo," he evolved both in his life and ideas. He expressed sorrow for the suffering of the peasants, excitement for the political awakening in the countryside and joy for the emancipation of the peasantry. Ai Qing endured the shackles of the old society and shared the joy of liberation and land reform with the peasants. He wrote in sympathy for their plight: "The beauty in suffering is engendered by the notion that in this class society ... the suffering people are generally kind."* He thought their perspective should be depicted in Chinese literature which had previously reflected the lives of the upper classes. "This boundless country and the richest life in the countryside—both the old and new—all require an important position in modern poetry."**

Ai Qing's poems are always imbued with profound emotion. He depicted his melancholy, sorrow and grief in his poems and articles. Melancholy was conspicuous in many of his poems. It was not an indifferent or self-indulgent sorrow but an earnest contemplation of the miserable reality of China and its people. It was the deliberation before an answer could be found and, quite different from a sigh of hopelessness, it was the preparation for progress. This melancholy also reflected the heavy mental and emotional burden caused by the class into which the poet was born. His work showed the influence of the miserable rural life portrayed by some Russian writers. But along with the poet's changes in ideology in the course of the development of revolution, this melancholy disappeared and the tone of his poems became buoyant and bright.

Even when reflecting the misery in the countryside, Ai Qing always presented a gleam of hope in a scene of desolation. The sun, light, spring, dawn, life and flame are symbols appearing in many

* "Aesthetics" in *On Poetry*.

** "Preface to *A Poem Dedicated to A Village*."

of his poems. Ai Qing said: "All that prompts mankind to progress is beautiful, good and poetic as well."* Ai Qing's poems are full of vivid images. He said: "The poet comprehends the world in terms of imagery and explains the world to man through imagery."**

The imagery in Ai Qing's poems often benefits from his accomplishment in fine arts. His skill in using colour, light, composition and line in painting helps make his images more distinct and vivid. He paid great attention to technique: "If there is no novelty, colour, lustre and image in a poem, then where is the artistic life?"*** For instance, "Wheelbarrow" blends the scene with emotion, light, colour and images:

On frost-bitten, snow-chilled days,
In and around destitute little villages,
The wheelbarrow,
With its solitary wheel,
Carves out its deep ruts in the pale-yellow layers of earth,
Cutting through the vastness and the desolation,
From this road
To that road,
It knits together
The sorrow of the northern people.†

Ai Qing did not use ornate language, but rather simple and vivid language that was full of vitality. Ai Qing's accomplishments enriched modern Chinese poetry and enhanced its power of expression. Ai Qing is skillful at expressing his ideas in prose poems. His poems have vivid imagery and although they do not rigidly adhere to the rhyme and rules of poetic composition, they have an inherent melody and harmonious rhythm. Ai Qing's poetry marks an important step of the development of free verse after the May Fourth Movement in 1919.

---

* "Poetry" in *On Poetry.*
** "Imagery" in *On Poetry.*
*** "Technique" in *On Poetry.*
† *Ai Qing: Selected Poems*, p. 47, Foreign Languages Press, Beijing, 1982.

II. Tian Jian, He Qifang and Other Poets

Among the renowned poets in the late thirties are Tian Jian, He Qifang, Ke Zhongping and Guang Weiran who, like Ai Qing, also went to the anti-Japanese democratic base areas from the Kuomintang-controlled area in the early period of the War of Resistance Against Japan.

Tian Jian was born in 1916 in Wuwei County, Anhui Province and spent his early years in the countryside. In 1933 he went to Shanghai and later joined the Chinese League of Left-Wing Writers and became an editor of the magazine *New Poetry*. His first poetry collection, *Before Dawn*, mainly reflected the suffering of the workers, peasants, and soldiers.

Chinese Pastoral Songs and *Stories of Chinese Countryside* are two other collections written before the anti-Japanese war. The former focused its attention on the bitter life and struggle in the countryside and reflected the poet's increasing concern for the peasantry; the feeling in this collection was stronger than that in *Before Dawn*. Tian Jian loved the countryside, and longed for the vigorous life in the countryside. But the war had brought calamity to China, especially the northeast. *Stories of Chinese Countryside*, a long poem written in the summer of 1936, consists of three parts: "Hunger," "On the Yangtse River" and "Go Ahead." With incisive language, it denounced injustice in the countryside. The poet took the Yangtse River as the symbol of China and the Chinese people calling it to wake up and go into action, and believed that the "people's spring" would come with struggle. This poem was written at the time when the Chinese people's claim for national liberation was daily increasing. Through praising the peasants' army, Tian Jian "placed the hope on the Red Army."*

After the War of Resistance Against Japan broke out, Tian Jian made great progress in his poetry. In the article "On Eulogizing Our Age"** written in early 1938, he declared that he would write more poems to reflect the sufferings and struggle of the people. Before long he went to Yan'an and in the winter of that same year he fled

* "The Family," *Anhui Literature*, No. 4, 1962.

** In the article used in lieu of a preface to the poetry collection *To the Fighters*.

the enemy blockade and moved to the Shanxi-Chahar-Hebei Border Area where he lived and fought for a long time. Both in Yan'an and the border area, Tian Jian was active in the movement of "street poetry" (popular poetry). He wrote many influential poems. For instance, "A Volunteer" which was widely read:

In the places by the Changbai Mountains,
The Chinese sorghum
Is growing in blood.
In the sandy wind,
A volunteer
Passes his hometown on horseback,
He's come back:
Atop his rifle
Hangs the head of an enemy.

With these few lines, the poet drew a vivid picture. The triumphant volunteer was the image of a hero, as well as a symbol of the hope of the oppressed people, which inspired them.

A large number of Tian Jian's poems written during this period were collected in *To the Fighters*, and showed the progress he had made after he plunged into the actual struggle, as well as new development in his poetry. This collection was divided into six parts which consisted of lyrics, short narrative poems and other forms, for instance, "To a Stockman":

Oh stockman,
Take good care of the horse,
For you should understand
The master of the animal,
Neither you nor I,
Is
China!

Later, when Wen Yiduo talked about Tian Jian's poems, he used some short poems from this collection as examples to prove that the author was the "drummer of the age" during the War of Resistance Against Japan, and he pointed out that there was a desire for life in Tian Jian's poems which "inspires you to love, to hate and to live, to live with ultimate warmth and strength, in this land."* "To the Fighters" recounted in simple and powerful lines the fate of China and called on the people "to triumph or die in the struggle." This poem reflected the realism and love for China in Tian Jian's poetry as is shown in the following stanza:

In China
We cherish a deep love
For the wheat wine
In May,
The rice-flour noodles
In September,
The fuel
In October,
The tobacco
In December,
From each village household,
From the dreamland of four hundred and fifty million souls,
Sending forth
The fragrance
Of the motherland.

Compared with the poems written before the anti-Japanese war, the poems in *To the Fighters* portrayed the struggle of the peasants more concretely. They left their villages and joined the battles, "sowing the seeds of new life of mankind."** A number of short narrative poems written in 1939 depicted soldiers and civilians of the anti-Japanese democratic base areas, their fighting life and their growth to maturity in the struggle. Most of these poems reflected the ideas and demands of the peasants.

In *Chinese Pastoral Songs* and *Stories of Chinese Countryside* the poet began to explore new poetic forms and in *To the Fighters* his skill had matured. He was adept in using short, succinct and powerful lines to reflect militant fervour and at the same time frequent repetition was used to heighten the momentum of the

* "Drummer of the Age—After Reading Tian Jian's Poem," *The Works of Wen Yiduo*, Vol. 3, Kaiming Bookstore, 1948.
** "The Earth," *To the Fighters*.

poems. This terseness and repetition created a sense of rapid rhythm.

During the same period, Tian Jian published two other collections, *To the People Rushing About in Windstorm* and *She Will Kill Too*. The former, written between March and May in 1938, consists of twenty-five poems. Most of the poems in this collection depict the work when he was in the Northwest Field Service Troupe.

The long poem "She Will Kill Too" depicts the miserable fate of a country woman in north China, and also shows that the Chinese people were becoming more conscious of their oppression. Bainiang was raped by the Japanese while her son was killed and their house burned. She refused the idea of committing suicide and took up a knife and ran towards the field shouting, "I will kill!" This action reflected the character's awakening to her own anger. Tian Jian denounced the invaders and showed his trust and hope in the broad masses of suffering people: "The flames of the masses are spreading here," "In front of her/ China's forests, rivers and mountains and paths in the field.... / Have taken up arms." This poem had a rapid rhythm, but lacked well-developed character and depth.

During the later period of the War of Resistance Against Japan and the War of Liberation, Tian Jian published more poetry collections including *Poems Written in the Resistance War*, *Rong Guanxiu*, *Short Songs* and *The Carter (part I)*, which marked a new path both in content and style. *Poems Written in the Resistance War* were mostly short poems composed after the Yan'an rectification movement in literature and art circles, among which some short narrative poems used simple and concise works to depict a short story, portray a simple scene or create an image. *Rong Guanxiu*, a long poem written in 1945, showed how a woman who had been kept at the bottom of society became a heroine.

Great progress was made in *The Carter* written in 1946. It was a narrative poem, in which the protagonist Shi Bulan was a poor, but rebellious peasant. At first he fought individually against the backward society, but failed. Then he went to the Shanxi-Chahar-Hebei Border Region where he saw that under the leadership of the Chinese Communist Party "there is a way out for the poor in the world." He understood if the suffering people tried to free themselves, they must change their thinking and unite under a strong leadership. So he went back to his hometown and worked together with his friend Jin Buhuan, a Communist, to mobilize the masses, organize the peasant association and launch a movement for reduction of rent and interest. Thus the poor people could be emancipated. Both he and Jin Buhuan recognized that the struggle of individuals could get them nowhere, "You've used a sharp knife, / While I a blunt one, / But neither did any good, / Our hands have bled in vain." This poem adopted some techniques of folk songs. But there is too much elaboration that is not connected with the main plot and weakens the central theme. Because the poem was written in regular lines, each line consists of about five characters, and some of the lines are awkward, thus reducing the appeal of the poem.

He Qifang (1912-77) was a native of Wan County, Sichuan Province who began to write free verse in the vernacular in the early thirties. He and Li Guangtian and Bian Zhilin cooperatively published a poetry collection entitled *Poems of the Han Garden*, hence the name of "three poets of the Han Garden." In those poems they expressed their personal sorrows, suffering and disappointment of the society. He Qifang's prose collection, *Records of Painted Dreams*, is influenced by poetry. His early poems were later compiled into a collection entitled *Prediction* and most of them reflected the wishes and aspirations of a young intellectual. He tried to seek beauty and love. But he only explored it secretly and quietly waited for affection without any ardent pursuit.

When he started composing poems, He Qifang paid special attention to form, rhythm, metre and particularly to the imagery. The feeling in He Qifang's poems was subtle, sentimental and melancholic, but later reality began to intrude on his inner life. In the poems written in the following years, there was not much longing for youthfulness; but more adult loneliness. Even if there were some dreams, they had lost their original illusory beauty, as the author examined reality. His poems written right before the Resistance War began to reflect the atmosphere of the times and the injustice and misery in the cities and countryside. Meanwhile he began to change his aesthetic artistic principles. In the poem "Could" he wrote:

From now on I'll say my opinions:
I'm willing to have a thatched roof,
I'll not love the cloud and moon,
Nor the sparkling stars.

From 1940 to February of 1942, He Qifang continued to write many poems which were later published in a collection entitled *Night Songs.* The poems in *Prediction* are mostly floating images,* but *Night Songs* is much more realistic. "Chengdu, Let Me Wake You Up," written in 1938, tried to raise the consciousness of the people, which reflected that the poet himself had awakened from his earlier fantasies. More obvious progress can be seen in the poems written after he went to Yan'an. In *The Story of a Bricklayer,* written in 1939, He Qifang praised the hero who had sacrificed his life for national interests. This was unprecedented in his early poetry, hence attracted general attention. Most poems in this collection were written between 1940 and 1942. The author once pointed out that there was a contradiction between the "old self" and the "new self," which were "the contradiction of an old-type intellectual."** These contradictions were clearly reflected in the seven poems in this collection. In comparison with *Prediction,* this collection displayed a completely new world. Just as seen in "The Joyful People," "North China Is Aflame" and some other poems, changes can be seen from individual to collective, from fantasy to reality, marking the poet's change of world view.

The poem "Revolution—a March Against the Old World," written in 1941, extolled the revolutionary struggles and anticipated the coming victory. The ten short poems including "I'm Singing for the Boys and Girls" and "All-Embracing Is the Life," written in 1942, have a bright and optimistic note about the masses, the youth as well as the poet's own changes during the revolution.

Ke Zhongping (1902-64) joined the Creation Society (a literary organization formed in 1921) when he was young and began to

---

* "Postscript (I)," *Night Songs.*

** "Postscript of the First Edition," *Night Songs.*

publish poems around the period of the May 30th Movement in 1925. His long poem "Songs of the Seaside Night" and short poems "Greatness Lies in Daring to Die," "Running in the Snow" and "To a Hero in Jail" reflect the patriotic tide at that time. In 1929 he wrote *The Mountain of Wind and Fire*, a poetic drama in five acts, to reflect the grim struggle during the Agrarian Revolutionary War (1927-37), but the content in this poem was vague and superficial. Later he stopped writing for some years. Then the War of Resistance Against Japan inspired him and his life after he went to Yan'an enriched his work. In 1938 he wrote two long narrative poems, "Self-Defence Corps in Border Areas" and "The Sabotage Detachment of the Workers Along the Beiping-Hankou Railway." The former related the story of how the people's forces in the border areas captured a traitor and praised the resourcefulness and bravery of the soldiers. The poem showed the struggle and life in the border region.

Ke Zhongping paid much attention to style in poetic form and used the techniques of folk songs, and colloquial language. Literary devices such as metaphor and simile were used in the long poems and the rhythm was even and lively which made the poems easy to recite.

During this period Ke Zhongping also composed many short poems which were later compiled in a collection entitled *From Yan'an to Beijing*. Small in number, they were original and like his longer poems these short poems were inspirational.

Guang Weiran (Zhang Guangnian), born in November 1913, is another poet who wrote some outstanding poems during the War of Resistance Against Japan. He is good at writing poems for recitation and song lyrics. In August of 1935 he published the poem "Flowers in May," written in a lyrical style:

> *The flowers in May are in bloom all over the field,*
> *They have covered up the blood of the martyrs.*
> *In order to save the nation that is in imminent danger,*
> *They fought staunchly to the end.*

After the war broke out Guang Weiran took part in the propaganda work for the resistance against Japan. Having witnessed the horror of war, and the fighting morale of the people, in March 1939 in Yan'an he wrote an epic, *The Yellow River Cantata*. At the beginning of the poem, the poet depicted a boatman on the Yellow River battling desperately with the waves to symbolize the Chinese nation's life-and-death struggle against the Japanese invasion. The poem is powerful and moving. Guang Weiran closely linked the image of the Yellow River with the fate of the Chinese people. *The Yellow River Cantata* was set to music by the famous composer Xian Xinghai.

In 1940, under the repressive political atmosphere after the Kuomintang's first anti-Communist upsurge, Guang Weiran wrote in Chongqing *Qu Yuan*, a long narrative poem about the patriotic poet of the Warring States Period. Through this historical story Guang Weiran expressed the people's commitment to the Resistance War. During the democratic mass movement in the forties, he also wrote a number of satirical poems with political themes to expose the oppressive rule in the Kuomintang areas. The combination of lyricism and a narrative approach made Guang Weiran's work very popular.

Chapter 11
Literature During the War of Resistance Against Japan

I. Novels on the Resistance War and Works by Lu Ling and Other Authors

During the initial period of the Resistance War Against Japan, there were fewer novels than poems published. However, quite a number of short stories on the theme of the Resistance War appeared, such as "A Company Commander's Experience in the War" by Qiu Dengping, "Half-cart of Wheat Straw Short" by Yao Xueyin, and "The Death of Liu Cuigang" by Xiao Qian. A number of novelle and full-length novels emerged, which showed changes in the attitudes of the people during the struggle against Japanese aggression.

Qiu Dongping (1911-41) took part in the 1928 Uprising in Hailufeng in Guandong Province led by Peng Pai. After the Soviet movement in Hailufeng failed, he led a hard and vagrant life. Later he worked for the Nineteenth Route Army, taking part in the January 28th battle against the Japanese invaders in Shanghai and in a similar battle in Rehe (now in Hebei Province). These experiences provided a basis for his literary work. Nurtured and educated by the League of Left-Wing Writers, he began in 1932 publishing his short stories, including "The Messenger." His descriptions of revolutionary life in the countryside won the attention of the public. His *The Battle in Changxia* and *The Gloomy City of Meileng* are collections of short stories describing events in the revolutionary area.

At the beginning of the Resistance War Qiu Dongping published short stories in the magazine *July* about the bloody and bitter struggle of the soldiers and the people. "A Stormy Day" was about a young guerrilla who stuck to his post during a big storm. "A Company Commander's Experience in the War" described company commander Lin Qingshi's courage when he faced an attack by powerful enemy artillery.

Having taken part in the August 13th battle in Shanghai, the author witnessed the heroism of the Chinese who resisted the Japanese aggressors. His writing was vivid and realistic, showing the Chinese resistance against the aggressors during the initial period of the war and the impotence and corruption of the Kuomintang authorities.

Lin Qingshi's company, which fought bravely against the Japanese troops, was destroyed during the retreat upon orders from above. The tragedy exposed the non-resistance of the Kuomintang authorities.

Apart from the novella *The Donator* written in collaboration with Ouyang Shan (1908-), Qiu Dongping wrote the novel *At the Foot of Mount Mao* during this period. This novel was based on his own experiences in the New Fourth Army. Although he only wrote five chapters of this novel, he succeeded in depicting the national struggle interwoven with class contradictions in the anti-Japanese base area in southern Jiangsu Province with the Mount Mao area as the centre. Unfortunately Qiu Dongping died when covering the retreating students during the Japanese attack in 1941, leaving the novel unfinished.

Yao Xueyin's work attracted attention because he used the colloquial language of the Chinese peasants to describe their awakening at the beginning of the Resistance War. His short story "Half-cart of Wheat Straw Short" describes a peasant guerrilla who was known by this nickname. He was very straightforward, simple and kindhearted, but was also backward in his thinking and habits. He joined the guerrillas in the simple belief "If the devils (an abusive term for foreign invaders) are not driven out, we won't be able to bring in the crops." When he first joined the guerrillas he thought that "bullets have eyes that can see. So long as one doesn't do anything bad, there is no need to be afraid of anything." Since he had always used oil sparingly, he secretly put out the burning oil lamp in the barracks at night, and it caused confusion. In spite of this thinking and behaviour, he was attracted to the common struggle and gradually got used to collective life. He fought bravely and was seriously wounded in a battle. At a crucial moment he showed bravery and was not afraid of death. When this novel appeared in the magazine *Literary and Art Front* in 1938 it won widespread popularity because of its realistic characters.

The novella *Niu Quande and Carrot* similarly describes wartime changes in characters who came from peasant families. The theme shows the development of gallantry of those who defended the poor in the old Chinese society to the sense of responsibility towards the revolution.

Images in this novel are vivid and the language is lively. Together with "Half-cart of Wheat Straw Short" this novel is an excellent work, a conscious effort by the author to popularize literature during the Resistance War.

Yao Xueyin also wrote *Warm Spring and Blossom Time*, *Wartime Romance* (*Jin Qianli*), *Young Seedling* (*Bright Summer*) and other novels during this period. They reflect the fervent patriotism of the young generation during the war. Children and young people play a leading role in many of his novels. *Warm Spring and Blossom Time* describe the activities of young people's study groups at the foot of Dabie Mountain during the anti-Japanese war. The novel also describes the corruption of the Kuomintang authorities, the savage forces of feudalism in the locality and the network of the Kuomintang special agents.

In the War of Liberation period Yao Xueyin published a full-length novel *Long Night*. It describes the life of a group of bandits headed by Li Shuimo through the eyes of a young student, who was seized for ransom on his way home. The scene was set in a mountain district in west Henan Province in 1924, when warlords fought against each other. The book exposes poverty, bankruptcy and starvation in the countryside that forced many peasants to become bandits. Novels like *Long Night*—a realistic account of the characters and life of Robin Hood-type heroes —were seldom seen in the new literature of China after the May

Fourth Movement. Yao Xueyin also wrote the novella *Lu Rongxuan*, a biographical novel about a patriotic scientist. His short story "Recovery of Human Nature" exposes the cruelty of the Kuomintang special agents in suppressing progressive intellectuals.

The New Emerging Generation by Qi Tong (1902-50) is a novel which appeared early in the Resistance War period. The author originally planned to write a trilogy. He intended to write about the ideological changes among the youth in north China starting from the student movement of December 9th in 1935 to protest the occupation of northeast China by the Japanese, to the Marco Polo Bridge Incident on July 7, 1937, when the Japanese attacked Beijing which spurred a nationwide resistance against Japanese aggression.

Qi Tong had by then completed the first two parts of the novel, but published only one. The novel describes vividly the two demonstrations of Beijing students in December 1935 and their propaganda work among the peasants in the countryside. In the book the author portrayed different types of intellectuals. There were those who grew matured in the course of the struggle. There were scholars who talked a great deal, but were afraid of actual fighting and also some who even went so far as to betray the revolution. Still, there were professors who actively took part in the patriotic movement, but who could not put their theories into practice.

The hero of the novel Chen Xuehai, a young student, ignored politics at first, but later was active in political struggle. The novel gives a realistic account of the ideological changes of the student. The novel's drawback, however, was the description of the contact of the students in the countryside with the peasants was too simple to be convincing. In this respect the novel lacked authenticity, since the author did not have such experience himself. Nevertheless, *The New Emerging Generation* is still considered to be a good novel at the early stage of the War of Resistance Against Japan.

The novella *War Torn Couple* by Yu Ru appeared in *New Edition of Literature Field* edited by Mao Dun in 1944. Shortly after it was published in book form and received the attention of the literary world and young intellectuals. The novella has a lucid style, a boldness of vision and good characterization. Its heroine Luo Weina, who was from a petty bourgeois family, made a break with her small world and embraced the large cause of national liberation.

As was pointed out by Mao Dun: "The reason why we are glad is that this novella has described a new type of woman in this great age.... Through careful analysis of struggle in her mind we see a new woman steadily on the march, catching the main stream of the age. She has contributed all she has to the nation."*

The novella has certain structural flaws. Apart from Luo Weina, all other characters were written with a formula and were too general. However the character Luo Weina and the story inspired intellectuals at that time.

Lu Ling's *Sons and Daughters of the Rich* was completed in 1945 as one of the longest novels of this period. It shows the features of Chinese society in the ten years after the Japanese troops attacked Shanghai on January 28, 1932, using the separation of a big landlord-capitalist family in south China as the focal point. The family split up because of different ideologies held by family members. This reflected the divisions in Chinese society as a whole. It raised the question: What path should the young intellectuals take in this turbulent age? The author had just started writing. He had studied Western literature which influenced him to some extent; he also studied China's new literature since the May Fourth Movement. During his studies he learned novel writing techniques.

The novel is divided into two parts. The first part is loose in structure. The story focuses on the family of Jiang Jiesan, the richest in Suzhou, which disintegrated because of various reasons. The author also described in this part activities of the sons and daughters of the Jiang family in Shanghai, Nanjing and Suzhou.

Part Two concentrates on the complicated experience of Jiang Chunzu, the youngest son of Jiang family in the turbulent years from the Marco Polo Bridge Incident to the outbreak of the Second World War. It is interwoven with the meaningless and apathetic

---

* Mao Dun, "On the Novella *War Torn Couple*."

life of the other sons and daughters of the family behind the scenes of the war.

Placing these young intellectuals from an exploiting class background into their times, when class contradictions were growing sharp, the author showed their ideology and inner world.

The author said, "What I examine, criticize and affirm is the material and spiritual world of Chinese intellectuals. This involves the complicated life of China, in which a great storm—the war for national liberation—is developing rapidly."*

This attempt has positive results. The novel realistically described the luxurious life of a rich family and the struggle going on inside the family, each tried to cheat or outwit the other. It also exposed the decadent society in the Kuomintang areas. A character in the novel, Jin Suhen is similar to the woman character Wang Xifeng in *A Dream of Red Mansions*, one of the four best known Chinese classics. With this woman in the centre, a struggle for the right of inheritance of property developed within the Jiang family. The book has a very vivid description of this struggle, but its description of intellectuals is not so accurate. At that time large numbers of intellectuals went into the midst of the workers and peasants and into the heart of the actual struggle. In so doing intellectuals not only remoulded themselves, but also became integrated with workers and peasants. The novel fails to reflect this reality, but rather advocates Jiang Chunzu's individualist thinking, which separated him from the people and from the actual struggle. The novel, however, still has its historical significance as it has shown the inevitability of the anti-imperialist and anti-feudal democratic revolution in China.

Apart from this novel, Lu Ling wrote the novelle: *The Hungry Guo Su'e*, *A Snail on Thistles and Thorns* and two collections of short stories *Blessing to Youth* and *Wooing*. He wrote more than other young writers at that time. His works draw material from a wide range, and characters appearing in them include miners, peasants, soldiers, vagrants, exploiters as well as various types of intellectuals. They reflect from different angles the backwardness of the society

* Lu Ling, "Foreword to *Songs and Daughters of the Rich*."

then and the suffering of the people. The style of writing shows traces of European influence. Generally speaking, his portrayal of the exploitive characters and intellectuals is more realistic, while his characters of workers and peasants are not as well-done.

The novel, *On the Frontier*, written by Luo Binji before the War of Resistance Against Japan and his reportage, "Special Detachment on the Eastern Front" written at the outbreak of the war, had impact on readers. Afterwards he wrote the novel *Chaos* (Part One of *A Family History of Jiang Buwei*), and short stories which were later included in his collection entitled *Spring Comes to Beiwang Garden*. "Spring Comes to Beiwang Garden" in the collection best represents his artistic style. The story was set in Guilin, the rear area during the war. It described the lonely secluded life of intellectuals in Beiwang Garden, showing their dejected spirit.

The author shows in the book the inner life of his characters through detailed descriptions of their thoughts and feelings, effectively helping the reader to feel the impact of the suffocating atmosphere of the time.

In contrast to the gloomy life of these intellectuals, in his short story, "Fellow Villager—Kang Tiangang," the author portrayed a peasant of the late Qing Dynasty, who pursued stubbornly his ideals. He also described the beautiful snow-covered scenery of the Northeast. "The 1944 Incident" is about the tragic life of a petty civil servant, who was forced by poverty to become a thief and was sentenced to death. It criticized and condemned the Kuomintang government's legal system.

Chaos is an autobiographical novel set against Chinese society between 1918 and 1921. It described the life of Jiang Buwei who came from a landlord-merchant family. Through the observations and feelings of Jiang Buwei as a child, the novel revealed the social customs and the way of life in a northeast border town near the Soviet Union and Korea. But the description of society does not go beyond the viewpoint of a child and therefore does not reflect the broader social problems.

Shi Tuo (Lu Fen), born in 1910, started to publish short stories and essays in the thirties. The collection of his short works, *Miscellaneous Reporting on Old Home*, reflects the harshness of the land-owning class in his hometown in Henan Province and the suffering of the peasants. At times his writing is quite sarcastic and he had his own unique writing style. This style manifested itself at first in *Crops*, *Setting Sunshine* and *A Collection of Wild Birds*, which were published before the Resistance War. This style was even more apparent in works published during the war years. They were collected in a book in 1946 entitled *The Orchard Town*.

The Orchard Town is a collection of eighteen related short stories.

In the preface the author says, "The hero of this book is a small town which lies in my imagination. I have deliberately described the small town to represent all small towns in China. To me, it has life, character, thought, understanding, and a life span, like a living person."*

The author vividly described the life of this town, the rise and fall of various people in the town during a span of thirty years. He described feudal landlords, who had been wealthy but went bankrupt later, and peasants who worked hard all their lives and yet died in a tragic manner. These people include unfortunate young women from good families, and prostitutes well known in the town, as well as in port cities. These characterizations were realistic and served as a commentary on the tragedy of life.

However, the author failed to probe into the social factors responsible for these tragedies. He showed sympathy to the common people and contempt and irony towards the "big shots." Apart from his short stories, Shi Tuo also wrote novella *A Residence Owner in Wuwang Village* and two novels *Ma Lan* and *Marriage*. The artistic technique of these works is skillful, but the style is not as lucid as that of *The Orchard Town*.

II. Works by Xia Yan and Other Playwrights

Chinese theatre developed quickly following the outbreak of the Resistance War. Three short plays, "Good-Stratagem-Whip" for short—*Sanjiang is Good*, *The Last Stratagem* and *Put Down Your*

* Shi Tuo, "Preface to *The Orchard Town*."

Whip—were staged in various places and were inspirational in the struggle against Japanese aggression. *Defend Marco Polo Bridge*, *Taierzhuang* and *Eight Hundred Heroes*, were also about the anti-Japanese war. In the early stage of the war, the one-act play was the main form of drama being staged. According to an incomplete estimate, 142 plays had been written by the end of 1938, most of them were one-act works.*

When the war reached a stalemate the centre of the theatre moved gradually to the rear, where multiple-act plays were increasingly staged. The Kuomintang government stepped up its persecution and suppression of progressive drama. In spite of this, many playwrights emerged, including Xia Yan, Yu Ling, Song Zhidi, Yang Hansheng, Chen Baichen, Shen Fu, Yuan Jun and Wu Zuguang in the period from the Resistance War to the War of Liberation.

Xia Yan was born in Hangzhou, Zhejiang Province in 1900. He took part in the organization and leadership of the Left-wing drama movement. His writing began with his earliest one-act play written in 1934, entitled *A Corner in Metropolis*. *Sai Jinhua*, an allegorical historical play, was his first multiple-act play, written in April 1936. The author said he attempted to "paint a picture of lackeys with the Boxer Uprising of 1900** as the background in order to expose the Chinese traitors and thereby arouse the attention of the masses to national defence in areas under the Kuomintang control."***

The prostitute Sai Jinhua was the main character of the play which condemned the decadence of the upper ruling class members of the Qing Dynasty, such as Li Hongzhang, Sun Jianai and Wei Bangxian. The play was an allegory of the situation at that time using the historical theme. Consequently this play was banned by the Kuomintang.

The heroine, Sai Jinhua, was originally the focus of his allegory,

---

* Ge Yihong, "List of Plays on the Resistance War, An Appendix to *On Wartime Plays*."

** An anti-imperialist armed struggle waged by north China peasants and craftsmen in 1900.

*** Xia Yan, "History and Allegory," first issue of *Literary Circles*, 1936.

but as the author showed more sympathy to her, she had in the author's opinion, retained more or less some good qualities.*

The author praised her in his play, which lacked a comprehensive view and appraisal of the historical revolutionary role of the Boxer Uprising. Lu Xun criticized *Sai Jinhua* in his essay, "This Too Is Life." In the winter of 1936 Xia Yan wrote his second historical play called *Soul of Freedom*, but changed the title later to *The Story of Qiu Jin*. The theme of the second play was the heroic deeds of Qiu Jin, a heroine in the 1911 Revolution. At the same time the play ruthlessly condemned the traitors and the Qing Dynasty rulers, who cruelly suppressed the Chinese people but fawned on foreign powers.

Between April and May 1937 Xia Yan wrote a three-act play *Under the Eaves of Shanghai*. After the Xi'an Incident (Chiang Kai-Shek was arrested in 1936 by two of his generals and forced to make a coalition with the Communists to resist Japanese aggression) the Kuomintang government was forced to release a number of political prisoners. Some of the revolutionaries were freed from jail. There were tragic departures and happy reunion, which moved the author, who wrote the play named *Reunion* at first. Written in a realistic style, the play described what happened in five households in a Shanghai lane on one day, showing the suffering of Shanghai residents on the eve of the outbreak of the Resistance War. In a gloomy political climate that was like the rainy season in China with its unpredictable intermittent rains, every family had its own worries. Shi Xiaobao was a deserted woman driven to prostitution, the lonely old newspaper vendor drank to drown his worries.

An employee of a foreign firm, Huang Jiamei, having lost his job, was beset with poverty and illness. His father, who had managed to support his college education, came for a visit from the countryside. Huang Jiamei and his wife tried to borrow money and pawn their possessions to cover up their predicament. But the father finally discovered the truth. He returned to the countryside, secretly leaving with his grandson a small amount of money,

* Xia Yan, "History and Allegory," first issue of *Literary Circle*, 1936.

which was his last savings.

Zhao Zhenyu, a primary school teacher, was quite used to poverty and resigned to fate, but his wife was worried about their poverty and complained all the time.

The main thread of the story, however, was the family of Lin Zhicheng and Yang Caiyu. Lin Zhicheng, as sublessor, worked very hard in a factory. He was gloomy and cross all the time.

Caiyu used to sympathize with the revolution. She left her family to marry Kuang Fu, a revolutionary. After Kuang was arrested, poverty and loneliness forced her to retreat. Under the wrong impression that her husband had been executed, she married Lin Zhicheng. When Kuang was set free from the prison he met his good friend Lin Zhicheng and his former wife. The situation caused conflicts for all three. The play showed the audience that the characters' feelings and thoughts were closely connected with their social circumstances and conflicts were brought about by the political climate that suffocated people. It was through the sad fate of the characters that the play condemned the backward society and Kuomintang rule. The author, however, still placed hopes on the future of these people, especially on the children.

Various types of people were brought together in this play and the story of each person was coordinated with the others. The climax at the end of the story was the departure of Kuang Fu. *Under the Eaves of Shanghai* shows that Xia Yan has become a realistic writer with a unique style.

In the first three years of the war Xia Yan moved from one place to another. He wrote *During One Year*, (*Heaven and the World*) in Guangzhou and *Psychological Defence* and *The Story of A City of Sorrow* in Guilin. The three plays all took place in Shanghai, after it fell into the hands of the Japanese.

The author explained in "Soliloquy of a Traveller" written as a preface to *The Story of A City of Sorrow* that he had persistently written about Shanghai because he knew Shanghai better than any other place, and because he was concerned about the fate of his friends who were struggling in Shanghai. Of the three *Psychological Defence* was the most successful.

The four-act play *Psychological Defence* was completed in May 1940. It vividly portrays the struggle waged by progressive cultural workers during the first two years after the occupation of Shanghai by the Japanese army. The gloomy and depressing atmosphere permeating *Under the Eaves of Shanghai* was now replaced by the storm of the age after the outbreak of the Resistance War. The hero, Liu Haoru, was a patriotic journalist who was a leading member in the field of progressive culture. When Shanghai first fell, he decided to go to the rear, but soon made up his mind to stay on. He thought that "the question before us now is how to establish a spiritual defence line in the hearts of five million people in Shanghai. Spiritually we must never be conquered by the enemy. This is the responsibility of cultural workers, remaining in Shanghai."

The struggle became more and more difficult because the Resistance War suffered a series of defeats and Wang Jingwei openly betrayed the nation and surrendered to the enemy. Liu Haoru stood firm before the threats and bribes of the Japanese aggressors and Chinese traitors. He inspired his comrades to have confidence in their victory and to persist in the struggle. He was eventually killed by the enemy.

In the summer of 1942 Xia Yan completed the four-act play *A Chant on the Waterside Village* and the five-act play *Fascist Germ*. The former was about the guerrilla war in the villages by the river in west Zhejiang Province. Xia Yan, however, was not familiar with this kind of life, so the play was not so successful. The latter was a realistic and moving account of the ideological changes of a scientist in the war.

Fascist Germ—the name was once changed into *The Seventh Wind Ball*, shows the awakening of the political consciousness of a scientist, Yu Shifu, and exposes the reactionary nature of fascism as an enemy of all things progressive and the corruption of the Kuomintang. The play was set against the political events between 1931 and 1942.

Yu Shifu studied medicine in a Japanese medical college. Returning home from Japan he became a research fellow at the preventive medicine department of the Shanghai Institute of Natural Sciences. He hoped his scientific research would serve the nation and mankind.

The Resistance War had a strong impact on his family. Because his wife was Japanese, his maidservant resigned from her job. People cursed his daughter as "The little Japanese." He was forced to live in Hong Kong, where he decided to do research on typhus. When the Pacific War broke out Japanese aggressors broke into his home, destroyed his research and subjected him to humiliation. They killed a young patriot Qian Yu in his presence. This event awakened him at last to the realization that "if the greatest disease—the fascist germ—is not destroyed, it would be impossible to build China into a modern state." Thereupon he left Hong Kong and went to the revolutionary area, where he made up his mind to fight fascism. He started all over again. He decided to stop his work until a victory was reached, then he would continue his research. The description of the process of Yu Shifu's political awakening was very convincing. Two other intellectuals, Zhao Antao and Qin Zhengyi, portrayed as foils to Yu Shifu, also left a deep impression on the audience.

Towards the end of 1944 the author wrote *Li Li Cao*. He wanted to show the persistent struggle against Japanese aggression in northeast China. But the scenes of the struggle in northeast China were entirely fictitious. The characters were superficial, lacking authenticity and the power to move people.

From *Under the Eaves of Shanghai* to *Fascist Germ* Xia Yan's plays have a unique realistic style and the themes are closely linked to real struggles. They are imbued with patriotism and revolutionary optimism. In exposing backwardness and corruption Xia Yan pointed out the way to a bright future.

The plays of Xia Yan are rich and vivid and his language is simple and concise. His plays are different from Cao Yu's, which have more intense conflicts and are more colourful. Xia Yan's plays are also different from Guo Moruo's plays, which are more poetic and impassioned. His works are like watercolour sketches, expressing serious themes and exposing the dark elements of society and human nature. In some places the influence of Chekov and Gorky can be discerned.

Apart from play writing Xia Yan also wrote many essays, which have been collected in *Collection of This Time and This Place*, *Long Distance*, *The Border Drum* and others. He was a major writer for *Weeds* published in Guilin and Hong Kong during the Resistance War and the War of Liberation.

Song Zhidi (1914-56) wrote one-act plays *A Speck of Dust* and *Going on an Expedition*. He also wrote multiple-act plays, such as *Self-Defence Corps*, *Torture*, *Whip*, and *The Motherland is Calling*.

The five-act play *Whip*, also known as *Foggy Chongqing* was written in 1940. It describes several university students living in exile in Chongqing, heading for a downfall.

The play describes what happened to young people in areas under the Kuomintang control. It criticizes the weakness and vacillation of young petty bourgeois intellectuals and condemns the political corruption of the Kuomintang. The conflict and experiences of the main characters were based on reality. The characters are vivid, and the story is complicated but well-organized. It was well-received by audiences in Chongqing and elsewhere.

The Motherland is Calling, a five-act play, was written and performed in the spring of 1943. Song Zhidi went to Hong Kong during the War of Resistance Against Japan but returned to Chongqing when the Pacific War broke out. The play was set in the upper class society in Hong Kong during the Japanese occupation. It is about an intellectual, Xia Wanhui and her husband, a noted surgeon, Lu Yuanfang, who left the enemy-occupied area and went to the rear with help from revolutionaries. It describes the struggle between the revolutionaries and the enemy in Hong Kong. The revolutionary Wei Kegong was the former husband of Xia Wanhui. The climax is reached when Wei Kegong was seriously wounded and then died.

During the War of Liberation Song Zhidi wrote a one-act play *A Flock of Monkeys*. Characters representative of various cliques of the Kuomintang assembled at the home of a mayor of a borough. The story was set against the background of the "election" of representatives of the Kuomintang national congress. The secretary generals, directors and congress members used all kinds of tricks to get votes. Though lacking in depth, the play scathingly satirized the political corruption of the Kuomintang bureaucrats, the hypocrisy of the "democratic constitution" and the struggle between various political cliques.

Yu Ling (1907-, pennamed You Jing) is an important playwright, who wrote in Shanghai during the early years of the Resistance War. His works include *Female Lodging House*, *Weeping Flowers*, *Shanghai at Night*, *Female Kingdom*, *Apricot Blossoms in South China During Spring Rain*, *Journey During the Long Night* and *Heroes of the Ming Dynasty*. Most of these plays drew their themes from life in Shanghai during the Resistance War. In exposing the crimes of Japanese imperialists they reflect the suffering and resistance struggle of the Chinese people. The dialogues in the plays were suggestive and restrained, but the plots were not well-edited in some plays and there seem to be too many threads all at once.

Shanghai at Night, a five-act play written in 1939, is a representative work of the author. Focussing on the family of Mei Lingchun after the outbreak of the Shanghai battle on August 13, 1937, the play reflects attitudes of various social classes in Shanghai at the time, as well as the suffering of the people and their growing feelings of resistance against Japanese aggression.

Mei Lingchun brought his family to seek refugee in Shanghai. He went through many worries and tribulations. His eldest son and daughter-in-law were killed by the Japanese. His daughter Mei Ehui married a playboy Qian Kaizhi, out of her gratitude to him for helping her family enter a settlement in Shanghai. In the end she was abandoned by him. Though the family endured many problems, the Meis retained their integrity and moral courage. They refused to yield to threats or bribes from the enemy. Finally the family decided to return to their hometown.

The continuation of *Shanghai at Night* is the four-act play *Apricot Blossoms in South China During Spring Rain*. It is the story of Mei Lingchun's family after they left Shanghai and returned to their hometown. Together with local anti-Japanese national salvation army they put up a struggle to protect their hometown. Due to the author's lack of experience of the struggle portrayed in the play, it was not so successful.

The four-act play *Journey During the Long Night*, written in 1942, largely reflected the struggle between patriotic intellectuals, and the Japanese imperialists and the bogus regime, before and after the fall of Shanghai, and also the suffering of the poor people.

The leading character of the play Yu Weixin and his wife, Ren Landuo, were both honest and patriotic intellectuals. "Life is like going on a journey in the dark night. One can't afford to lose one's footing and fall." With these words Yu Weixin warned himself to always be vigilant in his stand against oppression. Poverty, sickness, threats or bribes could not prevent him from his struggle against oppression.

Heroes of the Ming Dynasty is a five-act historical play, written in 1941. Set against the battle at Caishiji, the play describes Liu Baiwen, Su Jiaojiao, Tang Lixing, Xiugu and other leaders of the rebellion and masses of people who were determined to overthrow the Yuan Dynasty.

Shen Fu's plays include *Twenty-Four Hours in Chongqing, The House Full of Gold and Jade* and *A Nobody's Rhapsody*, which describe the society in towns and cities in the rear during the stalemate of the Resistance War.

The three-act play *Twenty-Four Hours in Chongqing* deals with characters and events in an ordinary two-storey building in Chongqing on the eve of the Pacific War. The story centres on a young woman from northeast China, who was innocent, weak and living in exile in Chongqing. She was helped by people working in progressive drama. She saw through the schemes of those who tried to turn her into a prostitute and then she joined the anti-Japanese progressive theatre.

The four-act play *The House Full of Gold and Jade* describes the decline of a landlord family which had a scroll inscribed "House Full of Gold and Jade" at a small township near Chongqing. Three generations of the family lived under one roof. Because the men of the first two generations died, a woman now managed the family estate. Hope had been placed on the third generation to continue managing the estate. The grandson was clever enough, but utterly immoral. Not only had he failed to keep the estate, but he lost his life. The author did not quite understand the class struggle in rural areas, so some of the details in the play were not realistic, but the play exposed the crimes caused by the wealth of landlords. Both plays contain intense dramatic conflict and were written with high technique.

Yuan Jun's four-act play *One of Exemplary Virtues for All Generations*, written in 1944, is also a major work during the Resistance War period. Set in two different epochs, the May Fourth Movement in 1919 and War of Resistance Against Japan, the play portrays the character of Professor Lin Tong, praising him for maintaining his integrity in a period of social and political upheaval. The plot is not intriguing and does not have grand and spectacular scenes, but portrays the stubborn spirit of the professor who devoted himself to his work. The play is nevertheless quite moving despite its simple theme. Drawn from real life it is a faithful portrayal of the path travelled by many just-minded intellectuals from the May Fourth Movement to the Resistance War period.

Yuan Jun also wrote the multiple-act plays *Story of a Small Town*, *Story of a Border Town*, *Story of a Mountain City*, and *SS American President*. The dialogue is witty, and the dramatic conflict, intense and suspensive; but the play fails to illustrate the theme clearly and deeply. The achievement and impact of these plays are not as great as that of *One of Exemplary Virtues for All Generations.*

III. Poetry Praising the Resistance War and National Liberation

After the outbreak of the War of Resistance Against Japan, poets joined the struggle to resist Japanese aggression. They left their individual world to participate in the movement in which the masses of people struggled for existence. Many poets travelled all over China and saw for themselves the danger and poverty facing the people. Many went through years at the front, seeing the suffering caused by the war. Poets went from frontline to the rear, living through various stages of the war. Still other poets went to the anti-Japanese democratic base areas from the Kuomintang-controlled areas, going through many difficulties and dangers. These experiences increased their understanding of the plight of the Chinese people and broadened their horizons all of which influenced their work.

Poems popular during the initial period of the Resistance War were mostly short ones written by young poets, of which poems for recitation were the most popular. In the first issue of *Voice of the Times* Feng Naichao wrote in Wuhan his poem "Declaration," advocating poets' going to the streets and the impoverished villages and using living language to sing for national liberation.

In Wuhan poetry recitals became a movement. Feng Naichao, Xi Jin, Gao Lan and other poets promoted this movement. Ai Qing's "Against Aggression" was a poem for popular recitation at that time. In Yan'an and other anti-Japanese base areas, recitation poems and street poems appeared in large numbers, inspiring the people in their struggle against aggression.

Guang Weiran's *The Yellow River Cantata* was very popular as a recitation poem in the anti-Japanese democratic base areas. As the war reached its stalemate, the content of the poems changed from vehement anti-aggression themes to a description of people's suffering and their longing for the bright future of China. There was a good variety of poems, including short poems and long ones, lyric and narrative poems. Li Yang's "The Tiger Shooter and His Family" is a long narrative poem which appeared at this time.

Before and after V-J Day many political satirical poems were written in the Kuomintang areas. This was closely connected with the political circumstances of the time. The Kuomintang ruling clique were fascist dictators and the broad masses of people not only had no share in the benefits of their victory over the Japanese, but were once again plunged into suffering and oppression.

Since the reactionary authorities put strict shackles on cultural expression, poets who used verse to fight their battle had to change their strategy. The result was emergence of satirical political poems. *Ma Fantuo's Rustic Song* is representative of this type of poetry. From the beginning of the Resistance War to the victory of the

Liberation War, many poems were written on anti-aggression and anti-oppression themes. Apart from the works by Ai Qing mentioned in Chapter 10, poems by Li Yang, Lu Li, Lü Yuan, Zhou Difan and Yuan Shuipai should be mentioned.

Li Yang (1908-64) wrote poems which were included in three collections *Shackles and Freedom*, *My Harp* and *The Tiger Shooter and His Family*. Li Yang's poems are rich in feeling, reflecting an intellectual's serious pondering over life, his hope, ideals and longing for change. His images are creative and his language is simple, fresh and rich.

When the Resistance War broke out, the author devoted his poems to China's turmoil and fight. "The people bravely broke the chains in storm ... loudly proclaim the new emerging sun. They acclaim spring has finally come."

Having lived for a long time in the rear under the Kuomintang control, the author persisted in his faith and optimism even in the face of difficulties. He sowed the seeds of hope and the seeds of struggle. As he walked along the road in winter, he pined for the return of spring.

In this period Li Yang explained his responsibility as a poet in poems such as "Foggy Season Poems—Why Don't We Sing?," "My Harp," "To Poets" and so on.

In "Short Song" he wrote, "I have ground my life into a dagger. I regard the people's voice as the most treasured classic. Forward I go as I sing for the morrow." Many of his poems expressed his deep feelings for the struggle of the people.

"The Tiger Shooter and His Family," a long narrative poem appeared in *Literary and Art Front* in 1942, was an important work of Li Yang. It described the tragic story of a rural family in old China. The family toiled their whole life, but suffered tragically. The only heritage left behind was an intense hatred. This poem recorded the oppression of the landlord class.

Like other poems by Li Yang, this poem expressed his deep and sincere feelings in forceful and convicing language.

I am a descendant of a tiger shooter

......

Though I can't inherit
Their mighty physical strength,
But what reason is there to prevent me from
Inheriting their only heritage
—An eternal hatred?

In old China this hatred was shared by all oppressed classes and people.

The fortnightly *July*, *July Poems* and *July Essays* edited by Hu Feng had a great impact on readers. Apart from the noted poets Ai Qing and Tian Jian, Lu Li, Lü Yuan and other young poets also wrote for these magazines during the Resistance War.

Poems by Lu Li were published in two collections, *When I Wake Up* (included in the *July Poems* series) and *Tempering* (included in the *July Essays* series). *When I Wake Up* contains mostly short poems, simple and fresh in style. They describe the poet's experiences in the anti-Japanese base areas. They praise spring and sunshine, land and labour. "Sing Outside the Yanmen Pass" praises the people who have undergone the most intense suffering. "Trees" and "Red Coloured Snow Flakes" praise soldiers who died for their country. These patriotic poems express a youth's longing for bright future and progress. In the poem "New Epoch" the poet wrote:

On the other side of the horizon,
There is yet no news about the sun.
*I return again to lie on the kang.**
I remember mother's words of long ago:
"The sun will soon come out.
It won't be buried underground for long."

In *Tempering*, a collection of verse, the long narrative poem by the same name describes a young soldier of the Eighth Route Army who was seized by the Japanese. He went through many tribulations and was rescued from death. Lu Li's poetry, which is mostly free verse, is simple and natural.

Lü Yuan's poems were collected in *Fairy Tales*, which first

---

* A *kang* is a brick bed which can be heated in winter.

appeared in the *July Poems* series, and *Another Starting Point*, which first appeared in the *July Essays* series. The poems in *Fairy Tales* praise the workers and the revolution. They include "Fog" and "Flag," which are vigorous and fresh. Many poems describe in a gloomy tone the sorrow of a vagrant youth.

In *Another Starting Point* the thoughts are clear and the writing more realistic. With deep feeling the poet described the suffering of the people under imperialism, feudalism and capitalism. Poems such as "People Filled with Grief and Indignation," "Yoke" and "Who Are You?" were very popular.

In the long lyric poem "Who Are You?" the poet wrote about China.

The cruel sea of bitterness,
With its hungry claws,
Tear open China's embankment.
China, my motherland
Shines under angry waves of bitter sea.
We shall always remember
Your shadow with teeth biting into hair.

In his poems the poet expressed his hatred for the oppressors who brought suffering to the Chinese people. However, he did not stop at describing the suffering of the people, but inspired them to rise up and struggle against their oppressors. Revenge and resistance make the theme of many of his poems in the book. "The Philosophy of Revenge" and "People Filled With Grief and Indignation" are poems permeated with this theme.

Lü Yuan was influenced by the forms of modern foreign poetry. Not confined to one style, most of his poems adopt a free style. The poems are rhymed and easy to recite. Lü Yuan had a positive influence on young intellectuals at that time.

Collections of poems by Zou Difan include *Timber Mill*, *Gambler of Will*, *Blue Sky and Forest*, *Snow and Villager*, *Striding Over* and *Memoire of Nightmare*. The author was known for his gift at political lyrical poems.

"Ode to Chinese Students" contained in the book *Striding Over* is a famous long lyrical poem. With impassioned lines the poet described the heroic struggle of the Chinese student movement since December 9, 1935. He angrily exposed and condemned the rule of fascist agents, who suppressed and destroyed the student movement. He compared the revolutionary students to brave seagulls and heavenly birds.

You stand up
Like seagulls braving a storm.
Like heavenly birds
Spreading wings in a remote sky.
I hear your whistles
......
You have already sounded
The death knell for reactionaries.
What you are calling
Have come in roaring.
Tomorrow that is bright
Will be forever yours!

The poem dedicated to Lu Xun "Striding Over Ah Q" addressed those people who had not yet become politically conscious and who had gone through endless suffering.

Come out of the Temple of Land and Grain
Like a huge tree standing right up
Stand up like the mountain
And walk on the street in broad daylight!

Yuan Shuipai's poetry collections include: *People*, *Sunflower*, *Winter*, *Years Seething with Excitement* and *Folk Songs on Liberation*. But the poems that had the most influence on readers were his political satirical verses, written under the penname Ma Fantuo. They had been collected into two volumes: *Ma Fantuo's Rustic Songs* and *Ma Fantuo's Rustic Songs Continued*—"Rustic Songs" for short. In these poems the poet expressed sympathy for the suffering and the insecure political circumstances experienced by people in cities under the Kuomintang rule. These poems aroused readers' dissatisfaction, resistance and desire to work for a new future.*

On the inflation which had brought terrible economic difficulties to the cities, the poet wrote "Rein in the Wild Horse," "The Booming Price Rise in Shanghai," "Worshipping Rectangle," "Too Costly to Live," "Everything Is Expensive Nowadays" and "Paper Tiger—*Fabi*" (*fabi* is the paper currency issued by the Kuomintang government). In his poetry the author used satire against the financial and economic policy of the Kuomintang, which brought difficulties to the people.

In "Rein in The Wild Horse" the author compared the spiraling prices to the movements of a wild horse. The poem voiced the demand of the people that prices be brought under control. "Rein in the wild horse quickly! Rein in this mad wild horse! Put the soaring prices under control!"

"Rustic Songs" did not stop short with a description of social problems, but also attacked their source, making readers see that the origin of the problems lay in the reactionary rule.

"A Fairy Tale of Three Hundred Million American Dollars," "The Rhapsody of Big Shot," "The Master Wants to Resign," "A Cat," "Ten Thousand Kinds of Taxes," "Strange Tales Within the Four Seas" and "The World Is Upside Down" satirize the Kuomintang ruling clique.

The poem "The World Is Upside Down" reads:

The world is upside down,
A ten thousand yuan note is worthless,
Blood is shed for making an appeal for peace,
Safeguarding human rights costs imprisonment.

The world is upside down,
"Free elements" change their countenance,
Ban newspapers amidst "freedom of speech,"
And turn democratic constitution into martial law.

"Folk Songs" satirized the Kuomintang dictatorship, but is by

* Mao Dun, "The Development of Revolutionary Literature and Art in the Struggle Against the Oppressive Reactionary Forces," *Essays in Celebration of the National Congress of Literature and Art Workers.*

no means only a series of slogans. The poet used realism, composing images from common social problems to expose various political and social contradictions.

The master in "The Master Wants to Resign," the civil servant in "Civil Servant Applies for Price Rise," Wang Xiaoer in "Wang Xiaoer's Adventures," the big shot in "The Rhapsody of Big Shot" are all characters reflecting social contradictions of the time.

"Stick the Invoice on the Revenue Stamp" was not only a satirical attack on exorbitant taxes, levies and inflation, but also exposed the violent acts of Kuomintang rulers against the people:

The head bumps against the bullet,
And peace rests on a bayonet,
Where's China's destiny?
It hangs on the high-arched nose.

"Rustic Songs" was a successful attempt to popularize new poetry. The poet drew upon techniques from folk songs, ballads, and children's rhymes, using five or seven characters to the line, which were very popular in Chinese poetry. The language of "Rustic Songs" was simple and popular, easy to recite. Some poems were set to music and sung by the people during the democratic movement and some were adapted to skits and performed. "Rustic Songs" represented a new progressive tendency in poetry. Progressive newspapers at the time published many positive critiques on these poems.

There were poems however which were shallow and vulgar. For instance, "A European Widow Cries Over the July 7th Incident" drew criticism for this reason. When "Rustic Songs" was reprinted after the establishment of New China the poet made some cuts in the book.

Zang Kejia, who became a famous poet in the thirties was active in promoting political satirical poems during the latter part of the forties. *My Precious One* and *Zero Degree in Life*, collections published in 1946 and 1947 contained many political satirical poems. Included in these collections were poems like "The Wind of Victory," "What Is People?", "The Bore of the Gun Is Still Hot," "Staff Reduction," "Precious Baby," "Thank You, Representatives of the Kuomintang National Congress," "Policeman, Tell the People," "Only the Bore of the Gun Is Hot" and "Zero Degree in Life," criticizing the Kuomintang ruling clique's reactionary rule which brought disaster to China. Zang Kejia wrote that the "democracy and freedom" much trumpeted by the Kuomintang reactionaries were nothing but a "poor straw shed that could not stand up to rain nor give shelter from wind." In "The Wind of Victory" Zang Kejia wrote:

Political prisoners are in prison,
Freedom is under chains,
Refugees roam the streets, and
With "big sale" flags blowing,
Industry and business precarious,
All these—adorn "victory."

This is a faithful description of the Kuomintang-controlled areas after the victory of the Resistance War. It satirizes the "democracy, freedom, prosperity and wealth" propagated by the Kuomintang. The satirical poems of Zang Kejia and those of Yuan Shuipai are similar in that they both combine politics with art. But their styles differ. Yuan Shuipai is better known for his long narrative poems and Zang Kejia's poems are lyrical and full of feelings. In order that his poems might be better accepted by the general public, Zang Kejia changed his former style which was more embellished and refined, and wrote in simple and natural language. He said: "I have used an ornate style for fifteen years. Now I wake up to find the beauty of simplicity. I try to free myself from a pattern I have set for myself. I am happy that the field of poetry is so vast!"*

Zang Kejia's "Thank You, Representatives of the Kuomintang National Congress" and "Policeman, Tell the People" were biting satires of the Kuomintang's false democracy and exposed its dictatorship in popular and easy to understand language.

Following the publication of *The Creation of Poetry* and *China's New Poetry* in the latter part of the forties a small new school of poetry emerged in Shanghai. Apart from a few elderly poets, they

* Preface to *Zero Degree in Life.*

were mostly young people. They included Xin Di, Chen Jingrong, Du Yunxie, Hang Yuehe (Cao Xinzhi), Zheng Min, Tang Qi, Tang Shi, Yuan Kejia, Mu Dan (Zha Liangzheng). Each had his or her own style, but all tried to reflect the mood of the epoch. They were opposed to "exaggerated propagandism" as well as to the empty talk of Chinese-styled aestheticism. They absorbed various techniques of modern Western poetry, enriching and developing new poetry. Facing the oppression the poets bravely took the stand of the people and expressed their protests.

Xin Di's poem "Cuckoo" expressed the suffering of the people. During the early years of the forties Mu Dan's "Eulogy" expressed his fervent hopes for China. Tang Qi's "Prison for Women" criticized the harshness of prison life. Tang Shi's "An Excited Town" vividly described the struggle of the people of his hometown against hunger and civil war. Hang Yuehe's long poem "Land Reborn" portrayed various characters in the old society. He showed sympathy for the suffering people and revolutionary martyrs and expressed hope for the future.

There were also contributions by two women poets, Zheng Min and Chen Jingrong. In her poem "Spring," Zheng Min wrote that she "heard spring" from a few new leaves on withered branches "like an unfolding scroll and like music." In "On Bridge at Winter Dusk" Chen Jingrong wrote that the dark night would expose reality, and dusk was the prelude of this exposure. Their poems were clever, lively, fresh and beautiful, expressing their patriotism and sympathy for the people.

Various nationality poets also wrote poems against oppression. The Mongolian poet, N. Sainchogt and the Uygur poet L. Mutarif wrote many poems during the turbulent years of war. They had wide influence in Inner Mongolia and Xinjiang.

IV. Reportage, Essays and Other Miscellaneous Writings

Reportage flourished during the early days of the War of Resistance Against Japan. At that time almost all literary magazines carried a considerable amount of newsletters and reportage. The two most influential periodicals *Wartime Literature and Art* and *Literature and Art Front*, for instance, published two to six newsletters and reportage every issue in 1938 and 1939. Many collections of these articles were also published. *A Series of Battlefield Life* edited by Yi Qun printed eight editions for its first issue. *July Essays*, edited by Hu Feng, published many reportage collections. *Collection of Battlefield Reportage*, *Mini-Collection of Battlefield Literature*, *Wartime Literature and Art Series*, *Selection of Wartime Reportage* and *China in the War of Resistance* were also reportage collections. Many famous writers such as Qiu Dongping, Bi Ye, Xiao Qian and Cao Bai also wrote articles about the struggle against Japanese aggression.

Qiu Dongping's articles carried in wartime periodicals had a big impact on readers. He wrote about the Shanghai battle on August 13, 1937. He strongly criticized the crimes committed by the enemy and praised the enthusiasm of the Chinese army and people in their resistance against the Japanese aggressors. In the article "I Come to Know Such An Enemy" a woman refugee told of the revolting massacre of Shanghai residents by the Japanese. It also showed how Shanghai citizens rose in self-defence against the enemy.

"The Seventh Company" and "There We Were Defeated" expressed the patriotism and militant spirit of the Kuomintang lower-ranking officers and soldiers in battles against the Japanese. They showed how the Kuomintang was forced to put up resistance hastily with inferior arms and little military training, which led to their defeat. The author witnessed the corruption and impotence of the Kuomintang military leaders and his reportage depicted the tragic atmosphere of defeat in war.

The author joined the New Fourth Army in the spring of 1938, and accumulated new material from his life experiences for his writing. He wrote newspaper articles about the people's resistance against Japanese aggression. His articles no longer had a heavy and gloomy tone, but were full of optimism and confidence in victory.

"Skirmish at Wanglinggang" was about the fighting of the New Fourth Army, which was totally different from the Kuomintang army. "A Battalion Commander of the Friendly Army" and "On the Road to Liwu" contrasted the difference between the New Fourth Army and the Kuomintang troops and praised the life and struggle of the army and people in the anti-Japanese democratic base areas.

Many articles written in the early stage of the war merely recorded the passing events and neglected the portrayal of people. Qiu Dongping wrote about people and their ideology and character. He described Kuomintang officers and soldiers at the front. He mostly used the first person in his writing, so that Kuomintang officers or refuges would thus narrate their own stories. People were portrayed against the background of intense conflicts and battles.

Bi Ye's reports from the battlefield described peasant guerrillas in battle under the guidance of the Eighth Route Army on the vast plain of North China. After the outbreak of the war, Bi Ye following the troops to the Hutuo River and to the foot of the Taihang Mountains for six months. His articles describing this journey were collected in two books: *Beside the Taihang Mountains* and *The Northern Plain*. The articles were short and the writing forceful.

The Northern Plain was about military life of the Eighth Route Army and the peasants' armed resistance against Japanese aggression.

Bi Ye's writing was spontaneous, bold and unrestrained. The writing sometimes contains poetic descriptions and picturesque scenery. Besides his reportage, Bi Ye wrote many novelle, *Night Sacrifice Offered at Wulanbulang*, *Three Testaments*, *Love Stories from Battlefield*, *Flowerless Spring* and others.

Xiao Qian published short stories, essays and newsletters during the thirties. These were included in *Under the Fence*, *Chestnuts* and other collections. He became a correspondent for the newspaper *Da Gong Bao* after the outbreak of the war. He travelled in China and abroad to cover his stories and wrote many feature stories. They were first included in *Wartime Book Series* as the tenth book of the collection called *What One Sees and Hears*. It was enlarged into a second edition *Reporting on Life*.

In "Yunnan-Burma Road Built with Blood and Flesh," he described in a moving manner the oppression of the 25 million peasant workers, recruited to pave the road. He praised the workers who built the road and exposed Kuomintang authorities who disregarded the interests of the workers, causing thousands of deaths.

Xiao Qian also wrote articles in praise of the people's army and the people's war. In autumn 1938 he wrote "Soliloquy of a Demolition Brigade Leader," in which he told of the impact of the guerrilla war behind enemy lines.

In this period he visited Britain, the United States of America and Indo-China. He wrote "Symphony of Contradictions," "Bloody September" and "London Under Silvery Kites" with rich and colourful descriptions of wartime London. Xiao Qian reported on the support of the British people and the people of many other countries for the Chinese Resistance War Against Japan.

His articles were very timely and newsworthy, packed with information. He skillfully used typical events and his language was lively and easy to read. His articles had a strong convincing quality and artistic appeal.

Cao Bai's book *Breath* contains articles and essays written between 1937 and 1941. The first part of the book was called *Articles of Breath.* It was mainly devoted to Cao Bai's experiences in a refugee camp in Shanghai following the outbreak of the battle on August 13, 1937. It exposed Japanese aggression and the corrupt administration of refugee camps. Cao Bai strongly condemned the tragedies that happened to the refugees. The second part of the book *Articles on Successive Battles in Different Places* is about his experiences as an armyman in different guerrilla areas south of the Yangtse River after the fall of Shanghai showing the complicated political and military circumstances in the guerrilla areas. An important thread running through the whole book was the active participation of the revolutionary youth in the Resistance War and the heroic struggle of the guerrillas under the influence of the New Fourth Army. In "Here, Too, Breathes Life" he described the coldness and cruelty of a cinema owner towards refugees, who were eager to go to the front to fight the Japanese aggressors.

In "Under the Dark Shadow of the God of Death," Cao Bai described bombing by enemy planes. Refugees had a precarious life, not knowing in the morning what might happen to them in the evening. "In the Morrow" was set in a refugee camp to mark the sixth anniversary of the Japanese occupation of northeast China. "Seizing Living Souls" exposed and condemned those who managed refugee camps and treated refugees as profit-making objects. "Yang Kezhong" and "In Memory of Wang Jiayin" were dedicated to the memory of these two noble-minded ordinary people.

"The Recovery of Human Nature" by Shen Qiyu was a reportage about life in the Resistance War in the Kuomintang-controlled rear. It was better written and more lengthy than most articles. It dealt with the reform of Japanese prisoners of war. It mainly described how a group of Japanese prisoners of war in a camp near Chongqing changed their aggressive stand. Dedicated to transforming prisoners of war the author, who had earlier studied in Japan and knew Japanese customs well, gave a vivid account of the contact with Japanese prisoners.

During the early part of the Resistance War, essays and other forms of writing did not flourish as much as reportage. But during the latter part of the Resistance War and the War for Liberation essay writing became popular. This was especially true in the period when the Kuomintang stepped up its fascist rule. In the tradition of essays since the start of the Left-wing literary movement, many writers exposed the cruelty and injustice of the aggressors and the oppression in the Kuomintang-controlled areas. They praised progress and revolution.

The supplements to the progressive newspapers like *Wen Hui Bao* and *Yi Bao* as well as *The Style of Lu Xun* published in Shanghai, and the supplement to *Xinhua Daily* published in Chongqing as well as *Weeds* published in Guilin and Hong Kong, all carried a large number of essays. Essays by Guo Moruo, Mao Dun, Ba Jin, Zhu Ziqing, He Qifang and Li Guangtian had a great impact on readers during this time. Apart from these writers, Feng Xuefeng, Nie Gannu, Song Yunbin, Meng Chao, Qin Si and Lin Mohan were among those who also wrote essays.

Feng Xuefeng (1903-76) joined the Riverside Poetry Society during the twenties when he began to write poems. He mostly did revolutionary work in the following decade and at the same time he dedicated himself to literary theory. He worked closely with Lu Xun. In 1941 after the Southern Anhui Incident in the Resistance War he was locked up in the Shangrao Concentration Camp in Jiangxi Province. When he left the concentration camp he continued his revolutionary work. Apart from literary theory, literary criticism and verse, he wrote essays. He published *Prevailing Practices in Village and City*, *Forward, No Retreat* and *The Day on Which to Step Across*. These books contained 120 essays written by Feng Xuefeng in Chongqing and Shanghai from 1943 to 1946. There was also another book by Feng Xuefeng, *Three Hundred Fables*.

The essays in the first two books were usually political exposes hidden behind social criticism. The essay "Again on Soul" deals with soul, conscience and evil. The author wrote about the ruling clique and social system, pointing out that the unequal social system and oppressive ruling class was at the root of social problems. In "On Philistinism" and "On Mediocrity" he criticized philistinism and mediocrity. He warmly praised revolutionaries who fought for the interests of the people. *The Day to Step Across*, a collection of essays, mostly contained short and terse political comments. "The Characteristics of Fascism and Fascism in China," "Military Force," and other satirical essays attacked fascist dictatorship. In essay writing Feng Xuefeng studied Lu Xun's writings to learn style and technique.

Nie Gannu was one of the main writers for *Weeds*. He wrote under the names of Xiao Jindu and Er Ye. In each issue of *Weeds* he had one or two articles. He published collections of essays, such as *Muttering*, *Mystery of History*, *White Snake and Leifeng Pagoda*, *Wake Up Early*, and *Letter Written in Blood*. The first two belonged to the *Weeds* book series. *The Mystery of History* was a book of fifteen articles. An article by the same title was a comment on Trotsky and the traitor Wang Jingwei, who had formed a government at Nanjing in 1940. Together with "Zhou Fohai Recalled," this article discussed current events and people. The author sought to educate people with his writings. Nie Gannu wrote "Shakespeare Should Regret" and "The Loss of Nanjing Brings About Endless Things," which were humorous satires.

White Snake and Leifeng Pagoda contained thirteen miscellaneous writings. The article with the same title as the book dealt with the legendary story of the suppression of White Snake (a woman who had been turned into a snake). All articles in the book were about women and their problems, in the same vein as "A Debate on Women's Rights," which he later edited and published as a book.

Wake Up Early contained fifteen articles of varying lengths. *Letter Written in Blood* consisted of forty articles in two volumes. Volume one was entitled *On Courtesy*, criticizing erroneous views spread by some people in the cultural circles. Volume two, *Letter Written in Blood*, dealt with politics and the rulers of old China, who were satirized by the author.

The language of most of the writings in this book is fresh and the style biting. Social and political problems were well reasoned out by the author. In the "Letter Written in Blood," the author paid tribute to the document issued by the Central Committee of the Chinese Communist Party on Land Reform as "a sacred writing in blood." Though his arguments were in places inaccurate, the author showed his support for the peasants in breaking the shackles of the feudal system of land ownership.

Other writers who edited *Weeds* with Xia Yan and Nie Gannu, were Song Yunbin, Meng Chao and Qin Si. They also wrote many essays.

Song Yunbin published two collections of essays, *Breaking the Commandments* in 1940 and *Gu Geng Ji* as a series in the *Weeds* books in 1942. *Breaking the Commandments* had fourteen articles, including "A Study of Xianbei People's Customs," "Zhang Taiyan and Lu Xun" and "A Declining Advisor." His second collection consisted of twenty-four articles, including "On Slavery," "Thoughts After Reading History," "The Qidan Politician in the Eyes of Tao Xisheng" and "On Tao Yuanming."

The author wrote in a simple manner and used many quotations. Nie Gannu said that Song Yunbin's articles were hidden beneath calm sketches, almost detached from the world at times.

However, one finds passion in them too.*

Meng Chao wrote two collections of essays, *Long Night* and *Unyielding Grass*. He wrote about many subjects from ancient to modern times.

His book *Long Night* includes "A Brief Account on Treacherous Officials and Rebellious Officials in the Song Dynasty," "Liang Shanbo and Intellectuals" and "Jiao Da and Qu Yuan." His other book *Unyielding Grass* includes "A Brief Account on the Style of Men of Letters and the Style of Warriors," "A Slave Girl and A Lady" and "The Window Paper of History."

Qin Si wrote *Sound of Sensation*, a collection of thirty-two articles, in a style similar to that of "decorative literature" of the thirties.

Lin Mohan's essays were contained in the collection *The Lion and the Dragon*. The writing had clear viewpoints and lucid language. An article under the same title and written during the Liberation War described the duel between the dragon—symbolizing the reactionary rulers and the lion—symbolizing the people. "Victory had been decided beforehand—it belonged to the lion," which meant the writer believed that the people would win the Liberation War.

V. Satirical Novels by Sha Ting and Other Writers

Sha Ting was a novelist who joined the Left-wing literary movement during the early period of the thirties. His novels were highly successful, contributing to the anti-Japanese struggle and to the struggle against the Kuomintang oppression in the forties.

Sha Ting's real name was Yang Zhaoxi. Born in Anxian County, Sichuan Province in 1904, he was influenced by the new thinking of the May Fourth Movement and by new literature during his school days. Following the failure of the First Revolutionary Civil War (1924-27) he dedicated himself to revolution in Sichuan. He came under the guidance of Lu Xun when he started writing in Shanghai in the early thirties. From 1935 onward he wrote about

* "Reply," *Wake Up Early*.

the life in the countryside and small towns in Sichuan, with which he was familiar.

After the outbreak of the Resistance War, Sha Ting returned from Shanghai to Sichuan. At first he wanted to write about the atmosphere of his home province in the Resistance War. Much of what he now saw in backward Sichuan was dedicated only on the surface to the Resistance War. Some people were exploiting the situation to make money. Sha Ting decided to exposed the corruption that stood in the way of the Resistance War, and the factors which held back reform.* During this period Sha Ting's novels humorously satirized the corrupt officials and the landed gentry who made large fortunes out of the Resistance War.

Written on the eve of the fall of Wuhan, "Air Defence—A Corner at Kamchatka" described a scene in which the gentry in a county town fought with each other for the position as the head of air defence society. After its publication in *Literary and Art Front*, Mao Dun, its chief editor, wrote in his "Epilogue": "It used humour to cover up painful feelings. The more you read and think it over the more bitter you will feel."

Sha Ting's later works were not so sharply satirical. Somewhat cooler in tone, his criticism was cloaked in descriptions of the difficulties facing the Chinese people.

Unlike the caricature method of exaggeration, the short works of Sha Ting had a simple and clear style. Sha Ting was very good at describing ordinary events that often went by unnoticed. In the *Qixiangju Teahouse*, written in the latter part of the 1940s on the theme of draft system, was a famous short satirical story. Fang Zhiguo, the director in a county joined security office, let out the secret to the county government that the new magistrate intended to reform the draft system. As a result, the local tyrant Xing's son, who had been exempted four times from service, was pressed into service. Fang and Xing openly quarrelled in the teahouse and ended up in a fight. The fight resulted in the loss of face of the bigwigs of the town. The ending of the story suggested that the military reform of the new magistrate was nothing but a fraud.

---

* "My Literary Creation in the Past Three Years," *Wartime Literature and Art*, No. 1, Vol. 7, January 1, 1941.

Having accepted a bribe, the new magistrate dismissed the son of the tyrant Xing from military service on the lame excuse that he was unqualified to fight the national war because he gave a wrong number when the new recruits were asked to line up and number off. This story revealed that the root cause of the problems in the draft system lay in the Kuomintang government.

Many of Sha Ting's short stories dealt with corruption. "Pastime of the Director of the Joint Security Office" and "Substitute" were stories that characterized Kuomintang rulers, who exploited the people and undermined the resistance efforts. These works combined exposure of political corruption with an analysis of the oppressed society.

Sha Ting's satirical comedies were influenced by classical Chinese novels, especially *The Scholars.* He had also profited from reading Lu Xun and the Russian authors Gogol and Chekov. Sha Ting's novels criticized corruption and brutality, and were sympathetic to the oppressed and persecuted people.

"The Story of Old Yan" dealt with a man who tried to avoid taking a political stand. The story was set in a dangerous political situation caused by the diehard Kuomintang reactionaries who launched an anti-Communist campaign. The man suffered from a neurosis because he was in a constant state of anxiety, thinking that political persecution might suddenly fall upon him. He died of sickness in the end. The author levelled more criticism than sympathy at this character for his lack of strength in the face of adversity.

Sha Ting's three other works "Storm in a Small Town," "Two Brothers" and "Spring Tide" exposed the crimes committed by Kuomintang secret agents. Sha Ting's "Magnetic Force" described youth in the Kuomintang-controlled areas, who yearned for progressive cause and journeyed to the anti-Japanese democratic base areas. The same is true with his "A Small Scene in Kamchatka" (later renamed "One Autumn Night") which described the touching friendships among the poor who were in distress. These people showed faith in life despite a gloomy reality.* In telling how a

* "Epilogue to *Collection of Sha Ting's Short Stories.*"

young woman was humiliated and persecuted, the story revealed the nature of class exploitation.

From 1938 to 1939 Sha Ting spent some time in the enemy rear area. From Sichuan he travelled to Yan'an. He accompanied the army to northwest Shanxi and other North China anti-Japanese base areas. His experiences were narrated in the famous biographical reportage. "Sketches Written While I Was with the Army" and the collection of essays, *Notes Written in Enemy Rear Areas.* Later he wrote *Breaking Through the Pass*, a novella about the struggle and life in the base areas. This novella was also named *Strange Journey* and *On Both Sides of the Blockade Line.*

Sha Ting's novel *Prospecting for Gold* showed the harsh reality in the countryside and a small town in Sichuan during the Resistance War. It was written between 1941 to 1942, when the author returned from the base area to his home province. The novel first appeared in two magazines under the titles: *Shao Ji Bei* and *Beidou Town.**

Based on an incident during excavation at the Shao Ji Bei gold mine, the novel centred on the conflict among landlords and the gentry, who fought each other to make fortunes from the Resistance War. Among the landlords struggling for power in Beidou Town was the eldest son of the gangster leader of the Society of Brothers,** Lin Yao. There was also the local despot, Bai Jiangdan, who attached himself to the upper class in the local society, and Widow He, a landlady, whose fortune was now declining. Bai Jiangdan hid his brutality with kindness. But he not only exploited the gold mine at Shao Ji Bei for private gain, but also defended the decadent, reactionary system. Bai Jiangdan was presented as a brutal, ugly and shameless political hoodlum nurtured by the Kuomintang reactionary rule. He was also the support that buttressed the dying and decadent social system. Longge, director of the joint security office, was another character successfully portrayed in the novel. He represented the Kuomintang political power in the countryside.

---

* *Shao Ji Bei* appeared in *Literary and Art Front*, Nos, 2 and 3, Vol. 7. *Beidou Town* appeared in *Literary Creation*, No. 5, Vol. 1.

** A secret society created in the Qing Dynasty to restore the Ming Dynasty.

Sha Ting combined characterization and plot development with description of the Sichuan countryside during the Resistance War and depicted the atmosphere of the time in the Kuomintang areas.

Prospecting for Gold was the first novel which fully showed Sha Ting's life experience and the maturity of his artistic technique. Sha Ting succeeded in presenting the Sichuan countryside with its rich rustic atmosphere and local dialect. He had observed, analyzed and unravelled relationships, therefore he was familiar with the psychology of various kinds of people and with the local customs. His characters were well-rounded compared with similar characters in his short stories.

He paid particular attention to the use of language—a pause, a retort or a certain emphasis—all these had been carefully worked out by Sha Ting. What the novel lacked, however, was a positive perspective. The masses of labouring people portrayed by Sha Ting were largely ignorant people, who showed not even the slightest sign of resistance. The novel failed to give any hint as for how to solve their problems. Consequently, the tone of the book was a bit too gloomy.

Beasts at Bay, Sha Ting's other novel, written between 1943 and 1944, unravelled the problems of intellectuals who became despondent following reversals in the war. It was about the indignation, depression and yearnings shared by progressive intellectuals in Kuomintang-controlled areas. The novel depicted the heavy oppressive atmosphere prevailing among intellectuals in the latter part of the Resistance War.

Sha Ting studied Mao Zedong's *Talks at the Yan'an Forum on Literature and Art* in Chongqing in 1944, which influenced his ideology. Both before and after the victory of the Resistance War and during the Liberation War period, the peasants' political struggle and resistance in Sichuan Province gained momentum. The democratic movement in cities continued in spite of serious suppression by the Kuomintang reactionaries. This provided the basis for Sha Ting's portrayal of popular democratic demands and the resistance and struggle against oppression in the novel.

Notes on a Journey Home, written in 1946, was about the sharp class contradictions in the Sichuan countryside. The setting was in Linqingou, a mountain village with a tradition of peasant struggle. The impoverished peasants sank into misery and found themselves at an impasse, following the suppression of a peasant uprising thirty years earlier. The author described the ideological development of a poor peasant, Feng Dasheng under serious oppression, from resistance on his own to participating in collective struggle. Having suffered setbacks on many occasions Feng Dasheng came to understand from his own experience the real nature of reactionary regime and became disillusioned. When he took part in the struggle to oppose despotic landlords who conspired to seize bamboo grown by peasants, he defended the peasants very strongly.

Due to Sha Ting's limited political view his novel *Notes on a Journey Home* failed to point out the way for peasants in their struggle. There was, however, no longer any trace of the mood of depression found in this novel. He vividly described peasants' life and their struggle. Although this novel did not reach the same level of artistry and characterization as *Prospecting for Gold*, it had introduced new themes and new characters.

His collections of short stories entitled *Wailing* and *Doctor*, appearing at the end of the Resistance War and during the Liberation War period, reflected the sharp social contradictions and the demands of the people in the democratic movement. "Mr Fan, the Elderly Teacher" and "Wailing" were realistic and with good characterizations. Some stories were biting satires on reactionary authorities by using well-chosen incidents. One-act satirical comedy, "Doctor" was such a story.

Apart from these works Sha Ting wrote "Bombardier," which described the disintegration of the Kuomintang. "Disaster-Ridden Election" was another satire of the hypocrisy displayed in the election of the Kuomintang's national congressmen.

Generally speaking, Sha Ting's novels depicted the life and struggle in the countryside under the Kuomintang control since the Resistance War. Artistically he had developed a unique style of his own; however, his political horizon was somewhat narrow and his experiences limited which adversely affected the depth of his works. However, he was good at making order of the events of the time and unravelling the complexity of the society. He reflected the main social contradictions through satire and expose. He successfully depicted the security organizations as a grass-roots establishment of the Kuomintang's reactionary rule in the country-side, secret societies and the landlords' despotism. He was also successful in using the form of the short story to describe the unique customs of the Sichuan countryside.

Jin Yi (1909-59) edited literary magazines and wrote many short stories during the thirties. His works, written in the Resistance War, were included later in the collections of *Deluge*, *A Faraway City*, *An Assembly of Gods* and *Survival.*

Unlike his earlier works which dealt with love themes, his later works were broader in scope, using different literary techniques. In "A Couple Separated by War" Jin Yi condemned the undemocratic political environment by describing a young couple who were arrested for participation in resistance work.

In "An Assembly of Gods" the author used a romantic technique, describing a millionaire whose soul after his death met an assembly of gods in paradise. In this way the story exposed the speculation, hoarding, smuggling and the licentious and decadent lifestyle of bureaucratic capitalists during the Resistance War.

"Evening Party" condemned traitors and those who undermined the Resistance War through a character who got drunk at a party. The exposure was relatively shallow and the exaggeration was such, that sometimes one felt it was a bit unreal.

Another short story of Jin Yi's, "Survival," was a social criticism. The story was about a fine arts professor, who kept his integrity, and would not go along with evil-doers despite his poverty.

Jin Yi's novel *The Eve* reflected the three years of turmoil following the outbreak of the Resistance War, describing the lives of different members of a big Chinese family against a background marked by major political events. With its lengthy description of the epoch, the book was informative and educational and provided an insight into the times. However, it lacked clear characterization and artistic appeal. Besides this novel Jin Yi wrote many essays, which were collected into the book *A Hundred Scenes from Human*

World. Like his novels, the essays exposed the corruption and oppression in areas under the Kuomintang. Zhang Henshui's novels *Eighty-One Dreams* and *Five Sons Passed Imperial Examinations*, exposing the backward society in areas under the rule of the Kuomintang also had a major impact on readers.

Zhang Henshui (1895-1967) was a prolific novelist and representative of the Mandarin Duck and Butterfly School (or love stories) and later he wrote progressive new novels. After the September 18th Incident in 1931 and, particularly, after the outbreak of the Resistance War, some members of the Mandarin Duck school wrote novels on the calamity that had befallen the nation.

Zhang Henshui was an outstanding novelist who made this change. Written in 1939, *The Night of Street Fighting* (also known as *The Charge* or *Defend Tianjin*) was a work about the Resistance War. It described the wanton bombing and bloody slaughter of Chinese people by the Japanese invaders who took Tianjin by force. He wrote about the resolute resistance put up by petty officers of the Kuomintang army and the people of Tianjin against the Japanese aggressors.

Zhang Henshui also wrote social satire which had a great impact on readers during the resistance. His novel *The Eighty-First Dream* deals with the luxurious lifestyle and corruption of Kuomintang officials and the Chinese gentry in the enemy rear area. It was written from the view of a poor urban petty bourgeois in the form of dreams. The method he used was the same as that used by writers of the classical novels such as *Journey to the West*, *Flowers in the Mirror* and *The Scholars.* After the victory of the Resistance War he wrote another book of similar themes, entitled *Five Sons Passed Imperial Examinations.* It exposed the corruption of the Kuomintang commissioners, who took office after the Japanese had surrendered and indulged themselves in "money, women, houses, cars and bullion."

The novel, *A Beleaguered City* by Qian Zhongshu dealt with intellectuals in wartime. It was first carried in part in the magazine *The Renaissance.* Qian Zhongshu had earlier published essays and short stories. His major achievement was in literary criticism which he wrote with a great range of knowledge and profundity. *A*

Beleaguered City was published in book form in 1947.

The novel was centred on the character of Fang Hongjian, a student who had retuned from France. He was in milieu of intellectuals who had been far removed from the war. Jockeying for social position, these intellectuals tried to outwit or cheat each other when the country was engulfed in war.

The book showed their daily life and work. With puns and satire the book showed their emptiness and meanness as well. The novel compared marriage to a besieged city. The people outside tried to break in while those within wanted to get out.

Qian Zhongshu was particularly good at psychological description, and he portrayed the inner world not only of the chief characters, Fang Hongjian, Zhao Xinmei and Su Wenwan, but also of minor characters, such as Tang Xiafu, Mrs Wang and Miss Fan. Witty remarks abounded in his novel. However, sometimes he overdid it, so that the average reader had difficulty in understanding his work. This prevented the book from reaching a wider audience.

The appearance of *The Story of Xia Qiu* (*The Story of Prawnball*) by Huang Guliu brought vitality to a suffocating literary world during the dark days before the collapse of the reactionary Kuomintang rule. The novel was published in serial form in the supplement to *The Chinese Merchant* in Hong Kong from 1946 to 1948. It was later printed separately as *Spring Wind and Autumn Rain*, *Mount White Cloud and Pearl River* and *High Mountains and Long Rivers*. It reached a wide audience in the Kuomintang-controlled areas, particularly in the southern part of China.

Huang Guliu (1908-77), whose works were published as early as the beginning of the Resistance War, led a bitter life in the old semi-feudal and semi-colonial society. The novel, *The Story of Xia Qiu* was an artistic achievement which had great breadth of vision. It successfully portrayed the character of Xia Qiu, who led a vagrant life as a boy and grew up to be a revolutionary.

Xia Qiu was also known as Prawnball. He came from an overseas Chinese worker's family. He had been an unskilled worker and pedlar in Hong Kong ever since his childhood. He left the family at the age of sixteen because of poverty and became a street urchin. He often went hungry. In the old society, however, there was no paradise for the poor. Xia Qiu was detained in custody, tied up and beaten. From Hong Kong he went to Guangzhou and other places in southern Guangdong. After a precarious life with many twists and turns, he joined the revolutionary forces—the Communist-led guerrillas, where he became a good soldier. The story's message was that to fight oppression the poor people must get themselves organized. The novel did not present the adventures of Xia Qiu as an isolated experience, but gave a general picture of the colonial society in old China, based on the observations of Xia Qiu and his junior partner, Niu Zai while working for Hong Bin, a leading gangster in Hong Kong. Huang Guliu unravelled the corruption of Hong Bin, as well as his superiors and colleagues. Hong Bin had wormed his way into Hong Kong at first. He stole and robbed in broad daylight. Later he went to Guangzhou, where he became captain of a ship and then commander of a regiment. He worked in collusion with officials, merchants and the local gentry, committing many crimes. Hong Bin and his company was a microcosm of the reactionary ruling circle then. Through description of the rise to power and the downfall of Hong Bin, the novel predicted that the final collapse of the reactionary forces was near at hand.

Works that depicted the life of the urban poor were among the many new novels that had emerged since the May Fourth Movement. *Camel Xiangzi* by Lao She represents this type of novels. However, modern Chinese literature had hardly touched on urban crime and the suffering of the vagrant adolescents in cities. The appearance of *The Story of Xia Qiu* broke fresh ground for this topic. Influenced by classical novels and folk literature, the plot of the novel was moving and the language plain and concise. The novel was very popular. As Mao Dun said in his comments on novels including *The Story of Xia Qiu*, they broke through the limits of the traditional form to create a new form which popularized literature.* Huang Guliu had made an important step in this direction.

* Mao Dun, "The Development of Revolutionary Literature and Art in the Struggle Against the Oppressive Reactionary Forces."

VI. *Annals of Heavenly Kingdom, Promotion in Officialdom* and Other Drama Works

The progressive theatre movement was subject to increasing oppression and persecution in the Kuomintang-controlled areas, during both the Resistance War and the Liberation War. As a result many playwrights turned to write satirical plays and historical themes. Such noted playwrights as Guo Moruo and Ouyang Yuqian wrote historical plays. Other noted writers were Yang Hansheng and Chen Baichen who wrote satire. In addition, Wu Zuguang's mythological plays were influential in the movement against oppression and for democracy.

Yang Hansheng wrote novels in the thirties and worked for the Left-wing theatre movement. His major works included his multiple-act plays, *Frontier War*, *Double Dealer* (also known as *The Beginning of the Universe*) and his historical plays, *The Death of Li Xiucheng*, *Annals of Heavenly Kingdom* and *Heroes of the Wild Grassland*. *Annals of Heavenly Kingdom*, however, remains his representative work. This play was completed in September 1941, immediately after the Southern Anhui Incident. Said the author: "At that time I wished to denounce the flagrant crimes of the Kuomintang reactionaries and expose their insidiousness, brutality and viciousness. Since I couldn't write on realistic themes, I selected the historical themes as a weapon to wage my struggle."*

The play *Annals of Heavenly Kingdom* used the incident that led to the collapse of the Taiping Heavenly Kingdom as a basis and presented the three characters of Yang Xiuqing, Wei Changhui and Hong Xuanjiao. Yang Xiuqing held a high responsible position in military and political affairs in the Taiping Heavenly Kingdom. Wei Changhui, a political speculator and conspirator, formerly a wealthy man, joined the revolution as a speculator and held an important position as the northern king in the Taiping Heavenly Kingdom. When the Heavenly Kingdom established its capital in Nanjing, Wei slipped back into his old ways. He not only collided with the rich and powerful, but was

* Yang Hansheng, "Epilogue to *Selected Plays of Yang Hansheng*."

also involved in smuggling and forcibly took other people's wives. He led an immoral and decadent life. He employed traitors, conspired and sowed discord among people and framed innocent people. He was responsible for the slaughter of Yang Xiuqing and the massacre of over twenty thousand men of the Taiping revolutionary army. This tragic event greatly weakened the revolutionary forces. As a result the Taiping Heavenly Kingdom was more seriously split.

Hong Xuanjiao, who was largely responsible for the tragic event, repented for her murderous act in the end. Towards the end of the play she said: "Confronted with a formidable enemy, we should stop killing each other! We are the real criminals, guilty of an unpardonable crime!"

This incident in the play reminded the audience of the Southern Anhui Incident. The performance of this historical play caused a deep stir and played a major political role in exposing the reactionary nature of the Southern Anhui Incident plotted by the Kuomintang.

Heroes of the Wild Grassland was completed in October 1942. It was about the struggle on the eve of the 1919 Revolution by the people of southern Sichuan who waged a struggle to protect their railways from foreign infringement and from being nationalized by the Qing government. Luo Xuanqing and Chen Sanmei were the people's heroes in the play. They fought resolutely against the enemy, but lacked vigilance towards the enemy hidden within. They were easily carried away by success and disregarded the good advice from others. They believed enemies who pretended to surrender to the revolutionaries, but were assassinated by them. The revolution was seriously undermined. The lesson the author had drawn from this historical event through his drama had its immediate significance at that time.

Chen Baichen became noted for his satirical comedies. He wrote some short stories in the thirties, which were collected in *Datura Collection*, *Xiao Wei's Domain*, and *A Woman Tea Sorter*. He wrote several one-act plays: *Street Scene at Night*, *Father and Son*, *and Brothers*, *Imperial Concubine Yuji* and others. He also wrote a multiple-act play *The Last Day of Shi Dakai*. His plays were well-received by audiences. After the outbreak of the Resistance War he wrote two one-act plays: *Husband and Wife Who Are Yet Unmarried* and *It is Forbidden to Pass Water* (this play was included in the book *Short Comedies in Rear Areas*). His multiple-act plays included *Den of Monsters, Men and Women in Troubled Times, Spring Is Here Again, The Wedding March* and *Dadu River*. These works signified a new stage in his creative work as a playwright of realism.

Men and Women in Troubled Times, written in 1939, was a well-known satirical play of three acts. In this play the author described various kinds of social "dregs" living in the cities. These social dregs had escaped from Nanjing to the rear area when the Resistance War broke out. Qin Fan, a character in the play, was earnestly determined to work for the war. He provided the contrast between those dregs of the society and the Resistance War fighters. The social dregs in the play were objects of contempt and ridicule. The author failed to analyse the social problems that led to the degraded situation of these people.

The Wedding March, a five-act play written in 1940, was based on a previous play *Husband and Wife Who Are Yet Unmarried*. It dealt with a young educated woman, Huang Ying, who failed to find a job. It exposed the corrupt society in the Kuomintang-controlled areas. Unwilling to be a mere appendage to a man, Huang Ying looked everywhere for a job, but could not find any opening for women. She ended up becoming a housewife and mother, living in poverty. Weighted down by hard life, her husband Liu Tianye became decadent and took to drinking to forget his sorrows.

Unfortunately the play tended to trivialize its serious social content, especially in the first three acts.

Chen Baichen had written *A Cold Winter Scene* and *Promotion in Officialdom*. The first play was published at the beginning of 1945. It was about the life of a noble-minded intellectual in adverse social circumstances. The play was set in a hospital attached to a private medical college in a city in the rear area during the Resistance War.

The leading character was Li Zhusun, a physician, who was devoted and loyal to his duties. Li Zhusun was a professor at the medical college and head of the tuberculosis department at the hospital where he had worked for twenty years. He was so dedicated to his work that he often went without meals and sleep to treat his patients.

Knowing that four million people died of tuberculosis in China each year he developed a programme for the prevention of tuberculosis. Under the programme he hoped to put an end to tuberculosis in his city within three years and wipe out the disease in the whole country within ten years. However, this goal could not be achieved under reactionary rule. Finally Li Zhusun realized that the trouble lay with the whole social system. As long as the whole social problem remained unsolved, it was impossible for him to carry out his plans.

The play praised the integrity of scientific and cultural workers in China and was very critical of the old society.

Promotion in Officialdom was written in October 1945. It brought the house down when the play was performed in Chongqing, Shanghai and other cities in 1946. In order to pass censorship the author set the play at the beginning of the Republic of China in 1912, when warlords were terrorizing the people. However, by looking at the past, the audience and readers could see the correlation between the past and present oppression.

The play exposed and satirized the bureaucracy as seen through the dreams of two bandits. In a night of bitter wind and rain, two bandits broke into an ancient residence to avoid pursuit and arrest. The two intruders went to sleep and dreamed that they got promoted as officials and made a large fortune.

In riot in the dream the two bandits posed as the magistrate and secretary-general as the real magistrate was wounded and the secretary-general died. Officials and even the wife of the magistrate, blinded by greed, acknowledged the two fake officials as genuine officials. The real magistrate was put into military service.

Apart from the two fake officials, there were many other characters in the play, including the head of the police station who claimed that he would exterminate the entire population of the city, yet he had only six policemen under him. There was the obese head of the finance bureau. The head of the education bureau was listless and gloom, yet he could play twenty rounds of mahjong in one go. The head of the public affairs bureau was always dressed in a well-pressed foreign suit with a painted face and oily hair. The magistrate's wife was a highly seductive woman, who was always seen in the company of the head of the finance bureau. Lastly, there was Miss Ma, who became a prostitute for a five-karat diamond ring, a car and a European-style house. All these characters were depicted as greedy and evil.

News came that the provincial governor was coming to the city on an inspection tour. The city officials immediately began a farce in which they showed their true colours. The fake magistrate tried to memorize a welcome speech in which he said "We've got rid of corrupt officials and established an honest government." The head of the police station used beggars to augment his police force. The head of the public affairs bureau collected 100,000 yuan from each household for the whitewashing of walls. The provincial governor talked a great deal about honesty and simplicity, but he was corrupt too, and took bribes. He had a peculiar kind of headache and he wanted gold bars to be burned in smokes as a remedy.

The governor received enough gold bars and got a wife too, free of charge. He announced that the inspection tour had completed. Everything was okay. The real magistrate who escaped from the army was shot. The governor promoted the fake magistrate to the post of provincial inspector. The head of the finance bureau was promoted to the office of magistrate. Everyone was satisfied. But just when the governor and the magistrate were having their weddings together an angry crowd arrested them. The two bandits were rudely awakened from the dream. Promotion in officialdom was a dream, but it reflected reality. Using fantasy the author depicted the corruption of the Kuomintang rulers.

The technique used by the Russian writer Gogol in his *The Government Inspector* and in traditional Chinese dramas. The author used exaggeration to reveal the decadent characters.

Following Chen Baichen's *Promotion in Officialdom*, Wu Zuguang's *Catching Ghosts* and *Chang'e Flying to the Moon* (changed to *Chang'e* when it was staged) attracted the attention of audiences and readers with new concepts and a unique style. *Promotion in Officialdom* was a play that portrayed reality in dream form. Wu Zuguang's plays used ghosts and celestial beings from legends and myths to criticize politics by innuendo.

Catching Ghosts, a three-act play based on the legendary tale of Zhong Kui, was a biting satire of the corruption under the rule of the Kuomintang. Zhong Kui was a scholar from Mount Zhongnan, who lived in the Tang Dynasty over one thousand years ago. He passed the imperial examination and became the top scholar in the country. But he was refused an official position because he was too ugly. In anger he stormed into the emperor's audience hall, bumped against a pillar, and died.

When Zhong Kui met the King of Hell, he expressed his determination to wipe out all demons, catch ghosts and make the world pure. He led a force to the human world to capture the Bull Demon King and other devils among the mortals. The success of his campaign led him to believe that his task had been fulfilled. He drank and got so drunk that he became petrified. Over one thousand years later, so the legend says, he was awakened by ghosts and found ghosts everywhere. Seeing no hope to catch all the ghosts, he withdrew.

The play exposed the Kuomintang in collusion with imperialists to oppress the Chinese people. They forced people into military service to wage civil war. Corrupt Kuomintang officials received bribes and committed many bad deeds.

In the play the ghosts had not been rounded up by Zhong Kui. The poor oppressed ghosts, shop assistants, and the inn proprietor remained in their low and humble position as before. The play suggested that the only way out for the oppressed people was to double their efforts in their resistance.*

Chang'e Flying to the Moon, a three-act play adapted from a legend, had its realistic significance. The author said that "shooting at the extra suns" was the symbol of resistance against oppression, and "flying to the moon" was a symbol for freedom. The story

* "Postscript to *Catching Ghosts*."

described in the play represented the struggle between progress and reaction.

The play described Hou Yi shooting at the extra suns to get rid of disasters for the people. When he enthroned himself as king, Hou Yi became a great dictator. He forcibly took Chang'e as his queen. Chang'e, who was dissatisfied with living a life under lock and key, stole celestial herb. When she ate the herb, it enabled her to fly to the Palace of the Moon.

Feng Meng and Wu Gang represented the forces of progress and reaction. In the play Chang'e's parents and three sisters were oppressed and starving. They represented the broad masses of people who were good, honest and innocent. The people endured suffering but resisted in the end.* The play ended with Feng Meng leading the people to overthrow the dictatorial rule of Hou Yi.

Based on his own interpretation, the author combined the simple and beautiful legend with the heroic struggle of the people against oppression. His play reflected the desire of the people for freedom and liberation. The second act of the play adopted Lu Xun's version of "Flying to the Moon" in the *Old Tales Retold*.

In addition to these plays, Wu Zuguang wrote a four-act play *He Returned on a Snowy Night* and adapted the legend *The Cowherd and the Maiden Weaver* as a play. Both of them proved to be very successful.

---

* "Preface to *Chang'e Flying to the Moon*."

Chapter 12
Zhao Shuli and the Literature of the New Era

I. Zhao Shuli

After the forum on literature and art was held in Yan'an and the publication of Mao Zedong's *Talks at the Yan'an Forum on Literature and Art* in 1942, literature in the anti-Japanese base areas and the liberated areas (later on both are referred to as liberated areas) changed both in content and style. Quite different from the hard conditions of the writers in the Kuomintang-controlled areas, the writers in the liberated areas enjoyed the freedom of going among the people and into the thick of life where there was ample material and scope for them to display their literary talents. Therefore, authors wrote about new subjects featuring peasants and workers as protagonists and at the same time writers began to use popular language more and more. The literature reflected the new era of the people in the liberated areas. Zhao Shuli was an outstanding writer of the that period.

Zhao Shuli (1906-70) was born in a poor peasant family in Qinshui County, Shanxi Province. He worked on a farm and led a hard life in his childhood. He loved folk songs, ballads, storytelling, local operas and other folk arts when he was still very young. He learned to play various musical instruments in the local peasants' amateur troupe. In 1925 he entered the Fourth Provincial Normal School in Changzhi, where he was influenced by the new-vernacular literature of the May Fourth Movement in the magazines published by the Creation Society and the Literary Research Society. Later he was inspired by the proletarian revolutionary literary movement. Because of the persecution of the reactionary authorities, he was forced to leave school and became a vagrant. In 1931 he began to write short stories and other works for the literary supplement of some newspapers in Taiyuan. He used simple everyday language which peasants with little schooling could read and the illiterate could understand. He published "Iron Ox Resumes His Post," "The Curling Dragon Valley" and some other works which voiced his views that literature and art must serve the people. Zhou Yang pointed out later that Zhao Shuli entered the literary field as "a writer well-equipped in ideology and experience of life, who was fairly mature before he became known, a people's artist with a fresh, original and popular style."*

After the Resistance War broke out in 1937, Zhao Shuli took part in revolutionary work and in 1941 he went to work in the North China Party School where he specialized in popular literature. Later on, when he was an editor for the supplement of *The Yellow River Daily*, the newspaper *Chinese People* and *New Masses Daily*, he wrote many short stories, plays, ballads and other popular articles. He also wrote and directed plays for a country troupe which performed for villagers. In May 1943, he completed his well-known short story "The Marriage of Young Blacky" and finished *Rhymes of Li Youcai* in October that year, which was rated highly as "a representative work of the literature and art in the liberated areas." In the winter of 1945, he completed the novel entitled *Changes in the Li Village*. During this period and the later years, he also wrote many novelle and short stories, such as "The Emancipation of Meng Xiangying" and "The Floor" (1944), "Fu Gui" (1946), "A Young Manager" and "The Evil Can Not Overwhelm the Just" (1948). "The Heirloom" and "Widow Tian Keeps Watch by the Melon Patch" (1949). In a few years Zhao Shuli became the most successful writer in depicting the lives of the workers, peasants and soldiers. In August 1946, Guo Moruo and Zhou Yang published articles in Shanghai and Yan'an to recommend Zhao Shuli and his works. Commenting on *Rhymes of Li*

* Zhou Yang, "On Zhao Shuli's Literary Creation," first published in Yan'an's *Liberation Daily*, August 26, 1946 and later included in the collection of essays entitled *To Reflect the New Era of the People*.

Youcai, Guo Moruo wrote, "I was completely intoxicated by the novel and its simple contents and style. It reflected a new world, new characters, a new meaning and way of life as well as a new culture. I believe that whoever reads it will take an interest in it."* In July 1947 the Federation of Literary and Art Circles in the Shanxi-Hebei-Shandong-Henan Border Region held a meeting to call on writers and artists to follow the direction of Zhao Shuli. In August that year, the government of the border region awarded the only special prize for literary and education works to Zhou Shuli's stories, and Zhao Shuli became one of the most renowned writers in the liberated areas.

The Marriage of Young Blacky depicts how a young couple, Young Blacky and Little Celery, were persecuted by the local despot and opposed by their parents when they tried to break through feudal tradition and fight for freedom in marriage. They struggled and, with the support of the democratic government, finally won the right to marry. The parents of the young couple and other backward people were mocked and criticized in the story and began to remould their thinking as a result. From the failure of two young city intellectuals in their struggle for freedom in marriage depicted in Lu Xun's *Regret for the Past* to the success of two young country people in the same struggle reflected in *The Marriage of Young Blacky*, it is shown that great progress had been made in the Chinese revolution in two decades' time. *The Marriage of Young Blacky* praised the democratic government, the development in the countryside and the growth of the new generation of peasants; therefore it was well-received in the countryside, especially by the young people, who wanted democratic reform.

Through an election of a village administration and the reduction of land rents and of interest on loans in a mountain village, the novel *Rhymes of Li Youcai* showed the class struggle in the countryside during the War of Resistance Against Japan. The Yan Family Village epitomized Chinese villages under the deep-rooted feudal rule. The village became a base area behind the enemy lines after the war broke out, but the despotic landlord Yan Hengyuan

---

* Guo Moruo, "*Rhymes of Li Youcai and Other Stories*," *Wen Hui Bao*, Shanghai, August 16, 1946.

still relied on his power and tried to maintain his domination over the villagers. The story exposed the reactionary nature of the cruel landlord; for instance in the chapter "Measuring the Land" Yan Hengyuan's cunning schemes were exposed. But under the influence of the Communist Party, the consciousness of the peasants had begun to develop. Li Youchai was a straightforward and sober-minded peasant in the story. When the balance of class forces was unfavourable to the peasants, he expressed his grievances through ironical remarks. He was also a gifted folk singer who used ballads to protest oppression. A group of young peasants in the story were enthusiastic disseminators of Li Youcai's ballads. They were politically active and more militant in the struggle. As a new generation of peasants, they played an important role in the democratic revolution in the countryside.

The fact that the emancipation of the peasants in the Yan Family Village was incomplete was closely related with the mistakes of Zhang, a cadre in charge of the work there. Instead of relying on Li Youcai and the young peasants, he fell into the power trap of the landlord and his followers. The author portrayed Old Yang, another cadre in the village to contrast with Zhang. Being a hired-hand himself before becoming a cadre, Old Yang always identified himself with the people. He discovered the revolutionary elements among the peasants and relied on them to mobilize the people and it only took them three days to defeat the landlord, thus liberating the peasants from feudal rule. Though the *Rhymes of Li Youcai* only depicted the struggle in a mountain hamlet, its implications were far-reaching and thought-provoking.

Changes in the Li Village is a novel depicting the changes of a village in the Taihang Mountains in about twenty years from the defeat of China's First Revolutionary Civil War to the victory of the War of Resistance Against Japan in 1945. It reflected on a broader background the turbulent situation of Shanxi under the reactionary rule of Yan Xishan, a warlord, and its influence on the life of the peasants.

The story started by showing the cruel feudal oppression and depicted a series of events leading to the climactic struggle between the landlord and peasants. From the massacre in "Bloodshed at the Dragon King Temple" to the victory of the peasants by punishing Li Ruzhen, and finally to the inspiring scene in which the young peasants vied with one another to join the army, the novel vividly reflected the long fight of the people's revolution led by the Communist Party. It portrayed a number of rebellious peasants including Tiesuo, Lengyuan, Baigou and many other characters of different class origins. Among them, Tiesuo was most vividly portrayed. The author depicted Tiesuo's ideological changes in the different periods of the revolution. Oppressed politically and economically by Li Ruzhen, Tiesuo had taken a sceptical attitude towards the unjust society and hoped to seek revenge and freedom. When he failed to do so, he met Young Chang, a Communist who aroused his class consciousness and persuaded him to join the revolution. The development in the latter part of the novel was a bit too fast and the portrayal of Tiesuo after he joined the revolution lacked depth, therefore the image of this leading character was impaired. Similar deficiencies existed in the portrayal of other characters.

The other short stories of Zhao Shuli reflected the social changes in the countryside of the liberated areas. "The Emancipation of Meng Xiangying" depicted a young woman in the Taihang Mountains who was ill-treated by her mother-in-law, but finally became a heroine in helping to tide over the famine. "The Heirloom" also reflected a relationship between a mother-in-law and daughter-in-law. In the former story, Meng Xiangying's mother-in-law did not allow her to take part in social activities because the democratic political power was not stable; the conflict between them contained a political element, while the conflicts in "Heirloom" reflected the changes in households caused by economic development after the political power in the liberated areas had been consolidated. "Fu Gui," "The Evil Can Not Overwhelm the Just," "A Young Manager" and "Widow Tian Keeps Watch by the Melon Patch" criticize the old conventions in the countryside, as well as certain mistakes in the Party's rural work. Meanwhile they praised new people, and new things emerged in the countryside.

Since the May Fourth Movement in 1919, many writers depicted the life of the peasants. Lu Xun was the first one who depicted the poverty-stricken peasants with sympathy. In the thirties, along with the development of the revolution in the countryside, some Left-wing writers began to write about the new generation of young peasant rebels. But because those writers had not yet shared the life of the peasants, they could not fully show the reality that peasants had to face. Zhao Shuli's important contribution to modern Chinese literature is that he created characters which genuinely represented the peasants.

His understanding of rural life and peasant psychology enabled Zhao Shuli to write effectively on their position. He said, "When I was doing popular work, I encountered some problems that must be solved but could not be easily solved, which later became the themes in my works."* The reason why he wrote *Rhymes of Li Youcai* is that "at that time our work lacked depth in some places, especially the schemes of the landlords were not fully revealed and there were many party workers like Zhang, but few like Old Yang. In order to encourage Old Yang's style of work, I wrote this novel."** Before the people were mobilized in the land reform movement, some bad guys often took advantage to worm their way into the revolution and some of the cadres in authority were easily corrupted. In order to draw people's attention to guard against such things, he wrote "The Evil Can Not Overwhelm the Just" so that "the cadres and masses will heighten their vigilance after reading the story."*** Zhao Shuli's stories depicted the class contradictions between the peasants and feudal landlords and reflected the social changes in the countryside during that period and the transformation of the old rural society after the problem of political power was solved. He depicted the changes of social status and ideology and the internal relations of each family. In "The Marriage of Young Blacky," "The Emancipation of Meng Xiangying," "Fu Gui" and "The Heirloom," he wrote about the changes of the relations between the old and young generations,

* "Maybe This Is My Experience," *Selected Works of Zhao Shuli*, People's Literature Publishing House, 1959.

** "Problems Existed in Present Literary Creation," *San Fu Ji*, Writers' Publishing House, 1962.

*** About "The Evil Can Not Overwhelm the Just," *People's Daily*, January 15, 1950.

of the changes in marriage and between mothers and their daughters-in-law. Instead of evading contradictions, Zhao Shuli boldly analysed the problems and backwardness of the countryside. Zhao Shuli portrayed the historical process of change in the countryside. His stories mirrored Chinese rural society in the tide of revolution in a down-to-earth style popular with the public.

Zhao Shuli created many characters in his stories, using the style of character portrayal of Chinese classical literature and adapted his works to popular taste by letting his characters unfold their personalities through the plot and dialogues. For instance, in *The Marriage of Young Blacky*, the author brought out the superstitions, pedantic and timid but honest and kind nature of Young Blacky's father through a series of incidents.

Zhao Shuli's stories have simple plots, and the personalities of the characters are displayed through simple and succinct description. This gives the stories a realistic touch. Zhao Shuli's stories are well-linked and develop step by step, unfolding several short stories within a long story. He introduced the characters at the beginning of his works, then developed their characters along with the plot, so that the reader can easily follow the whole story from beginning to end.

There were few writers who had used the colloquial language of the peasants in northern China, but in Zhao Shuli's stories all the characters used the everyday speech of the peasants and even the narration was sometimes written in this form. However the language is simple and easily understood, while the description is vivid and true to life. Zhao Shuli's works appeal to both refined and popular tastes because the author had combined popular writing with artistry. He drew upon the tradition of folk literature, absorbing techniques from it to create a new folk form rather than merely imitating the established folk literature. He was clearly aware that there were some gaps in folk literature which should be remoulded. In order to reflect modern life and to appeal to the taste of modern readers, he adopted the strong points of both Chinese classical literature and the new vernacular literature since the May Fourth Movement in 1919 to create his own style which influenced later writers and helped to form a new school of literature called "The Potato School."*

II. *The Sun Shines Over the Sanggan River, The Hurricane* and Other Works

As well Zhao Shuli's stories, Ding Ling's *The Sun Shines Over the Sanggan River* and Zhou Libo's *The Hurricane* also depicted the peasants' struggle for emancipation and reflected the great changes in China's countryside. They won the second and third place in the Stalin Prize for Literature in 1951.

After the Yan'an forum on literature and art, Ding Ling went further into the midst of the masses and the revolutionary struggle and gained many new ideas for her works. From 1946 to 1948, she went several times to the countryside to take part in the Land Reform Movement in North China where she gathered plenty of war material, then wrote the famous novel, *The Sun Shines Over the Sanggan River*. This novel depicted the initial stage of the Land Reform Movement in the countryside of North China after the Central Committee of the Chinese Communist Party had issued the "May Fourth Directives" concerning the Land Reform in 1946. It was the first part of a trilogy she planned to write. Set in the Warm Water Village in North China, the novel depicted the class struggle in the countryside, and showed that under the leadership of the Communist Party, the peasants had hope.

The story begins with Gu Yong, a well-to-do peasant who was later wrongly classified as a rich peasant, and who heard of the Land Reform in a nearby village. Ding Ling showed the reaction of the people in the Warm Water Village on the eve of the sweeping storm of class conflict.

The characters were vividly portrayed and true to life. Zhang Yumin was the first Communist in the Warm Water Village. The

* Meaning that their works were down-to-earth and popular with the reading public.

novel highlights his cool-headedness, shrewdness and loyalty to the revolutionary cause. He enjoyed high prestige among the cadres and villagers and occupied an important position in the village. Cheng Ren was a hired-hand like Zhang Yumin, who had been exploited by the landlords since he was a little boy. He was simple and honest and hated the landlord class. Because of his relation with Heini, niece of landlord Qian Wengui, he was indecisive about the conflict at the beginning, but he took a firm stand with the masses in the struggle against the landlord class. The portrayal of despotic landlord Qian Wengui as one of the major characters in the book is not so successful, but he illustrated how the landlord class resisted the Land Reform Movement. The author neither exaggerated his ability, nor underestimated his abuse of power, but had a sense of balance in the characterization. As well as Qian, Ding Ling also portrayed several other landlords with different characteristics, for instance, the timid and despairing Li Zijun, the sinister and ferocious Jiang Shirong and the fiendish Hou Diankui who bore a bitter hatred against the peasants.

The significance of *The Sun Shines Over the Sanggan River* lies in its realistic portrayal of the peasants. Ding Ling created her characters from real life and placed their struggles in a historical context. She showed their search for emancipation, but at the same time she also showed the influence of traditional feudal relations on them, their shortcomings and misgivings before taking part in the revolutionary struggle and their feelings when suffering setbacks.

Ding Ling's characters are very life-like, for example, Zhang Zhengguo, the head of the militia unit was stable and upright; Li Chang, in charge of the propaganda work of the village administration and the Party branch, was active, lively and sober-minded; Liu Man was a brave activist, but a little bit rash; Dong Guihua, the efficient director of the women association and Zhou Yueying, a shepherd's wife who was shrewd and capable. Each one had a distinct personality. Through these characters, the author brought to light the relations among the people and reflected the circuitous development of the Land Reform Movement. The characters grew with the development of the struggle and their fate was closely linked with it. For instance, the change of Cheng Ren's attitude towards Heini reflected the progress of the struggle in the Land Reform Movement as well as his own consciousness. Thus the novel embodies that the great mass movement of Land Reform not only changed the old social order that had existed for thousands of years in the Chinese countryside, but also influenced people's thinking and psychology. This is the reason why this novel is more substantial than other works with the same theme of the Land Reform Movement.

The Sun Shines Over the Sanggan River portrayed nearly forty characters and the whole process of the Land Reform Movement from the beginning stage to the mobilization of the masses to the defeat of the landlord class. With one climax following another, the plot is complex but well organized. At the beginning, the novel showed the influence of the Land Reform Movement on the people from different classes. Then the work team's entry into the village created a tense atmosphere, which grew even more so with the gradual unfolding of the struggle.

The Sun Shines Over the Sanggan River also has certain defects. For instance, the character of Heini is not well portrayed and a bit detached from the actual class struggle; the language, especially in depicting the inner world of the characters, is not colloquial enough. But generally speaking, this novel is a fine work reflecting the struggles in the Land Reform Movement and its artistic success indicates that the technique in novel writing had reached a new level after the Yan'an forum on literature and art in 1942.

The Hurricane, a novel that has also strongly influenced both Chinese and foreign readers like *The Sun Shines Over the Sanggan River*, is the representative work of Zhou Libo (1908-79). A native of Yiyang County, Hunan Province, Zhou Libo began his literary career in the early thirties. He joined the Chinese League of Left-Wing Writers, wrote prose and literary reviews and translated foreign literary works such as *Secret China* by a Czechosolvak writer E.E. Kisch and Sholokhov's *The Reclaimed Virgin Soil*. After the War of Resistance Against Japan broke out, he went to the Shanxi-Chahar-Hebei revolutionary base area and wrote many news reports which were later collected into *Impressions of the*

Shanxi-Chahar-Hebei Border Region. After the victory over the Japanese, he wrote *Marching to the South*, a collection of feature articles, and from 1946 to 1948 when he took part in the Land Reform Movement in the liberated area in northeast China, he wrote *The Hurricane.*

In *The Hurricane* there are not so many characters and the plot is rather simple, yet it reflects the broad scale and complete process of the Land Reform Movement. The novel begins with a work team entering a village to launch the Land Reform Movement. As well as the struggle against the despotic landlord, the novel also depicts the reexamination of the Land Reform, sharing out the land, confiscating the firearms of the landlords and suppressing bandits. It ends with a vigorous recruitment for the army. The novel is divided into two parts: the first reflects the initial stage of the Land Reform after the Central Committee of the Communist Party issued its "May Fourth Directives" in 1946, while the second shows the situation after the publication of *Outline Land Law of China* in late October of 1947. Set in Yuanmao Village on the bank of the Songhua River in northeast China, it unfolds the revolutionary struggle which enables readers to see clearly great political and economic changes as well as changes in the thinking and customs in the Chinese countryside, which had been fettered for hundreds of years by feudalism.

The Hurricane successfully portrayed Zhao Yulin, Guo Quanhai and other poor peasants. Under the twofold oppression of Japanese imperialism and the local despotic landlord Han, Zhao Yulin's mother starved to death, his wife became a beggar and he was imprisoned and cruelly tortured by landlords. Guo Quanhai's father was murdered by Han and he himself became a groom for the Han family when he was only thirteen years old, thus he had a bitter hatred against the landlord. Before the work team entered the village, the peasants were still helplessly oppressed and enslaved; but when they were aroused an awareness of their situation, the sparks of revolution flared into flames. The author emphasized the peasants' desire for Land Reform Movement and the inevitability of this process. The author also depicted the weakness of the peasants, as well as their good qualities to show the obstacles they had to overcome to win their newfound social consciousness.

The characterization of the cart-driver, Old Sun, is very good. He was a peasant of the older generation who had the shortcomings of backwardness and selfishness, but at the same time he was eager for liberation. He was somewhat timid, boastful and concerned about saving face, but when he saw that the power of the landlords was really crumbling he took active part in the struggle. The portrayal of Old Tian, another representative of the old peasantry, was also a very good characterization.

The novel showed the leadership of the Communist Party through the activities of Xiao Xiang, leader of the work team. From the development of the plot we can see that Xiao Xiang was actually the key character of the whole novel. The author did not portray him as a saviour who placed himself above the peasants, but as a leader who understood the peasants and supported and helped them at the critical junctures of their struggle. The character of Liu Sheng, another member of the work team was detached from the peasants and reality to set off Xiao Xiang who was in close contact with the peasants and understood them very well.

The Hurricane had its distinct features of the times and vivid local flavour. At that time the Kuomintang reactionaries tried desperately to seize the Northeast and defend their position there. In order to accelerate the development of the War of Liberation, the central leadership of the Communist Party pointed out that it was necessary to arouse the masses, expand the revolutionary forces and establish solid revolutionary base areas in the Northeast. The Land Reform Movement in northeast China was actually closely linked with the suppression of bandits and the struggle against local despots and was directly related to the War of Liberation.

Realism and idealism are well combined in *The Hurricane.* Zhou Libo was adept at depicting typical events and details in a simple and succinct style to reveal the personalities of the characters. There is seldom any lengthy and gloomy narration and the style of the whole book is straightforward and lively. The author used flashbacks to show how Zhao Yulin was sent away as a forced coolie and how he met his wife, who was reduced to a beggar.

With the development the Land Reform Movement as the main plot, the author spiced the novel with lively episodes and details. He used the colloquial language of the peasants in the Northeast, which made the novel vivid and expressive. The dialogue brings out the personality of each character.

The novel does have some flaws however. The second part is rather loosely structured and there are too many events in it. The first and second parts are not closely linked, so the novel seems somewhat disjointed. As for the characterization, some major characters, such as Zhao Yulin, are too simple while the villains, such as the landlord Han and Philanthropist, are rather similar and superficial. But generally speaking, this novel is still a great success and occupies an important place in the history of modern Chinese literature like *The Sun Shines Over the Sanggan River.*

As well as *The Sun Shines Over the Sanggan River* and *The Hurricane*, many other novels and novelle were written in the liberated areas, including *Uncle Gao, Sowing, Ten Days in the Jiangshan Village, Earthshaking Changes, The Story of Ironbucket, Heroes on the Lüliang Mountains, Daughters and Sons* and *The Motive Force* which greatly influenced readers.

Ten Days in the Jiangshan Village, written by Ma Jia, is a novella reflecting the same theme of the Land Reform Movement in the Northeast. Based on real people and events, it reflected the tremendous changes in a village ten days after the Land Reform. Before he went to the Northeast, Ma Jia had written a novel, *Along the Hutuo River Valley,* and some short stories including "Reduction of Land Rent," "Over the Ridge" and "Mother." Like the novel, Ma Jia's short stories also depicted life and struggle in the liberated areas, but they are better than the novel.

Uncle Gao is among the earliest novels about rural life in the liberated areas. The author, Ouyang Shan began his literary career during the period of the First Revolutionary Civil War. He later joined the Chinese League of Left-Wing Writers and published "The Seventh Anniversary" and other works. The life of the peasants depicted in those works was not authentic and profound enough. During the War of Resistance Against Japan, Ouyang Shan went to Yan'an where he plunged into the thick of struggle. *Uncle*

Gao described how Renjiagou Village in northwest China set up a supply and marketing cooperative in the hardest days during the War of Resistance Against Japan. Gao Shengliang, known as Uncle Gao, was a village cadre in the novel who was loyal to his duties and worked untiringly among the people. Gao fought against feudal and reactionary forces and at the same time broke through the obstacles set by the bureaucrats, thus enabling the cooperative to flourish. Besides Uncle Gao, other characters were also vividly depicted; the language is simple and lively. The use of colloquialisms of the peasants in northern Shaanxi makes the characters in the book true to life and the novel more realistic.

Sowing is a novel written by Liu Qing (1916-78) about the early stage of mutual aid and cooperation in the countryside of northern Shaanxi. The story was set in Wangjiagou Village where the peasants organized themselves in mutual aid teams and sowed the millet collectively. Because the author was familiar with the rural life in northern Shaanxi his depiction of the local conditions and customs were realistic and vivid; but the development of the plot is too slow and some detailed depictions are rather tedious.

Unlike the above-mentioned works, *Earthshaking Changes*, *The Story of Ironbucket*, *Heroes on the Lüliang Mountains* and *Daughters and Sons* were written in the traditional form of Chinese novels, with each chapter headed by a couplet giving the gist of its content. The contents of these books include class struggle in the countryside and the armed struggle in the War of Resistance Against Japan.

The author of *Earthshaking Changes*, Wang Xijian, was a young writer who began to write after the Yan'an forum on literature and art. He had experienced the struggles and changes in the countryside so the novel is true to life. It depicted the class struggle in the countryside of Shandong Province during the War of Resistance Against Japan and the tremendous changes afterwards. The plot of the story is very complicated and absorbing and the language is simple and easy to understand, but the characters are not vivid enough.

The author of the novella *The Story of Ironbucket*, Ke Lan, was also a new writer who emerged after the Yan'an forum on literature and art. The story is about a local hero nicknamed "Ironbucket" who led a militia detachment to fight the Japanese and eliminate hidden traitors. The language is plain and lively, but like *Earthshaking Changes*, there are too many conventional terms and patterns adopted from traditional Chinese novels.

Compared with *Earthshaking Changes* and *The Story of Ironbucket*, the two novels *Heroes on the Lüliang Mountains* and *Daughters and Sons* are better at adapting the form of traditional novels to reflect new contents. *Heroes on the Lüliang Mountains*, written jointly by Ma Feng and Xi Rong, was based on the heroic deeds of the militiamen who attended the Conference of Combat Heroes in the Shanxi-Suiyuan Border Regions. Set in Kangjia Village at the foot of Lüliang Mountains, the novel reflected the people's armed resistance in the Shanxi-Suiyuan Border Regions. The novel has a very interesting and complicated plot, but some of the stories are not well-connected. Ma Feng also wrote many news reports and short stories. His "Village Rancour" written in the later period of the War of Liberation is a short story reflecting the class struggle in the countryside. Compact, well-organized and written in a lively style, the plot is interesting and all the characters have distinctive personalities. Xi Rong also wrote some news reports and short stories, among them is"The Happy Event" about the love story of young peasants.

Written together by Kong Jue and Yuan Jing, *Daughters and Sons* depicted the heroic anti-Japanese struggles of the people in the area around Baiyang Lake in central Hebei Province under the leadership of the Chinese Communist Party. The authors used traditional forms to reflect the days and nights in the struggle against the Japanese invaders. There are still some artistic defects in this novel, yet among the novels reflecting the same theme of the anti-Japanese struggles published during that period, it had a great impact on readers. Before the Yan'an forum on literature and art, Kong Jue published a collection of short stories entitled *The Suffering People* and after the Yan'an forum he wrote another short story, "The Story of a Woman's Emancipation."

One of the features of the Chinese revolution was to encircle the cities from the rural areas and then capture them, so the writers in the liberated areas lived for a long time in the countryside and there were few works on industrial themes written during that period. Cao Ming's *The Motive Force* is the earliest novella of that kind. The author began to write short stories and novelle in the thirties to reflect the miserable life of the workers and went to Yan'an during the War of Resistance Against Japan. After the victory of the anti-Japanese war, she worked in the factories and power stations in the Northeast. Based on her life there, she wrote the novella in 1948. It depicted how the workers of a hydraulic power plant in the Northeast tried to repair the machines which were damaged by Japanese invaders and Kuomintang reactionaries to get the production going again. Characterized by the distinctive atmosphere of the times, the story is well-knit, the plot complicated and the language simple. Although it is a bit immature artistically, it is meaningful as the first literary work reflecting the life of liberated workers.

III. Works of Sun Li, Liu Baiyu and Others

After the Yan'an forum on literature and art, fiction flourished in the liberated areas, especially short stories, with new writers and new works emerging in large numbers. Sun Li, Liu Baiyu, Kang Zhuo, Qin Zhaoyang, Shao Zinan, Yang Shuo and many other writers were notable.

Sun Li was famous for his short stories dealing with the people's struggle against the Japanese invaders in the rural areas in central Hebei Province. His works were notable for their distinctive and original style. His short-story anthologies such as *In the Reed Marshes*, *Lotus Creek*, *Parting Advice*, and *Caiputai* are set in his birthplace the Central Hebei Plain. His works vividly depicted the people's struggles in the War of Resistance Against Japan in the base areas under the leadership of the Communist Party. All the stories were written in an elegant, lucid and poetic style and were optimistic in spite of the bitter struggles.

Sun Li (913-) is especially adept at portraying peasant women, who were faithful, lively and considerate of their families, but brave and unyielding to the enemy. Fearing neither hardship nor sacrifice, they shouldered the heavy load of family responsibility and the struggle, demonstrating the strength of the emancipated woman. Sister Shuishen in both *Lotus Creek* and *Parting Advice* was industrious, capable, lively and simple; she was rather wayward at first but through the trials of war gradually became brave and resourceful. In *Lotus Creek* she organized a boat-guerrilla team with some other women, while in *Parting Advice* she skillfully drove a sled to send her husband back to the front though he had just come back and stayed only overnight at home after eight years in the Resistance War. During both the War of Resistance Against Japan and the War of Liberation women proved themselves to be as much the backbone of Chinese history as men. In *Caipu Platform*, Xiao Hong and her mother were ordinary women, but they were industrious, tenacious and optimistic embodying the indomitable spirit of Chinese working women. Xiumei in "Honour" was bold and vigorous and firm in her class stand. The director of the village's women association for national salvation in "Wormwood Ridge" was energetic and enthusiastic, and treated the soldiers as brothers.

Sun Li depicted both the activities and the inner world of the characters. He brought out the persistence, courage and wisdom of the people, their happiness and hopes, as well as the hard struggles they launched to destroy the old order and welcome in the new. He was good at describing important themes through everyday life. Sun Li's style is simple and straightforward, but vivid and realistic, especially his depiction of the people and scenery in the region of the Baiyang Lake is well done. His language is terse and graceful, mainly using the language of ordinary people, so his works could be read by everyone.

Kang Zhuo and Qin Zhaoyang are also famous for their short stories on rural life, but they differ from Sun Li in their choice of theme and their artistic style. Most of Kang Zhuo's works reflect the tremendous changes in the liberated countryside through family relations and character development. With the love and marriage of Jinfeng and Shuanzhu as the main thread of the story, "My Two Host Families" showed how the young people in the liberated areas dared to smash the shackles of traditional ideas in marriage and take their destiny into their own hands. Through this story, readers can see how the new ideas and ethics struck root in the family life of the peasants. Through the change of an old man who had outdated conventional ideas, but who taught by reality eventually redressed his thinking, "Early Spring" reflected the profound changes in the liberated countryside. In an early story, "The Disastrous Tomorrow," which is rather lengthy and loosely-structured, Kang Zhuo illustrated the superiority of the new society and the strength of the more democratic system through the changes in the relationship among the three members of Xiangbao's family. In his other works such as "In-laws" and "Winter Plum Blossom," life in the liberated countryside was also realistically shown. Kang Zhuo was skilled at characterization and depicting the inner world of the characters, as well as unfolding important themes, especially the problems and relations in peasant families. His style is simple and original, serious but not dull; meticulous, but not boring. Not long before the Liberation in 1949, Kang Zhuo also wrote another short story "The Worker Zhang Feihu" and a novel *Romance of the Heishipo Coal Mine* to show the life of workers, but artistically they are less successful than his works about peasant life.

Some of Qin Zhaoyang's works praised the new life of the emancipated peasants. For instance, "The Old Man Liu Mantun" and "Happiness" reflected the changes in peasant life. Qin Zhaoyang's stories have interesting plots and are vividly written in a unique style. "The Story of the East and West Li Villages" tells the story how the peasants of Li Village, incited by the landlords, divided their village into two, and how they ended their estrangement because they came to realize their common class interests after the Land Reform Movement, reflecting the changes of relationships after the people had seized the political power. "The Cook Xiong Laotie" is about army life.

Qin Zhaoyang's early works, such as "Mother," "Hatred," "The Road" and "He Huaxiu" are about the people's struggles in the War of Resistance Against Japan, and were later collected in his short-story anthology *On the Plain*, but most of them read like sketches and are insubstantial and the writing technique is not as good as his later writings.

Among the short stories reflecting the struggle in the Resistance War and extolling the people's war, "Land Mine Warfare" by Shao Zinan (1916-55) was the most popular. The author began to write in the mid-thirties and published a short story, "Qingsheng," about the miserable life of the miners. In the early days of the Resistance War, he actively advocated "street poetry" (popular poetry) and wrote quite a few poems. Later he switched to story writing. "Land Mine Warfare," whose protagonist Li Yong was based on a real person, depicted the mine warfare in the Shanxi-Chahar-Hebei Border Region which badly battered the Japanese. Li Yong was very good at land mine warfare and guerrilla warfare. He invented the tactics of "combing guns with land mines," which was praised and awarded by the authorities and the army troops. He created various tactics in land mine warfare.

In the narration and description in the story, the author used techniques of folk literature, especially the ballads and rhymes, which made the work more popular and widespread, thus playing an effective role in arousing the people. "Yan Rongtang's Narrow Escape from Death" is another story about a storekeeper who remained faithful and unyielding under the cruel torture of the enemy. It is realistic and very touching. Although these works described the severe trials the Chinese people underwent during hard times, they are permeated with optimism and a bright tone. This optimism is apparent in Shao Zinan's stories.

Short stories written during this period by Yang Shuo (1913-68) are included in his anthology entitled *In the Moonless Night* after one of the stories. Most of the stories tell about the efforts of the army and the people in fighting against the Japanese invaders. The title story of this collection, "In the Moonless Night," is about an old man, Grandfather Qing, who led the villagers to escort an Eighth Route Army detachment across the river and was later captured and killed by the enemy. When the armymen came back after fulfilling their mission and heard the news of Grandfather Qing's death they were deeply moved by his heroic deeds and sensed his inspiring strength. In the early period of the anti-Japanese war, Yang Shuo wrote a lot of prose as well as a novella, *Offshoots of the Pamirs*, which depicted the struggle against traitors in the northwestern border region, but the characters in this novella were not so lifelike as those in his later book of *In the Moonless Night*.

Apart from the above-mentioned stories, many short stories extolling the new life in the liberated countryside emerged after the Yan'an forum on literature and art, such as Shu Wei's "The First Harvest," "Selling Chickens" and "Red Contract," Wang Li's "A Sunny Day," Fang Ji's "Aunt Wei," Hong Lin's "Li Xiulan," Wang Ruowang's "Stationmaster Lü," Ge Luo's "Health Inspector," Lin Lan's "Red Cotton-padded Jacket" and Yu Lin's "Old Zhao Goes to the Countryside."

One of the major themes in the fiction written in the liberated areas is the life and battles of the people's army and the portrayal of the soldiers and officers. Liu Baiyu is the most notable writer in this field. Before the anti-Japanese war he published a short-story collection under the title of *On the Grassland*. He went to an anti-Japanese base area after the war broke out and there he wrote a reportage collection, *In the Guerrilla War*, recording the heroic deeds of the guerrilla fighters against the enemy. He also wrote a few short-story collections, including *At the Foot of Mount Wutai*, *A Story of Longyan Village* and *Happiness*, most of which reflected the awakening of the class consciousness of the peasants. After the Yan'an forum on literature and art, he wrote many short stories about life in the people's army, such as "The Political Commissar," "Three Invincible Fighters," "Amidst the Flames of War" and "The Consanguinity" (all of them are included in the anthology entitled *Amidst the Flames of War*). Owing to his keen political insight and rich life experience, the characters in his works are well-defined. Liu Baiyu was familiar with the life of the soldiers and their thoughts and feelings, so the characters and battle scenes portrayed in his works are lifelike. Except the short stories, he also wrote many reportage collections during the period of the Liberation War, such as *Travelling Around the Northeast*, *The Light Is Shining Over Shenyang*, *The Storm of History* and *Fighting for the Motherland*, which depicted the historical changes in the Northeast and the swift development of the war. Liu Baiyu's stories and prose writings capture the atmosphere of the times through artistic images, vividly reflecting the events.

Other works reflecting the battles and the life of the people's army include Tan Hu's "Four and Half Catties," Liu Shi's "The Real and Sham Li Bantou," Hu Tian's "Growing Up" and Li Erzhong's "An Old Fogey" which showed the life of the troops on the march and portrayed soldiers with different ideologies and personalities. Other works depicted brave and resourceful children such as Hua Shan's "A Letter Attached with a Chicken Feather," Guan Hua's "Yulai Is Still Alive" and Jun Qing's "Little Scouts." The workers' life in the liberated areas was shown in Zhou Jiefu's "The Master and Apprentice," Lu Mei's "Two Red Banners," Li Na's "The Coal" and Lei Jia's "Eels." The relationship between the intellectuals and the workers and peasants were depicted in Si Ji's "My Teacher" and Wei Junyi's "Three Friends." These short stories were written after the Yan'an forum on literature and art.

As compared with the early works and those written in the Kuomintang-controlled areas, the stories written in the liberated areas are distinctive for their vigorous style and bright and colourful tone. Both the characters and events reflected in these works have an inspiring appeal that enhanced the people's morale. These stories presented a completely new life, new themes and new characters paving a new path in the history of modern Chinese literature. Most of the stories are not written in an ornate style, but rather in a simple and natural style. The writers knew their readers well and some of them had done revolutionary work themselves, so they were able to draw a lot of material from their own experiences. These stories appealed to popular taste and helped develop new forms of folk literature written in vivid colloquial language. In spite of some deficiency of breadth and depth, they were the newest and most important works written in the vernacular since the May Fourth Movement in 1919.

IV. *The White-Haired Girl, The Hatred of Blood and Tears* and Other Plays

In the years after the Yan'an forum on literature and art, the theatre movement was in full swing in the liberated areas, which was unprecedented in the history of modern Chinese theatre. Both the quantity and scale of playwriting and performance greatly surpassed the previous records and changes had taken place both in content and style, which were propelled forward by the mass movement of new *yangge* (a folk dance of the Han Chinese developed by the peasants in North China).

At the Spring Festival of 1943, new-styled *yangge* dances and operas were put on in Yan'an, and among which was *Brother and Sister Reclaim Wasteland*. It was choreographed jointly by Wang Dahua, Li Bo and Lu You and performed by the theatre troupe of the Lu Xun Art Academy. In an editorial headlined "The New Direction of Literature and Art as Seen from the Propaganda Activities on the Spring Festival," the *Liberation Daily* said that *Brother and Sister Reclaim Wasteland* was "an excellent new type of short song-and-dance drama." The initial success of the new *yangge* opera showed that the new *yangge* form reflected the new social conditions as well as the new ideas and was well-received by the public. The Spring Festival of 1944 saw an upsurge in the *yangge* dance and opera movement and more than one hundred and fifty *yangge* pieces including *Niu Yonggui Is Wounded in Action* were performed by twenty-seven amateur *yangge* troupes from factories, army units, administrative organizations and schools, which created quite a sensation in Yan'an and "turned the New Year into an art festival of the masses."*

The experience of the new *yangge* movement in Yan'an and the whole Shaanxi-Gansu-Ningxia Border Region spread quickly to the other anti-Japanese base areas and the new *yangge* pieces were popular everywhere and many new *yangge* operas including *The Joy of the Poor* emerged. Learning from the experience of the new *yangge* movement, other local arts and traditional operas were

---

* Zhou Yang, *To Manifest the New Era of the Masses.*

transformed and many new operas were created which greatly enriched theatre-goers. The new *yangge* movement started in the liberated areas was significant in the history of modern Chinese literature. It greatly expanded the popularity of literature and art with the public, especially the millions of peasants. The new *yangge* movement explored the relationship between the reform of traditional operas and the development of new drama. It combined revolutionary ideology with traditional theatrical forms and linked professional and amateur cultural activities as well as adapting folk literature and art.

With the development of the new *yangge* movement, cultural workers, both professional and amateur, reformed and adopted other forms of folk art and opera and created many plays of different types. They incorporated *yangge* operas into their works, and also drew upon other operas and folk art and combined them to create a new national opera with rich and colourful variety. *The White-Haired Girl*, *Wang Xiuluan*, *Liu Hulan* and *The Red Leave River* were among these new operas. With rural women as their protagonists, these operas were about the bitter suffering under feudal oppression. The operas praised the struggle for a new life and depicted the battle from misfortune to liberation.

Liu Hulan performed by the Combat Theatrical Company was written by Wei Feng, Liu Lianchi, Zhu Dan, Yan Jizhou and Dong Xiaowu and is based on a true story. Liu Hulan was a 17-year-old woman Communist in the countryside who heroically gave her life to guard the secrets of the Party. When her heroic deeds were spread throughout the liberated areas, the authors began to collect material and the play was performed right after the first draft was finished. At first the playwrights intended to highlight the girl's integrity, so the first draft of the play centred on how she faced the execution bravely. Later, her efforts in supporting the front and her other revolutionary activities were added to the script, which portrayed her character more deeply so that her death aroused stronger sympathy and respect from the audience. The last scene was added to the revised script, in which the People's Liberation Army (PLA) men shot Liu Hulan's murderer. Because Liu Hulan's heroic deeds reflected the noble qualities of the Communists and the fighting will of the army and people in the liberated areas and exposed the cruelty of the reactionaries, the play had a strong appeal even though the script was artistically rather crude.

Wang Xiuluan written by Fu Duo depicted the parting and reunion of a peasant family in the liberated area of central Hebei Province. The dramatic conflicts were unfolded between the ferocious and lazy mother and her kind and hardworking daughter-in-law. Because the mother was imperious, gluttonous and lazy and refused to see reason, the family broke up. But Wang Xiuluan, the daughter-in-law, worked hard in spite of the difficulties and complaints, and not only bettered the life of the family, but also became a model worker. Later the mother was moved and returned home and the family was reunited at last. Though the play reflected few new ideas of the times, it advocated building up a family fortune through hard work which played a positive role at that time.

Steel Bones and Iron Sinews, written collectively by Su Li and others, depicted the heroic struggle of a platoon leader and soldiers of the Eighth Route Army after they were captured by the enemy. They remained unyielding though the enemy tried by all means, coupling threats with promises, to get secrets of the Eighth Route Army from them. In the play the cook, Old Wang, indignantly denounced the traitor who had betrayed them and Little Liu, an orderly, wounded the interrogator with a pen. The enemy tried to force the platoon leader to reveal the secrets by killing his mother and son on the spot. The play portrayed the different personalities of each person and reflected the revolutionary spirit of the fighters of the people's army who would rather die than surrender. One of the best films made shortly after the establishment of New China, *Dauntless Fighters*, is adapted from this play.

Among the new operas, one of the best ones is *The White-Haired Girl*. Based on the initial work of the teachers and students of the Lu Xun Art Academy, He Jingzhi and Ding Yi wrote the libretto. In 1945 when the Northwest Battlefield Service Troupe returned to Yan'an from the front, they brought back the folk story about "the white-haired goddess" which was wide-spread in the area around Fuping County, Hebei Province, in the early forties. The story is about a village girl who escaped into remote mountains because of persecution by a landlord. She lived in a cave for several years, and her hair turned white from lack of sunlight and salt. She went to a temple at night to eat the offerings. Thus she was called "White-Haired Goddess" by the villagers. Later she was rescued by the Eighth Route Army. The vivid story attracted immediate attention of the teachers and students of the Lu Xun Art Academy and they produced *The White-Haired Girl*, a full-length new opera based on the story.

The White-Haired Girl successfully portrayed the characters of Yang Bailao, Xi'er and other peasants. Yang Bailao returned at the New Year's eve after he had hidden himself to avoid the creditor. This industrious and kindhearted peasant longed to break away from the oppression of the landlords and lead a peaceful life. But this humble desire of Yang Bailao could not be satisfied. He committed suicide after he was forced to sell his daughter Xi'er. He did not discuss the matter with anyone to find an alternative, which showed the weak side of his nature. Through his experience of several decades, he had seen clearly that "the magistrates and moneybags are wolves and tigers," but he dared not to think of overthrowing them. Yang Bailao was typical of the old generation of peasants who had long been oppressed by the landlord class, but had not yet become conscious. His tragedy is a powerful exposure of the evil landlord class, therefore this character has always gained sympathy from audiences.

Xi'er, the protagonist of the opera, was a peasant woman with an increasingly rebellious spirit, different from her father. At the beginning of the opera she was a simple and naive girl, but after suffering and setbacks, her rebellious spirit strengthened. After she was raped by the landlord Huang Shiren, she tried to commit suicide. But she was rescued, then changed her mind and was determined to break the pattern of humiliation her father and the older generations of peasants had undergone. In the development of her character, it was her suffering that had nurtured her hatred against the landlord class. With a strong wish of vengeance, she held out in remote mountains. Depending on her rebellious spirit, indomitable will and determination for revenge, she survived several years of hard life in the mountains. Xi'er confronted Huang

Shiren in the Goddess' Temple. When she recognized him, "in towering rage she rushes at Huang Shiren and the others, and throws the sacrificial fruit at them with a shriek." This episode shows Xi'er's hatred. The story of "the white-haired goddess" provided a fantastic plot and the opera writers adopted the plot and successfully portrayed Yang Bailao, Xi'er and other characters based on their own experience of rural life.

The White-Haired Girl profoundly reflected the basic conflict in the countryside between the masses of peasants and the landlord class. The despotic landlord Huang Shiren hounded the honest and kindhearted Yang Bailao to death, kidnapped and raped his daughter Xi'er who later ran into remote mountains and led a miserable life. These episodes exposed the cruel, cunning, rapacious and decadent nature of the landlord class and showed the tragic lot of the poor peasants. In the feudal society there were thousands of poor peasants who shared the fate of Yang Bailao and Xi'er. Through the heart-stirring plot the libretto strikingly reflected this common fate so that the opera aroused strong sympathy from the public. Xi'er's determination to live on and avenge her family is an expression of the peasants' rebellious spirit. Through its description of the suffering of the peasants the libretto aroused hatred for the landlord class, while praising the dauntless fighting spirit of the peasants. At the end of the opera, the authors depicted how the peasants overthrew the feudal rule and won their liberation under the leadership of the Communist Party and how Xi'er became a member of the new society.

In May 1945, *The White-Haired Girl* was put on the stage. The audience of the première were the delegates to the Seventh National Congress of the Communist Party of China and leading members of the Central Party Committee. The troupe gave more than thirty performances of this opera in Yan'an, which won an unprecedentedly warm welcome. In 1946 the opera was performed in Zhangjiakuo and some important changes were made in the libretto according to the opinions of the audience. In the process of later performances, the opera was revised again. Very soon the libretto of this opera spread to the Kuomintang-controlled areas and was highly praised by progressive literary and art circles. When Guo

Moruo read the libretto, he immediately wrote a letter, praising warmly its success.

The keynote of the opera is romanticism, reflected in its characterization, plot and arias. Through these aspects the libretto reflected the ideals and wishes of the people. In the portrayal of Xi'er, her rebellious spirit was highlighted. Xi'er's life in the mountains and her encounter with the landlord demonstrated her unswerving resolve and the scene in which she threw the sacrificial fruit at Huang Shiren reflected the fury of thousands of victims in the old society. The opera was like the eruption of a volcano that stirred the people's hatred for the landlord class. In the history of modern Chinese literature, there are not many such works like *The White-Haired Girl* in which realistic portrayal is combined with bold romantic techniques. The first half of the opera is more realistic and the second half romantic.

The White-Haired Girl is the cornerstone of a new Chinese national opera. It inherited the tradition of folk opera and at the same time used techniques of both Chinese classical operas and Western opera so that it represents a new national art form based on that of *yangge* opera, opening up a new path for operas. It adopted some folk songs and melodies of local operas. But it is neither an expansion of the small folk operas nor a copy of the patterns and modes of traditional operas. It drew on the techniques of Western opera which is good at portraying characters and used Chinese music and melodies to reflect the distinct characteristics of each role in the opera. The Hebei folk song "Little Cabbage" was originally a children's rhyme about a cruel stepmother. The authors wanted to use this folk song to express Xi'er's depression when she was tortured by the landlord's mother. But the melody was too melancholy to fit in with Xi'er's innocent and lively character, so the lively and buoyant melody of another Hebei folk song was chosen. When Xi'er lived in the remote mountains and confronted Huang Shiren in the Goddess' Temple, the sonorous and vehement melody of Shanxi *bangzi* (a kind of opera) was adapted to express the outburst of her hatred. The music of this opera not only played an important role in portraying the temperament of the character but was also very popular among the people. It had the traditional combination of singing, chanting and monologue in classical operas. For instance, when Xi'er first appeared on the stage, she used an aria to tell the audience the background of the story. Then she told about her family and life experience in a soliloquy. Other characters, such as Yang Bailao, Huang Shiren and Mu Renzhi, also introduced themselves to the audience by singing an aria and monologues were used in many places to explain the events. Dialogue as well as techniques from traditional operas were used. The arias were used to explain events, recall past experiences, introduce characters, set the atmosphere and to delineate the inner world of the characters. Because the transition from recitation to singing was natural, the opera had unity. Most of the arias in the opera are verses, which had characteristics of folk songs. For example:

The gale is blowing hard and the snow's heavy,
Nine households out of ten are dimly lit.
We're celebrating the New Year as others,
But the celebration of the poor is different from that of the rich.
There're wine and meat in the landlord's house,
While we tenants have neither rice nor flour.

Poems like these set to music made *The White-Haired Girl* popular far and wide among the masses because it addressed their suffering. It became one of the most influential and welcomed theatre pieces in the liberated areas. During the Land Reform Movement and the War of Liberation, *The White-Haired Girl* continued to appeal to the people. It was unprecedented in the history of modern Chinese literature that a theatrical work could influence so many people.

The unfolding of the new *yangge* movement increased the interest of theatre workers in reforming other traditional theatrical forms. In popular amateur theatre, local operas and folk theatre familiar to the people were adapted to reflect the new life and new themes. Among the changes of various theatrical forms at that time, the most successful and influential ones were the changes of Beijing Opera and *qinqiang* (Shaanxi opera).

Beijing Opera has a long history. The Yan'an Beijing Opera

Theatre was the first troupe which combined those parts of Beijing Opera that consist of folk forms with ballads and songs selected from other theatrical forms and created a new opera. Among the new works created during that period was the historical Beijing Opera *Driven to Join the Liangshan Mountain Rebels*. It has three acts, twenty-seven scenes in all. It was first created and performed in 1943 by Da Zhong (Popular) Art Research Society, an amateur art unit formed by a number of Beijing Opera enthusiasts in the Central Party School in Yan'an. The libretto, written by Yang Shaoxuan, Qi Yanming and others, was adapted from an episode in *Outlaws of the Marsh*, which tells how Lin Chong was oppressed by evil forces and driven to join the rebels in the Liangshan Mountain. New content was added to the old plot.

In characterization, *Driven to Join the Liangshan Mountain Rebels* broke free from the conventional roles in old Beijing operas, although retaining certain performing techniques of Beijing Opera. It did not rigidly adhere to the traditional stylization. The opera caused a sensation in Yan'an when it was first staged around New Year's Day of 1944. Ai Siqi (a well-known Chinese philosopher) published an article on January 8 in *Liberation Daily*, praising *Driven to Join the Liangshan Mountain Rebels* as "a marvellous historical opera" and "it is the most successful work in the reform of Beijing Opera." Mao Zedong read the libretto and went to see the performance on January 9. That night he wrote the following letter praising the opera:

> Comrades Shaoxuan and Yanming,
>
> Having seen your performance, I wish to express my thanks to you for the excellent work you have done. Please convey my thanks to the comrades of the cast! History is made by the people, yet the old opera (and all the old literature and art, which are divorced from the people) presents the people as though they were dirt, and the stage is dominated by lords and ladies and their pampered sons and daughters. Now you have reversed this reversal of history and restored historical truth, and thus a new life is opening up for the old opera. That is why this merits congratulation. Guo Moruo has done an excellent work in historical play and you have done this work in old opera. The initiative you have taken marks an epoch-making beginning in revolutionizing the old opera. I am very happy at the

thought of this. I hope you will write more plays and give more performances, and so help make this practice a common one which will prevail throughout the country.

The success of *Driven to Join the Liangshan Mountain Rebels*, especially Mao Zedong's letter to the Yan'an Beijing Opera Theatre, helped the Beijing Opera reform movement. In January of 1945, *Three Assaults on Zhujia Village*, another revised historical Beijing Opera performed by the Yan'an Beijing Opera Theatre, won praise again. Having seen the performance, Mao Zedong also wrote a letter to congratulate the playwright, director, cast and stage workers. He pointed out, "Having seen your performance, I feel it is very good and educational. After *Driven to Join the Liangshan Mountain Rebels*, the success of this opera has consolidated the road of revolutionizing Beijing Opera."

The Popular Opera Troupe led by Ke Zhongping and Ma Jianling was also successful in reforming traditional *qinqiang* opera. Ma Jianling's representative work is *Hatred of Blood and Tears*, a full-length opera. Using the strong points of traditional opera which set no restrictions on time and space, the librettist unfolded a very broad picture of the society. The opera has thirty scenes and nearly fifty characters, covering the areas from the Kuomintang-controlled countryside to the Shaanxi-Gansu-Ningxia Border Region. With the help of the bold and buoyant characteristics of *qinqiang* opera, the playwright created more new ideas than in his earlier works in *Ardent Youth* and *Checking Travel Permit*. The opera described the tragic experience of the three generations in Wang Renhou's family, who led a vagrant life after the family broke up. The opera reflected the bitter hatred of the broad masses of peasants against the reactionary ruling class. It also reflected the concern of the people's government in the border region for the refugees. The opera also exposed the crime committed by a spy sent to the liberated area by Kuomintang troops. The opera ended with the capture of the spy and reunion of the Wang family.

As compared with the vigorous mass movement of new *yangge* and the flourishing of new operas, the reform in modern drama was a bit late and smaller in scale. After the Yan'an forum on literature and art, the first modern dramas that became popular were several one-act plays which appeared in the Shanxi-Chahar-Hebei Border Region. In 1942 the Japanese invading troops in this area launched the "May 1 Mopping-up Campaign," and their barbarous burning, looting and killing challenged the Chinese army and people in the rear to a severe test. All these plays reflected the struggles when double-faced authorities were established in the countryside of that area. The best-known play among them is *Set Your Vision Further* created collectively by the Central Hebei Frontline Drama Troupe. Hu Danfei did the actual writing of the libretto. Through a dispute between two brothers who had different attitudes towards their sons' joining the Eighth Route Army, the elder brother firmly supported his son to fight the enemy to the finish, while the younger instigated his son to desert and go home. The play praised the peasants and satirized the short sightedness of some rich people. *Grain*, written by Luo Ding, Zhang Fan and Zhu Xingnan, and *Sixteen Rifles*, created collectively by the Central Hebei Frontline Drama Troupe and compiled by Cui Wei, depict how the resistance army and the people sent grain and rifles to the Eighth Route Army. *The Struggle Against a Comeback* written by Li Zhihua, which appeared shortly afterwards, is a one-act play that had a greater impact. It depicted the situation after the Land Reform whereby landlords were still waiting for an opportunity to regain their power and plotted to frame the activists. *To Press Recruits*, a play written in 1938 by a drama troupe formed by Sichuan actors who were touring the country, drew material from life in the Kuomintang-controlled areas. The script was revised in 1943 by Wu Xue, Chen Ge, Ding Hong and Dai Bixiang in Yan'an. The play, written in a vivid and pungent cartoon style, is an exposé of the landlord and a local official who worked in collusion with each other to bully the people.

The people's army used theatre for propaganda. After 1942 more and more dramatists went to the army units and wrote many plays about battles and army life. *Li Guorui* written by Du Feng is such as play. The play depicted how Li Guorui changed from a backward and undisciplined person into a good soldier. *Heroes on Jiugu Mountain*, a joint work by the Propaganda Team of the New Fourth Brigade and the Combat Theatre Troupe edited by Lin

Yang, Yan Jizhou and Liu Lianchi, described the war to defend Yan'an in March 1947. Lu Yi and Zhang Jie's *United to Win Merit* also had the transformation of backward soldiers as a theme. It depicted the daily life in a company and the close relations between the army and the people.

Comrade, You've Taken a Wrong Road! written by Yao Zhongming, Chen Bo'er and others is also about army life. But unlike those works reflecting life in army companies, it showed the audience the sharp conflicts in the headquarters of a detachment of the Eighth Route Army. Though it lacked ideological depth and was artistically unrefined, it was successful in handling the subject and the many characters and the complex relations between them.

Growing Up Amidst Battles, a play written collectively by Hu Peng and others and later adapted by Hu Ke, showed the victory of the people's war and the emancipation of the peasants through the story of three generations of Zhao Tiezhu's family. The play depicted how Zhao Tiezhu and his son changed from ordinary peasants to revolutionary fighters who regarded the liberation of the whole country as their duty. The play reflected the common experience of the broad masses of peasants, so it was socially relevant.

Along with the victory of the people's war, big cities were liberated one after another, thus providing new material for modern drama. The première of *The Song of Red Flag*, a joint work by Liu Canglang, Chen Huaikai, Chen Miao and others and the libretto written by Lu Mei, had a strong impact in literary and art circles, and was especially well-received by workers. When it was performed in Nanjing, it "broke the box office record of modern drama in this city";* "when *The Song of Red Flag* was staged in Shanghai, there were about five hundred reviews published in the newspapers."** The story took place in a factory in a newly liberated city, when a labour emulation drive had just been launched in the factory. The significance of the play lies in the question: after the workers, once slaves of the old society, had

* Zhou Yang, "On *The Song of Red Flag*."
** Lu Mei, "Preface to *The Song of Red Flag*."

become masters of the new society, what should their attitudes be towards the factory, work and their fellow workers? Although the play still had some shortcomings, it was the first play dealing with the life of workers and marked a good beginning in modern drama.

V. *Wang Gui and Li Xiangxiang, The Zhanghe River* and Other Poems

Like the flourishing new *yangge* movement, poetry writing was also unprecedentedly prolific in the liberated areas. China has a long tradition of folk songs and rhymes. After the May Fourth Movement of 1919, many new folk songs and ballads emerged during the workers' movement in cities; however, most of the new poetry appeared in the revolutionary base areas during the period of the Agrarian Revolution (1927-37). Emancipation, hatred for landlords, local despots and the reactionary army, love for the Communist Party and Red Army and the longing for a bright future were all themes of the folk songs and ballads. For example, *To the Frontline, Longing for the Red Army, He Long's Troops, Ten Sendoffs, When the Gentle Breeze Blows in March* and other famous folk songs were widely spread among the people in the base areas. During the War of Resistance Against Japan, especially after Yan'an forum on literature and art held in 1942, professional organizations of writers and artists devoted more attention to the popularization of literature and art. The representative works of this period are those poems included in the poetry collection *The East Is Red*. The title poem was originally written by the Shaanxi folk poet Li Youyuan and later polished by some professional poets and set to music, which has become a very famous song in China.

The development of popular poetry not only gave impetus to the people's struggle and production, but also profoundly influenced professional poets. The long narrative poems *Wang Gui and Li Xiangxiang* and *The Zhanghe River* and many other poems all assimilated techniques from folk songs.

Wang Gui and Li Xiangxiang by Li Ji (1922-80) first appeared in Yan'an's *Liberation Daily* in September 1946. He was born in Tanghe County, Henan Province. In 1938 he went to study in the Anti-Japanese Military and Political College in Yan'an and after graduation he worked in a grassroots army unit in the Taihang Mountains area. In the winter of 1942 he went to northern Shaanxi where he became a primary school teacher, secretary of the district and county governments and then editor of a small local newspaper. He was interested in literature and art and collected many folk songs. Before this long narrative poem, he had written *The Old Geomancer Angrily Beats the Lord of Insects* in a popular folk style and published *Romance of Palm Village* and other works in lithographic form. He also published many news dispatches, stories and poems in the *Liberation Daily*.

Wang Gui and Li Xiangxiang, containing three parts and thirteen chapters, reflected the struggle around 1930 waged by the peasants in northern Shaanxi under the leadership of Chinese Communist Party and unfolded the love story between Wang Gui and Li Xiangxiang. The poem vividly reflected the close relation between the liberation of the poor peasants and the victory of revolutionary struggle, and praised the young couple's loyalty to the revolution and their love.

The poems unfolded before the reader, a series of pictures of class oppression in the countryside of northern Shaanxi:

On every side stretched yellow sand,
But all of it was rich men's land.

The year of 1929 saw a drought, and all crops were scorched. The following year witnessed a spring famine:

With weeds gone people searched for leaves and roots,
Not a single shoot of green could be found near and far.
With no grass left they began to eat tree branches,
Into powder the branches were ground.
Those who died in February and March were buried in coffins,
There'll be nobody left to bury those who die in May and June.

When the countryside was strewn with bodies of the starved, the grain in the barns of the despotic landlord Second Lord Cui was rotting away. Instead of helping the starving peasants, he pressed for payment of the rent. Wang Gui's father was beaten to death by Second Lord Cui because he could not pay the rent and Wang Gui was forced to work for the Cui family when he was only thirteen. On the one hand Wang Gui was cruelly oppressed by the landlord class, on the other hand he was helped by Li Derui and his daughter Li Xiangxiang, who were also oppressed by the landlord. As time elapsed, Wang Gui and Li Xiangxiang grew up in the bitter circumstances and fell in love with each other.

Red wild lilies are delicate and fair,
Xiangxiang has grown charming and shapely.

Her big black eyes, a limpid pair,
With dewdrops on the grass compare.

Millet must be husked again and again,
Xiangxiang loves peasants plain.

The willow at the edge of the field grows green and gay,
A proper youngster is Wang Gui.

Five feet tall, and all of it brown,
A match for two peasants he was born.

Maize will flower when it's half grown,
He's always wanted Xiangxiang for his own.

But in the old society, it was not easy for the couple to lead a happy life; the despotic landlord tried to obstruct and sabotage their marriage. The reason why the landlord dared to bully the local people was that he owned a lot of cattle, sheep and land and had the backing of the reactionary government.

Wang Gui's character was decided by his social status. His father's tragic death, his terrible life and the landlord's interference in his marriage served as the source of his hatred against Second Lord Cui and the starting point of his conscious revolt. When the revolutionary struggle came to northern Shaanxi, Wang Gui was the first one at Dead Goat Bay who joined the Red Guards. Educated by the revolutionary forces, his personal revolt gradually developed into a wider political consciousness of revolution, and he plunged into the struggle. When Second Lord Cui found that Wang Gui had joined the revolution and subjected him to severe torture, Wang Gui denounced the landlord's threats:

No need, old dog, to put such airs on,
We'll have your life before three days are gone!

What does death matter in my case,
Millions of others will take my place!

Li Xiangxiang is another successful character portrayed in the poem. The only daughter of Li Derui, her mother died when she was a little girl and her family led a very poor life.

Like a moulting sparrow in winter's sleet,
No clothes to wear, no food to eat.

She was beautiful, kindhearted, valiant and industrious and had a staunch rebellious spirit. She fell in love with Wang Gui. The poem depicts her loyalty to love and gradual awakening in the struggle. When Wang Gui was tortured and she was eager to save him, she became aware that only the guerrillas could save him. When Second Lord Cui came back to the village together with the White Army and sent her father away and tried to marry her by force, she rebelled and angrily scratched the landlord "till both cheeks bleed" and sharply denounced him:

The day will come when my wish I gain,
And by my knife you will be slain!

When she was locked up by the landlord and cut off from help, she realized that she and Wang Gui shared a common fate. She eagerly looked forward to the victory of revolution and hoped that the guerrillas would fight and win the revolution. Her rebellious spirit reflected Li Xiangxiang's awakening and the growth of her political consciousness, as well as her loyalty to her love.

The poem also vividly portrays Second Lord Cui, the representative of the landlord class who had a vicious character. Relying on the reactionary authorities and colluding with the reactionary troops, he gathered a bunch of thugs together to establish a reactionary force of his own. He savagely exploited and oppressed the villagers and attempted to take advantage of Li Xiangxiang. Confronted by the peasants' revolution, he panicked, but was stubborn and foolish enough to put up a last-ditch struggle. Finally, he met with his downfall together with the feudal rule he had tried to save.

Wang Gui and Li Xiangxiang represented the enlightened peasants who took part in the revolutionary struggle under the leadership of the Chinese Communist Party. Since the May Fourth Movement of 1919, modern Chinese poetry has experienced a long process of evolution and change. In order to reflect the voice of the masses and praise their heroic struggle, poets have done their best, but the common shortcoming of revolutionary poetry was that its form and expression were still distant from the labouring masses. Though *Wang Gui and Li Xiangxiang* appeared a bit later than such excellent works as *Brother and Sister Reclaim Wasteland*, *The White-Haired Girl* and *Rhymes of Li Youcai*, still it may be said that it has made a unique contribution to poetry in adopting the form loved by the labouring masses, reflecting their life and struggle. It was just because of this that Guo Moruo praised this poem as a clear signal from "the liberation of people" to "the liberation of literature and art."*

The poem consists of nearly one thousand lines, all written in the form of *xintianyou* (literally, "free flight"), a popular form of folk songs in northern Shaanxi. The poem skillfully combines several hundred *xintianyou* folk songs together. The poet adopted many wonderful terms and phrases of the folk songs. The use of metaphor is the main characteristic of *xintianyou* folk songs. There are many vivid metaphors and similes in this poem. For instance, "Red wild lilies are delicate and fair" refers to Xiangxiang's good looks and "Wild lilies bloom in the meadows here" indicates Wang Gui and Li Xiangxiang's love. Such metaphors and similes widely used in the poem strengthen the charm of the language and the power of expression. The rhythm of the verses is fluent and lively, natural and harmonious. This shows that the poet was familiar with *xintianyou* folk-song form. He used the colloquial language of

* Guo Moruo, "Preface to *Wang Gui and Li Xiangxiang*."

the masses imaginatively so that the simple language became musical and poetic.

The Zhanghe River is another long narrative poem produced in that period. The author Ruan Zhangjing was born in a poor family in Zhongshan County, Guangdong Province, and took part in the revolutionary work before the War of Resistance Against Japan broke out. In 1938 he went to the Taihang Mountains area where he began his literary career and wrote many plays. In the spring of 1947 he composed the long poem *Traps* and some short poems including *A Sendoff* and *Looking Forward to Happy Tidings. Traps*, as the poet himself pointed out, is a story told in popular folk-song form. Written in a simple and lively style and colloquial language, it reflected the class struggle in the Land Reform Movement. The poem exposed the malicious intent and reactionary schemes of the landlord class and at the same time depicted the influence of traditional ideas upon the peasants and their shortcomings. The class enemy used the influence of traditional ideas against the peasants. Through struggle, the enemy's plots fell through while the peasants won the victory. *A Sendoff* presented a moving scene when an old woman sent her son off to fight in the War of Liberation. *Looking Forward to Happy Tidings* is about a soldier's wife who wrote to encourage her husband to fight bravely. The mutual concern of the husband and wife and their patriotism made the poem very appealing.

Written in March 1949, *The Zhanghe River* is about the suffering of women in the Taihang Mountains area under the feudal traditions and savage oppression, extolling their emancipation and new life under the leadership of the Communist Party. The three heroines, Hehe, Lingling and Zi Jinying, were lifelike with different characteristics. When they were still carefree girls, all of them had the ideal and longed to have happy family life in the future. But under feudal rule, their fate was like "a kite with the string snapped off" and their marriages were like "a gambling game." As a result, their dreams were shattered and all of them landed in adverse circumstances. They protested plaintively:

Tearful cries shake the mountains,

Asking the Zhanghe River whose fault it is.
Through the Peach Blossom Basin, by poplars and willows,
The Zhanghe River flows whimperingly along.
Drum's beaten and the operas are shown,
Vicissitudes of all times are sung.

Vicissitudes of all times are sung,
But not a word of what women have undergone!
How we wish we could lift the mountain,
So we could smash the outmoded conventions.
......

Then the revolution was won, the people were liberated and the feudal shackles were smashed:

The Zhanghe River has ninety-nine turns,
Chairman Mao leads us to rearrange heaven and earth.
......
Women have shaken off the feudal bonds....

Hehe was the most advanced and the militant person among the three girls. She was the first one to divorce her husband who was vicious and much older than she was. She took an active part in the farm work of the mutual aid team and remarried a man she loved. She also helped liberate other women and helped them start a new life. Lingling was a liberated woman of another type. She was bright and capable, lively and humorous, and also very active in farm work. From the way she sponsored a "family training class" to fight against her husband's male chauvinism, we can see that she was very intelligent. Zi Jinying was a widow who led a more tragic and helpless life and suffered much more from the traditional ideas and old customs than the other two women. Therefore, the awakening of her political consciousness was slower and more complicated. Encouraged and helped by Hehe and Lingling, at last she extricated herself from her old way of life, took part in collective productive labour and began a new life.

Women's liberation is the yardstick of the liberation of the society. The poem vividly depicted the emancipation of three different types of women from feudal conventions and pointed out that to participate in collective productive labour was a correct way for women to win liberation. The poet depicted at great length how Lingling's husband was educated to change his thinking; and through criticism against the idea of looking down upon women, the poem reflected how the labouring people gradually freed themselves from traditional ideas after they won political emancipation.

The poem not only succeeded in vividly portraying the different characters, but also broke fresh artistic ground. In the poem the poet adopted the forms of many folk chants and ballads popular along the Zhanghe River, such as "The Blossom," "For Profound Hatred," "Harvesting Vegetables," "The Ditty to the Zhanghe River" and "Grazing Sheep." Though different techniques were used in *The Zhanghe River*, the poem reads smoothly and harmoniously. The ending of the poem is optimistic praising the new society, which forms a striking contrast with the tone of the previously-mentioned stanzas in which the three girls poured out their sorrows:

The Zhanghe River has ninety-nine turns,
The water sings merrily along:
Peach Blossom Basin, trees evergreen,
On the banks of the river appears a broad road;
The age-old dungeon is shattered!
The age-old cage is smashed up!
Liberated birds fly freely in the sky,
Liberated Zhanghe River will laugh heartily forever!

The poet skillfully used the colloquial language he had learned from the masses to reflect their life, in a fluent and expressive style with a colourful vocabulary.

Before *The Zhanghe River*, Ruan Zhangjing wrote an opera in September 1947 called *Red Leave River*. Set in the Taihang Mountains area in the thirties, the opera depicted the miserable life of peasants under the oppression of the landlords, as well as their struggle for liberation in the Land Reform Movement.

Except *Wang Gui and Li Xiangxiang* and *The Zhanghe River*, the poems written by Zhang Zhimin, Li Bing, He Jingzhi, Yan Chen and some other poets also succeeded in adopting the forms of folk song and ballads to reflect the life and struggle in the countryside.

Zhang Zhimin's three long narrative poems, *Wang the Ninth Pours Out His Grievances*, *The Story of an Emancipated Hired-Hand* and *An Unruly Daughter*, were written in a similar style, which depicted the suffering of the poor peasants under the oppression of the landlord class and their struggle for liberation in Land Reform Movement. The poem reflected the tragic lot of the oppressed:

On entering the village you need not ask,
All the stones, big and small, belong to Sun family.

Landlord Sun worked his abacus pitter-patter
He ruined the peasant families one after another.

The condemnation made by Wang the Ninth in the struggle for liberation vividly revealed his grief and anger:

Wang the Ninth was boiling with fury,
His long years' grief flowed out like a stream:

"You hounded my father to death,
You drove my wife into suicide!"

"Landlord Sun, You must pay with your life for the murders!
Landlord Sun, Your debts of blood must be paid with blood!"

The poem reflected the society and struggles at that time and as well as the emancipation of the masses in the Land Reform Movement. All three poems are easily understood without any elaborate description and the main characters are bold and realistic, thus their condemnation of the landlords for their suffering is forceful and true to life. But the description of the characters' inner world lacks depth and the plots of these poems are very similar. In his later poems, such as *The Delight* and *Receiving a Report of Good Tidings*, the poet depicted the bright atmosphere and the exultation of the people in the liberated areas.

Li Bing's *Zhao Qiao'er* portrays Zhao Qiao'er, a working woman who became more politically conscious and matured in the Land Reform Movement. The description of the evolution of her rebellious spirit is vivid, and by way of psychological depiction and flashbacks, the poem presented many major events from the beginning to the end of the Land Reform Movement. Though there are so many events, the poem is well-structured. Li Bing's poetry collection *Flowering Season*, includes many of his short verses written during the War of Liberation. Among them "Aunt," "A Broad Road," "Red Lantern" and some other poems praised the peasants' support to the War of Liberation. In a lively tone "Red Lantern" depicted the peasants' enthusiasm in joining the stretcher-teams to support the front and praised a stretcher-team of women. His language is natural and fluent.

As well as co-writing the opera *The White-Haired Girl*, He Jingzhi has also written many poems. His poems written between 1942 and 1949 were collected in two poetry anthologies entitled *Smile* and *Flowering Towards the Sun*. Most of these poems were written in the form of folk songs; some are themselves beautiful songs or poems that can be sung and the others are lyrics. The poem "Smile" is about the peasants' emancipation in the Land Reform Movement through the eyes of a poor old peasant. Written in a lively style it expressed the joy and excitement of the liberated peasants. "An Emulation Between Villages" is a narrative poem depicting how young people in the liberated areas vied with one another to join the army. The poet praised the thousands of heroes who marched to the front and the heroic spirit of the people in the liberated areas and their determination to carry the revolution through to the end. "Crossing the Yellow River at Night," another narrative poem by the poet, depicted Liu Zhidan, commander of the Red Army in northern Shaanxi Province, leading his troops across the Yellow River to the east to fight. "Verses Written on a March" is a group of short poems written on the march from Yan'an to North China, which showed the tremendous changes that had taken place in the Shaanxi-Gansu-Ningxia Border Region. Compared with the poet's early poems collected in *Night in the Countryside*, these poems are marked by great changes both in content and form. They are realistic and full of revolutionary optimism and written in a simple style and different forms.

Most of Yan Chen's poems were collected in *Singing to the*

Yanhe River, *The Spring of Life*, *Morning Star* and other anthologies. The most remarkable ones among them are "A Crack Company" and "Jiang Bo Detachment" which vividly depicted how the anti-Japanese guerrilla forces grew thanks to the support of the people. "A New-style Marriage" written in 1947 expressed the joys of the emancipated peasants. In the poem the newly-wedded couple contrasted their past misery with present happiness and felt satisfied with their new life.

> *The Jade Maid marries the Gold Boy in the heaven,*
> *The nun who suffered greatly now weds a hired-hand.*

This great change in life was brought about by the victory of revolution, therefore it is natural that the people leading a new happy life supported the revolution wholeheartedly. The plot of the poem was ingeniously conceived and the form of *xintianyou* folk song was skillfully adopted.

Another celebrated and active poet in the liberated areas is Xiao San (1896-83) also known as Emi Siao. In his early years when he was in the Soviet Union he had written some poems, such as "A Letter Written in Blood" and "Gifts," to praise the revolution in China and the international proletarian struggle and condemn fascist aggression. After he came back to Yan'an in 1939, he edited the magazine *Modern Poetry* besides continuing to write poetry. In the preface to his poetry selection he advocated that modern poetry "must learn from folk songs and classical poetry. His "Congratulatory Message to the 25th Anniversary of the October Revolution," "I Come to Nanniwan Again," "The Carnival in Yan'-an," "Seeing Chairman Mao Off to Chongqing" and other poems are examples of such poems.

The poets in the liberated areas used the form of folk songs to express the new life of the masses, thus popularizing poetry. There were also many poets who continued to use various free verse forms which had appeared since the May Fourth Movement of 1919 to express the new life and struggle, which also played an important role of education and inspiration in wartime. The gifted young poet Chen Hui (1920-44) for example, depicted the life and struggle in the liberated areas in his two poetry collections, *Songs from the Plain* and *Short Verses Written on the Plain*, and expressed the heroism and optimism of the guerrillas. *The New Garden of Eden* is another group of his poems praising the revolutionary life and struggle:

Who said that,
"The North is sad"?
No!
My Shanxi-Chahar-Hebei Border Region,
Your simple and plain fields,
Your unadorned countryside,
Your earth burning with flames of war,
They are
More beautiful
Than the Garden of Eden!

In these poems the poet expressed the people's resolve to devote themselves to China. He described the character Nie Rongzhen, a commander of the Eighth Route Army and praised the heroic deed of a girl who protected a revolutionary cadre. He also described a night raid launched by the people's army and the mass movement for production in support of the revolutionary war. Through these descriptions, the poems praised the heroic struggles waged by the people in the liberated areas for the new life of the country. After Chen Hui died, Tian Jian collected his works into a book and published it under the title of *The Songs of October*.

Wei Wei's anthology *Spectacles at Dawn* comprises most of his poems written during the War of Resistance Against Japan and the War of Liberation. He wrote many short narrative poems in folk song form, such as "Song of a Good Couple," "Three Combined Villages" and "Song of Good Brothers," which exposed the crimes of the Japanese and reactionary troops against the people and praised the people's heroic struggles. He also used the free verse form that was familiar to him to write many lyric narrative poems. "Sorghum Crops, Grow Up Quick" expressed the high morale of the guerrillas and their eagerness to fight. "A Knock at the Door" presented the guerrillas' triumphant return from a night raid:

Mother, open the door
Our troops have come back
The morning star will rise soon
The Threshing ground
Is covered with frost
......

After the establishment of the Inner Mongolia Autonomous Region in May 1947, the Mongolian poet Sayntsogt was inspired by the prospects of a new life and he made a great change in his writing style. His poems "The Desert, My Native Place," depicted the lovely scenes and history of "The desert covered with glistening golden sand" and the poet expressed his hopes for the future:

The storm sways the willow branches,
Shaking my wrathful heart;
We'll never let the claws of the Kuomintang reactionaries
Plunder our fat sheep and cattle.

Oh, the desert, my mother,
Our native place!
Advance in the direction pointed out by the Party,
And let freedom radiate with splendour!

He also wrote "In Commemoration of the Exploits of the People's Hero Tao Gao" and other poems to praise the heroes of the War of Liberation.

Besides the above-mentioned poets, Guo Xiaochuan, Gong Mu, Ge Bizhou, Liu Yu, Ke Gang, Bai Ren and many others also wrote many noteworthy poems in different forms at that time.

VI. Reportage and Other Works

The struggle in the liberated areas was an inexhaustible source of literary inspiration and provided a wide range of material for reportage. In the forties reportage in the liberated areas made much headway. As compared with reportage written in the early thirties, these works were different both in content and form. They were no longer superficial propaganda, but writings which had combined militant spirit with realism; the protagonists depicted in these works were no longer "wronged souls of slaves," but politically conscious soldiers and civilians under the leadership of the Communist Party. Distinct improvement was achieved both in the ideological content and the style of these works as compared with those written in the early days of the War of Resistance Against Japan.

Modelled on *A Day in China* edited by Mao Dun in the thirties, two huge volumes of reportage, *A Day in Central Hebei* and *A Day During the Battle to Cross the Yangtse River*, were published in the liberated areas. The former consists of over two hundred short reports on the battle of May 27, 1941. Among them "She," "A Martyr Killed by Bayonet," "A Brave and Steady Young Squad Leader," "A Common Story," "Crossing Beiping-Hankou Railway at Night," "A School Near an Enemy Stronghold," "Half a Day in a Car" and "Smile" all depicted the life and struggle of the people in central Hebei. *A Day During the Battle to Cross the Yangtse River* comprises 120 reportages, written by officers and soldiers of the Third Field Army of the People's Liberation Army (PLA) in 1949 when they forced their way southward across the Yangtse River. Among them the reports gathered under the title of *Bombarding the River Defences* vividly reflected how the people's artillery quickly destroyed the defensive positions the Kuomintang troops had painstakingly built up by the Yangtse River. Another collection of articles under the title of *The Artillery Captures Enemy Warships* depicted how the PLA artillery severely punished the imperialist naval vessels which ran wild along the Yangtse River and defended the sovereignty of China. All these works, from *A Day in China* to *A Day in Central Hebei* and *A Day During the Battle to Cross the Yangtse River*, are historical records of the miserable life of the Chinese people and the victory they won through arduous struggles.

Besides writing fiction, many writers in the liberated areas including Ding Ling, Zhou Libo, Sun Li, Liu Baiyu and Ma Feng, also wrote articles showing the life and struggle of the army and the people. Among the writers who wrote news articles Hua Shan and Zhou Erfu had a notable impact on readers, and those written by Wu Boxiao, Zeng Ke and Han Xiliang were distinctive for their unique style.

Hua Shan's "Positional Warfare in Cave Dwellings" is a comprehensive dispatch written in a pithy style to record how the militiamen positioned themselves in caves and defeated the Japanese invaders. "Along the Blockade Line of Pillboxes" centred on the story of Liu, an 18-year-old guerrilla team leader who fought resourcefully against the enemy and at the same time reflected the struggles waged by the people in the enemy-controlled areas under the leadership of the Communist Party. The author did not make his protagonist a solitary hero, but presented him as a representative of the masses. This reportage showed the generation growing up in the anti-Japanese guerrilla war. The author's long dispatches written during the War of Liberation, such as "On the Snowy Banks of Liaohe River," "Combat Heroes in Qitamu Battle" and "The Heroic October," depicted battle scenes in the Northeast. These pieces were written in a lucid and lively style and the accounts of events are vivid. Hua Shan also wrote the well-known short story "A Letter Attached with a Chicken Feather." This story is about a brave and resourceful shepherd boy Haiwa.

Zhou Erfu's most famous reportage is "Episodes of Norman Bethune." It is an account of the work of the Canadian doctor, Norman Bethune who worked at the anti-Japanese battlefront in China to help the wounded and support the liberation cause of the Chinese people. When Dr Bethune came to China from Canada, he brought large quantities of medicine and medical supplies. He toured the frontline and revolutionary base areas behind the enemy lines to give medical treatment to the soldiers and civilians in difficult conditions. He once said that the aim of medical treatment "is not only for saving today's China, but also for bringing about a great, free and classless new China in future." In order to suit the needs of war, he trained large numbers of medical workers and founded the International Peace Hospital. He always thought about the sick and wounded and criticized irresponsible work and set strict medical standards. In the winter he gave his own quilts to wounded soldiers; he fed a severely wounded soldier with the food the cook had prepared especially for him. He gave blood for transfusions and performed many operations in the battlefield. He rescued many soldiers and cured many sick people in the Shanxi-Chahar-Hebei Border Region. On hearing the news of his sudden death on November 12, 1939, everyone in the region was saddened. The Chinese people had been deeply touched by his spirit. The author depicted Doctor Bethune mainly through recording episodes in his life and work on the anti-Japanese frontline. Mao Zedong wrote an article, "In Memory of Norman Bethune," calling upon Communist Party members and the Chinese people to learn from Dr Bethune's spirit.

As well as "Episodes of Norman Bethune," Zhou Erfu is also an important co-author of the reportage "Encounters on the Sea"; his collection of short news stories, *Short Songs on the Plateau*, written in the middle period of the War of Resistance Against Japan depicted the reclamation movement in the border region.

Wu Boxiao's *Black and Red Dots* is a collection of news stories and sketches written in the later stage of the War of Resistance Against Japan. The stories, short, but well-organized, depicted the guerrilla fighters as well as the bumper harvests and prosperity brought about by the movement for production. The title story consisted of a few short sketches about the people in the enemy-controlled areas of southern Hebei who kept a book about the traitors and puppet troops, using black dots to record their evil deeds and red dots for good ones. The stories in the second part of the collection, such as "Nanniwan," "Planting Trees on the Flaming Mountain" and "A New Village," are about the movement for production, the afforestation in the Shaanxi-Gansu-Ningxia Border Region and the new settlements arranged for people from outside the region. The collection entitled *Starting Off* comprises the author's works written after 1946. The first part consists of prose writings, among which "Starting Point" is a prose poem written to extoll the Yan'an spirit when Wu Boxiao (1906-) was about to leave there. Wu Boxiao is well versed in literature and has experience in the struggle bringing immediacy to his writing, and his works are compact, well-organized and skillfully written.

Zeng Ke's *The Glorious People* is a collection of news stories written in Yan'an and the Taihang Mountains area during the later stage of the War of Resistance Against Japan. Many protagonists in her sketches are unknown people who had gone through the hardships of the Resistance War and the movement for production and they reflect the keen observation and special sensitivity of a woman writer. "Working Women" described the simple character and staunch spirit of the country women in the Taihang Mountains area; "Life in the Countryside" recorded the author's experience in the countryside and expressed her love for the people. "Advancing into the Area of Dabie Mountains" comprises six groups of sketches written in a lively style to record the Chinese People's Liberation Army's victorious march to the south. Among them "A Sendoff," "In the Desert," "Eternal Glory to Comrade Shi Yulun," "A Surprise Attack," "The First Battalion Commander I Know" and "Across the Wohe River" are especially vivid with good descriptions of both scenery and the emotions of her characters.

Han Xiliang's "A Rapid March in the Yimeng Mountains" and "Sixty-Eight Days" are two long reportages reflecting the battles to liberate east China. Both of these works centred on the growth and the role of an artillery unit in the Menglianggu battle of the Huaihai Campaign, during the Liberation War. The author was then a company political instructor and familiar with army life, so his works were true to life and touching. The first story reflected how the artillery company overcame various difficulties, such as the enemy's obstruction, the steep mountain path, hot weather and shortage of rations and water, and how they finally thrust into the area behind the enemy lines together with the field corps. In cooperation with other army units, they wiped out one of the Kuomintang's five crack forces, the 74th Division, at Menglianggu. The latter reflected how this field corps and its artillery company set off from the Yimeng Mountains and drove southward along the east section of the Longhai (Lanzhou-Lianyungang) Railway to enter the Huaihai Compaign. Written in a simple and vigorous style, these two articles recorded the author's personal experience.

Many other articles written during that period reflected the heroic deeds of the people during the War of Resistance Against Japan and the War of Liberation. Zhou You's "The Battle at Song

Village in Central Hebei" depicted the fierce battle in the area around Song Village to smash the enemy's operations in 1942, where the guerrillas won the victory against heavy odds. Zhou Yuanqing's "Rescue" vividly depicted a triumphant night raid of the guerrilla forces against the Japanese troops. Ding Fen's "The Bomb Without a Spring," written in lively colloquial language, is a true story of a resourceful scout. Li Hou's "Song Jiliu" recorded the heroic deeds of Song Jiliu, a guerrilla fighter in Shandong Province. Li Li's "Forty-Eight Days" is a long dispatch written in diary form, recording how the People's Liberation Army troops led by Wang Zhen broke through the enemy encirclement, fought in the area around the Hunan-Guangdong Railway and finally joined forces with the troops from the north. Hong Lin's *A Grain Transport Corps* vividly depicted how the liberated peasants supported the War of Liberation.

The reportage written by the writers in the liberated areas, as well as the fiction, drama and poetry, reflected a new era and showed the struggle to reach that new era by the resistance against imperialists, the Kuomintang reactionary rule and feudalism.

Conclusion

In July 1949, during the days when New China was being established, the First National Congress of Literary and Art Workers was held in Beijing (known as Beiping then). This congress marked the end of the history of literature in the period of China's new-democratic revolution and the beginning of the history of literature in the socialist period.

The preparations for the congress started shortly after Beijing was liberated. In February 1949 a large number of literary and art workers came to Beijing from the liberated areas in north China, and later many writers and artists from the Kuomintang-controlled areas arrived in the ancient capital too. They united with those who had stayed in Beijing, thus forming the first assembly of China's new writers and artists. On March 22, Guo Moruo proposed to a national congress of literary and art workers and that a new national organization of literary and art circles be established.

After about three months' preparations, the congress held its preparatory meeting on June 30 and was inaugurated on July 2. Eight hundred and twenty-four delegates participated in the congress,* representing over seventy thousand new literary and art workers and several tens of thousands of traditional opera singers and folk artists throughout the country. Mao Zedong attended and spoke at the congress. Zhu De delivered the message of congratulation on behalf of the Central Committee of the Communist Party of China and Zhou Enlai made a political report. Guo Moruo, chairman of the congress, gave a speech on "Struggle for the Construction of the Chinese People's Literature and Art," while Mao Dun and Zhou Yang, vice-chairmen of the congress, gave reports

* The preparatory committee originally invited 753 delegates, but after the opening ceremony the number of delegates increased to 824.

respectively entitled "The Development of Revolutionary Literature and Art in the Struggle Against the Oppressive Reactionary Forces" (about the literature and art in the Kuomintang-controlled areas) and "The New People's Literature and Art" (about the literary and art works in the liberated areas). The congress listened to various reports and speeches on special topics and there was a lively discussion and exchange of opinions. The meeting agreed to found the China Federation of Literary and Art Circles and associations in literature, theatre, film, music, dance, fine arts and other fields. It came to a successful close on July 19.

This congress was a grand assembly of literary and art workers from all parts of China. It joined the two literary and art contingents that were forced to work separately in the Kuomintang-controlled areas and the revolutionary bases after the failure of the First Revolutionary Civil War (1924-27). "It also joined the forces of the representatives of the new literary and art troops and the representatives of the old literary and art workers and it is the joining of the three literary and art contingents from the countryside, cities and the army. This is a wide-ranged unity and assembly under the banner of new democracy and in the new direction for literature and art pointed out by Chairman Mao."* The New Culture Movement since 1919 was a movement of the proletariat-led united front. The participants in this congress consisted of those long-established progressive literary and art workers, as well as writers and artists of different tendencies and classes, including writers of the Mandarin Duck and Butterfly School, who had been criticized by the ranks of the new culture, but later were inspired by the struggle to join the united front and wrote some progressive works. In some countries the victory of proletarian revolution caused some writers to go into exile, but the victory of the revolution led by the Chinese proletariat made most writers and artists happy and many writers who had lived abroad for a long time came back to China. Zhou Enlai pointed out in his political report, "Except for a few reactionary elements who are eliminated,

---

* Zhou Enlai, "Political Report at the National Congress of Literature and Art Workers," *Essays in Celebration of the National Congress of Literature and Art Workers*, p. 33.

almost all the members of the Federation of Chinese Writers and Artists founded in the Kuomintang-controlled areas during the War of Resistance Against Japan, which is one of the sponsor organizations of this congress, have united under the banner of new democracy and almost all its chief representatives are present at the meeting today." This clearly shows that the First National Congress of Literature and Art Workers was a success.

This congress is also a general review of the achievements of the new literature and art. Modern Chinese literature and art had accomplished much in the thirty years since the May Fourth Movement of 1919 and many works played a supporting role in the struggles of different periods, encouraging thousands of young people to rebel against the old order and the imperialists in order to improve the lives of the Chinese people. Revolutionary writers and artists experienced the same suffering and struggles as the masses. "In different historical periods the main trend of China's new literature and art was always an important component of the revolutionary political movements at that time. In order to win the victory of political revolution in the period of the new-democratic revolution, many Chinese writers and artists sacrificed their lives together with the heroic people. During the Agrarian Revolutionary War (1927-37), some Left-wing writers and artists were killed by the Kuomintang reactionaries. During the period of the War of Resistance Against Japan and the War of Liberation, there were still more writers and artists who died on the battlefield and in Kuomintang prisons or murdered by Kuomintang special agents."* Zhu De, commander-in-chief of the People's Liberation Army, pointed out in the message of congratulation, "It is the honour of modern Chinese literature and art that writers and artists have such an inseparable relationship with revolutionary struggles." Mao Zedong highly praised cultural workers in his speech, "You are all needed by the people; you are people's writers, people's artists, or organizers of people's literature and art. You are of benefit to the revolution and the people. Because people need you, we have

* Guo Moruo, "Struggle for the Construction of the Chinese People's Literature and Art," *Essays in Celebration of the National Congress of Literature and Art Workers*, pp. 41-42.

reason to welcome you."

The congress was also a summing-up and exchange of the basic experience of modern literature and art since the May Fourth Movement of 1919. The development of new Chinese literature and art in the thirty years was on the one hand a period of learning from the world's progressive literature and art and modernizing both the content and form, and on the other hand it was a period of popularization of literature and art drawing upon traditional forms. The real starting point of the modernization of Chinese literature is the literary revolution which began with the May Fourth Movement. Only through this revolution, did Chinese literature begin to incorporate ideas from modern democracy, science and scientific socialism and to have a common language with the world's progressive literature.

The congress held on the eve of the birth of New China was an important meeting in the history of Chinese literature for carrying forward tradition and forging ahead into the future. It summarized and developed the achievements and experience of the past thirty years, affirmed Chairman Mao's guiding principles for literature and art as the "common programme" in literary and art circles, organized a large contingent to build up a new socialist literature and art and opened up new prospects for Chinese literature and art.

INDEX

图书在版编目(CIP)数据

中国现代文学史:英文/唐弢主编. —北京:
外文出版社,1993 (1998 重印)
ISBN 7-119-01459-5

Ⅰ.中… Ⅱ.唐… Ⅲ.现代文学-文学史-中国-英文
Ⅳ.I209.6

中国版本图书馆 CIP 数据核字 (97) 第 21328 号

责任编辑　郑其平　孙之龙

中国现代文学史
唐弢　主编
*

外文出版社出版
(中国北京百万庄大街 24 号)
邮政编码 100037
北京外文印刷厂印刷
中国国际图书贸易总公司发行
(中国北京车公庄西路 35 号)
北京邮政信箱第 399 号　邮政编码 100044
1993 年(大 32 开)第 1 版
1998 年第 1 版第 2 次印刷
(英)
ISBN 7-119-01459-5/G·36(外)
02950(平)
7-E-1879P